The Dangerous Philosophies of Michael Jackson

His Music, His Persona, and His Artistic Afterlife

Elizabeth Amisu

Forewords by Joseph Vogel, PhD,
and Karin Merx

 PRAEGER™

An Imprint of ABC-CLIO, LLC
Santa Barbara, California • Denver, Colorado

Library of Congress Cataloging-in-Publication Data

Names: Amisu, Elizabeth.
Title: The dangerous philosophies of Michael Jackson : his music, his persona, and his artistic afterlife / Elizabeth Amisu with forewords by Joseph Vogel, PhD, and Karin Merx.
Description: Santa Barbara, California : Praeger, [2016] | Includes bibliographical references and index. | Description based on print version record and CIP data provided by publisher; resource not viewed.
Identifiers: LCCN 2016020927 (print) | LCCN 2016020710 (ebook) |
    ISBN 9781440838651 (E-book) | ISBN 9781440838644 (hard copy)
Subjects: LCSH: Jackson, Michael, 1958–2009—Criticism and interpretation.
Classification: LCC ML420.J175 (print) | LCC ML420.J175 A8 2016 (ebook) |
    DDC 782.42166092—dc23
LC record available at https://lccn.loc.gov/2016020927

ISBN: 978-1-4408-3864-4
EISBN: 978-1-4408-3865-1

20 19 18 17 16   1 2 3 4 5

This book is also available as an eBook.

Praeger
An Imprint of ABC-CLIO, LLC

ABC-CLIO, LLC
130 Cremona Drive, P.O. Box 1911
Santa Barbara, California 93116-1911
www.abc-clio.com

This book is printed on acid-free paper ∞

Manufactured in the United States of America

*For all who "danced" with MJ,
mourned his passing, and
celebrate his life. With love.*

When a great poet dies, the immediate critical question is often where to bury him. In the choice between the public tomb and private resting place, a prominent quarter in Westminster Abbey or the wood-choked corner of a foreign graveyard, posterity makes its first decision about how the poet will be remembered. And often enough the result has been a scandal. . . . Not even a proper burial can guard against infamy. Milton's bones, for instance, were dug up at the end of the eighteenth century for souvenirs, just as fragments of his early poems had been exhumed and confiscated by minor poets. Neglected at first, eventually competed for, like Homer, by contending cities, the poet goes to meet his shades. But not unsung. With his dying breath, frequently, an industry springs up around him—memorialists, literary undertakers, chisellers, epitaph-makers. The custodians of his fame take charge of manuscripts and the will. He enters his tomb.

—Lawrence Lipking, *The Life of the Poet:*
Beginnings and Endings

Contents

Foreword

J ust over 10 years ago, when I began writing about Michael Jackson in the midst of his 2005 trial, books and articles on the artist were hard to come by. I emphasize the word "artist" because, as Elizabeth Amisu makes abundantly clear in this book, much had been written and spoken (superficially) about Jackson the celebrity, the caricature, the freak. But for a figure who had such a demonstrably seismic impact on global culture, it was remarkable how little serious coverage existed on the artist. Consider this: At the time of Jackson's death, the most widely available books about the pop icon included *FREAK!: Inside the Twisted World of Michael Jackson* (2005) by David Perel and Suzanne Ely; *Be Careful Who You Love* (2009) by Diane Dimond; *Unmasked: The Final Years of Michael Jackson* (2009) by Ian Halperin; and of course, J. Randy Taraborrelli's biography, *Michael Jackson: The Magic and the Madness* (2009). The most widely read articles were written by gossipmongers like Roger Friedman and Maureen Orth. More talented writers who had covered Jackson in the 1980s and early 1990s, like Nelson George, Michele Wallace, Kobena Mercer, and Michael Eric Dyson, had moved on to other subjects. One could count the total pieces of scholarship dedicated to Jackson on one hand— maybe two.

Fast-forward 10 years: There is now a substantial enough body of work on Jackson—from Spike Lee's acclaimed documentaries (*Bad 25* and *Michael Jackson's Journey from Motown to Off the Wall*), to college courses offered by professors Mark Anthony Neal and Marie Plasse, to Susan Fast's brilliant *33 1/3* study on *Dangerous*, to an explosion of books, essays, and articles— enough to prove that Michael Jackson Studies is not only a thing, it is a thing that is thriving. Elizabeth Amisu's intelligent and illuminating book, *The*

Dangerous Philosophies of Michael Jackson, not only adds to this growing field; it documents in great detail how much important work has been done in this short amount of time.

I will leave the particulars of what now constitutes Michael Jackson Studies to Elizabeth—her second chapter, "A Critical Survey of Michael Jackson Studies," offers an excellent introduction to the field and how it has developed over time. The broader point I would like to make, however, is that in spite of the influx of new work on everything from Jackson's music, to his short films, to his dancing, to his cultural impact, Michael Jackson Studies is still in its infancy. It is an exciting time of exploration, innovation, and possibility. No single individual or lens can tell the whole story—nor should they. Indeed, if anything, the most refreshing thing about Michael Jackson Studies at this stage is its embrace of complexity and variety. Pushing back against decades of reductive narratives, Michael Jackson has once again become dynamic, paradoxical, and mysterious.

A multifaceted human being and artist is precisely the portrait of Michael Jackson that emerges in Elizabeth Amisu's book. Her study covers considerable territory—not only spanning Jackson's career, but also the many different forms he used and the many historical, social, cultural, and artistic contexts in which he was operating. Her passionate, keen, and often daring interpretations combine to create a kind of mosaic, with each chapter offering a different color or shape or piece of the picture.

Over the course of his career, Jackson was often dismissed as a serious artist by the cultural gatekeepers. See, for example, the critical commentary of heavyweights like Dave Marsh, Greil Marcus, and Jon Pareles, which consistently reduced Jackson to a commercial phenomenon. In a 2009 interview with NPR, prominent cultural critic Stanley Crouch summed up the conventional wisdom, when he was asked if Jackson should be classified as an artist or an entertainer:

> I think he was an entertainer. I don't think he was an artist because his material doesn't contain much human understanding or human value beyond an adolescent vision of life, you know, like, which is like, we would all be better if people would just treat each other right. Well, you know, that's nice, but that doesn't tell you much of anything.

In *The Dangerous Philosophies of Michael Jackson*, Elizabeth Amisu proves how deeply misinformed such an assessment is. Michael Jackson was an artist *and* an entertainer (as with so many things, he refused the either/or terms). What his creative life and work tells us, it seems, largely depends on what one is able to see, hear, and feel. One thing's certain: He did not aim low. He was not content with a niche audience, and he despised limitations. His art was intended for everyone, yet it managed to be as singular and subversive as anything pop music had seen. A dangerous philosophy indeed.

Joseph Vogel, PhD
Author of *Man in the Music: The Creative Life and Work of Michael Jackson; Featuring Michael Jackson: Collected Writings on the King of Pop;* and *Earth Song: Michael Jackson's Magnum Opus*

Foreword

This is an amazing book. I have seen this book grow from an essay first published on the Internet to what it is now—an indispensable source for all who wish to know about Michael Jackson's art and who seriously want to study this multitalented artist. Elizabeth has an eloquent writing style, combining her literary qualities as an author with her academic writing, which makes the book very pleasant to read. I have great admiration for Elizabeth because she dared to take the opportunity to write this academic book on Michael Jackson and his art. Especially since writing about Jackson is a delicate subject for many, and there is not that much academic writing about him available, I would say that the task she took at hand was a sign of courage. However, I am also sure that everyone who reads this book will be pleasantly surprised. *The Dangerous Philosophies of Michael Jackson: His Music, His Persona, and His Artistic Afterlife* is a considerable volume that gives so many starting points for those who wish to expand their knowledge and study of Jackson's catalogue. In fact, for me, this book **is** the place to really start studying, listening, and reading.

So many books were published about Michael Jackson in the last seven years, but this is truly one of a kind. It is actually the first academic book on the art and life of Michael Jackson that uses his work has its main source material. Elizabeth has written 21 unique and compelling chapters. Each chapter has a different approach and answers a specific question: whether it's about the significance of a specific work Jackson created; how he was a storyteller able to engage an enormously wide and diverse world audience; his influence on culture then and now; his clothing; his short films; the use of his voice; or how he related to other artists. Elizabeth comes to informed and academic conclusions and insights about Jackson's life, art, and artistic afterlife that I am sure people will have never heard before. If you are a fan, or academic of musicology, art history, black history, history, culture, philosophy, religion, dance, fashion, film, literature, or just interested in the life and work of an incredibly versatile artist, this book definitely is something for you. It is so inspirational that I am sure you will not be able to do anything but start your own research in earnest and explore again the stunning art of Michael Jackson.

Karin Merx
Editor of *The Journal of Michael Jackson
Academic Studies* and author of *A Festive Parade of Highlights:
La Grande Parade as Evaluation of the Museum Policy of Edy De Wilde*

Acknowledgments

In the publication of any book, there are countless people who have played a vital role. Firstly, I would like to thank the artist, Michael Jackson, for his dream and his creations, into which he poured his laughter, joy, and tears. I also appreciate the many talented and inspired individuals Jackson collaborated with during his career. Without them, his greatest works could not have been possible.

I would like to thank Joseph Vogel, for his continuing encouragement of my research, his thoughtful foreword to this book, and his many contributions to the field of Michael Jackson Studies. I also owe great thanks to my fellow academics and authors in the field: Michele Wallace, Francesca T. Royster, Willa Stillwater, Toni Bowers, Susan Fast, Lisha McDuff, Sylvia J. Martin, Michael Eric Dyson, Marjorie Garber, Constance Pierce, Julian Vigo, Aneta Ostaszewska, Jochen Ebmeier, Veronica Bassil, Mary A. Fischer, Raven Woods, Jeremy Gilbert, Matthew Delmont, Mark Fisher, Michael Bush, Zack O'Malley Greenburg, Andy Healy, Margo Jefferson, Syl Mortilla, Harriet J. Manning, Kobena Mercer, Susan Woodward, Armond White, and countless others whose research has informed mine.

I would also like to thank my editors at Praeger: Catherine Lafuente and Anthony Chiffolo, as well as Elana Place and Rebecca Matheson, for guiding this book from proposal to print. I am especially beholden to the sponsors, supporters, members, and readers of the *Journal of Michael Jackson Academic Studies* (*MJAS*) online and my web site, *Writing Eliza*. To all the early adopters of the journal and my work, especially MJJJustice, Tahkiya Brady, Ale Huerta, Marisa Ramirez, Ilke Lenz-Nolte, Poli Brückner, Jamilah Bourdon, the MJCast

(Q and Jamon), and so many others on Facebook, Twitter, and Instagram. It's all for love.

My gratitude goes to the entire English Department at King's College London, currently led by Richard Kirkland, who provided me with the tools to expand my research. I am especially grateful to Rivkah Zim, Gordon McMullan, and Lucy Munro for going the extra mile to enable me to complete my research. A great debt of thanks goes to the wonderful Elizabeth Scott-Baumann, Sonia Massai, and Sarah Lewis, three of the greatest educators a scholar could ask for.

All the staff in Rare Books and Manuscripts at the British Library, where I spent so much of my time during this project that it feels like a second home, and the marvelous staff at the Maughan Library, with its beautiful round reading room, and those at the Lambeth Palace Library. To Arnold Hunt and Giles Mandelbrote, who gave me a love of rare books that I will treasure for the rest of my life. To my former students and colleagues for their engaging conversation and dedication, especially Carolyn Jordan, Gemma Smith, Wendy Shorter, and Neil Smith. My dearest and oldest friend, Jenny Stapleton, who has been a beacon of love and support for 15 years—keep smiling and keep shining. I am very grateful to be standing on the shoulders of so many amazing people, without whom this book could not have been written. The final word of heartfelt love and thanks is reserved for my joyful co-creator, Karin Merx, for her continual unwavering belief in me and for the magical portrait of Michael gracing the cover of this book.

Michael Jackson:
A Selected Chronology

This chronology has been compiled from a range of sources. It aims to provide an overview of Jackson's career to accompany the academic criticism that has emerged and focused on his career.[1]

1958	Michael Joseph Jackson born on August 29 in Gary, Indiana, to Katherine Esther Scruse and Joseph Walter Jackson, eighth of 10 children.
1963–1968	The Jackson 5, a musical group consisting of Jackson and his brothers—Jermaine, Tito, Jackie, and Marlon—perform at several talent shows. They also perform at the Apollo Theater in Harlem, New York, and on the "chitlin circuit."
1968	The Jackson 5 release their first single, "Big Boy," with Steeltown Records. In the same year they are signed to Motown Records.
1969	The Jackson 5 perform on the televised *Ed Sullivan Show*.
1970	The Jackson 5's first four singles, "I Want You Back," "ABC," "The Love You Save," and "I'll Be There," peak at No. 1 on the Billboard Hot 100. Jackson is the youngest artist to reach No. 1.
1971	ABC-TV airs an animated television series based on The Jackson 5.
1972	Jackson's first two solo albums, *Got To Be There* and *Ben*, are released. The latter includes his first No. 1 single, "Ben." Subsequent solo album releases at Motown are *Music & Me* (1973) and *Forever, Michael* (1975).

1969	The Jackson 5 release several albums, including: *Diana Ross Presents The Jackson 5* (1969); *ABC* (1970); *Third Album* (1970); *Jackson 5 Christmas Album* (1970); *Maybe Tomorrow* (1971); *Goin' Back to Indiana* (1971); *Lookin' Through the Windows* (1972); *Skywriter* (1973); *The Jackson 5 in Japan* (1973); *G.I.T.: Get It Together* (1973); *Dancing Machine* (1974); and *Moving Violation* (1975).
1976	The Jackson 5 leave Motown and move to CBS Records. Motown's ownership of the band name causes the group to rebrand as The Jacksons. The Jacksons release several albums, including: *The Jacksons* (1976), featuring Michael Jackson's first published song, "Blues Away"; *Goin' Places* (1977); *Destiny* (1978); *Triumph (1980), The Jacksons Live!* (1981); and *Victory* (1984).
1978	Jackson stars as the Scarecrow in his first feature film, *The Wiz*, directed by Sidney Lumet, and meets the film's score composer, Quincy Jones.
1979	Jackson releases his first adult solo album, *Off The Wall*, produced by Quincy Jones, the highest-selling album of all time by a black artist to date. Number 1 singles from *Off The Wall* include "Don't Stop 'Til You Get Enough" and "Rock With You."
1982	Jackson releases his second adult solo album, *Thriller*, coproduced with Quincy Jones, which becomes the highest-selling album of all time. Number 1 singles from *Thriller* include "Billie Jean" and "Beat It."
1983	Jackson debuts "the moonwalk" on the televised NBC special *Motown 25: Yesterday, Today and Forever*. "Say Say Say," a duet with Paul McCartney for McCartney's album *Pipes of Peace*, is released. The 14-minute *Thriller* short film, directed by John Landis, airs on MTV. *The Making of Michael Jackson's 'Thriller'*, directed by Jerry Kramer, is released on video. Along with *Beat It* (directed by Bob Giraldi) and *Billie Jean* (directed by Steve Barron), these short films serve to break down racial barriers.
1984	While filming a commercial for Pepsi, Jackson is burned in a pyrotechnic accident and rushed to the hospital. He wins eight Grammy Awards in 10 categories for *Thriller*. In the same year, he receives a Special Achievement Award from President Reagan at the White House. Jackson embarks on

The Victory Tour with The Jacksons and announces that he is leaving the group.

1985   *The Making of Michael Jackson's 'Thriller'* wins a Grammy for Best Video Album. The charity single "We Are the World" is released and peaks at No. 1. It is estimated to be the highest-selling single of the 1980s. Jackson purchases the ATV catalogue of music publishing rights for $47.5 million. This catalogue includes 251 Beatles songs. Kobena Mercer's essay "Monster Metaphors: Notes on Michael Jackson's 'Thriller'" is published in *Screen*.

1986   Jackson stars in *Captain EO*, a 17-minute short film, codirected by George Lucas and Francis Ford Coppola for a new 3D-ride at Disneyland.

1987   Jackson releases his third adult solo album, *Bad*, and becomes the first artist to have five No. 1's from one album: "Bad," "The Way You Make Me Feel," "Man in the Mirror," "I Just Can't Stop Loving You," and "Dirty Diana." Jackson embarks on his first solo tour, which breaks several records of attendance. He uses the tour to visit several hospitals and orphanages.

1988   Jackson is commended for his generous financial contributions to the United Negro College Fund through the Michael Jackson Scholarship Fund. He releases his first autobiography, *Moonwalk*, published by Doubleday and edited by Jacqueline Onassis, which becomes a New York Times Best Seller. Jackson moves to Neverland Valley Ranch in the Santa Ynez Valley near Los Angeles, California, and performs at Wembley Stadium in London with Prince Charles and Diana, Princess of Wales, in attendance. He also donates several hundred thousand dollars to the Prince's Trust, Great Ormond Street and the Motown Museum Historical Foundation. Jackson also releases *Moonwalker*, an anthology film directed by Jerry Kramer, Jim Blashfield, and Colin Chilvers.

1989   Jackson appears on the cover of *Vanity Fair*, photographed by Annie Leibowitz. He also befriends Ryan White, a teenager hemophiliac, who became a poster child for AIDS after contracting HIV from a transfusion. Michele Wallace's essay "Michael Jackson, Black Modernisms and the Ecstasy of Communication" is published in *Third Text*.

1990   White dies of AIDS-related complications. Jackson immedi-
            ately flies to Indiana to console White's bereaved mother,
            Jeanne. In this year, Jackson is briefly hospitalized for stress-
            related illness.

1991   Jackson co-writes and coproduces the song "Do The Bart
            Man," for the character of Bart (voiced by Nancy Cartwright)
            in *The Simpsons*. He also appears in the episode "Stark Rav-
            ing Dad," under the name John Jay Smith. Jackson signs a
            new recording contract with Sony Records worth approxi-
            mately $890 million, and receives a royalty rate of 25 percent.
            The widely referenced biography *Michael Jackson: The Magic
            and the Madness*, by J. Randy Taraborrelli, is published by
            Citadel. David Lynch directs the television ads for Jackson's
            fourth adult solo album, *Dangerous*. Number 1 singles from
            Dangerous include "Black or White."

1992   Jackson tours Africa and is given the title King of Sani in
            the Ivory Coast. He publishes his second book, *Dancing the
            Dream: Poems and Reflections* with Doubleday and begins
            his second solo world tour. He also launches the Heal the
            World Foundation and performs at the Super Bowl halftime
            show. *The Jacksons—An American Dream*, a televised mini-
            series based on the Jackson family, is aired on ABC-TV.

1993   Jackson gives a live interview entitled "Michael Jackson
            Talks . . . To Oprah," his first televised interview in over a
            decade. He also receives the Grammy Legend Award, pre-
            sented by his sister Janet. The Los Angeles Police Depart-
            ment begin a criminal investigation of Jackson, based on
            accusations by a 13-year-old named Jordy Chandler. The
            international press begin disparaging coverage of the alle-
            gations, and Jackson cancels his tour in order to begin treat-
            ment for painkiller dependency. *Dangerous: The Short Films*,
            is released on video. Jackson's four-minute statement of
            defense airs on American television.

1994   Although no corroborating evidence has been found, rep-
            resentatives of both Jackson and his accuser settle out of
            court for an undisclosed sum. In the same year, Jackson
            marries Lisa-Marie Presley, the only child of Elvis. Delores
            Martez Jackson, the former wife of Jackson's brother Tito,
            is found dead at the bottom of a swimming pool. Donald
            Bohana would be convicted of her murder in 1998.

1995   *GQ* publishes the landmark article written by Mary A. Fischer, "Was Michael Jackson Framed?" Jackson releases his fifth adult solo album, *HIStory: Past, Present and Future Book 1* in a double-disc format with 15 of his greatest hits. Its commercial success is widely ignored by the mainstream media, but it remains the highest-selling double album of all time. Number 1 singles from *History: Past, Present and Future Book 1* include "You Are Not Alone" and "Earth Song." Robert Burnett and Burt Deivert's essay "Black or White: Michael Jackson's Video as a Mirror of Popular Culture" is published in *Popular Music and Society.*

1996   Jackson and Presley divorce. Jackson begins his third solo tour. His short film *Ghosts* (directed by Stan Winston) premieres. Jackson marries his second wife, Debbie Rowe, a dermatological nurse.

1997   Son Michael Joseph Jackson, Jr. is born. Jackson releases his sixth solo adult release, *Blood on the Dance Floor: HIStory in the Mix*, a remix album. Jochen Ebmeier's monograph *Das Phänomen Michael Jackson* is published in Hamburg.

1998   Daughter Paris Michael Katherine Jackson is born.

1999   Jackson and Rowe divorce. Jason King's essay "Form and Function: Super Stardom and Aesthetics in the Music Videos of Michael and Janet Jackson" is published in *Velvet Light Trap.*

2000   Jackson enters the Guinness Book of World Records for supporting more charitable organizations than any other individual.

2001   Jackson delivers a speech called "Love: The Human Family's Most Precious Legacy" at the Oxford Union, and appears with the band N'Sync at the MTV Video Music Awards. He also reunites with his brothers for the *Michael Jackson: 30th Anniversary Special* at Madison Square Gardens. The day after the final performance, September 11, terrorists attack the World Trade Center. A month later, Jackson releases his seventh adult solo album, *Invincible.* Christopher Lynch's essay "Ritual Transformation through Michael Jackson's Music Video" is published in the *Journal of Communication Inquiry.*

2002   After its initial success, *Invincible*'s promotion becomes embroiled in a feud between Jackson and Sony Records

	executive Tommy Mottola. Jackson stars in *Men in Black II*. Son Prince Michael Jackson II is born.
2003	*Living with Michael Jackson*, a controversial documentary directed by Martin Bashir, is broadcast on ITV in the United Kingdom. It is soon followed by *Michael Jackson—The Footage You Were Never Meant to See* and *Michael Jackson—Private Home Movies* on FOX in the United States. Jackson is nominated for a Nobel Peace Prize. A compilation CD/DVD album, *Michael Jackson Number Ones*, is released. Shortly thereafter, the Los Angeles Police Department formally charges Jackson based on accusations by a 13-year-old named Gavin Arvizo, who was featured in the documentary *Living with Michael Jackson*. Jackson's Neverland Valley Ranch is raided by the police.
2004	Jackson features in *Miss Cast Away and the Island Girls*, directed by Bryan Michael Stoller.
2005	After a lengthy trial, Jackson is acquitted of all charges. Francesca Royster's essay "'Hee hee hee': Michael Jackson and the Transgendered Erotics of Voice" is published online via the *National Sexuality Resource Center*.
2006	*Thriller Live*, a musical showcasing the music of Michael Jackson and The Jackson 5, premieres at the Dominion Theatre, London. Margo Jefferson's monograph *On Michael Jackson* is published.
2007	Three articles are published about Michael Jackson in the journal *Social Semiotics*: "Michael Jackson Fans on Trial? Documenting Emotivism and Fandom in *Wacko About Jacko*," "The Face of Ruin: Evidentiary Spectacle and the Trial of Michael Jackson," and "Presenting Michael Jackson™.".
2008	*Thriller 25*, the 25th anniversary special edition of *Thriller*, is released.
2009	*Thriller Live* begins its run at the Lyric Theatre in London. Jackson announces *This Is It*, a 50-concert residency at the O2 Arena, in North Greenwich, London. *This Is It* sells out approximately one million tickets. Michael Jackson dies on June 25 of acute propofol and benzodiazepine intoxication. His sudden death provokes an unprecedented outpouring of grief. Several of Jackson's albums chart highly around the world. In the same year, Jackson's autobiography *Moonwalk* is published in a new edition by Doubleday, with a foreword by Berry Gordy. An edited collection, *The*

	Resistible Demise of Michael Jackson, and a new edition of Adrian Grant's *Visual Documentary*, are both published.
2010	Conrad Murray, Jackson's personal physician, is charged with involuntary manslaughter. Ubisoft releases *Michael Jackson: The Experience*, a multiplatform game based on Jackson's choreography. Armond White's collection of articles, *Keep Moving: The Michael Jackson Chronicles*, is published, and the *Journal of Pan-African Studies* devotes an entire issue to Michael Jackson. Charles Thomson writes a series of articles regarding Jackson's coverage by the mainstream press.
2011	Cirque du Soleil performs *Michael Jackson: The Immortal World Tour*. *Immortal*, a compilation soundtrack to the tour, is released. *Man in the Music: The Creative Life and Work of Michael Jackson* by Joseph Vogel is published by Sterling. The posthumous album *Michael* is released. Murray is convicted of the involuntary manslaughter of Jackson. Joseph Vogel's monographs, *Earth Song: Inside Michael Jackson's Magnum Opus*, are also published. The *Journal of Popular Music Studies* devotes an issue to essays on Michael Jackson.
2012	The posthumous album *Bad 25* is released. Jackson features posthumously in the documentary *Bad 25*, directed by Spike Lee. Joseph Vogel's collection of articles, *Featuring Michael Jackson: Collected Writings on the King of Pop*, is published, along with Francesca Royster's landmark monograph, *Sounding Like a No-No: Queer Sounds and Eccentric Acts in the Post-Soul Era*. The edited collection *Michael Jackson: Grasping the Spectacle*, is published by Ashgate. Michael Bush's monograph *The King of Style: Dressing Michael Jackson*, is also published this year.
2013	Cirque du Soleil performs *Michael Jackson: One*.
2014	The posthumous album *Xscape* is released. The first academic journal dedicated solely to Jackson's life and creative work, *The Journal of Michael Jackson Academic Studies*, is founded by Elizabeth Amisu and Karin Merx. Susan Fast's monograph *Dangerous* is published as the 100th edition of Bloomsbury's *33 1/3* series. Susan Woodward's *Otherness and Power: Michael Jackson and His Media Critics* and Zack O'Malley Greenburg's *Michael Jackson Inc.* are also published this year.

2015   Jackson's former home, Neverland Valley Ranch, is put up for sale by Colony Capital and the Michael Jackson Estate. Joseph Vogel's essay "'I Ain't Scared of No Sheets': Re-Screening Black Masculinity in Michael Jackson's Black or White" is published in the *Journal of Popular Music Studies*. Karin Merx's essay "From Throne to Wilderness: Michael Jackson's 'Stranger in Moscow' and the Foucaldian Outlaw" is published in the *Journal of Michael Jackson Academic Studies*. The journal also publishes the first *Companion to Michael Jackson Studies* for free online.

2016   Seven years after Jackson's death, *The Dangerous Philosophies of Michael Jackson: His Music, His Persona, and His Artistic Afterlife*, the first comprehensive academic monograph entirely dedicated to Michael Jackson's art, is published by Praeger.

PART I

Art as Life

This section focuses on Jackson's artistic output. It is investigative in that it seeks to deeply consider aspects of Jackson's work that may have been overlooked in the past. It also engages with the current body of discourse on Jackson's creative output and draws links to cultural, film, and literary theory and criticism.

CHAPTER 1

Introduction:
Reading, Writing, and
Rewriting Michael Jackson

> "Thou art a monument without a tomb. . . . And art alive still while thy book doth live. And we have wits to read and praise to give."
>
> —Ben Jonson[1]

I, like countless others, was born into a world filled with the music of Michael Jackson. One of my most wonderful memories is of listening to Jackson's final studio album, *Invincible*, for the first time. There were fireworks at my boarding school in 2001, and as I watched them, my ears were alive with the electricity of his songs. I was transported to a new world. It would be another 13 years before I would begin to tackle one of the most prevalent questions in Michael Jackson Studies: Where are all the books? No, not the celebrity biographies, not liner notes and sheet music, but the actual books—the academic books, the celebratory books, the ones on Jackson's art and his inspiration, the edited collections focused on his filmmaking, composition, clothing, and artistry. The kind of books of which there are dozens on artists like The Beatles and Elvis Presley. Then I discovered that "books on Elvis Presley alone outnumber titles on Chuck Berry, Aretha Franklin, James Brown, Ray Charles, Marvin Gaye, Stevie Wonder, and Michael Jackson combined."[2]

I was not, by any means, the first academic to realize how few books and journal essays had been written on Jackson, whose "career, cultural impact and artistry deserve—and reward—serious exploration."[3] As further illustrated in Chapter 2—"A Critical Survey of Michael Jackson Studies," "the only way Michael Jackson could get covered was if he was presented as a freak, a curiosity, a spectacle," and precious few pieces written used his actual music, short films, and interviews as their primary sources.[4] However, much like the pioneering academics who paved my way, I took this challenge as an incredible opportunity to model what Michael Jackson Studies could be. As Jonson writes in his elegiac poem to William Shakespeare, Jackson's work may yet live, while "we have wits to read and praise to give."[5] In other words, the only enduring method by which to venerate any great artist is to write about their creations.

When I began my research in 2014, one of my most pertinent unanswered questions about the world-renowned artist, Michael Jackson, remained—who was he? While completing academic research in Early Modern English Literature at King's College London, I found myself asking similar questions about the 17th-century playwright, Shakespeare.[6] What truly shocked me was that—though the artists were born four centuries apart—aside from the bodies of creative work they left behind, their contemporary audiences knew little about who they were. Despite this fact, images of Michael Jackson and William Shakespeare remain fixed in public consciousness. In light of this, I have chosen similar methodologies (approaches) as those employed in the study of Early Modern (Shakespearean) English Literature. I specifically chose a Cultural Materialist approach because it allowed me to construct a narrative from a wide range of sources and convey a clearer account of specific concepts, such as Jackson's personas.[7]

There are those who argue that the popularity of Jackson's work undermines its artistic value, and others who claim that to write about Jackson is to profit from the materialism that stole his life. However, to them I put this argument: William Shakespeare's work was also predominantly created for a mass audience, and this does not in any way diminish his contribution (see Figure 1.1).

Moreover, while Shakespeare's genius will forever be shrouded by untold stories, Michael Jackson Studies has a rich catalogue of compositions, cinematic works, autobiography, poetry, fashion, live performances, and collaborative material, as well as numerous interviews to draw from. There has been much discussion about Jackson's legacy in the past seven years, especially with regard to how his art has been presented in his absence.[8] Academic study may well fulfill Jackson's most heartfelt wish, to be respected for the artist he was: "I always want to do music that inspires . . . to escape death, I attempt to bind my soul to my work"[9]—hence, the use of the original portrait of Jackson by artist Karin Merx, in order to further reiterate Jackson's regality and the respectful nature of this work (see Figure 1.2).

This book is a collection of original essays focused entirely on the art, music, and life of Michael Jackson. It seeks to emulate accessible and informative academic books like Kim F. Hall's *Things of Darkness: Economies of Race and Gender in Early Modern England*, Sonia Massai's edited collection *World-Wide*

Figure 1.1
William Shakespeare, 1564–1616.
One print: photograving. (Photograving/Typographic Etching Co./
Library of Congress)

Shakespeares, and Francesca Royster's *Sounding Like a No-No: Queer Sounds and Eccentric Acts in the Post-Soul Era*.[10] It also imitates Joseph Vogel's *Man in the Music: The Creative Life and Work of Michael Jackson* and Susan Fast's *Dangerous*, by utilizing Jackson's art as primary source material.[11] The first section, *Art as Life*, focuses on case studies from Jackson's canon (back catalogue), ranging from the 1997 short film *Ghosts*, to his use of clothing as costume. The second section, *Life as Art*, explores Jackson's life, especially in terms of his representation and personas. The final section, *Art Beyond Life*, explores Jackson's artistic afterlife, and discusses his posthumous releases and legacy. This book also proposes several models for further study of Jackson's creative works. It has been written primarily for those interested in or studying music, art, film, popular culture, literature and African American heritage.

This book uses the following primary sources: musical compositions, interviews, books, articles, and performances produced by Michael Jackson in life. Posthumously released works are not used as primary sources; however, some demos are occasionally referred to. The secondary sources include

Figure 1.2
A Portrait Drawing of Michael Jackson, 2014.
Ink pen on watercolor paper, Frame & Sight 44.5×34.5 cm. Private Collection of
Elizabeth Amisu. (Artwork by Karin Merx)

monographs, edited collections, journal essays, news, and blog articles that focus chiefly on Jackson's art, life, and cultural significance. The use of secondary sources is a form of recognition of wider discourse in which this book exists. Throughout the chapters that follow, all albums and songs performed, written, composed, arranged, or recorded by Jackson during his lifetime and released in Jackson's life are considered canon. Posthumously released songs are not. As a result, songs that have been altered or revised after Jackson's death are used sparingly. Songs from the solo adult album releases, for which Jackson was executive producer, were chosen by the artist to depict themes, ideas, and concepts he wanted to present to the wider world. Though not all of these songs were written by the artist, they are referred to as *his*. I have elected to use the artist's own autobiographies, *Moonwalk* and *HIStory: Past, Present and Future, Book 1*, because they illuminate the artist's life.[12] I have chosen not to use biographies that rely on undisclosed sources because it is difficult to ascertain their authenticity. Nevertheless, the accounts of relatives and colleagues of Jackson are used only when their version of facts corresponds with the artist's. Lastly, all term dating, definitions, and etymological references (unless otherwise stated) have been taken from the *Oxford English Dictionary (OED) Online*.

CHAPTER 2

A Critical Survey of Michael Jackson Studies

T his chapter is a critical survey.[1] Its aim is to familiarize the reader with the emerging critical field of Michael Jackson Studies. It also illustrates the critical "conversations" about Michael Jackson, which various academics have engaged in, and how these conversations have shifted between 1986 and now. After outlining its key terms, this survey examines the rapidly growing study of Michael Jackson as an artist, and it concludes with a brief discussion of the future of Michael Jackson Studies.

> "In the beginning was the word . . ."
>
> —John 1:1, *NIV.*

The story of Michael Jackson Studies is doubtless a story about words. In the biblical book of John, a mysterious connection is made between what is spoken and written and what becomes a living, breathing being. Likewise, in Michael Jackson Studies, words very much made the man in question, and words unmade him. The first series of words to which I am referring are those of the masses of tabloid ephemera published during Jackson's lifetime.[2] However, the second set of words are the books, academic and otherwise, that circulated primarily between 1986 and today. What remains remarkable, though, is the stunning lack of words devoted to one of the most superlative musicians of modern times. At the time of the artist's death, there were absolutely no published academic books dedicated to Jackson's art in the English language. The single book with an academic focus this survey uncovered was first published in 1997 by an academic named Jochen Ebmeier in German.[3]

The primary use of a word to describe the study of Michael Jackson was the term "Jacksonism" in 2009. This was at least four years before the academic, Joseph Vogel, introduced the term "Michael Jackson Studies" as the title for his unique online resource page.[4] "Jacksonism" was used to describe the artistic contributions of Michael Jackson in an article by Mark Fisher that argues emphatically that Jackson's "mass-mediated demise" was symptomatic of a disease that had been present at the earliest moments of his career.[5] The article is an interesting example of much of the literary discourse that emerged about Jackson posthumously, and it incorporates the well-worn notion that: a) Jackson's only vital art was the "soul to sell your soul for" *Off the Wall* and *Thriller* albums, and b) Jackson's changing appearance to a "repellent white sepulcher" was, in Fisher's opinion, synonymous with an artistic decline.[6] What is particularly interesting, however, is Fisher's use of the suffix "ism" in addition to Jackson's name. For "ism" denotes a movement that commands action, and this is particularly true in Jackson's case. Jackson's art persistently required action from those who engaged with it. Audiences were galvanized into listening to Jackson's music, watching Jackson's short films, emulating his moves, focusing on his physical appearance, and investing in his products.

Throughout this book, Michael Jackson Studies is used as a proper noun that describes the entire canon of Jackson's artistic creations and the artist himself, as well as how both were received by audiences. This definition, *all that pertains to Michael Jackson and how he was presented*, has been employed because it enables the reader to examine 1) how Jackson was both a product and producer of popular culture and 2) how the very same culture constructs and enacts notions of ethnicity, gender, consumerism, and celebrity.[7]

1986–2008

Though he was born in the late 1950s, Jackson's early musical catalogue spans the breadth of the late 1960s and 1970s. Academically speaking, however, the critical analysis of his work begins in 1986 with Kobena Mercer's essay, "Monster Metaphors: Notes on Michael Jackson's 'Thriller'," published in a leading academic journal of film studies, *Screen*.[8] Mercer has been cited here as the first key example of criticism, rather than the monograph by Dave Marsh, *Michael Jackson and the Crossover Dream*, published a year earlier.[9] The main reason for this is the negative bias in Marsh's account, and several more detailed explanations are provided by Susan Woodward in the second chapter ("American Messiah") of her 2014 monograph, *Otherness and Power: Michael Jackson and His Media Critics*.[10] She writes, "Marsh was left with a feeling of profound betrayal" and "compares Jackson to performers in a minstrel show."[11]

Mercer's essay was an early example of emergent academic discourse of both Cultural Studies and Film Studies. After providing a significant introduction to both Jackson and his LP, *Thriller*, Mercer launches into a detailed reading of the film text that deconstructs *Thriller*'s narrative aspects, its characterization, and its mise-en-scene.[12] Jackson's *Thriller* short film provides ample ground for analysis, especially since it is a pioneering short film of a field that would become known as the music video. Mercer argues that "in the absence of a direct economic imperative . . . its use of cinematic codes and structures provides a framework for Jackson to act."[13] Mercer's essay is a particularly useful one for those studying Film Theory and Film Language, both as a resource and as an example.

Building upon Mercer's focus on African American Cultural Studies was Michele Wallace's 1989 essay, "Michael Jackson, Black Modernisms and the Ecstasy of Communication."[14] Originally published in *Third Text*, it would be included in her landmark 1990 monograph, *Invisibility Blues: From Pop to Theory*, a critically acclaimed, unique, holistic, black feminist manifesto. In this collection, Wallace ties together studies of popular culture, film theory, and gender. Michael Jackson's *Bad* had been released a few short years before, and Wallace gives a laser-sharp focus to it, including short films and public performances like the Grammy Awards, arguing that Jackson "must constantly struggle for space alongside considerations of consumerism and televisual postmodernism."[15] Wallace's article remains one of the most fruitful offerings of criticism in Michael Jackson Studies and is an integral source for any essay on Jackson, quite simply because it contextualizes him so aptly: "American television still keeps one unfathomable secret: this country's Afro-American presence."[16] Black presence is also a focus in "Michael Jackson's Postmodern Spirituality" by Eric Dyson, published in 1993 as part of *Reflecting Black: African-American Cultural Criticism.*[17] Both Dyson and Wallace use the lens of postmodernism when discussing Jackson's art and representation, and both are far ahead of the critical curve, taking into account both Jackson's influence and context, and also his artistry: "Jackson's videos may be capable of playing a key role in evolving public discourses of race, sex, and class."[18] However, Dyson's perspective takes into account, to an even greater extent than Wallace's, the cultural connections between Jackson's music and performance, African American culture, and spiritualism: "Jackson's concerts thrive on call and response" and "mediate ritual structures of an antiphonal oral and verbal exchange between artist and audience."[19]

In terms of primary sources, Jackson released autobiographical material alongside his studio albums: *Moonwalk*, a monograph published by Doubleday in 1989, a collection, *Dancing the Dream: Poems and Reflections*, in 1991, and *HIStory: Past Present and Future, Book 1,* a musical autobiography, which gives his account of the events that transpired between 1989 and 1995.[20] The 1990s were a fertile season for the artist who, "in the midst of the circus that surrounded him . . . managed to leave behind one of the most impressive catalogs in the history of music."[21] Jackson drew from a huge intellectual and artistic library and, at key moments in his career, based his art on both the aesthetics of Tchaikovsky and of black children from the ghetto, while crossing the boundaries between ethnicity, gender, and class.[22]

During his life Jackson's art achieved mainstream success, as evidenced by countless awards, accolades, and records, but this lucrative production of popular music and popular culture in short films and albums was often misrepresented and misunderstood. In order to give context to these misconceptions, and to how they are perpetuated through academic criticism, it is necessary to contextualize the wider discourse, particularly in the mass media.

The journalistic criticism produced during Jackson's career, primarily after *Thriller*'s huge success, would go on to determine the perceived quality of his art. This criticism was not produced by academics. It was produced by music critics, whose goal was often not to give well-researched appraisal of the work but to discredit the artist and largely sideline the art by discussing widely circulated rumors about his personal life.[23] Music critics had the preserve of evaluating "some of the most substantive music ever to have been obliterated by personal scandal."[24] Throughout Jackson's later career, especially after 1993, the damning critique of journalists would repeatedly counter the value of his work; as Vogel states, "reviews of the albums, post-*Thriller*, focused on the sensational and were overwhelmingly patronizing, when not outright hostile."[25] A particularly useful resource for those interested in how the criticism of journalists, reviewers, and tabloids made the man, Vogel's 2011 monograph, *Man in the Music: The Creative Life and Work of Michael Jackson*, is an indispensable resource. It boasts a comprehensive and detailed bibliography of contemporaneous reviews.

To many of the aforementioned music critics, subject to the dominant ideologies of white heterosexual patriarchy, a black, androgynous, socially powerful man who toppled the crowns given to the Beatles and Elvis was, at best, a nuisance. *Thriller* remains a testament to Jackson's success, though the label "commercially successful" has now acquired negative connotations. Furthermore, this negatively biased criticism that dogged Jackson's career also exists within the wider context of African American heritage; as critic Margo Jefferson remarks, a black man, "William Henry Johnson was still playing the missing link between man and ape in 1906, when a group of anthropologists arrived in New York with Ota Benga, a central African Batwa . . . scientists put Ota Benga in the monkey house at the Bronx Zoo."[26]

Jackson's career between 1979, with the release of *Off the Wall*, and his last studio album, *Invincible*, in 2001, played out like an ancient myth. It was as though Jackson had opened Pandora's Box and suddenly, after *Thriller*, MTV had no choice but to play black artists' music videos.[27] Icarus-like, Jackson flew higher than anyone had before him, especially in terms of album and ticket sales, and like Prometheus, he passed to his African American brothers and sisters a fire that could not be taken from them. However, both Icarus and Prometheus suffered for their transgressions: Icarus lost his wings and plummeted to his death, while Prometheus was brutally punished for eternity.[28] Jackson, too, would face a unique punishment; in his words, "overnight they called me a freak . . . They called me a child molester. They said I bleached my skin. They did everything to turn the public against me."[29]

Between 1985 and 2009 there was an intensive attempt by the mainstream press to refer to Jackson as anything but an artist, "the only way [he] could get covered was if he was presented as a freak, a curiosity, a spectacle."[30] In later years he would be negatively characterized in many ways, from megalomaniac to pervert, from liar to racist, in what Vogel terms as "cultural abuse" in his article, " 'Am I the Beast You Visualized?': The Cultural Abuse of Michael Jackson." Jackson's vulnerability created the environment in which he became a target for extortion, and in 1993 tabloid fabrications were universally accepted in one of the most sensational accusations in popular culture. By 1993, Jackson's name was synonymous with scandal, to the extent that to write about Jackson academically was seen as far more trouble than it was worth. There were too many versions of Jackson's story. Not until his death would he once again begin to "engender more respect from the intelligentsia."[31] This is partly why there is such a relatively small amount of academic criticism in Michael Jackson Studies between 1986 and 2009.

Both Susan Fast and Joseph Vogel have described the barrenness of critical discourse at this time: "I couldn't find *one* serious book focused on Jackson's creative output," and "I started looking for writing on his music and found . . . practically nothing! I was stunned that an artist of his caliber had been so little considered by academics."[32] Hence, also, the fragmentary tone to the criticism produced between 1990 and 2008, and many of the essays consult a popular biography, J. Randy Taraborrelli's *Michael Jackson: The Magic and the Madness*, rather than Jackson's *Moonwalk*, and often, Jackson is used as a metaphor for an entirely different argument, which has little to do with him.[33] One key example, however, of valuable criticism produced during these years, is Francesca Royster's " 'Hee hee hee': Michael Jackson and the Transgendered Erotics of Voice," an article published online in 2005 and later included in Royster's monograph, *Sounding Like a No-No: Queer Sounds and Eccentric*

Acts in the Post-Soul Era.[34] Royster, like myself, is an Early Modernist, and her unique perspective of 17th-century literature would enable her to make key connections between Jackson and cultural studies, as well as the semiotics of representation. This trend of academics from fields such as English Literature and Musicology, using their prior knowledge to engage in the discourse of Michael Jackson Studies, would spark a fascinating trend in the years to follow.

From academics Robert Burnett, Bert Deivert, Elena Oliete, and Radan Martinec the 2000s offered a continuing critical analysis of Jackson's short films: *Black or White*, *Smooth Criminal*, and *Jam*.[35] In these works Jackson is presented as a product of his popularity and a symptom of society's celebrity culture. At once, the same artist becomes both the maker of the culture, under which he is a victim. Margo Jefferson's monograph, *On Michael Jackson*, illustrates the challenge of writing about Jackson in the early 2000s. Jefferson explores Jackson through the prism of the xenophobic culture into which he was born, "circus owners couldn't find genuine dark-skinned specimens," and childhood stardom, "a national sex object—a sex toy, really."[36] Furthermore, Jefferson draws connections between Jackson's personal familial history and the personas that had been attributed to him by 2006. The chapter "Freaks" is particularly poignant, presenting Jackson's "cultural abuse" as originating from a disturbing freak-show heritage at the heart of Americana. The essay was republished in 2012 in the edited collection *Michael Jackson: Grasping the Spectacle*.[37]

2009–2015

Much in the same way that William Shakespeare's death in 1616 spurred John Heminges and Henry Condell to publish the First Folio in 1623, Michael Jackson's death spurred Michael Jackson Studies on to a previously unknown height. Suddenly, after several years, the public was asking questions about Jackson, and questions needed answers. At the moment of the artist's unexpected death, untethered cultural critique and a myriad of "academic" discussions of *Thriller* as allegorical abounded, as in Reid Kane's "The King of Pop's Two Bodies, or, *Thriller* as Allegory."[38] In 2010 critic Armond White published *Keep Moving: The Michael Jackson Chronicles*. It was a limited print, privately published, and a compelling collection of critiques that, although not strictly academic, more than made up for it in its immediacy and consistency. The collection employs a subtle academic tone that dissects Jackson's art within the wider context of critical analysis and cinema. White's essays were written during the mid-1980s and they continue until 2009, which give a real sense of fluidity to his work. As White highlights in the article,

"Screaming to Be Heard," for most of his adult life Michael Jackson was deemed unworthy of serious academic attention.[39]

Two essay collections, *The Resistible Demise of Michael Jackson* and *Michael Jackson: Grasping the Spectacle*, were published in 2009 and 2012, respectively. Though outwardly seeming to offer objective criticism, several articles in each perpetuate fabrications. Although these collections bear Michael Jackson's patronym, they are rarely about the artist himself. More often than not, they are about public perceptions of the artist and should be cited with this in mind.[40] These collections are also dotted with diamonds, such as Amy C. Billone's "Sentenced to Neverland: Michael Jackson, Peter Pan, and Queer Futurity," and Jeremy Gilbert's "The Real Abstraction of Michael Jackson," essays that discuss Jackson's art and the circumstances in which it was created, in depth and with sensitivity. Gilbert introduces the concept of a simulacra of Jackson emerging as a result of his overexposure, while Billone contradicts the dominant reading of "dreams" in Michael Jackson's work as solely a positive.[41]

In 2010 *The Journal of Pan African Studies* provided a plethora of well-researched, academic essays on Jackson, in an issue devoted entirely to him.[42] Where *The Journal of Pan African Studies* really revolutionizes the critical conversation about Jackson as artist is with its publication of Jackson's entire 2001 speech given at the Oxford Union—"Love: The Human Family's Most Precious Legacy."[43] For the very first time in print, Jackson's own words were placed in an academic context, side by side with the critics who wrote passionately about him and his work.

Several conferences took place at American universities in the five years following 2009.[44] Then, in 2011, Sterling published Joseph Vogel's *Man in the Music: The Creative Life and Work of Michael Jackson*. *Man in the Music* is an incredibly important text in Michael Jackson Studies because it was the first and most comprehensive meeting of all the primary material and the secondary material, criticism by academics and journalists alike. Vogel's book also presents Jackson's work in a highly specific context of production and reception, divided into sections for adult solo albums, from *Off The Wall* to *Invincible*, and it goes further than the canon to chart some of the prospective work from his later years. Furthermore, *Man in the Music* provides, for the first time, a truly comprehensive bibliography for further research,—"academia is currently blossoming with new scholarship on Jackson (from a variety of fields), music journalism has yet to catch-up."[45]

Vogel's second and third books, *Featuring Michael Jackson: Collected Writings on the King of Pop* and *Earth Song: Inside Michael Jackson's Magnum Opus*, followed the substantial inroads from his first book, and they are integral reading for every researcher in Michael Jackson Studies.[46] From the 2011 publication of *Man in the Music* onward, essays and monographs on Jackson gain a new sense of cohesion, as shown in *Popular Music & Society*'s 2012 special issue, which featured a wide range of insightful essays focused on recontextualizing Jackson.[47] More mainstream publications, such as Zack O'Malley Greenburg's *Michael Jackson Inc.*, provided more source material for academics to use in their analytical discussion of Jackson's art as an economic entity and of his posthumous success, while the publication of Michael Bush's *The King of Style: Dressing Michael Jackson* provided a source for those who wished to explore Jackson's use of fashion and clothing to create character and connection.[48]

In 2014, Susan Fast's *Dangerous* was published as the hundredth book in Bloomsbury's *33 1/3* series. This was a new type of academic writing devoted to Jackson, which deftly packs its small pages with musicological analysis, cultural study, key context, and film analysis to produce a clearer picture of Jackson's *Dangerous* album than has ever been seen before. While staying very close to the primary sources of Jackson's own words and music, Fast draws repeatedly from a range of critics such as White, Vogel, as well as wider criticism.[49]

Meanwhile, among readers there grew a need for further academic conversation. This academic community of Michael Jackson Studies was spurred on by the formation of the *Journal of Michael Jackson Academic Studies* in 2014, a nonprofit online peer-reviewed journal; through the journal, articles, essays, and publications that were lost are being reclaimed, and there is now a means for comprehensive references and new academic works on Jackson to find a public voice.[50] This book, *The Dangerous Philosophies of Michael Jackson: His Music, His Persona, and His Artistic Afterlife*, is a product of Praeger publishing's progressive outlook and the academic community's tireless contributions. The first of its kind, the book is an ambitious publication that draws upon all the academic criticism that has come before it. It is able to do so because there is now a body of critical discourse on which to base answers to some questions.

2016–FUTURE

The interest of fans, readers, librarians, and academics in learning about and studying Michael Jackson has resulted in publications that are slowly eroding Jackson's "delinquent" status and repositioning him as artist and auteur: "I'm going to tell different stories about Michael Jackson . . . hopefully allowing Jackson's mature artistic vision to emerge from the shadows."[51] The academic study of Jackson is now present in several fields, and criticism of

Jackson's art has now been published in the contexts of film, fashion, art, music, popular culture, and African American studies.[52]

Despite all this newfound criticism, there is still very much a need to write about Michael Jackson. He remains part of the very fabric of popular culture, his music an ever-present facet of daily living, as are his dance moves, his fashion, and of course, the short films that pioneered the music video. An academic discussion of Michael Jackson is an exploration into who and what we are. We are the consumers of his work, who spur his records on to continue to break records posthumously as they did during his lifetime. Among the much-needed criticism required in Michael Jackson Studies are academic reviews of a range of books that have been published in the last decade on Jackson, as well as Jackson's connections with the study of dance, performance, and the Renaissance artist. Of all Jackson's work, his later albums—*HIStory: Past, Present and Future Book 1*, *Blood on the Dance Floor: HIStory in the Mix*, and *Invincible*, in particular, seriously require academic discourse. Apart from the insightful essay by Karin Merx, "From Throne to Wilderness: Michael Jackson's 'Stranger in Moscow' and the Foucaldian Outlaw" published in the *MJAS* in 2015, discourse on Jackson's later work remains sparse.[53] There is very much a requirement for: analysis of Jackson's work in the fields of Film, African American Heritage, Musicology, Culture, History, Art History, Theatre, Literature, Live Performance; research on Michael Jackson as Composer, as Persona, and as Auteur; research on Jackson's posthumous representation and his legacy, and on the management of his estate; and research on his creative process and fashion. Alongside these topics is a range of source material that includes all the album releases produced as part of The Jackson 5 and The Jacksons (1968–1978), *Off The Wall* (1979), *Thriller* (1982), *Bad* (1987), *Dangerous* (1991), *HIStory: Past, Present and Future, Book 1* (1995), *Blood on the Dance Floor* (1997), and *Invincible* (2001), along with Jackson's numerous tours and their global impact, and the misappropriation and remixing of his work.

A useful piece of advice for prospective researchers is to decide on their approach by virtue of the source material. For example, the theme of oblivion throughout Jackson's career can be fruitful; however, an examination of oblivion in three key texts of a similar medium can be even more illuminating. In this case, one might choose two short films, *Billie Jean* and *Who Is It*, and focus on Jackson's disappearing act in both these works, discussing the ways in which these short films were constructs of the audiences who received them and the artist who starred within them. Context is key in Michael Jackson Studies, and context expertly and methodically integrated will make a good essay truly great.

A recent survey of London's British Library catalogue boasted precious little academic discourse on Michael Jackson, showing that the access to this research is still limited. However, owing to the mass-cultural appeal of his art, and the speed with which academic discourse has developed since 2009, it is with optimism that I conclude this survey.

CHAPTER 3

On Michael Jackson's
Dancing the Dream

Michael Jackson's words were disseminated in liner notes, magazines, and even a blog. His first published book was a 1988 autobiography, *Moonwalk*; the second, a children's storybook based on the film *Moonwalker* (dir. Jerry Kramer, 1988); and the last, a 1992 publication called *Dancing the Dream: Poems and Reflections*. This chapter contextualizes the latter collection within Jackson's career, and it positions a work as autobiographical as *Moonwalk* as a pivotal and hitherto uncelebrated moment in his artistic career. The chapter poses and answers the following questions: What is *Dancing the Dream*? How is it significant? and How should we read it?

"We are such stuff as dreams are made on . . ."
—William Shakespeare[1]

There is a pervasive misconception that Michael Jackson did not leave much more behind than "a few scattered memories."[2] This presumption stems from an acceptance of him as simply a commercial product, rather than as an artist; a person who sold records through controversy and spectacle rather than through dedication and learning.[3] It is a symptom of the reductions his life was plagued with. In truth, the Jackson canon consists of several released songs and albums, upwards of forty short films, three books (including an autobiography), and hundreds of unreleased songs.[4]

Dancing the Dream is, arguably, one of the best-kept "secrets" in Michael Jackson's artistic back catalogue. So secret, in fact, that 22 years after its publication, *Rolling Stone* did not include it in its 2014 tribute issue.[5]

Nevertheless, it showcases the author's most personal feelings about children, mortality, and the human condition.

WHAT IS *DANCING THE DREAM*?

Dancing the Dream is not like other books. Although it has a title, pages, and illustrations, the similarities stop there. In order to fully appreciate the considerable aesthetic depth of the collection's 46 entries, we must consider the title, the text's discourse features, and its content.

What does it mean to "dance the dream"? Is the poet dreaming of dancing, or is dancing his dream? The title boasts a dynamic verb, followed by a definite article and an abstract noun, creating a sense that dancing is dreaming and dreaming is a dance. Both are transient and transformative, and were of great importance to Jackson, who regarded his dance as a "divine union" between the spiritual and the physical and his dreams as integral to creativity and aspiration.[6]

In terms of structure, focus, and layout, *Dancing the Dream* bears more resemblance to the early modern (17th-century) commonplace book than the modern-day anthology. To "commonplace" is the art of taking extracts from one's reading and placing them under specific headings (*OED*). For an early modern reader, who might frequent the playhouse for a new Shakespeare play, reading was an active experience. It was commonly said to be wasteful to read without taking notes.[7] This type of reading culture is very evident in Ben Jonson's *Timber: Or, Discoveries Made Upon Men and Matter*, a chaotic combination of ideological matter from 1641.[8]

The commonplace book is a fiercely personal item; in fact, its only unifying feature is usually the person who has collated it. The same is true for *Dancing the Dream*. Although it has 46 works and several illustrations, it does not have a contents page, and the entries, without subdivision, are presented in a stream-of-consciousness style, like spontaneous conversation or the piecemeal expressions of a dream state.

A contents page (see Table 3.1) has been given here for clarification, and the entries have been categorized as a) Parables, b) Philosophies, and c) Poems. Much like Margaret Cavendish's *The World's Olio* (1655), this publication requires the reader to engage in an unusual way. Jackson described it as "thoughts" and "essays."[9] We are encouraged to consider congregated ideas as a form of spiritual and intellectual nourishment.

Doubtless inspired by Jackson's incredible personal library, it has been written in a low to middle language level, enabling a wide demographic to engage with its content[10]—from young children, for whom there are a plethora of illustrations, to adults, who can interpret the complexities of the poetry.

Table 3.1
The Contents of Michael Jackson's *Dancing the Dream*

Title	Page Number
Dancing the Dream	1
Planet Earth	4
Magical Child Part 1	7
Wings Without Me	13
Dance of Life	14
When Babies Smile	18
But the Heart Said No	20
Children of the World	23
So the Elephants March	26
The Boy and the Pillow	28
Enough for Today	31
Mark of the Ancients	34
Heal the World	39
Children	45
Mother	46
Magic	50
Fish That Was Thirsty, The	54
Innocence	58
Trust	60
Courage	63
Love	66
God	69
How I Make Music	70
Ryan White	75
Elusive Shadow, The	78
On Children of the World	80
Two Birds	85
Last Tear, The	86
Ecstasy	90
Berlin 1989	92
Mother Earth	96
Wise Little Girl	98
I You We	103
Angel of Light	105
I Searched for My Star	110
Child Is a Song, A	114
Child of Innocence	119
Will You Be There?	121
Magical Child Part 2	125

(*continued*)

Table 3.1 (Continued)

Title	Page Number
Are You Listening?	129
Breaking Free	132
Once We Were There	135
Heaven Is Here	137
Quantum Leap	140
That One in the Mirror	143
Look Again, Baby Seal	148

Although Jackson's personal religious beliefs are a unifying current that runs through *Dancing the Dream*, they are offered in the form of universal truths rather than rigid dogmas.[11]

THE PHILOSOPHIES

A personal philosophy denotes a way of being, a mantra, or a code, however the word's etymology lies in alchemy and magic (*OED*). The predominantly philosophical entries in *Dancing the Dream* comprise approximately 26 percent (12/46) of the entire collection (see Table 3.2).

Four of the philosophies are specifically about children: *A Child Is a Song*, *On Children of the World*, *Children*, and *Innocence*. Extracts from *Children* formed Jackson's acceptance speech in 1993 when he received his Grammy Legend Award at the 35th Annual Grammy Awards.[12] The illustrations in the collection also depict Jackson as father, friend, and protector of children of a range of ethnicities.[13]

Courage, *Innocence*, *Love*, *Magic*, and *Trust* extol the virtues of each eponym as integral to living, thriving, and achieving. In these panegyrics, there is a world that is saturated with "magic," while self-trust is tied in with allowing oneself to be fearful. Here, courage and bravery are tied to the "promise of love," which, in turn, is "everywhere."[14]

The entry *Dancing the Dream* corrals imagery of the dead and the dying, the history of slavery, victory from oppression, the fight for intimacy, and a search for something more than we already are. It creates a vignette of life through the metaphor of a performance, just as Shakespeare did in many of his works: *As You Like It*—"All the world's a stage | And all the men and women merely players" (2.7.140–141), and *Macbeth*— "Life's but a walking shadow a poor player, | That struts and frets his hour upon the stage | and then is heard no more" (5.5.23–25). These quotes tie in beautifully with "the dance lives on."[15] The latter quote uses the exact same phrase as the Bible

Table 3.2

The Philosophies in Michael Jackson's *Dancing the Dream*

Philosophies	
Child Is a Song, A	Innocence
Children	Love
Courage	Magic
Dancing the Dream	On Children of the World
God	Trust
How I Make Music	

when the "trumpet shall sound, and the dead shall be raised incorruptible."[16] It is also repeated in the song "Gone Too Soon" and the poem "Are You Listening?"

The philosophies regard life as a wider experience we are encouraged to align with, and to connect with its energetic flow as our collective existence speeds on.[17] The music, with which Jackson is so synonymous, is both within him and around him. It is not unique; perhaps only his ability to tap into this all-encompassing infinity is. The joy of this literary sojourn culminates with the dancer being unified with the dance itself and leaving both the reader and himself behind.[18] In *Dancing the Dream* death is presented as a smile, rapture, and cosmic reunification between the being and the universe.

THE POEMS

Poetry is concerned primarily with the voice, that indefinable nuance or style that characterizes one person's physical or literary self-expression as unique. One of the strongest elements in *Dancing the Dream* is its 17 poems, which form 37 percent of the whole collection (see Table 3.3). Again, children are a predominant focus. However, "When Babies Smile," "Magical Child Part 1," and "Magical Child Part 2" can be easily interpreted as Jackson referring to himself.

"Ryan White" correlates directly with the songs "Gone Too Soon" and "Will You Be There?" on the *Dangerous* album. "Gone Too Soon," written by Buz Kohan, became a requiem for the real Ryan White, who was immortalized through the short film of Jackson's song, directed by Bill DiCicco. Ryan, a hemophiliac, contracted AIDS in the 1980s and was persecuted because of the disease. He died aged 18.

"Are You Listening?" and "Will You Be There?" challenge the reader with rhetorical searching, and words from the latter are spoken passionately on the *Dangerous* album. Through the repetition of the phrase "dream of another

Table 3.3
The Poems in Michael Jackson's *Dancing the Dream*

Poems	
Are You Listening?	Magical Child Part 2
Breaking Free	Mother
Child of Innocence	Once We Were There
Children of the World	Planet Earth
Ecstasy	Quantum Leap
Elusive Shadow, The	Ryan White
Heal the World	When Babies Smile
Heaven Is Here	Will You Be There?
Magical Child Part 1	

tomorrow" in both "Ryan White" (poem) and "Will You Be There?" (song), the works exorcise grief at losing a friend whose life became symbolic of an undesirable life experience.[19] *Dangerous* was released 18 years before Michael Jackson died, and when he did die, the song "Gone Too Soon" became his requiem, too. For both Jackson and White, the words were symbols of unfulfilled promise, and although they were so visible, they bore the heavy burden of being vilified instead of treated with compassion.

"Heal the World," "Mother Earth," and "Planet Earth" are parts of the conservation theme, where "one touch of nature makes the whole world kin" (3.3.176).[20] "Heaven Is Here" complements them, while "Breaking Free" and "Ecstasy" exalt freedom and flight into the limitless vault of the heavens.[21] "Quantum Leap" highlights unsung songs and an ongoing search for a realm where death no longer exists.[22] This is Jackson reaching into the transom of his mind for a dream of the celestial and eternal. It is truly a unique, intensely spiritual outlook on the world, interwoven with fantasy, hope, and reservation. It is the work of one who knows their dream is as distant as the stars but chooses to dream it anyway.

"Mother" is something altogether different. Accompanied by a beautiful full-page picture of a young Katherine Jackson, it is an expression of love from the poet to the one woman he places above all others. It also attributes his life's success to his mother, who "fashioned" his soul out of "fragments."[23]

THE PARABLES

Thirty-nine percent (18/46) of the entries in *Dancing the Dream* are parables (see Table 3.4). The *Oxford English Dictionary* defines a parable as "an

Table 3.4
The Parables in Michael Jackson's *Dancing the Dream*

Parables	
Angel of Light	Last Tear, The
Berlin 1989	Look Again, Baby Seal
Boy and the Pillow, The	Mark of the Ancients
But the Heart Said No	Mother Earth
Dance of Life	So the Elephants March
Enough for Today	That One in the Mirror
Fish That Was Thirsty, The	Two Birds
I Searched for My Star	Wings Without Me
I You We	Wise Little Girl

allegorical or metaphorical saying or narrative." It is synonymous with the words "fable" and "proverb." Although other entries have an educational purpose ("Ryan White," "Heal the World," "Trust"), the parables in particular are allegories that utilize the familiar to exemplify the unknown. In the Bible, Jesus Christ spoke frequently in parables to teach the masses about abstract concepts like salvation and the kingdom of heaven.[24]

Michael Jackson was particularly fond of two biblical lessons.[25] The first, The Parable of the Talents, was integral to Jackson's method of working.[26] He often claimed that it was his duty to perform. It was, in effect, what he was "sent to do."[27] In other words, to the artist, the very fact that he had so much talent meant he had to work very hard to create a significant return on the investment of his creator.

The second biblical lesson that recurs throughout *Dancing the Dream* is The Little Children.[28] In the biblical books of Matthew and Luke, parents arrive with babies for Jesus to bless. Those whom the disciples see as least in society are elevated by Christ, who not only rebukes his disciples for turning the children away, but also brings the children close by, declaring that his kingdom is for them. This sentiment of humility is echoed throughout the New Testament: "so the last will be first, and the first will be last."[29]

Much of Jackson's work elevated children above adults: In the opening sequence of *Black or White* (dir. John Landis, 1991), the guitar riff that Macaulay Culkin plays is so powerful it throws a belligerent adult into the African wilderness; in Kramer's *Moonwalker*, children are Jackson's only honest and faithful sidekicks in a world filled with vicious adults; in *Badder* (dir. Jim Blashfield, 1988), the diegesis from *Bad* (dir. Martin Scorsese, 1987) is inhabited solely by children. Jackson's songs "Heal the World," "Little Susie," and "The

Lost Children" highlighted the plight of the needy, and millions of his hard-earned dollars would go to supporting sick and underprivileged children in remote corners of the world.[30]

In *Dancing the Dream*, children are elevated from unfinished adults to the wise inheritors of everlasting paradise, with a "natural wisdom." They have not yet learned prejudice or hatred, and they live out solely their "simple goodness."[31] This view of childhood is, on one level, idealistic and romanticized, a rose-tinted perspective of a playground environment where one is as likely to be punched as hugged.[32]

Jackson's unique perspective of "this wondrous age" is that it is one he considered himself to have been "deprived of." His relationship with children stemmed from his traumatic childhood and ongoing battles with the mirror. In those extremely challenging circumstances, "transforming" in the public eye from a cute cherub to a gangly teenager with chronic acne, children were the ones who saw Michael Jackson as the same person, whether he was singing "I Want You Back" or "Dancing Machine." The fact that he had changed physically during adolescence did not change the way children treated him. He drew strength from this and would devote much of his life to helping them.[33]

"The Boy and the Pillow" and "Wise Little Girl" emphasize the inner wisdom of children in realizing that what truly matters is the value of the heart, not material wealth. "In their innocence, very young children know themselves to be light and love. If we allow them, they can teach us to see ourselves the same way."[34] "The Fish That Was Thirsty" and "I Searched for My Star" are about searching for important things in the wrong places, not understanding that they are within us and that we are the ones who "miss what is everywhere." The anthropomorphic nature of the thirsty fish is particularly aimed at children.

Each of the parables in *Dancing the Dream* is unique. "Angel of Light" concerns itself with an inner greatness that has not been fully realized: "I have caught sight of glory." Angels are the metaphor here, and in "Wings Without Me" the semantic field of heavenly imagery abounds: "spirit," "saint," and "sacred."[35]

"Berlin 1989" personifies the Berlin Wall and, employing a third-person narrative, describes what can be achieved when a "million hearts find one another." "But the Heart Said No" offers a similar sentiment, arguing that the heart has a wisdom the head has not. Things that logic deems necessary, human emotion sees as barbaric: "villagers . . . buried in rough wooden coffins."[36]

"Mark of the Ancients," "So the Elephants March," "Look Again, Baby Seal," and "Enough for Today" all follow conservationist themes. Animals teach humankind a lesson, or those that were here before us teach the same, encouraging us to treat our planet and its creatures with respect. For Jackson, nature is part of the same dance as all mankind. "I can't keep the dance from being killed, but at least I can pause in memory."[37] The dance Jackson is dreaming goes beyond his stage prowess and moonwalk to a symbiotic coexistence of all living creatures.

Eighteenth-century poet Samuel Taylor Coleridge shares this Romantic notion in his lyrical ballad *The Rime of the Ancient Mariner*, an extended phantasm from which there is no escape. In the mariner's wanton destruction of an innocent albatross he seals himself and an entire ship's crew to a terrible fate. Not until he finds respect for nature does he receive redemption, though it is still tinged with misery—"forthwith this frame of mine was wrench'd | With woeful agony, | Which forc'd me to begin my tale | And then it left me free."

In "The Last Tear," an altercation between two lovers leaves one bereft. Loneliness is only relieved after shedding a last tear, one made from "love," not "frustration" or "despair." Similarly, the mariner is unable to pray until a single moment where he recognizes the beauty of nature and blesses it: "a spring of love gusht from my heart | And I bless'd them unaware!" In the book *Dancing the Dream*, as in *The Rime of the Ancient Mariner*, "he prayeth best who loveth best, | All things both great and small: | For the dear God, who loveth us, | He made and loveth all."[38] "Two Birds" and "The Last Tear" are vignettes, drawn out of emotional conversations, many of which are showcased throughout the *Dangerous* album. In *Dancing the Dream* children are pure, innocent, and simple, while women are typically wanton, exasperating, or saintly mother figures.

A third of the *Dangerous* liner notes comprise content found in *Dancing the Dream*. In both, love interests are often unnecessarily cruel. Sexually charged arguments and deceptions continue in the songs "Can't Let Her Get Away," "Who Is It," "She Drives Me Wild" "In the Closet," and "Dangerous."[39]

"Two Birds" ("the world hears your song in mine") could be interpreted as requesting a revelation of a love affair, reminiscent of the love poetry of Keats. However, Stillwater and Collins discuss the birds as possible representations of two halves of the same psyche, one repressed and hidden, the other fully expressed.[40]

"Dance of Life" is very much about death. The writer analogizes life as a dance, a sojourn that, once over, results in silence: "it's the unheard music that never dies." Once all the excitement, the "molecular jiggle," and the "cells" have faded, the narrator is left looking at the light cast by stars long since gone. Much like watching Michael Jackson himself on celluloid, we as viewers are aware that he no longer lives. Instead of being morose, the narrator reiterates that "a star can never die."[41]

"That One in the Mirror" is the last parable in *Dancing the Dream*. It is a parting message that carries on where the songs "Man in the Mirror," "We Are the World," and "Heal the World" left off, where "the planet was being used up."[42] Instead of looking to others to "make a change," the mythological character of Narcissus is summoned, and after a radical conversation with the "one" in the mirror, the narrator acknowledges they "never feel alone" as "earth's child." It ends with a reaching into the mirror, asking the reader to join in this new realization and to be a partner and friend.[43]

Lacan's mirror stage ties in uniquely with this final parable, a fact of which Jackson was most likely well aware. The mirror, a place of self-reflection and heightened self-awareness, is where Jackson's narrator sees the version of himself who doesn't think enough about love. It is a battle between the basest parts of the psyche, which must be convinced to do what is right, without clinging to personal interests.[44]

DANCING THE DREAM AND *DANGEROUS*

Dancing the Dream is synonymous with the author's album *Dangerous*, as they share five of the same works: "The Dance (Dancing the Dream)"(poem and liner notes), "Heal the World," "Will You Be There?" and "Planet Earth." For Jackson, as for Shakespeare, "if music be the food of love, play on."[45] The two works of art are symbiotic. They feed from one another metaphorically, semantically, and lexically. Words from the book are echoed, repeated, and re-presented in the album, while songs in the album extend motifs and themes that are introduced in the book.

By 1991 and the release of *Dangerous*, all of Jackson's artistic and professional aspirations had been reached. He already held many of the records with which he is still synonymous: biggest-selling album of all time, most number ones from a single album, and several others.[46] He had also created a successful follow-up, *Bad*, to the behemoth that was *Thriller*—no small feat, considering the incredible pressure he had put himself under.[47] *Dangerous* became another attempt at fulfilling a seemingly impossible dream—an album to eclipse *Thriller*'s success.

The pursuit of this new dream would spur on the artist to keep creating, when, materially, he had everything he could possibly want. He reveled in newly acquired independence. His new album had been created without the producer who had helped him forge *Off The Wall*, *Thriller*, and *Bad*; he had moved out of his family home and into a magical place Deepak Chopra called a "modus vivendi" purposely built "to counter the tidal wave of stress that accompanies mega-stardom."[48] What he did not have were children of his own to share it all with, which had been a lifelong dream.[49]

Dramatic biblical imagery abounds throughout the album, with "two-edged swords" and "honey-combs" echoing "false prophets," the "river Jordan" and "hearts of stone," while a respect for nature popularized by the eighteenth-century Romantic poets, Wordsworth, Coleridge, and Keats is also prevalent on Shakespeare's glorious and transient stage. How else to describe the cryptic cover art of *Dangerous* than "the baseless fabric of this vision, | The cloud-capp'd towers, the gorgeous palaces, | The solemn temples, the great globe itself, | Yea, all which it inherit, shall dissolve | And, like this insubstantial pageant faded, | Leave not a rack behind" (4.1.151–156).[50]

The first entry in *Dancing the Dream* is included as "The Dance" on the opening page of the liner notes of *Dangerous*.[51] On the final page of those same liner notes is the poem "Planet Earth." The poetic lyrics of 14 songs, "Jam," "Why You Wanna Trip On Me," "In the Closet," "She Drives Me Wild," "Remember the Time," "Can't Let Her Get Away," "Heal the World," "Black or White," "Who Is It," "Give in to Me," "Will You Be There?," "Keep the Faith," "Gone Too Soon," and "Dangerous," are likewise nestled invisibly between pages one and five of *Dancing the Dream*. The world already knows this book; wearing *Dangerous* as its disguise, it has already made its way into the homes of millions.

This chapter began by asking the question, What is *Dancing the Dream?* It is an attempt to quantify the unquantifiable, to put in written form, emotions better captured in dreams. As Shakespeare wrote in *The Tempest*, "We are such stuff | As dreams are made on, and our little life | Is rounded with a sleep" (4.1.156–158).[52] Jackson closes the book with three words, "The Dream Continues," and an ellipsis. Academic Amy C. Billone counted the word "dream" no less than 49 times in Jackson's released records, and she argues that dreams and nightmares were synonymous with "Jackson's creative universe."[53] They were hopes to heal the planet and leave it better than he found it, but these were also dreams of anguish and despair. It is no secret that Jackson suffered from insomnia, and an irony is the fact that his aspirational dreams often kept him awake. These were dreams that became nightmares, the very dreams he was living into being.

According to Paul Lester, Michael Jackson's existence "could have been the dream of a lifetime but it ended up an American nightmare. But the soundtrack was sublime."[54] The rags-to-riches rise of the Jackson 5 was the typical expression of the American Dream, but, as a plethora of writers have reiterated, from Steinbeck to Miller and Fitzgerald, that dream is little more than an illusion itself. So dreams are broken as easily as they are made and as likely to be expressed through delusions as prophecies. *Dancing the Dream* is incredibly important because, like its musical twin *Dangerous*, it reveals Jackson as a poet who is acutely aware of all these interpretations.

What relevance does *Dancing the Dream* have in the wider context of Jackson's artistic canon? Well, it points us to the trajectory his work would have taken if not for the tumultuous period that birthed *HIStory: Past, Present and Future, Book 1; Blood on the Dance Floor: HIStory in the Mix* and *Invincible*. Why is *Dancing the Dream* so important? As the only book of its kind Jackson saw fit to publish, it is essential to how we understand his artistic intentions and personal motivations. It signifies the beginning of Jackson's artistic self-presentation as activist. Sentiments that were alluded to in "Can You Feel It," "Be Not Always," and "Man in the Mirror" are actively pushed to the fore here. No longer does Jackson encourage his listeners to "make a change"; he becomes the change, maturing into a voice crying out in a literal wilderness in the short film for "Earth Song" five years later. *Dancing the Dream* puts this journey into seamless context.[55] It is more than a collection of early nineties ephemera or even a gift for the fans; it is an experience in and of itself.[56]

CHAPTER 4

Narrative in Michael Jackson's *Bad*

T he years 1987–1988 saw an exponential growth in Michael Jackson's musical and artistic development. After *Thriller*'s meteoric success, Jackson was encouraged by his producer, Quincy Jones, to write as many songs as possible on his 1987 release, *Bad*. This chapter presents Jackson primarily as a storyteller, and gives an in-depth exploration of his ability to employ the aspects of literary narrative: plot, perspective, characterization, setting, language, and genre, in order to engage a wide audience.

> "This is the one where I'd asked him to write all the tunes. I could see him growing as an artist . . ."
>
> —Quincy Jones[1]

1987's *Bad* was a time of unmatched and unparalleled creativity for Michael Jackson. Jackson's anthology film was still being made, piecemeal, in between the dates of his *Bad* tour, which would successfully go on to break records of attendance throughout the globe. Jackson's tour, his first solo adult effort without his brothers, who had always been with him performing from the tender age of five, would be simultaneously one of the most difficult and rewarding experiences of the artist's life. As always, while on tour Jackson would visit as many hospitals and orphanages as he did stadiums. In every state he visited, Jackson would enquire about the welfare of children, how well they were taken care of, what looked-after children's experience was like in that city and in that corner of the world. This was Jackson's overriding reason for performing and touring. It gave him the platform from which to effect some social change. In the United Kingdom, Jackson's Wembley Stadium performance would be visited by the Prince and Princess of Wales.[2]

The *Bad* album is imbued with many narrative qualities and has been chosen for study because it is a singular expression of Jackson's creativity and composition, both collaboratively and independently. It provides a lynchpin for the narrative techniques Jackson began to employ early in his career, with *Off The Wall*, techniques that maintained throughout his career, right up to his *Invincible* album. This chapter uses supporting material from short films, as well as close textual analysis of the lyrics, to discuss the literary aspects in individual songs from the *Bad* album, in order to illustrate Jackson's unique ability to communicate narrative.

Jackson would often describe the making of his music using the rhetoric and the field-specific lexis of painting, or weaving a tapestry. The purpose of both these crafts is to present narrative and sentiment. In *An Introduction to Literature, Criticism and Theory*, Andrew Bennett and Nicholas Royle's definition of narrative corresponds with the way one views oneself and asserts that entire societal ideologies are constructed through the narratives which become dominant.[3] For example, a Princess being saved by Prince Charming can, over time, become a societal code for women being intrinsically weaker than men. Narrative is integral for how we are and how we experience our world. It is through stories, narratives, and allegories that we begin to make sense of who we are.

Michael Jackson's *Bad* album, though overshadowed by the success of *Thriller*, bears the fruits of his storytelling efforts. It is also an album relatively unburdened by a severe need for reinvention, or one mired in the politics of the mainstream press. Having been afforded the freedom to do so, *Bad* exchanges the literal for the evocative, leading the listener and viewer down paths of emotional discovery, much in the same way a novelist leads their reader into the depths of a mystery or the lofty heights of a love story.

PLOT

We will consider Jackson's use of plot in the *Bad* track "Dirty Diana."[4] Useful examples of particularly well known (and oft-recycled) plots are those from Ancient Greek tragedies such as *Oedipus Rex* and *The Theban Plays*.[5] Many tragedies of this nature, as noted by Aristotle, have unique moments, moments of equilibrium (where all is well and at rest); peripeteia, where the tragic hero (usually of noble birth) finds themselves in a great reversal of fortune, otherwise known as a fall from grace.[6] Value is often assigned to specific moments within a plot, based on where they are positioned. This value is assigned in terms of proximity to the resolution of the narrative. So plot, though it may lack the necessary detail of a narrative, often has very clear structure.

"Dirty Diana" follows the following plot structure:

A. Equilibrium
   a. A groupie, her name may be "Diana" but this may also be a pseudonym, often waits at backstage doors in order to provide sexual favors for musicians, in exchange, she hopes, for a life of affluence and notoriety.[7]
   b. A (male) musician has a girlfriend.
B. Conflict
   a. The musician is propositioned by Diana, but he refuses.
   b. Eventually the musician begins a sexual relationship with Diana.
   c. At some point in the course of their infidelity, Diana invites the musician to her home.
   d. The musician realizes that he hasn't called his girlfriend to confirm that he will be late.
C. Climax
   a. During the phone call Diana exposes the affair.[8]
   b. The ramifications of this revelation are most likely negative for the musician and his girlfriend, but not particularly for Diana.

As we can see, although the song does not provide a resolution or an anti-climax, a large part of what makes "Dirty Diana" such a compelling song are its basic plot points. The song begins in a state of equilibrium with, we assume, some element of faithfulness to the musician's partner, or at least with the fact of the musician's partner being unaware of his infidelities. These plot points are emphasized in the short film that accompanies the track, and we see conflict brewing in plot points B and C; however, it is interesting that Jackson and the film's director Joe Pytka, chose not to visualize the sexual scenes or conflict in the lyrics of the song and instead opted for having "Diana" wait for Jackson inside a limousine. In the short film, shots of a scantily clad woman are interspersed with live action shots of Jackson performing on stage; the space between Diana's silhouetted legs and the extreme shortness of her skirt are emphasized by the use of tight close-ups. The fact that she remains face-less gives the impression she is one of many. The visual world of Diana is visually dirtier and grimier than the world of Jackson's stage, while his white shirt contradicts the darkness of Diana's clothing.

Plot point C is, arguably, the climax of the short series of points, but its closeness to the end of the song gives the event of the disclosure of the musician's infidelity more gravitas than it might have, were to be found in the middle of the sequence of events. What is particularly powerful and engaging in this use of plot is the fact that we don't see what happens after the "cat is out of the metaphorical bag," and as listeners/viewers we are left to decide for ourselves what happens next. This leaves the reader with a cliff-hanger effect. The use of plot, however, is only one very basic feature of narrative; the next aspect this chapter considers is "perspective."

PERSPECTIVE

A "perspective" or a point of view is a particularly powerful aspect of narrative. It is one of the key aspects that builds a story or narrative out of the basic bones of a plot. **Who** is telling the story and the way **they** perceive a series of events is often far more intriguing than the events themselves. For example, the use of a young girl, Scout, in *To Kill A Mockingbird*, strongly requires the reader to believe that the narrator of the story is transparent and entirely honest, that she hasn't yet learned to lie.[9] This makes Scout's recollection of events credible in a way that the character Nick Carraway's from *The Great Gatsby* can never be. Nick is a very unreliable narrator, and the author, F. Scott Fitzgerald, leaves the reader unsure, while reading *The Great Gatsby*, as to whether Nick's entire summation of the novel's characters in the narrative are due to his own insecurities or to an infatuation with Gatsby.[10] In any case, this ambiguity makes for genuinely exciting reading, because the reader must continually assess the information that an unreliable narrator gives, in order to gauge our level of belief in the version of events we are given. If we are observant, we can see the story that lies behind the one we are told. Great storytellers often use this technique to keep the reader/viewer engaged with the narrative. An excellent example of this is the 2000 film *Memento*, written by Christopher Nolan, where the sequence of events keeps unraveling for the main character, whose memory is continually being wiped clean. The viewer is positioned similarly to this character, so we encounter every new plot point for the first time with him; hence, we are more likely to be engaged with the events as we try and piece together what is going on.

In four tracks from *Bad*, Jackson uses narrative perspective to achieve different aims. In the first, "The Way You Make Me Feel," the use of first- and second-person pronouns "I," "me," and "you" create a sense of character but still places the emphasis on a monogamous relationship. The word "me" is repeated 52 times, "my" 29 times, "I" 8 times, and "you" 54 times. The heavy repetition of these pronouns creates a sense of intimacy, reiterated by Jackson's line "ain't nobody's business."[11] The privacy of the ensuing relationship that the song describes is of paramount importance. However, the use of pronouns also indicates ownership. The first-person voice is the owner of the second person, "you."

In "Leave Me Alone", first and second pronouns are used quite differently. The word "me" is repeated about 47 times, "you" 28 times, and "I" 18 times.[12] The use of the pronouns to create perspective here builds a wall between the narrator and those that antagonize him; even the use of "you must fight" is used in a reflexive, generalizing way, as a writer might use "we" or "one" to indicate a general way of doing things.[13] The narrative perspective emphasizes isolation and a state of being continually rebuffed.[14]

In the track "Another Part of Me," Jackson utilizes perspective in order to bring a sense of harmony. The second person "you" is plural here and indicates unity. Jackson writes from the perspective of bringing together a "we" that the listener can be part of—a very adept skill employed in several of Jackson's songs. In the track "Bad," Jackson uses both forms of the perspectives used in "Leave Me Alone" and "Another Part of Me."[15]

CHARACTERIZATION

Characters are always avatars, expressions of an artist's creativity, or tools used to advance a particular idea. They can provide multiple perspectives through which we perceive plot. They can be the embodiment of great ideals, based on real human beings, or entirely figments of the author's imagination. However, what is particularly important about characters in narrative is that they are the conduits through which the reader experiences and engages. Characters are constructed from their external qualities, the physical attributes assigned to them by the author of any work, as well as their internal attributes, the trappings of humanity that make them plausible in a narrative. Hence, a character with a fear of enclosed spaces will have more of a compelling reaction when stuck inside a lift with strangers. There are also the overlapping moments when characters' internal and external worlds coincide: what the character says and what the other characters say about them. To return to *The Great Gatsby*, notions of who Gatsby is are created by what the narrator, Nick, and several other characters in the novel say and think about him, as much as by his own actions and words.

The fourth track on Jackson's *Bad* album is called "Liberian Girl," and it exemplifies beautifully Jackson's use of characterization in his songs. The eponymous character is clearly: a) an African woman held in high esteem, "more precious than any pearl," and b) the object of the author's sexual and emotional desire.[16] The character's Liberian heritage is a feature so dominant that she is not given any other name. Liberia is a unique "country along the coast of West Africa . . . home to a lush rainforest containing a rich diversity of flora and fauna." It is "Africa's oldest republic" and it "was established on land acquired for freed U.S. slaves."[17] In that respect, the character embodies the beauty of African nationality and African women in general. Jackson's beauteous invention sharply contradicts long-purported negative representations of black women, as discussed in Kim F. Hall's "'Object into Object?': Some Thoughts on the Presence of Black Women in Early Modern Culture."[18]

In his essay "'When You Have to Say 'I Do': Orientalism in Michael Jackson's 'Liberian Girl'," Jeremy Faust writes that "Jackson co-opts *Orientalism* towards implying a place for himself within the mainstream of dominant American society," and although his argument has much merit, he negates the fact that Jackson, although an American, is an African American with a vested interest in his African heritage.[19] The song can just as easily be read to be a love song to Africa. The Liberian girl is not given one of the many names Jackson utilizes throughout all of his back catalogue. Faust rightly asserts that Jackson does not give the Liberian girl a name, yet he is an artist who repeatedly uses female names in his songs.[20] A character is often defined first by their name, and second by their dialogue. The girl's Swahili speech is far more revealing.[21] She speaks only in response to Jackson's declarations of love. It is ironic that this girl, whose country's name is derived from the Latin word for "freedom" and from which we derive the word "liberation," is the object of affection for a male who is now free to express his affections after she has *changed his world*. She lacks liberation, existing solely as an extension of the singer's devotion. The internal-external elements of this character remain ambiguous, and the fact that she is prized primarily for her appearance and African-ness is awkward, as is the fact that she is not given a name of her own. "Liberian Girl" is a song about a character constructed entirely from a male perspective; she is an African object of love and desire. However, she is unique in that she is an evidently black African woman placed on the pedestal as the object of affection in a romance. The features that make her uniquely African are the features that make her uniquely precious and "more precious than any pearl."[22] The fact that a pearl is white and that African skin is predominantly a darker shade has resonance here.

SETTING AND TIME

In addition to plot, perspective, and characterization, setting and time can be extremely effective in engaging viewers and readers. Settings can, like characters, embody emotion, just as the weather does in cases of pathetic fallacy. In Emily Brontë's 1847 novel, *Wuthering Heights*, the wildness and power of the adverse weather on the English moors can easily be interpreted as a reflection of the wildness of the central characters' (Cathy and Heathcliff) love for one another, a love that is out of their control and dangerous. Likewise, Jackson's "Smooth Criminal" utilizes the ambiguous nature of both time and setting to create a sense of suspense and danger. The narrative of the song takes place in the apartment of what we assume is a single woman. This is an archetypical place for a murder to take place, and the song replays the series of events that "left the bloodstains on the carpet."[23] The crime scene is key here, as in the hardboiled crime-fiction novels of Raymond Chandler and James M. Cain.

The crime scene is a timeless setting, a place that is easily transported to various locales. However, our fascination with crime has deep roots in our fascination with both the macabre and the grotesque, a fashion that was expanded in the Victorian era with the publication of gruesome murders.[24] The artist Andy Warhol famously embraced newspaper printings of gruesome accidents in his silkscreen, *Orange Car Crash Fourteen Times* in 1963.[25] Jackson's transposes the events of the narrative into the 1930s in the short film for the song "Smooth Criminal," a time that is synonymous with glamorized mob crime. Fundamentally, crime is made fascinating in crime-fiction narratives, but the violence that is alluded to by the crime-scene narrative setting takes some of the danger out of the song because its use of tense is intermittently locked into the past. These events have occurred, and there is nothing the reader or viewer can do to alter them. We are passive watchers of a cocooned event. This ambiguity of time is powerfully exhibited in the short film, which in turn is an extract from the full-length movie, *Moonwalker*.[26] Jackson plays the character of Michael, an alien who is able to manipulate both time and space, to transport himself between forms and places. Why he chooses the glamorous, crime-riddled 1930s may be because this setting is both close to the present day in terms of style and yet distant enough to be part of a mythic past. Jackson uses setting and time to bring us close, but he sets us apart just enough to maintain the air of mystery

LANGUAGE

The song "Man in the Mirror," like several of the songs on *Bad*, was not written by Jackson, but since Jackson was executive producer of his work, I will assign him credit for the use of the song and for including it on his album. He retains credit for the song in terms of its delivery and its style. "Man in the Mirror" utilizes key language features: imagery and metaphor. The extended metaphor of the song's title is particularly evocative because it relates the idea of the distance between one's actions and one's thoughts.[27] Jackson explores, by the use of the metaphor that is extended through the narrative, the concept that people often want change to occur but do not wish to be that change, nor do they wish to effect that change in their own lives. The song repeats a demand that its listeners turn their gaze inwards.[28]

The use of imagery in the song is just as evocative as the use of the extended metaphor, if not more so. The narrative style is set by the imagery of a person walking through a street, wearing their preferred attire; we follow them on their journey as they see children playing, and the image resolves itself in a realization that the first-person narrator has been ignoring the needs of others. The power of the metaphor is heightened with a "broken bottle top," which leads the listener to wonder if the broken bottle is in fact a metaphor for a life that is falling apart. The lines often link back, by anaphoric referencing, giving the imagery of souls flying out of bodies into death, or simply of people living aimlessly due to neglect. The personification of inanimate objects (for example, the wounded willow tree) may indicate the unseen scars caused by emotional wounds. The scars are what produce faded dreams of those without any financial security at all.[29] Jackson reiterates the metaphor of the wind, which is incredibly emotive because it implies that the souls of these characters have been made synonymous with wind—incorporeal. They have been rendered as invisible as air by the refusal of others to look at them and truly see their pain, acknowledge it, and then attempt to ameliorate it.

GENRE

The final narrative aspect that Jackson utilizes throughout his work is genre. The word "genre" is derived from the French word for "type" and was employed primarily in the industrialization of film and literature. Films and books are often now marketed by virtue of their genre, to the extent that genre fiction is a commonly accepted term. However, many texts supersede contemporary notions of genre, while others combine so many genres that it is impossible to classify them. Genres offer opportunities for creativity by positioning the viewer to expect a certain theme, and to bring their prior conceptions of a specific theme into the understanding of this new work. So, a reader of science fiction may have expectations of imaginative worlds, which an author can use for heightened effect, as in Ursula Le Guin's *Left Hand of Darkness* or China Mieville's *Perdido Street Station*.[30] For example, "Just Good Friends" is very much in the genre of a buddy movie or rivalry movie, in which two friends fight for the affections of a single love interest, while "I Just Can't Stop Loving You" is clearly a romance. However, where Jackson is at his best is when he flouts genre conventions completely. "Speed Demon" defies genre. We are presented with a speeding character and left with just that. We are not told exactly where they are going, or exactly why, and instead we are given a sense of heightened urgency for the journey at hand.[31] Many of the key features of narrative aspect are forsaken for the tension, and the listener is encouraged to fill in all the narrative gaps.

Narrative is the driving force of all of Michael Jackson's music. However, what is particularly exciting is what occurs when we separate the narrative aspects in each of Jackson's individual works and examine how they create a sense of engagement for readers, listeners, and viewers. This narrative quality may account for the success of Jackson's short films, as they were, in so many ways, narratives set to music.

CHAPTER 5

Identity and Identification in Michael Jackson's *Dangerous*

Over the last three decades there has been much speculation and confusion over Michael Jackson's identity—that is, who he identified with and how he determined his own sexual, racial, and personal identity. Was Jackson proud of his African American heritage or was he ashamed of it? Did he prefer to be associated with children or adults, mortals or immortals, celebrities or laypeople, America or his global audience? This chapter answers the question, "How is the theme of identity expressed in Jackson's artistic canon?" It does so by exploring identity in Jackson's 1991 album *Dangerous*, using its liner notes as a literary source, and carrying out a close textual reading of its linguistic features.

> "I become the victor and the vanquished."
>
> —Michael Jackson[1]

Dangerous marks a departure that Joseph Vogel calls "the end of an era: the death of pop," and Susan Fast regards the album as "pushing all kinds of limits and boundaries."[2] Pre-1993, Jackson's *Dangerous* arrived before his "monster persona" took hold of public consciousness.[3] Even at this time Jackson had to face ongoing misrepresentation by the tabloid press, whose speculation over every facet of his life, from his sexual inclinations to his eating habits, were fed by his own massive success, bringing to mind the image of a monster that feeds upon itself. *Thriller* had made Jackson into a brand-new type of celebrity, the "superstar." Any copy about Jackson would and could sell, from mild speculation to outlandish lies—"this poor coverage wasn't only about race" and was "often more subtle, veiled and coded."[4] It was in this climate that Jackson continued to forge his own personal reinvention, one that revealed just how significantly his musical palette had matured. It also demonstrated that Jackson had newfound intentions for the influence of his worldwide fame. *Dangerous* is an album fueled by the all-important question for Michael Jackson in his early thirties: "Who have I become?"

It must be said that a relistening of Jackson's *Dangerous* is necessary to fully understand and appreciate this chapter. One may be particularly struck by the forcefulness of the music, the certainty of it. Fast calls this "the sonic equivalent of massive spectacle . . . thrilling, electrifying, exhilarating, but sometimes also threatening, angry, and ominous."[5] This "spectacle" integrates Jackson's identity as something that is far more ostentatious than the average, presumably more visible, and clearly more "out there." The *Oxford English Dictionary* defines "identity" as the "action or process of regarding or treating one thing as identical with another" and "the quality or condition of being the same." It also defines the word as "the action or process of determining what a thing is or who a person is." Closely linked to these definitions is "the state of being or feeling oneself." Here, we have "identification" as a clear and distinct property, easily seen and demarked, but also an ongoing process of determination, by which a person associates with outside factors. These definitions underpin this chapter and will be considered in turn, in terms of how they relate to specific tracks on Jackson's album. Firstly, we will consider Jackson's particularly evident sexual identification in the album, "a full-on assault of all things sensual, sexual, and romantic."[6] Secondly, we'll consider the album in relation to the sense of identifying with concepts, people, and things: "he saw God less as an authority figure and more as a creative energy."[7] Thirdly, we'll consider the album with regard to affinity and closeness, and lastly, in terms of the identification of the self as existing and having purpose, "a clearer vision of what he wanted to achieve with his music."[8]

THE ACTION OR PROCESS OF IDENTIFYING: SEXUALITY AND SEXUAL DETERMINATION

The first and most prominent process of determination we encounter in *Dangerous* is that of the masculine, which evokes the well-worn binary view of man versus woman, as defined by lust. Vogel's " 'I Ain't Scared of No Sheets': Re-Screening Black Masculinity in Michael Jackson's Black or White" goes in some detail to expand on this concept, and in it Vogel contextualizes race and racial expression in the context of stereotypes surrounding the sexuality of black women and men in American culture.[9] Here, Vogel asserts that these views stem from the dehumanizing portrayals fueled by hatred and slavery in prior centuries, which still have their cultural stamp on how blacks are portrayed and consumed in popular culture today. Early Modern research confirms time and again Vogel's views as having their roots deep in the 17th century.[10]

In "In the Closet," Jackson identifies as a man in a clandestine relationship, equating the sexual relationship between a man and woman as secret rather than sacred. A woman who is regarded as an intoxicating "lover."[11] The interaction is solely about sexual attraction, an abstract noun that the female in the song "wants to give," while the man "can't deny," because sexual desire is an "ache" that needs to be soothed.[12] The sexual dynamics are problematic here, especially with regard to how the female is stereotyped as simply an object of sexual gratification for the male. However, Jackson confounds expectation because he identifies with both genders in this lyrical dance. His yelps, grunts, and sighs on the track are orgasmic, and we may infer from them that he becomes both participants in this erotic transaction. Jackson becomes both the woman who is the object of the sexual desire, and the man who must have his ache soothed.

This is not the case in "She Drives Me Wild," in which Jackson takes the role of the voyeuristic heterosexual male candidly eyeing an attractive female. The lyrics of "She Drives Me Wild" are suggestive and objectifying, fully inhabiting the male gaze.[13] The song's lyrics are concerned primarily with the physical attributes of the female—"she's got the look"—and her worth is regarded solely with how sexually available she is deemed to be.[14]

In "Give in to Me," the female is again an object of masculine desire. However, this song identifies love as less a feeling and more a physical need; like hunger and thirst, love becomes desire that must be quenched. "Give in to Me" is filled with imperatives—these orders emphasize the struggle for control in a shifting dynamic. The line "love is a woman" implies that sexuality is something that one lover can surrender to another, to slake their thirst for physical intimacy. "Love" here is far less emotional than physical, even though the song reiterates the fact that "love" can only be given when it is wanted. The lyrics pertaining to "giving in" are also problematic because they position the masculine in a possessive stance.

Two further tracks that highlight the identification of sexuality and masculinity in the album are "Can't Let Her Get Away" and "Dangerous." In "Can't Let Her Get Away," the feminine object of affection, "her," is presented as a femme fatale, manipulative and cold-hearted.[15] Jackson recognizes the complexity of romantic relationships here; however, he is particularly masculine in his linguistic standpoint. In the repeated refrain of the title, "I" is the subject, while "her" is the object. "I" has the power, and what "I" wants, "I" must get. The masculine "I" refuses to allow the feminine "her" to get away, because doing so will reveal the male as a cuckold and a "fool."[16] In the lyrics of this song the female is imprisoned in the relationship. Again,

Jackson leaves ambiguity, especially when the track dissolves into elongated vowels, implying that the male is the one who cannot let go and who is in fact imprisoned by his own feelings and his inability to disengage from this relationship.[17]

Likewise, in both tracks, "Who Is It" and "Dangerous," the negative dynamics of sexual relationships are reiterated. Exchanges of secrets, money, passion, and time are fruitless, and we can interpret the "Who is it?" question to be related to the cuckolding of a male—a male who is trying to determine who has taken his object of affection away.[18] In "Dangerous," the skewed sexual dynamic is offered once more. However, all the blame is laid squarely with the female.[19] In this track the female is synonymous with her sexuality, which is predominantly physical and palpable. The sexual dynamic is played out here in terms of finance and transgression. The female is untrustworthy because her sexuality is a source of temptation, a "lust" that "can blind." Furthermore, this female is presented as an extramarital affair; she is a lover, and at no time does the subjective voice in the song take blame for his own transgressions. The breakdown of a relationship occurs because the "girl is bad." What is unusual here is that Jackson takes the narrative voice of the female and the male again, whereas in "In the Closet" he employs a female to speak the female's lines. Thus, "Dangerous" showcases a conversation between the two halves of the same whole.[20] Jackson is again both the male and the female, identifying with both sides, and sexuality is exciting because of both danger and transgression. These are themes that are also employed in the song "Dirty Diana" on the *Bad* album, where sexuality is titillating for both male and female because of its transgressive quality.[21]

Moving forward, "Remember the Time" offers us a whole new side of the sexual dynamic—playful nostalgia. In the song, Jackson asks repeatedly if the female object of affection, "girl," remembers events from the past.[22] This is nostalgia at its height: "in the spring . . . birds would sing." Love is completely contrasted with sex, rather than portrayed as the cause of it. Sex is simply physical need, while love is emotional connection.

There is an intense masculine identification in more than half of the songs on *Dangerous*, which is focused heavily on sexual relationships and sexuality in general. These are songs in which Jackson identifies the timeless tussle between the sexes and the dramatic nature of romantic relationships in general, a tension that playwrights and lyricists have found ample ground on which to create artistic works for millennia. However, what Jackson does, which is unique, is that he positions himself on both sides of every argument, making himself at times both the male and the female. Fast also asserts that "Jackson himself clearly viewed the boundaries between male and female as too confining."[23]

A SENSE OF IDENTITY WITH SOMEONE
OR SOMETHING

In a very different way, in the songs "Jam" and "Why You Wanna Trip on Me," Jackson's identification is entirely in the first-person singular "find my peace."[24] Fast's exploration of what it means "to jam" is extensive in her monograph *Dangerous*, and she interrogates the meaning of jamming, from its most colloquial sense of being about people performing music together in jam sessions, working collectively to produce music for the sheer joy of performing, and the carrying of this allegory further to Jackson's making of music as a personal sense of meaning and ambition in order to solve the world's problems.[25] The short film of "Jam" reiterates the point that for any given individual, jamming is whatever they enjoy and excel in. Therefore, for Michael Jordan, jamming is playing basketball, and for Michael Jackson, jamming is performing, singing, and dancing.[26] This metaphor can be extended to all the people who listen to Jackson's music, which encourages us all to "jam" and use our collective talents and abilities to make the world a better place. "Jam" positions Jackson at the forefront of this movement, a motion toward using personal talent to fight global issues and to make the world a better place.

In "Why You Wanna Trip on Me" Jackson again presents himself at the forefront of a political conundrum, identifying with the layperson by arguing that the world's attention should be focused on its ills and problems, rather than focused on celebrities like him. He attempts, in this track, to refocus the media glare on the real problems that the world faces, such as education, violence, homelessness, police brutality, violent crime, and gang violence. The purely rhetorical question, "Why you wanna trip on me?" requires the listener to identify with Jackson and then consider why they are more concerned with what he is doing and how he is living than with the state of their own political and social environment. The irony is that Jackson presents a spectacle in order to showcase his point, a spectacle that garners attention, and it is somewhat a moot point to use the sharp attention and focus on a person to showcase chagrin at the attention focused on a person. Jackson identifies here with a sense of himself, especially in terms of global and commercial popularity, which is of far less importance to him than the social problems that are pervasive in his surroundings.

CLOSENESS AND AFFINITY

In the tracks "Will You Be There?," "Gone too Soon," and "Keep the Faith," Jackson presents his identification as entirely personal: "love me like a mother."[27] He identifies with the all-too human condition of needing support, and encouragement in times of weakness, sadness and loss, "I'm only human," and suggests that the load of his public life is too much to bear.[28] Jackson uses several dynamic verbs, "hold," "carry," "love," "mold," "walk," "care," "fight," "heal," "bathe," "feed," and "free"; as well as several adverbs, "boldly," "slowly," "lowly," in order to explicate this desire for human inter-action and tenderness. The poem with which the song ends is a personal and direct communication of inner turmoil, laying out the emotional circum-stances in which this universal caring presence is required. It is in "trials" and "tribulations," "anger" and "despair," that the hope of another and the help-ing hand of another is most required.[29]

Jackson identifies with those in need of love and support, which is in turn identifying with the human condition of needing one another. Here, Jackson communicates that we are not separate, self-contained, or self-sufficient, for it is impossible to be. We can only exist and find meaning and purpose in our relationships. The same process of affinity and identification with needy humanity is emphasized in "Keep the Faith," during which Jackson uses a uni-versal "you," Jackson replies to the questions posed by "Will You Be There?" by emphasizing that the only way forward is to "keep the faith" and that the potency of love will lead to greatness because belief has a unique power.[30] The gospel core at the heart of "Keep the Faith" has its roots in the negro spiritual, and it provides an affirmation that identifies strongly with African American spirituality and faith; although, "to suggest that Michael Jackson art harbors religious significance and spiritual meaning is contentious for many observers of American culture."[31] Notions of a brighter future may well have far more resonance for African Americans, who have been defined by subjugation for much of their history. Jackson's track builds a crescendo, a sense of pushing forward and taking new ground. He preaches a sermon on how to rise above oppression, by advocating self-respect, while also staying level-headed.[32] Much of the faith Jackson discusses leans toward a specifically Christian ideal, a hope for redemption, eventual rapture, and delivery into a promised land.

"Gone Too Soon" is also included into this group of tracks centered on closeness and affinity, because it denotes a range of beautiful objects that, like all that is perishable, pass away in time. Jackson identifies here with all those who are bereaved and feel loss. He mourns not solely his friend, Ryan White—for whom Jackson included the song, and to whom the video is both a dedi-cation and an elegy—but mourns all that passes away too early. The song is saturated with similes that focus on universal experiences that a wide range of people can relate to: seeing a rainbow, watching a sunset, and building sand-castles that are washed away by the tide.[33] Despite its despondent tone, the song remains optimistic, because the death of a sunset is always proceeded by the rise of the moon. The lyrics do not present death as simply an ending but also as a natural progression, a metaphor for all that is wonderful and temporal, which is also, perhaps, made even more beautiful because of its transience. This transience applies to all of us who are aware of our mortality, for all who have ever experienced the loss of something valuable, a loved one, a friend, a relative, even a relationship or a home, or witnessed the dying of a dream.

THE FACT OF BEING, A CONCLUSION

The last process of identification in *Dangerous* are found in the poems, "The Dance" and "Planet Earth," and the tracks, "Heal the World" and "Black or White," which are found in the album's liner notes and in *Dancing the Dream: Poems and Collections*. In these works Jackson goes further to identify himself as part of a collective. He begins "The Dance" by merging with all existence, and in "Heal the World" he demarks a way in which we can get to a place where there is no pain.[34] Collectively, Jackson encourages us to heal our world, derived from "We Are the World," and asserts that to heal ourselves is to heal our environment. The world is us. Jackson identifies himself within that "us," which is the whole of humanity, thus introducing a radical playing field that considers the entire human race and the planet on which it lives as part of a harmonious physical interaction—a dance.

Similarly, in "Black or White," Jackson reiterates that fact that "we're one and the same." Vogel regards the song as championing racial equality, especially in terms of romantic relationships, "a powerful visual mythology about the nature of black men, the dangers they present to whiteness."[35] America has a specific history with miscegenation in particular when it comes to white women and black men, but the concept that "Black or White" proposes and supports fervently is the one that race is not a pertinent factor in forming relationships.[36] Again, Jackson contends that we are all the same because no matter the shade of our skin, we are not above one another, for we are all born and we all must die.

Jackson closes the album liner notes with the poem "Planet Earth." In this poem he defies the very basis of the pronouns "we" and "us." He challenges notions of race and division by arguing that the Earth itself is our home, making every single inhabitant part of the same family. Jackson personalizes his own relationship to the planet and personifies the Earth as his "sweetheart gentle and blue."[37] One of the most touching and fervent identifications in the album *Dangerous* is not with a person or an idea but with the planet itself.[38] Jackson identifies more with the planet than with any other thing, and he encourages his audience to do the same.

This chapter has explored the theme of identity as it is expressed in Jackson's canon. It seeks to refute the misconception that Jackson was confused about who he was, and to illustrate that, although Jackson did not often readily resolve misconceptions, we can find resolutions by close textual examination of his art. As mentioned in the introduction, the theme of identity is crucial in the consideration of Jackson because, through the prism of popular culture, his audience repeatedly identified with him. Therefore, this discussion of identity reveals even more about the public that consumed the album than it does about Michael Jackson the artist.

To conclude, Jackson identifies himself and his art most fervently with sexuality and positions himself on both the masculine and feminine aspects of sexual dynamics. He also identifies with the celebrity and the layperson, but most importantly he identifies himself as a human being with mundane needs—sexual, emotional and spiritual. Finally, Jackson contradicts the perception of him as alien and encourages his audience to draw new connections with him as an artist.

CHAPTER 6

"Liberace Has Gone to War": Undressing Michael Jackson's Fashion

Much has been written over the last 30 years about the semiotics (sign system) of clothing.[1] Critics like Roland Barthes have questioned how fashion creates identity and solidarity.[2] Although much journalism has been devoted to Jackson's unique sense of style and branding, relatively little academic attention has been given to how Jackson's use of clothing and costume created meaning. This chapter explores how Jackson used key costumes, accessories, and military jackets as symbols, which then became synonymous with the artist. It focuses on key accessories and outfits Jackson wore during his career, using the book by designer Michael Bush's *King of Style: Dressing Michael Jackson* as a primary source.

> "Michael's creativity transcended anything Dennis and I thought could be perceived in reality."
>
> —Michael Bush[3]

There is probably no subject more precocious and slippery than fashion. Fashion is unique in the fact that, like language, it is constantly changing in order to reflect those who wear and purvey it. In the words of Malcolm Barnard, "there are theories of class, gender and aesthetics underlying and presupposed by all fashion production and consumption."[4] Fashion is a mirror of who and what we all are, and since who we are keeps changing, the mirror changes also. Michael Jackson's use of fashion has been included in *Vogue*, *The Los Angeles Times*, and it was even referenced in a Balmain collection.[5] Clothes are often used to exhibit both conformity and rebellion. They can be representational of class, or they can instill a sense of pride and camaraderie among wearers. Furthermore, clothes, though a primary necessity for physical protection (like a warm jacket), are also used increasingly to ascertain class and financial status; Jackson did not use clothing to denote his class or his financial status, because those were evident by his reputation.

Jackson's clothing was personally designed by Dennis Tompkins and Michael Bush for decades. Bush's 2012 book, *The King of Style: Dressing Michael Jackson*, is a unique primary source, a 203-page folio-sized publication that boasts a plethora of color photographs of Jackson's clothing, along with Bush's designs, his thoughts on his designs, and anecdotes. It won two awards in 2013, including a Gold Medal at the 2013 Independent Publisher Book Awards and the 2013 PubWest Book Design Award.[6] Bush and Tompkins collaborated for decades to create clothing for Jackson, and many of his signature "looks" can be easily assigned to their partnership, resulting in "some of the most original and indelible clothing ever worn by a musical performer."[7]

This chapter begins by discussing Jackson's use of accessories, such as his single glove and fedora, which became instantly recognizable symbols of the artist and his performances. Then we consider how Jackson used costume to create a sense of character. The costume section begins with *Off the Wall*'s tuxedo (see Figure 6.1), then considers *Thriller*'s colored leather and letterman jackets, then *Bad*'s rough punky belts. It then moves into Jackson's releases of *Dangerous* and *HIStory: Past, Present and Future, Book 1*, and Jackson's ongoing use of the military jacket to create a dramatic performance out of every appearance and function, focusing on the symbolism within the military jacket and on its history. Finally, the chapter concludes with a look at the legacy of Jackson's use of clothing by considering Jackson's final ensemble, the one he was buried in.

TURNING ACCESSORIES INTO SYMBOLS

Accessories are complementary clothing or articles that often complete a wearer's outfit—a scarf, bag, hat, or even a ring, among other items.[8] Jackson's most recognizable accessory by far was his wearing a single glove, although his use of it far predates the 1980s. In *Moonwalk* Jackson writes, "I had been wearing a single glove years before *Thriller*, and this is confirmed by Bush: "I couldn't help but feel nostalgic for a young Michael Jackson sitting in his small Indiana home, pushing rhinestones into the right-handed waiter's glove."[9] The rhinestone glove (possibly worn to cover emergent vitiligo), would become synonymous not only with Jackson's mesmerizing dancing, but also with the song "Billie Jean" and the Jackson's performance of it in 1983 at the *Motown 25: Yesterday, Today, Forever* show. The use of Jackson's glove demonstrates how he knew the entrancing nature of magic tricks, illusions, and

Figure 6.1
A Sketch of Michael Jackson's
Off the Wall **Tuxedo.**
(Artwork by Karin Merx)

slight-of-hand, especially. The glove was actually sported by Jackson for several years in live performances, long before it became readily attributed to him through the power of television: "two gloves seemed so ordinary, but a single glove was different . . . an artist should let his style evolve naturally . . . I was wearing it on some of the old tours back in the 1970s."[10] White gloves are most well known for their attribution to mime artists and performances; however, in Jackson's case, studding the glove with rhinestones produced an accent on his movements and gestures on stage, reflecting the stage lights "dancing" upon the glove until it became a symbol of Jackson's magic.

Another particularly interesting use of an accessory that became a recognizable symbol was Jackson's fedora. The *OED* defines a fedora as "a low, soft, felt hat with a curled brim and the crown creased lengthways." The fedora is very much a staple of 20th-century cinematic costume. It can also be associated with the film noir movies of the 1940s and 1950s. Jackson's use of the fedora in his performances and short films serves to present him as part of the golden age of Hollywood cinema, "reminiscent of a dapper gentleman from the 1940s . . . the iconic white Smooth Criminal hat . . . functional and fun."[11] The word "fedora" originates in the United States, and with his donning it in key performances of "Billie Jean" and "Smooth Criminal," Jackson places himself within America's cinematic history. He becomes a specter that walks out of the silver screen and onto the stage.

Jackson, who often used accessories to maximum effect, was well aware of how to fluidly traverse the lines between the real and the virtual, and thereby he often crossed the shaky border between the physical and incorporeal. Jackson's own transience was reflected back to him by a world in flux. In the 1980s, when Jackson showcased both the single glove and the fedora, the world was on the very brink of the Internet, social media, and a new type of connectivity that altered communication and social interaction radically. Jackson preempted this change by turning his performances and short films into symbols, now the current lingua franca of an Internet-savvy audience. This is definitely one of the reasons why Jackson's appeal continues seven years after his death.

COSTUME AND CHARACTER

Costumes are used to denote both time and space in the cinema and on stage, and Jackson was no stranger to the visual power of costumes, especially in terms of expressing nonverbal meaning to a global audience. Publicly, Jackson would use costume to enact the performance of being "Michael Jackson, the star," or to present himself as a specific character, often directly related to those he played in his short films and a sharp paradox to the uniform he sported privately ("all he wore when he wasn't performing: corduroy shirt, usually red: black cotton pants with box pleats . . . and his loafers").[12]

Three items became a staple of his costuming throughout much of his career: His white t-shirt, Levi 501 jeans, and Florsheim shoes, illustrating the fact that Jackson's clothing palette grew to be far more than the sum of its parts.[13] The rhinestone glove grew to hold an air of mystery and magic, while the Florsheims were simultaneously a contradiction and extension of this: "he taught himself to dance in Florsheims . . . they were comfortable and were what he had worn as a child star."[14] Jackson's repeated wearing of simple white vests and t-shirts continued to identify him with the working everyman, in "a message of rebellion," along with his customized Levi jeans: "a handful of us knew the secret that Michael had spent thousands to have Dennis and me rig his 501s."[15]

Predating Jackson's use of the Levi 501s and white shirts was the *Off The Wall* era, between 1979 and 1981, during which Jackson sported the conventional tuxedo, "a short jacket without tails, for formal wear" (*OED*), to connote the fact that Jackson had become the life and soul of a disco party. The use of this costume also represented his new smooth, polished sound, as well as the frivolity of youth, as Jackson began branching out on his own into a new world of adulthood. This costume transformed Jackson into the coolest guy at the party, the boy every girl wanted to dance with and that every boy wanted to be. Jackson's costume here relied once again on distinctly American themes like the high school prom, and catered primarily to an American audience who would identify with his large black bowtie and his ruffled shirt.

By 1982, and the release of Jackson's *Thriller* album, he had become already the biggest selling black artist in history. However, upon receiving just two Grammy Awards in just two categories, and being snubbed by his peers (despite having the biggest-selling album of the year), Jackson was denied the artistic accolades he desired, "*Off the Wall* was well received by my fans and I think that's why the Grammy nominations hurt."[16] It is on the cover of *Thriller* that Jackson's clothing and costume take a left turn. Jackson still uses a suit for the cover of *Thriller* but presents himself, rather than as a prom date, as a gentleman. He inversely colors his suit jacket in white, rather than black, and his shirt as black, rather than white. This time his shirt material is sheer and he sports an open neck to reveal his chest, along with a snakeskin belt. The leopard-print handkerchief in his lapel pocket accentuates the tiger cub he sports on his knee in the full-spread of his LP sleeve.[17]

This marks a new phase where Jackson begins to clearly present himself as two separate halves. For Joseph Vogel, the cover "simultaneously projected innocence and sophistication . . . intended to present the singer as a youthful but mature artist."[18] The lines of Jackson's face are smoother and thinner, while his gaze belongs to the camera. This costume presents him as a gentleman, but the tiger presents as a sense of eccentricity and unusualness, causing the viewer to try to reconcile the image of Jackson with the image of the tiger cub. What does it mean? Why does he have it with him? Does it mean anything at all?

Throughout the *Thriller* era, Jackson wore several costumes that redefined his looks, the first of which was the letterman jacket, which again harkens back to the high school motif, to which a large majority of Jackson's American audience could relate. He also employed the letterman jacket and jeans as a costume in the *Thriller* short film, which was contrasted with the red leather jacket of the main dance number in *Thriller.* In the 1980s Jackson became synonymous with leather jackets, sporting them for a range of different videos and commercials. Jackson would continue to sport varsity jackets throughout the 1980s, and occasionally in the early 1990s.[19] What was particularly interesting about Jackson's clothing is how quickly the costumes were assimilated by his mass audience; they were instantly and easily imitated, and they quickly became so iconic that Jackson's style was easily recognized, even by just the simple lines.

It was also in this era that Jackson began to don the military jackets (which will be discussed toward the end of this chapter). Again, the lines of these jackets, similarly employed by recording artists like David Bowie and Freddie Mercury, were instantly recognizable and familiar, transforming Jackson, at a moment's notice, to a bandleader, dictator, or monarch. The leather jacket, once synonymous with criminality, tough guys, renegades, bike riders, and gang members, and known for its durable and hard-wearing fabric, became mainstreamed in part by Jackson's use, and it also served to toughen his image for the release of *Bad.*

In the late 1980s, and in the *Bad* short film, Jackson wore a multitude of leather accessories, primarily belts and buckles, with abandon. He can be credited, at least in part, for the wide usage of the leather jacket by recording artists and musicians today, apparel that's synonymous with being cool and enigmatic. During this period Jackson continued to blur the lines between stage costumes, worn predominantly for his live performances, and film costumes, worn to portray characters for specific dance sequences in his short films.[20] Jackson would also blur the lines for his mass audience, who continued to emulate his style, using an almost extravagant number of belts and buckles on one costume, reappropriating store-bought clothes and then having them reconstructed in a seamless way: "the pieces came from four or five stores off of Melrose Avenue . . . for some more "biker" essence, we severely embellished the jacket, pants, and gloves with twice as many buckles and straps."[21] Thus, by the late 1980s, Jackson's use of clothing transitions from costumes that identify him with the everyman, to costumes that mark him as spectacular, and this continued to be the case for the rest of his career. By 1991's *Dangerous* album, Jackson's costumes were no longer synonymous with his stage or short-film characters, since his characters had transitioned into an amalgam that represented Michael Jackson as a composite of many symbols.[22]

REGALIA

Throughout Jackson's career he would utilize timeless pieces of fashion that were crafted from practical uses in predominantly English aristocracy and culture: "I went through history books and reproduced the Renaissance Jacket using fifteen yards of soutache over German velvet and rhinestones."[23] The most evident example of this is Jackson's use of the military jacket, synonymous with royalty, discipline, conflict, and political power (see Figure 6.2).[24] Jackson's military jackets, though bedazzled with sequins and sparkling material, connote military power and presume that the wearer has ruling power enforced by a national armed force. Jackson's wearing the military jacket further identified him as a king, benevolently ruling over his fans with love. The military jacket is also a symbol of status, a status that Jackson enforced through his clothing time and again, declaring himself a black king and using the ultimate kingly accessory, the crown. Jackson was enamored with crowns and the insignia of British royalty: "Michael and we were looking at a book that he'd pulled from his extended library . . . a photograph of the Imperial State Crown of England."[25] This quote is from a particularly touching anecdote about the creation of a crown to commemorate Jackson's being named Entertainer of the Decade in 1990: "he taught us it was okay to celebrate ourselves."[26] Jackson was aptly designated the King of Pop for wielding influentially effective weapons in the form of vastly watched televised performances and short films, sold-out concert tours and record-breaking album releases.

Nowhere is Jackson's awareness of the power of his appropriation of military costume more evident than it is on the cover of his 1995 album *HIStory: Past, Present, and Future, Book 1.*[27] In the teaser, Jackson presents himself in the form of a "statue" Jackson, a benevolent dictator, a member of celebrity and musical royalty: "the cover reveals him standing like a militant prizefighter; bold, fists clenched, confident . . . the immortalizing of the body, the literal transformation of his likeness into a work of art makes sense."[28] Jackson uses this image subversively; it is still as much a costume as the tuxedo he wore on the cover of *Off the Wall* in 1979. Here he presents a rebellious image of a black dictator and king who rules benevolently over a global kingdom.

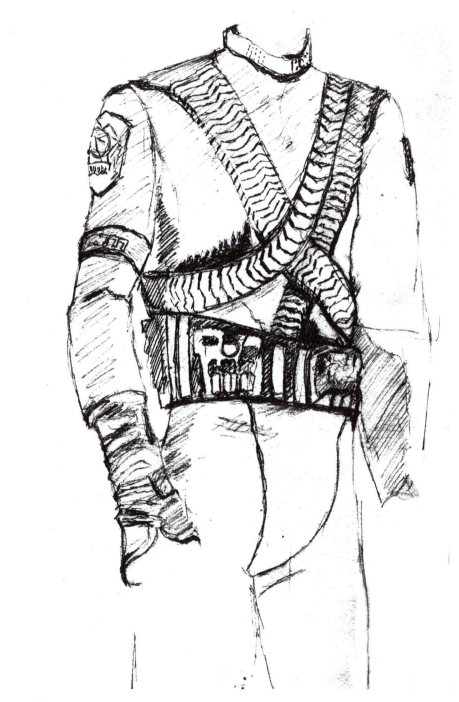

Figure 6.2
A Sketch of Michael Jackson's Military Jacket from the *HIStory* Album Cover.
(Artwork by Karin Merx)

Jackson's final ensemble is beautifully showcased in the last chapter of *The King of Style*.[29] He was buried in a costume uniquely designed after the jacket he wore to the Grammys in 1993, and received the Grammy Legend Award. Bush recalls, "I sewed hundreds of pearls in an effort to re-create what we knew was Michael's all-time favorite piece . . . I sewed a rhinestone Tinker Bell wearing a green dress and slinging a stream of the dust he so loved."[30] Jackson's final costume also included a "championship belt" and, of course, his beloved Florsheims. A crown was placed atop Jackson's "eighteen-karat, gold-plated casket" that boasted "rubies, emeralds, and sapphires," which "caught the moonlight that danced across the night sky." Bush quite rightly asserts that Jackson's death marked "not a funeral, but a coronation."[31]

There are surplus images of Caucasian kings and nobles in galleries and museums throughout Europe.[32] Since the emergence of transatlantic slavery in the 17th and 18th centuries, and the concurrent destruction of African dominions, there has been a disappearing act of the depiction of the black or African king (once so prevalent in depictions like the Adoration of the Magi), and a visual wasteland of blacks in positions of high status.[33] With repeated images of him in military regalia throughout the world's press and in his public appearances and short films, Jackson presented the image of himself as wielding both social and political power through the use of costume, which ascribed to him the appearance of social standing and black power in what was clearly a predominantly white world.

Clothing was a tool for artistic invention and, in later years, reinvention. Jackson mined history for archetypical images onto which he could craft his form and his unique style. In an interview with Jackson's creative team, his personal makeup artist Karen Faye and his designers Michael Bush and Dennis Tompkins were asked how they would describe Jackson's style, and their answer was, "Liberace has gone to war."[34] The "Liberace" connection has to do with Jackson's flamboyance, the glitter, sparkle, and shininess of Jackson's unique "brand" or style. Alternately, "goes to war" regards Jackson's embrace of military clothing as a person who may well have seen himself in a conflict, a battle for his own right to be a king, regardless of his ethnicity, and the right to be respected for the position of power he had earned with his dedication to his art.

In his fashion choices, Jackson regularly took the binary elements of the human body—a hand, a foot, a head—and attached significances to them that were entirely of his and his creative team's invention. Through his costumes, he endeavored to inhabit the human and supernatural, the virtual and physical. This chapter has aimed to open a conversation among fashion theorists about Jackson's clothing, accessories, and style choices, in order to encourage critics to explore the boundaries between what Jackson wore and who we are.

In Jackson's case, clothing was used not only to determine who Jackson was, but also to address who other people wished Jackson to be, as well as to emphasize how he presented himself, for effect, to his audience. Jackson's use of fashion and androgyny offers ample ground for further analysis and research, especially in the light of essays by Marjorie Garber on bisexuality and trans-vestitism, just two of the many topics that lie at the heart of modern popular culture. Jackson's use of fashion and makeup often defied and denied notions of the female/male dichotomy; and so, too, with fashion, Jackson's bucks the dominant idea that clothing is frivolous. He demonstrates the immense power of clothing and fashion to create character and to assume strength, poise, and social power. I sincerely hope that this chapter will serve to inspire many more academic conversations on Jackson's use of clothing, costume, and makeup. There are so many potential avenues for further discussion.

CHAPTER 7

"Instrument of Nature": The Voice of Michael Jackson

T his chapter begins with a brief overview of critical discourse relating to Michael Jackson's voice in terms of reception and recording production. It then explores Jackson's voice in terms of three key definitions: "music," "sound," and "opinion." This exploration begins with Jackson's voice as a component in his musical arrangements, followed by his voice as a sound or utterance produced in his language. Lastly, the chapter discusses "voice" as an expression of Jackson's personal opinions and attitudes, before concluding to focus on a collective definition of Jackson's voice as a crucial way by which he presents his authorial power (agency) and his perspective.

> "If I speak in the tongues of men or of angels, but do not have love, I am only a resounding gong or a clanging cymbal."
> —1 Corinthians 13:1, *NIV*.

Due to his considerable airplay through the past five decades, Michael Jackson's voice must be one of the most widely recognized of all time. The sound of his voice still permeates the airwaves throughout the globe and continues to be listened to via earphones and speakers, throughout the developed and undeveloped world.[1] The universality of Jackson's voice has interested academics and musicologists alike; as Susan Fast states in *Dangerous*, it is "exquisite to hear his intensity, this intimacy, to hear the human body laboring."[2] However, one of the earliest explorations into the resonance and impact of Jackson's voice was in Barney Hoskyns' 1983 article, "The Boy Who Would Fly: Michael Jackson," republished in 2009 in *The Resistible Demise of Michael*

Jackson.[3] Hoskyns focuses on the rhythmic, disembodied attributes of Jackson's singing voice, particularly on the *Thriller* album, and often describes Jackson's engaging use of vocal expression and its effect on the listener as being on a particularly personal level: "deep in the dark womb of the studio, Michael's voice is a vehicle of fantasy, an instrument ceaselessly running circles around itself, tripping itself up, playing make-believe."[4] For Hoskyns, Jackson's voice is so engaging and has such impact because it becomes an entity of its very own: "It's a voice which starts into every split spare second, stretching like rubber, filling cracks like water. It's not warm or sensual or 'black' but sharp, a squeezing of the throat's aperture, a voice of pure technique. Detaching itself, it gets lost in free flight. Its narcissism is almost not human."[5]

As the previous quote shows, debates surrounding Jackson's voice began long before the track "Speed Demon," which will be discussed in some detail in this chapter. These debates stem from a desire to explain and define, firstly, Jackson's voice, and secondly, its resonant qualities, which, because of their inherent intimacy, draw the listener in. For Hoskyns, certainly, Jackson provides an auditory seduction, "charging these words with the bitterest twists, bending and dragging them, winding vowels round his throat, spitting syllables like darts of poison . . . you can't escape, you're ripped by the voice's current."[6] Hoskyns interprets this inherent seductiveness as directly sexual and Jackson's voice as one that, "at a point of masturbatory orgasm . . . can all but shut out the world," and that, therefore, "to try to engage it in conversation seem[s] absurd, dangerous."[7] What this quote illustrates is the problematic nature of attempting to quantify the resonant qualities of Jackson's use of his voice, and to quantify the complexity of its reception by listeners who are seduced by it and then, of course, are required to rationalize their seduction and pull Jackson's voice into the realm of the unusual. Once Jackson's voice is transported, through any discourse, into the realm of "other," it then traverses easily into the realm of the dangerous and threatening. However, what Hoskyns' article does relate eloquently is the unique experience listeners often have upon first encountering Jackson's voice. Sam Davies echoes the same sentiment, asserting that "Jackson's voice, with its constant appeal to the unspeakable, its recourse to a spasmodic, tic-like, wordless vocabulary, carries the virus which disperses him into inhuman parts."[8]

In other words, Jackson's voice is often of such immense relatability that some critics regard it as entirely separate to the compositions it's part of. Clearly, how we perceive Jackson is inextricably connected to how his voice, and its impact, are received by the listener. How much this is due to Jackson's voice itself, and how much this is due to an idea of Jackson's voice and what it should signify, remain very complex questions. Much of the academic criticism on Jackson's voice centers predominantly around his earlier adult studio albums, 1979's *Off the Wall*, and 1982's *Thriller*—safe material for analysis, compared to the driven, heady, breathy sounds of *Dangerous* and the prickly synthesized sounds of *Invincible*, rife with technical manipulation and feedback.[9]

Joseph Vogel details his observations of Jackson's sounds succinctly, regarding each song as far more than the sum of its individual vocal parts, driven by the yelps, howls, guttural sounds, grunts, whoops, and screams that make up Jackson's musical vocal expression: "words aren't necessary—the deep emotion is communicated perfectly in his delivery. His voice *is* the music."[10] There is far more that Jackson seeks to reveal to his listeners than words could convey. For some critics, what Jackson is articulating with his voice is the sheer disembodied ecstasy of musical expression, while for others, Jackson's sounds create a sense of musical tapestry, a vocal painting, a splash of further color to punctuate his musical world.[11]

Francesca Royster writes about Jackson's voice in the chapter "Michael Jackson, Queer World Making, and the Trans Erotics of Voice, Gender, and Age" in her monograph *Sounding Like a No-No: Queer Sounds and Eccentric Acts in the Post-Soul Era*. Royster presents Jackson's voice as a medium that bends the perceived boundaries between genders and forces audiences to reconsider their prior notions around sexuality. For Royster, a self-attributed "queer" author, Jackson's *Off the Wall* was "a soundtrack for those [queer] desires which were floating around . . . for which I didn't have a name."[12] Royster assigned Jackson a "third sex" as early as 2005, the original publication date for her "Michael Jackson and the Transgendered Erotics of Voice," and she argued that the very act of using the throat to evoke sounds is inherently sexual, throats being "part of the erotic act."[13] However, what this chapter is more readily concerned with is Jackson's voice in relation not only to music and intimacy, but to meaning. Jackson's vocal performances are almost certainly far more than the sum of their parts, and the example we will consult as a case in point will be the track "Speed Demon" from Jackson's 1987 album *Bad*.

The reason for choosing this track is because "Speed Demon" (1987) is an example from the mid-part of Jackson's career, following his work on the 1979 *Off The Wall* and 1982 *Thriller*, where his vocal performances may be argued to be more concerned with audience and playability. The song also precedes a lyrical focus on false representation and slander in the albums *HIStory: Past, Present, and Future, Book 1* and *Blood on the Dance Floor: HIStory in the Mix*. Several other chapters in this book focus on *Dangerous* and *Invincible*, so it would be superfluous to focus on them again here.[14]

VOICE AS MUSIC

"Speed Demon" demonstrates Jackson's uncanny ability to showcase several parts of his vocal repertoire within his delivery of a song. The first definition of "voice" is as a vocal part in a composition. Within the first 10 seconds of the song's opening, which begins with the thrumming of an engine, Jackson's voice forms a "chuh" sound, a cross between a yelp and a grunt, which is immediately interlaced with the sound of Jackson breathing in unison with the engine's rhythm. Jackson's breath, and his rough intake of breath, become one with the pounding of a synth drum, as he begins the first line.[15] The vocal performance that continues in the chorus traverses the line between singing and speaking.

Jackson moves between the voice as a vocal part (a changing element of tone) and the voice as part of the instrumentals of the track, and he does so especially in terms of manipulating high and low pitch. During the hook and its repetition of the word "speeding," Jackson repeats the line "pull over boy." He stays in the lower part of his register, breath-singing his words, and this way his breath remains part of the song's instrumental. In the second part of the hook, where Jackson sings, he uses the falsetto register: "in the falsetto tradition there can be tremendous power, as well as vulnerability . . . a crack in the macho posture, the expression of need."[16] Jackson's voice also serves to create multiples of himself within this track and several others in his work. These multiples, stacked Jackson voices that often form his choruses, also provide a sense drama. Their dramatic function serves to give a rise in tension; they lift the dramatic stakes, and they provide depth. Simultaneously, Jackson's voice reaches new levels of expression, and when he crescendos the word "speeding" and repeats himself, he includes new nuances in every repetition, culminating in the final bars with yelping and grunting.

Jackson's vocal expression forces us to reconsider the relationship between vocal utterances and their meaning. The song seems to have far little to do with its semantics, and far more to do with the aural expression found in its vocal harmonies. The clue to this is in the driving progression of rhythms that originally serve to accentuate and highlight Jackson's voice. There is clearly a race on here, but who are the contestants, and is there truly a prize? Jackson's sound identifies with the rush of moving very quickly, and of being in control by being out of control.

MUSIC AS SOUND

Jackson's vocal expression can also be interpreted in terms of a "sound produced in a person's language" (*OED*), articulations that are made through their ability to sing. In "Speed Demon," Jackson articulates on many levels.

He utters the main verses, which use the first-person perspective ("**my** mind"); and he also articulates from another perspective, using the second person, which argues that he could be saving his own life by slowing down, to which Jackson replies that every moment will be lived as if it is the last.[17] Jackson is clearly demonstrating a desire and an ability to both speak and sing, but in doing so he is clearly developing something far more profound. The song is not explicit about the characters to whom it refers (for example, to whom we can attribute "pull over boy").[18] On one level, Jackson's voice provides his distinctive tone and style. However, in another, more literary sense, in which voice describes an author's unique style or flair, Jackson conveys his in his use of syncopated rhythms, a layered chorus, and a considerable range of pitches and tones. His use of multiple perspectives, in choruses, verses, and hooks, and, of course, in his use of synthesizers and found sounds and vocal sounds, which are incorporated into the main composition seamlessly. A voice is also a marker of what, who, and where we are—a means of identifying us. By the time of the *Bad* album, Jackson no longer relies on the "hee-hee" and "whoo" signatures, but he does give out one deep "whoo" scream toward the end of the track, as if he cannot quite contain the ecstasy of, or at least the energy within, the song's interactions.

For Royster, "through his cries, whispers, groans, whines, and grunts, Jackson . . . often undercuts his audience's expectations of erotic identification."[19] Jackson's breathy execution in many of his songs, the yelps and sighs, and the layering of breaths (both short and long), can contribute to a definition of what Jackson's unique vocal expression is, and can help us discover how we can distinguish his songs as entirely different and separate from the songs of other musicians and recording artists.

MUSIC AS OPINION

Continuing in the vein of Jackson's vocal expressions having a flair and flourish that make them distinctive to listeners, Royster also addresses "the power and dangerousness of Jackson's ability to make longing speak, and his ability to make it move across contexts and desires."[20] Jackson certainly makes longing speak in this track.[21] However, "voice," in terms of the expression of a particular opinion or attitude, is cloudy at best in "Speed Demon," as it is in so many of Jackson's songs where he relies heavily on analogy, allegory, and metaphor to express a wide range of meanings to his audience.

The first meaning Jackson may be expressing here is that of being a superstar, on the very edge, especially in terms of touring, flying from place to place, moving at breakneck speed, dancing on stage after stage on world tours, and being unstoppable. Even Jackson's severe burns in 1984 did not keep him down for more than a few weeks. Adrian Grant's *Visual Documentary* provides an excellent overview of Jackson's movements in the four years preceding "Speed Demon," and he truly was traveling the entire world on a grueling schedule of engagements, award ceremonies, performances, benefits, and recording commitments.[22] The sheer number of dates serve to illustrate Jackson's momentum, which may well have resulted in his feeling that he had been catapulted into his own life. Those who ask him to "pull over" are perhaps Jackson's detractors, commanding him to stop doing so well, stop earning so much money, and stop winning so many awards. To the detractors, Jackson gives the reply: There is no slowing down and no pulling over.

Another interpretation of "Speed Demon" examines the treatment and mistreatment of black men and women at the hands of the American police, news that has been in the mainstream press several times, like pulling over black people for alleged speeding offenses, and some events that have even resulted in violent beatings. This shameful, but longstanding, part of American culture, made iconic by the videoing of crimes such as the beating of Rodney King, blurs the line between reality and Jackson's inner visions, and it is reiterated by the short film for the song "Speed Demon," included in the *Moonwalker* anthology. The short film further underscores the words and helps us understand their meaning more fully. During "Speed Demon" Jackson morphs into several individuals, some of whom are famous, some who are not. In this short film, he is speeding away from hordes of fans, made, like him, of plasticine, in a claymation animation. Jackson escapes by disguising himself in rabbit costume, but fans hound him mercilessly until he flies away from them using a jetpack to launch himself into the sky, soaring into the heavens and into freedom.[23] Jackson speeds away from all those who have chased him and pursued him in a bid to get something from him, a chase that results in his escape. However, when he does escape he is accosted by a police officer for his "autograph," and when he claims that he was dancing with his friend, Spike, who morphs into reality after Jackson removes his costume and turns himself back from clay to human, the bunny has disappeared and Jackson is left alone. However, the word "boy" is reminiscent of the racist contingent that wishes to pull Jackson back and forces him to pay for going so fast and so far. He is not permitted to run, or, if he does so, he is constantly being told to get a ticket in order to continue on his way. At no point in the track does Jackson acknowledge his speeding as a crime for which he must atone. The concept of speed in this track may also well be an existential question; Jackson must speed because time is running out for him. What "Speed Demon" articulates most emphatically is a necessity to run with intense and immense speed and to escape a situation. It expresses a desire to run faster than those who give chase and to become a being who can always move fast enough to make their escape permanent. This notion of speeding is not leisurely, nor is it a result of hedonistic self-aggrandizing. Jackson is running for his life.

To conclude, in Jackson's case, the voice is not simply a single component in a musical composition; rather, it is like paint, which Jackson can and does apply in several colors through each composition. Often, the effect forms a cloud of meanings, ambiguous enough to leave listeners with a sense of deep emotional connection, sometimes a sense of urgency, immediacy, pleasure, or pain. Jackson's use of vocal expression is entirely unique, and it produces a highly distinctive tone and style in all of his songs, which helps the artist to express his own agency and perspective further. These opinions are often dressed beautifully by Jackson's flourishes, causing his voice to occupy Royster's "third space," totally free of gender but imbued with a great amount of meaning. Not only does Jackson have a voice like no other; he also uses it to express himself like an instrument of nature itself. Jackson uses his voice to convey narrative sentiment with a myriad of shrieks, whoops, guttural, and nonverbal sounds that are interpreted as a form of physical, life energy that Jackson uses in a form of vocal sculpture.

This chapter has presented a way of approaching Jackson's music in the light of his unique use of voice and vocal expression, presenting the three components of Jackson's voice as music, sound, and opinion. Jackson's use of voice creates a series of colors in an aural palette. These colors, through Jackson's use of vocal sculpture, breath, shrieks, whoops, and all his utterances, are integral components of Jackson's unique style. They are tools only he could wield, and they stamped his ownership mark on all of his work.

PART II

Life as Art

This section focuses on Jackson's life as an artist. It is biographical in that it concerns itself with how biography—real, constructed, or any combination thereof—figures predominantly in the life presentation and perception of Michael Jackson.

CHAPTER 8

Thoughts on Michael Jackson's Transformations

O ne of the most repeated themes in Michael Jackson's art is "transformation," a physical process of morphing from one state to another. Throughout many of his short films, Jackson regularly transformed himself between a living being and animals or inanimate objects, such as a werewolf (*Thriller*, 1984), a car, robot, and spaceship (*Moonwalker*, 1988), and a black panther (*Black or White*, 1991). Jackson often used these transformations to mesmerize his audience, using the most cutting-edge technology available and sparing no expense.[1] Shifting the dominant focus by critics on transformation in *Thriller*, this chapter first focuses its attention on Jackson's personal accounts of physical transformation before considering the 1997 short film *Ghosts*, directed by Stan Winston, in a close textual analysis of film language.

> "An actor's performance or a collective performance can transform me."
> —Michael Jackson[2]

Transformation is defined as "the action of changing in form, shape, or appearance" (*OED*) and has been a theme widely used by authors and filmmakers. An engaging example in English literature includes the birth of Victor Frankenstein's monster in *Frankenstein* by Mary Shelley and in Kafka's *Metamorphosis*, in which a salesman named Gregor Samsa wakes to find that he has become an insect.[3] Fiction aside, however, transformation is a vital component of every human life. We mutate physically from two-celled organisms in the womb to fully formed fetuses, from defenseless babies to precocious toddlers, from teenagers into adults, and then from adults to elderly pensioners. Very little in our transformative experience is in our control, and at many times during the growing experience we may endure "growing pains," "neuralgic pains in the limbs . . . during the period of growth" (*OED*).

For the artist Michael Jackson, much of this personal process of growing up and maturing took place within a context of continual pressure, surveillance, and criticism. As he stated, "show business and my career were my life . . . the biggest struggle was right there in the mirror . . . my identity as a person was tied to my identity as a celebrity."[4] His autobiography, *Moonwalk*, is particularly explicit about the turmoil caused by the intense adoration of his fans ("they don't realize they might hurt you") and the lack of connection with his father ("I still don't know him, and that's sad for a son who hungers to understand").[5] In addition to these personal problems, there were the public systems of attack, which are clearly outlined in Chapter 9—" 'Throwing Stones to Hide Your Hands': The Mortal Persona of Michael Jackson."

Many of the critical discussions around Jackson's physical changes (as discussed in Chapter 10—"Recontextualizing Michael Jackson's Blackness") are presented through a prism of misconception. For example, Jackson's use of cosmetic surgery to enhance his appearance is often cited by critics, such as Kobena Mercer, to support their assertions, and, of course, *Thriller* is often cited as a form of future allegory, implying that Jackson was purposely orchestrating all the changes that he underwent throughout his career.[6] Another perspective on these changes, especially with regard to transformation as a repeated theme in Jackson's early work, and the *Thriller* short film, in particular, is with the consideration that Jackson was a widely recognized child star, as discussed in some part by Margo Jefferson in *On Michael Jackson* and in the article from the *Journal of Popular Music Studies*, "Michael Jackson and the Jackson 5 Before *Thriller*."[7] Jackson's image as a child star was a commodity, and from this millions of dollars were made for him and the adults around him. However, in the mid-1970s, Jackson found his image changing drastically, out of his control, to such an extent that those who met him would express their disgust, "I was a gangly adolescent . . . not the person they expected or even wanted to see . . . imagine having your own natural insecurities about the changes your body is undergoing heightened by the negative reactions of others."[8]

This experience radically altered Jackson's personality: "I became subconsciously scarred by this experience . . . my complexion was so bad . . . [it] began to depress me . . . a devastating effect."[9] However, in conjunction with these paradigms about Jackson's appearance and its monetary value to his public, how his audience required Jackson to appear quickly became paramount to how successful his career would continue to be. Simultaneously, Jackson began to suffer severely from a skin condition, vitiligo, and this began an entirely new transformation, another one that was out of his control. Vitiligo causes splotches of pale skin to appear all over the body and may well have been what caused the theme of transformation to feature so heavily in Jackson's work, particularly in the *Thriller* short film, where Jackson's body is transformed from human to beast, character to actor, human to zombie, and back again to human. Furthermore, at the end of the *Thriller* short film Jackson's physicality remains fluid as he turns the camera with cat eyes rather than human ones.

Nevertheless, this chapter argues that it is not in *Thriller* where the theme of transformation is most evident in Jackson's work, but in his 1997 short film *Ghosts*, directed by Stan Winston. *Ghosts*, produced and directed 14 years after *Thriller*, includes all the events that had passed in the interim, most noticeably the allegations of 1993.[10] Jackson plays several characters in *Ghosts*, in which he stars as protagonist, accuser, and antagonist. The first character we meet in *Ghosts* is the Mayor, a character whose mononym shows his power in relation to the people of the town, a town satirically called Normal Village—"a lovely place to raise the kids."[11] In this role, Jackson's makeup draws close similarities to the Santa Barbara attorney, "Mad Dog" Sneddon, whose legendary vendetta against Jackson resulted in millions of wasted American tax dollars and Jackson's career and reputation in tatters.[12]

In playing the role of both attacker and victim, Jackson inhabits two sides of the human psyche, highlighting the fact that we are so often our own worst enemy, the ones who cause ourselves the most pain, and the very monsters who inhabit our own nightmares. Jackson also exhibits his ability to stand in the shoes of those who oppress him and to see the world from their perspective. From that perspective, his difference and eccentricity make him a threat. The transformative qualities of standing on both sides of the argument are what Jackson explores primarily in this short film, and "transformation" is key because it enables him to do this.

The place where Jackson's secondary character, the protagonist known as the Maestro, lives, is called Someplace Else, and the "townspeople" invade the Maestro's world, because, from their perspective, they find him strange. These sequences are reminiscent of those in Tim Burton's *Edward Scissorhands*, in which Edward is relegated to a dark place cut off from the main world, which is painted pastel pink to show the vapid, vacuous diegesis of suburbia in relation to the dark, more real world of Edward and his maker.[13]

The Maestro's large and imposing house is clearly foreboding to the townspeople, who include a cameo by the rapper, Mos Def, and three children who have been there before and do not find the Maestro's home terrifying in the least. What is particularly interesting in the opening sequence is that Jackson, in playing both the Maestro and the Mayor, transforms himself from a black musician to a white politician, highlighting two sides of a power struggle. The initial conversation between Jackson (the Mayor) and himself (the Maestro) concludes with insults, where he is called a "freak" numerous times, and the first transformation we are presented with is the ability of the Maestro to pull his facial skin in unnatural ways; perhaps referring to claims made in the press about Jackson's cosmetic surgery, he stretches out the bottom of his jaw to terrifying proportions (see Figure 8.1).

Figure 8.1
A Sketch of the Maestro's Elongated Face as in *Ghosts*. Based on a shot from Winston, "Michael Jackson's Ghosts."
(Artwork by Karin Merx)

This transformative quality is used specifically to instill fear in the Mayor. The Maestro exercises his power on his command of the human form, transforming from what appears human to something that is clearly superhuman or subhuman, bending the lines between what is possible and what is possible for Michael Jackson. This demonstrates Jackson's acute awareness of the thin veneer between his personas and the character he is portraying.

The Maestro proceeds to showcase his abilities to command the elements, and he presents himself as a being in the liminal space between the physical and the supernatural, issuing an ectoplasmic substance from his hands, from which emanates a light that creates and controls other beings with supernatural powers. Here, the Maestro's transformative powers extend to those he can create with his hands and mind, beings from a distant time, all of which look like zombies that have been plucked from the oblivion of death. Not only is the Maestro capable of great personal transformative power, but also of great creative power, extending his transformational abilities to those he creates, giving them the power of flight at will.

Death is one of the transformations that the Maestro easily transitions into; by simply removing his clothes and skin, he emerges as a living skeleton, able to dance, move, and communicate. His maniacal grin and form were designed using models of Jackson's own skull, so in many ways this skeleton is Jackson himself, his inner workings at play.[14] On one level, the skeleton is a reanimated corpse, which coincides with horror themes of reanimation of the dead and manipulation of the dead; however, what the dancing skeleton also represents in the short film is the bare bones of the Maestro and the Mayor, which are exactly the same. Human bones do not wear the same badges attributed to difference that our bodies and skins do; bones stay the same, and although bones are rarely seen in this form, once the flesh is gone, all bones are strikingly similar. The Maestro transforms himself to the barest essence of himself, his bones, and then gyrates and dances to entertain his viewers, who are both horrified and enthralled by this display. For amusement, Jackson retains his Florsheim shoes and his sparkly socks, for only through these items can we unequivocally accept that this living skeleton belongs to the celebrity, Michael Jackson, and to further reiterate this fact, the living skeleton does the moonwalk.

The next form that the Maestro employs in transformation is that of the beast. This beast is horned and his face is filled with ridges, like that of a demon (see Figure 8.2). Here, the Maestro takes the part of the monster (or the beast that the Mayor has said he is), conveying the most freakish elements that the Mayor has accused him of possessing. However, these elements are comical to the Maestro and terrifying to the Mayor. As a black musician and actor, Jackson's use of the beast character coincides with the concept of the "black

Figure 8.2
A Sketch of the the Maestro Transformed into a Beast.
(Artwork by Karin Merx)

devil" and the depiction of the devil as having black skin, thereby making black people synonymous with criminality and evil.[15] Stemming from medieval times, this notion is still endemic in Western tradition, as when the character Iago says of Othello, in Shakespeare's eponymous play: "an old black ram | has been tupping your white ewe" (1.1.87–88).[16] It is from this perception of black people as beasts that several other negative stereotypes about black people and criminality and sexuality emerged and coalesced.[17] However, these archetypes had very little to do with the real existence of black people in the medieval era, the 17th century, or today, and far more to do with negative perceptions of them by the slave owners in the Western world.

In the transatlantic slave trade and subsequent centuries, black Africans and African Americans were, in fact, sold as beasts of burden, and they were often given less rights than cattle. They were sold and bred at the will of slave owners and demeaned as second-class citizens, becoming part of an under-class that was dealt constant oppression and suppression by the ideological key-holders of the Western world.[18] A beast is also defined as a "contemptible person" or "something formidably difficult to control or deal with" (*OED*). It is no coincidence that Jackson chooses a beast to turn into, especially since it was a beast that he was accused of being through allegations of child molestation.

Once the Maestro transforms into the beast, he immediately proceeds to invade the Mayor character through the mouth, fusing all three aspects—Beast, Maestro, and Mayor—into one being. The transformative quality here relies on fusion of all positives and negatives into one and, especially, it releases the seemingly non-beastlike character (the Mayor) to be the most uncivilized and animalistic of all. Thus, the Mayor becomes what he hates most; he is his own source of revilement. Hence, the Maestro questions, "who's the freak now?"

The Maestro produces a mirror to reveal to the Mayor the new appearance that the Maestro has given him. The use of a mirror, to show the reflection of the inherent "beastliness" and the beastly behavior that the Mayor himself exhibits, expresses outwardly the inward attributes of prejudice, envy, and hatred. These are the Mayor's emotions, which have brought him to the Maestro's door with a lynch mob and lit torches. *Ghosts* also features the song "Is It Scary?" Throughout this song Jackson explores how American society, in particular, is duplicitous and hypocritical toward him, as discussed especially in the work of Joseph Vogel.[19] Jackson argues through the song and the short film that the behavior of those who attack him is in fact far more terrifying than he is presented to be, and that the lynch mob mentality that immediately marks him as a criminal, despite being falsely accused, is "scary."

The short film proceeds to take a drastic turn. The Mayor takes the Maestro's form and he uses it to dance, parodying Sneddon and the Mayor and simultaneously entertaining his viewing audience, both inside and outside of the film. After being ejected from the Mayor's body through a comedic fart, the Maestro seems to comply with the Mayor's request to leave. While on the ground, he proceeds to smash his face into the floor. The transformation here is once again fixated on the Maestro's face, the seat of most of the confusion and communication about the celebrity "Michael Jackson." However, in smashing his face, the Maestro reveals yet another transformational quality, that of the substance of himself. What seems to be, on first view, flesh and blood, is actually shown to be a porous, sandlike substance. The Maestro destroys himself until he dissolves into a heap of sand, becomes ashes, and crumbles away.

It seems that the Maestro has been defeated—well, at least, that the Mayor has convinced the Maestro to destroy himself and that the rejection of the

Mayor has destroyed the Maestro permanently. However, this is not necessarily the case, because of the beast's reemergence in the doorway as the Mayor attempts to leave. The Maestro cannot be destroyed. He will keep resurfacing, shapeshifting, and altering himself into new more complex and unexpected forms. The Mayor is eventually so terrified that he runs away, never to be seen again.

In conclusion, Jackson explored the theme of transformation in several of his works, most noticeably, in the 1997 short film *Ghosts,* and the exploration of this theme poses Jackson as both the antagonist and protagonist, able to transform himself repeatedly and to exert his transformative powers over beings that he creates. However, this depicted transformational power, often more commonly associated with Jackson's desire for personal difference and change—in terms of cosmetic and physical alteration—perhaps has far deeper roots in his youth and adulthood as an international music star and a sufferer of vitiligo. What is most unusual and exciting about *Ghosts* is that Jackson uses transformational themes to highlight the duplicity and hypocrisy of American culture, by highlighting the irony of accusing a stranger on the hill and of forcing him to reinvent himself to become normalized or leave permanently. The true monsters and beasts in the short film are those that lie dormant within the "normal" people who live in "normal village," the average everyday folk for whom attacking an innocent stranger has often been so easy and so much more preferable to actually seeking the real truth. Jackson also seamlessly includes themes of racial inequality in his use of transformational qualities, and by playing Mayor, Maestro, Skeleton, and Beast, fusing these characters and separating them, he shows that the art of transformation is so much more complex than *Thriller* as an allegory of personal change.

CHAPTER 9

"Throwing Stones to Hide Your Hands": The Mortal Persona of Michael Jackson

Drawing on a variety of critical resources relating to Michael Jackson Studies, the emerging scholarly study of the artist and his multimodal art, political impact, and cultural significance, this chapter deconstructs the varied personas of Jackson by exploring both his cultural deification and many subsequent attempts to degrade his deified status.[1] It employs the biblical story of Naboth as an allegory of Jackson's cultural denigration.

> "We are not stoning you for any good work," they replied, "but for blasphemy, because you, a mere man, claim to be God."
>
> —John 10:32–34, *NIV*

Stoning is a ghastly act of communal justice against one person, and it is still used as a form of execution in various parts of the Middle East and Africa. In the biblical book of Kings, two liars slander a virtuous man named Naboth, accusing him of cursing both the King and God. Although Naboth is innocent, he is still taken out of the city and stoned.[2]

There are several culprits in his demise: the king who wants Naboth's land, the queen who wants to please the king, the slanderers whose motivations for destroying Naboth are unclear, and the public who are easily led without evidence. The tale has all the makings of Shakespearean tragedy, but the parallels to Michael Jackson's life are unnerving. At the beginning of his story, Naboth is both wealthy and content. However, he is also in the wrong place at the wrong time, namely, a place called Jezreel with a vineyard near the palace of the King of Samaria. Similarly, 30-plus years ago in 1984, Michael Jackson was in America with a dream to become the biggest star who ever lived.[3] His deification as a solo artist began with the release of his 1979 album *Off The Wall*, which was, by 1981, "the biggest-selling album ever by a black artist," while the 1982 release of *Thriller*, its groundbreaking short films, and an iconic performance at *Motown 25: Yesterday, Today, Forever*, completed his veneration.[4]

Thriller would sell "a bigger number of copies than the number of human beings there have ever been, or will ever be, on Earth. Its numbers are bigger than the number of grains of sand or blades of grass or drops in the ocean or molecules or atoms."[5] In truth, the album has sold an estimated 110 million copies to date and, as a result of its unparalleled success, Michael Jackson would be hounded by fans and literally chased by paparazzi for the rest of his life.[6] He was often barricaded in his own home: "there've been a couple of scuffles at gate on Hayvenhurst, and they can get dangerous . . . it *hurts* to be mobbed. You feel as if you're going to suffocate or be dismembered."[7]

At this stage in his career he was given a superlative "idol" persona whose facets were unrecognizable from the man they signified. In many ways it was at this point that Michael Jackson became a trademark, a simulacrum of a person.[8] A confessedly shy, mild-mannered dancer, singer, and musician, he would be characterized as more godlike than human, with his military jackets and rhinestone gloves. However, in his own words, "accomplishments alone are not synonymous with who I am. Indeed, the cheery five-year-old who belted out "Rockin' Robin" and "Ben" to adoring crowds was not indicative of the boy behind the smile."[9]

Jackson was not equipped (it is questionable whether anyone could be) for the astronomical fame bestowed upon him. A friend and biographer claimed that as a child star and victim of domestic abuse he "arrived in adulthood with missing pieces . . . [who] tried to compensate for this through the home he built, his appearance, his music, and his interests."[10] The 1995 composition "Childhood," one of his most autobiographical, asks: "Have you seen my childhood?"[11] It is difficult to say whether anyone could have coped with Jackson's extraordinary renown. To some extent he had already started to become unreal as a human being, through the dominant overrepresentation of his image that pervaded throughout the world: it's "actuality . . . seemed to have been not merely distorted, but overwhelmed, drowned in a sea of his own images."[12]

Jackson wrote that "one of the side effects of the *Thriller* period was to make [him] weary of constantly being in the public eye," and the more famous he became, the more he became a target of vicious attacks by the press.[13] "There was a darker side to the media backlash. Jackson had become the most powerful African-American in the history of the entertainment industry . . . it is no coincidence that this was the precise moment when the tide began to shift."[14]

Academic Joseph Vogel gives a far more likely hypothesis for the creation of the malicious Wacko Persona. The "Wacko Jacko" moniker was coined in 1985. "Jacco" or "Jacco Macacco" is Cockney slang for "monkey." Its continued use can be interpreted as an insult to Jackson's ethnicity.[15] Jackson quite rightly reviled the nickname, the use of which was tantamount to discrimination by the tabloid press. In a 1997 interview he explained that he desperately wanted to shield his son from these cruel jibes. Poignantly, he remarked, "Did they ever think I would have a child one day . . . that I have a heart. It's hurting my heart. Why pass it on to him?"[16]

The gradual lightening of his skin from the early 1980s, which went unexplained until a televised 1993 interview, was manipulated to contribute further to the formation of this second false persona.[17] He was a sufferer of an aggressive, disfiguring medical condition which, since his personal identity was synonymous with his identity as a celebrity from childhood, was so emotionally crippling he rarely spoke of it: "it's a problem for me . . . something I cannot control."[18]

Jackson kept his arms covered at all times and always went out with an umbrella because the sun was toxic to his depigmented skin. He described himself as being "allergic to the sun" and was permanently covered in thick layers of cover-up to even out discolorations.[19] However, despite this true explanation, the dominant fabrication (which still spreads) is that he did not want to be black. As in Naboth's story, there were certainly slanderers who worked to defame him.

Due to the rumor mill, the "monster" persona was beginning to emerge, even though Jackson, a poster child for racial equality, took his signature move, the moonwalk, "from these beautiful black kids in the ghetto" whom he called "the real dancers."[20] We have to look no further for an affirmation of racial pride than his 1988 donations to the United Negro College Fund and his casting of women of color as leading ladies in short films, from Ola Ray (*Thriller*) to Naomi Campbell (*In The Closet*) with the only Caucasian exception being his then wife, Lisa-Marie Presley (*You Are Not Alone*).[21]

Significantly, the short film *Remember The Time* has an all-black cast and director, John Singleton. Set in ancient Egypt, it features Magic Johnson, Eddie Murphy, and Iman.[22] Ancient Egyptians are rarely depicted as full Sub-Saharan Africans, and the reason for this casting can be seen as putting an ethnic minority in power. Furthermore, most of Michael Jackson's leading males were also African American: Wesley Snipes (*Bad*), Michael Jordan (*Jam*), Eddie Murphy (*Whatzupwitu*), Taj, Taryll ,and T.J Jackson (*Why*), to name a few.

Elena Oliete exemplifies the perceived threat of a person who can cross cultural boundaries globally, through the universal mediums of song and short film, simultaneously crossing the physical divides between race and gender.

By the early 1990s he had already "been rejected by large numbers of both black and white people. The former consider him a traitor and the latter do not accept him as a white person . . . his skin change has served to show up the artificial cultural construction of social hierarchies based on racial distinctions."[23]

In Naboth's tale, the king first asks him to sell his lands, to which he replies that he cannot give away his family's inheritance. The king goes home, upset at not obtaining his quandary. It is then that the queen asks him why he is so unhappy, and on learning why, she decides to "fix" the situation. Events for Naboth have already begun to spin out of control and there is little he can do about it.[24]

The 1989 video for Jackson's "Leave Me Alone" is a parodist depiction of a man physically imprisoned by a media circus, which consists of several animated versions of the stories written about him.[25] By 1992, Jackson was similarly attempting to reclaim his public persona from the already extreme state it had been warped into: "I had no idea people thought I was so weird . . . it feels good to be considered as a person, rather than a personality," he said at the 35th Annual Grammy Awards.[26]

Despite a dominant discourse indicating his artistic and economic decline, *Dangerous* would outsell *Bad* by millions of copies, showing that in 1992 he was becoming, despite the fractured personas, more popular, not less. Through a candid interview at his Neverland home he laid to rest many rumors: "I've never had my cheekbones done, never had my eyes done, never had my lips done and all this stuff. They go too far, but this is stuff that happens every day with other people."[27] It was in 1993 that he was beset by salacious false allegations that would carry his representation into its most destructive and pervasive monster persona.

Jackson's close friendship with children, from Emmanuel Lewis to Gavin Arvizo, was well documented.[28] In no way had it ever been hidden from the public, because there had never been anything to hide. Jackson evidently treated these children as equals and considered them his friends. It is likely they were the friends he wished he had had as a child. They accompanied him to award shows and, with their families, spent time at his home.

However, "Michael's innocent childlike qualities had been warped into something pathological and creepy in the public's perception."[29] The fact that Jackson was clearly emotionally vulnerable, and that he had been an advocate of children's rights since the start of his adult career, were hardly reported by the press.[30] Despite this, in a 1993 poll, 88 percent of TV viewers believed his innocence and 78 percent were in favor of him.[31] The "stoning" that followed was clearly not orchestrated by the people, but by the press.

Jackson had always been very vocal about his affinity for young people: "children are pure and innocent and good." In his autobiography and in several interviews he explained that this affinity was rooted in his own sense of lost youth: "I remember my childhood as mostly work."[32] He gave millions of dollars of his own money to children's charities and very often visited orphanages and hospitals, giving away gifts to sick and dying children at his own expense.[33] There was significantly little coverage of Jackson's considerable humanitarian efforts, compared to coverage of unproven claims and wild conjecture, as Charles Thomson's articles illustrate ("One of the Most Shameful Episodes in Journalistic History" and "Michael Jackson: It's Time for Media Outlets to Take Responsibility in Covering the Rock Star").

The moment the allegations appeared, much like the two slanderers in Naboth's story, the press seized upon them, and the public, primed by the depersonalizing idol persona and the damaging wacko persona, was ready with stones. All they needed was a monster, and they would make one, if they had to. Jackson, who was categorically anti-drugs, would, from this point on, struggle intermittently with painkiller addiction.[34]

Repeatedly, Jackson attempted to explain himself, even appearing at the NAACP awards. "Not only am I presumed innocent, I am innocent! And I know the truth will be my salvation."[35] There was a wealth of evidence that he was guiltless, and much of this is expressed by Mary A. Fischer in her explorative article, "Was Michael Jackson Framed?"[36] As she looked into his accusers, she discovered a trail of prior wrongdoing. Not only was Jackson innocent, like Naboth, his accusers were guilty of both extortion and slander. Their reward would be millions of dollars. For sharing his talent with the masses and his money with sick children, his reward would be shame and disaffection. The queen in Naboth's tale probably paid her slanderers richly while they escaped unharmed.

Jackson, who was a high-profile and generous champion for disadvantaged children, would be typified as a child molester for the rest of his career. He would be, while attempting to restore his three false personas and depict his true mortal persona in a frank and honest documentary, *Living With Michael Jackson*, seized upon by the same lawyer and district attorney through a similar extortion case, after which he was summarily acquitted.[37]

Soon "Jackson's fruitful artistic career and musical denunciations of society's oppressive cultural constructions had been eclipsed by the widespread social condemnation of the singer as a monstrous child abuser . . . The zombie-like singer and author of *Thriller* had effectively become a real monster and, as such, he was accused of the most monstrous crime."[38]

The ritual process of stoning begins with slander. Jackson was effectively slandered repeatedly by the press and his accusers with lies that were disseminated among the public. Although in 1994 Jackson had not been found guilty of any wrongdoing and was further acquitted in 2005, the process had already

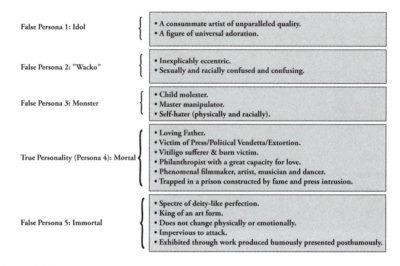

False Persona 1: Idol
- A consummate artist of unparalleled quality.
- A figure of universal adoration.

False Persona 2: "Wacko"
- Inexplicably eccentric.
- Sexually and racially confused and confusing.

False Persona 3: Monster
- Child molester.
- Master manipulator.
- Self-hater (physically and racially).

True Personality (Persona 4): Mortal
- Loving Father.
- Victim of Press/Political Vendetta/Extortion.
- Vitiligo sufferer & burn victim.
- Philanthropist with a great capacity for love.
- Phenomenal filmmaker, artist, musician and dancer.
- Trapped in a prison constructed by fame and press intrusion.

False Persona 5: Immortal
- Spectre of deity-like perfection.
- King of an art form.
- Does not change physically or emotionally.
- Impervious to attack.
- Exhibited through work produced humously presented posthumously.

Figure 9.1
The Multiple Personas of Michael Jackson.
(Illustration by Elizabeth Amisu and Karin Merx)

begun. Negative images and cruel words reduced him to an object, as far removed as possible from the compassionate human being he was. "Most people don't know me, that is why they write such things . . . I cry very often because it hurts and I worry about the children, all my children all over the world. I live for them . . . have mercy, for I've been bleeding a long time now. MJ."[39]

Jackson never concealed the emotional pain he felt at the libel of the world's press and the slander of the public. His appearance was an area of significant weakness for him ("the biggest struggle was right there in the mirror. To a great degree, my identity as a person was tied to my identity as a celebrity"), and there may be some truth in the hypothesis that he suffered from body dysmorphic disorder: "my appearance began to depress me . . . once I came offstage, there was that mirror to face again."[40]

Fame, like the concept of persona, is simply a figment of our imagination created in a generalized consciousness. "It's science fiction," Jackson said in a 1995 interview. "It's not true. I know myself and it's sad when other people have to read those things and they believe it. I know eventually the truth will prevail and I'm about truth."[41]

Therefore, we must consider a holistic representation of Michael Jackson, one that is not based on conjecture and tabloid sensationalism but on hard evidence. It is the literary academic's place and duty to write about Jackson the artist. For an artist is what he was. Only through academic study of his life and creative work can we gain insight into his genius and innovation.

To construct his mortal persona we must utilize his artistic canon in the form of autobiography, poetry, lyrics, musical composition, fashion, live performance, and cinematic works, supported with his collaborative material, extended body of posthumously released material, documentaries, and countless video and print interviews.

In a particularly moving speech at Oxford University, Jackson was unexpectedly candid in his revelations, when he said, "all of us are products of our childhood. But I am the product of a lack of a childhood, an absence of that precious and wondrous age."[42] The speech, though eloquent and moving, was given little press coverage and was considered still another oddity. Its valuable content in support of children's rights was generally ignored, and the 1993 allegations were mentioned to lessen the importance of the speech. Ironically, Jackson's uniqueness, lauded when moonwalking and when providing a sense of escapism for its audience, was now condemned for creating a theme-park home and befriending child stars. Everything Jackson said and did was given salacious nuance. How, then, could anyone benefit from his unique charm, talent, and perspective?

Jackson's mortal persona is of a human being who, despite his difficult upbringing and daily pressures, was still a loving father, devoted son, entertainer, philanthropist, and humanitarian. Jackson, his friends, and his family tried to promote his mortal persona and encourage a positive reception of the vulnerable man behind the art, but their cries mostly fell on deaf ears. For many it was not until the final moments of his televised memorial, during which his 11-year-old daughter described him as "the best father you could imagine," that his humanity really began to pierce the social consciousness. This man, though a simulacrum, though an idol, was still purely Paris Jackson's dad.[43]

When a victim is stoned in the modern world they are usually buried, leaving only the head exposed. Perhaps similarly, the public and press hide the signifiers of humanity, because it is evidence that these people are, in fact, living. They feel pain, and their image on a screen, album, magazine, or catwalk doesn't stop that from being the case.

The level of injustice Jackson endured in life was substantial, and his great success came at a terrible price. He sings prophetically in the *Bad 25* track "Price of Fame," "I'm living just to end . . . feeling all this pain."[44]

The real Michael Jackson continually fought a losing battle in a simulacra-infested celebrity culture. In his own words, the wall was "too high to get over" and "too low to get under."[45] He lay between a demonized representation of himself and an idolized representation. Nevertheless, it can be argued that the "people" did not hate Michael Jackson any more than they hated Naboth. They were a tool in the hands of his slanderers. Though the public carried Jackson out of the city, they could not stone him. Despite the powerfully negative press that had become daily fare, his *This Is It* tour sold at a rate of 11 tickets per second and 40,000 per hour. In March, just three months before he died, *The Essential Michael Jackson* album, consisting entirely of previously released material, was No. 1.[46]

Like the superhuman some thought Michael Jackson was, he resurrected his idol persona in preparing for a highly anticipated comeback at London's O2 in 2009. He was quoted saying, "his children are now old enough and want to see him on stage."[47] It would have been their first opportunity to see him perform live. Momentum and his own self-confessed "will of iron" kept him going when others would have abandoned public life entirely.[48] In this way he was truly unique. He was writing a classical release due to be recorded in London, was working on a new album, and his principal physical problem, despite his prior conditions, was an easily treatable lung infection.[49] By many credible accounts, Michael Jackson was a healthy, if slightly thin, 50-year-old man when he died. Apart from an incompetent doctor and an unfortunate propensity for the use of Diprivan (which should never have been administered to him), he could have lived long and given the world so much more. A needless death is Naboth's tragedy and, sadly, it is also Jackson's.[50]

When a person is stoned their torn, crushed, faceless body is taken out of the sand (in which it has been buried) and checked for signs of life. If a doctor confirms so, they are shoved back in and the stoning resumes. It is not the last stone that kills. It's a culmination of all those that went before. Instead of picking up stones to throw, we must, with careful consideration, decide whether we should in fact extend our hands in support.

Michael Jackson's 50 years on earth were a singularity. He was commoditized before starting secondary school, meaning many of his earliest memories were the roars of adoring crowds, which, unfortunately, were also the sound of stones being lifted and checked for the right weight and size. Understandably, his solo music professed alternate desires to escape his numerous problems ("Why You Wanna Trip On Me," "Leave Me Alone," "Xscape," "Fly Away," "They Don't Care About Us") and be strong in the face of adversity ("2 Bad," "Will You Be There," "HIStory," "Keep The Faith," "Heaven Can Wait").

It is possible that Michael Jackson's formative years grew to an almost painful need for love and caused him to regress in an attempt to regain his lost youth. These were things he could not help, and they should never have been used against him. Ultimately, it was the sharp focus of our cruel collective gaze that caused him the most suffering: "Does it affect me? Yes. But I've become immune in a way too. I'm very strong. I have rhinoceros skin. But at the same time, I'm human, so anything can hurt like that. . . ."[51]

The one facet of Michael Jackson's mortal persona that was not readily publicized before his death was his unparalleled capacity for love. He genuinely loved people he did not know, children especially. He showed that love through paying medical bills, taking entire families on holiday, giving away millions of dollars and thousands of hours. He never asked for recognition for this, and rarely, if ever, drew attention to it. This was the one extraordinary characteristic we could have drawn from most, and we still can now. We are all capable of looking to the truth before making judgments, of treating people as people, not as personas, whether they're on television or on a perfume bottle. Jackson reiterated throughout his career that the reason he loved children was because they treated him like a human being, not an idol, wacko or monster.

Jackson's last persona was created in his tragic and sudden death. One can imagine the crowd leaving Naboth, their work done, only to find he had not cursed the king or God. They see now that they have been misled, and their guilt is unbearable. What then becomes of all Naboth's children, family, and friends? For them, there is no reason, only an innocent man cruelly betrayed. In our case, it is the children Jackson so wanted to help, his grief-stricken fans, and all who loved him who suffer. The public, not the slanderers, created the final persona of Michael Jackson, and the world's press were forced to accept and conform to it—especially *The Daily Mail*, who regarded the artist as "a fairly minor figure . . . little more than a novelty act."[52] The outpouring of grief was, finally, an acceptance of the magnitude of Jackson's global artistic and social impact. The idol persona was now obsolete, and the immortal persona was appropriated with the release of the film *This Is It*, allowing audiences a cathartic opportunity to see him live one last time.[53]

Twelve fans reportedly committed suicide in Australia and over a billion people watched his memorial.[54] Everything in Jackson's life had been superlative except for the man himself. By contrast, he was soft-spoken, with a slender frame that had to be accentuated through clothing.[55] The people of the world beatified his immortal persona; their infinite King of Music sold millions in the year he died.[56] Ironically, he did not receive this fierce love in later life.

Michael Jackson sought immortality through his art. It was his dream that his work would stand the test of time and be as ubiquitous as Tchaikovsky's *Nutcracker Suite*.[57] None of us will live long enough to know if he achieves this dream. The sad fact is that the catharsis of the tragic contributes to timeless narrative. As in the preventable climax of *Romeo and Juliet*, Naboth's story, though thousands of years old, resonates with pathos. We are always moved by the loss of the innocent and resentful of what could have been.

What cruel force drove the king, queen, slanderers, and all who attacked Naboth? Was it a deep-rooted hatred for his success or simply a desire to acquire what was rightfully his? The questions of human nature remain unanswerable. However, Jackson, in his inimitable style, took his suffering and turned it into an artistic legacy. His death served, for a short time, to unify people of all races under his banner, and a song he had written to honor a friend became his requiem: "like a sunset dying with the rising of the moon . . . gone too soon."[58]

CHAPTER 10

Recontextualizing Michael Jackson's Blackness

This chapter begins with a brief overview of critical discourse relating to ethnicity and Michael Jackson, and it considers Jackson's representation and his perceived blackness (or lack thereof) as tied to a historic chain of events that often have very little to do with Jackson himself or his music. This chapter continues by outlining ideological constructions surrounding Jackson and Afrocentricity, a movement "centred or focusing on Africa or on cultures of African origin" in "North American black culture" (*OED*). Then it gives an overview of race and culture as presented in the short films *Remember the Time*, directed by John Singleton in 1992, and *They Don't Care About Us*, directed by Spike Lee in 1996, to illustrate Jackson's Afrocentric self-expression through his art in this period.

> "The African people had given us gifts of courage and endurance that we couldn't hope to repay."
>
> —Michael Jackson[1]

As early modern critics like Ania Loomba have regularly asserted, the legacy of race and racial representation has a long and twisted past, and it is mired in the racial stereotyping that began hundreds of years before Michael Jackson's birth.[2] As Loomba suggests, the history of "race" is "both protracted and erratic," and it consists of "a range of concepts, theories and mechanisms for assigning different values to human beings [that] arise and mutate, go dormant, resurface, relocate and adapt anew."[3] The study of ethnicity is complex at the best of times. The very notion that English, Dutch, and Spanish people came to the conclusion that the dark-skinned people of the African continent were, by virtue of their complexions, uncivilized, beastly, and oversexed, making them inherently less human than their white counterparts, remains at the heart of any debate, since "it was in fact the 'erasure of Africa from the civilized world, and the reinterpretation of "blackness" as monstrous and unnatural' that "allowed for the construction of a European race."[4] Academic Harvey Young, in the monograph *Race and Theatre*, explores how these centuries-old constructions of race connect to the 20th-century American presentation of race as a theatrical act: "race and racial thinking stem from a basic human desire for orientation," and "should not be dismissed as either a mere fiction or an anachronism"; while race "did not attain widespread use until the late nineteenth century," it is one of several factors that complicate representations of blackness.[5]

For Young, American culture made blackness a performative, and actors were applauded for the use of "blackface," which became particularly popular around 1830–1965 in the United States, further enforcing constructed ideas around skin complexion as a marker of difference.[6] However, what further complicates Jackson's story is the emergence of his skin condition, vitiligo, which transformed his brown skin to a translucent white.[7] This rapid color change flew directly in the face of the dominant blackface performative construction, in which white people, from the Queen of England in 1608, all the way to the stage actors of the 20th century, wore black makeup in caricature of black people for the entertainment of predominantly white audiences.[8] This is discussed in some great detail by Harriet Manning in *Michael Jackson and the Blackface Mask*.[9] However, it does serve to highlight the fact that "there is little truth in the blackface representation," but it became so popular that "black artists who wanted to perform on the stage frequently discovered that they too had to apply burnt cork."[10] Interestingly enough, "the black character, the caricatured performance of black folk, never aligned with the *actual* appearance, behavior, or presumably, style of speech of African-Americans, blackface performances required the same skill of black artists as they did of non-black artists."[11]

A real irony remains in Jackson being perceived as a traitor to his race ("you hate your race baby," he sings in the track "Morphine") for being perceived to have attempted to cross the boundary from black to white.[12] This irony is found in the fact that white people have been racially cross-dressing for entertainment purposes for centuries: "the ability of the white man to become black and to channel blackness was rewarded with thunderous applause."[13] The early modern period and the transatlantic slave trade were very much responsible for destabilizing the primacy, originality, and the early wisdom of African people in Western culture, commonly accepted by playwrights such as Ben Jonson in the early 17th century and reiterated by the depictions of a dark-skinned African king in the Adoration of the Magi.[14]

There is a common and almost persistent misconception that Jackson attempted, in both literal and metaphoric ways, to erase his ethnicity. This is clearly outlined by Oprah Winfrey's question to Jackson in his 1993 interview with her: "Are you bleaching your skin and is your skin lighter because you don't like being black?"[15] As Oprah's question illustrates, the arguments on the subject of Jackson's blackness consist of three false claims: 1) that Jackson purposely changed his skin from black to white; 2) that Jackson's music similarly shifted from being inherently urban (black) to mainstream (white); 3) that Jackson changed both his music and his skin because of a dislike of being black. The fact that all three of these claims were categorically false did not do anything to stop them gaining traction in the mass media and on the street. This chapter examines the ways in which these claims are inherently false, as well as their ideological origins.

A range of debates have circled around Michael Jackson and ethnicity for decades, and these are most clearly laid out in Joseph Vogel's article "Re-Screening Black Masculinity in Michael Jackson's 'Black or White'," in relation to the film *Birth of a Nation* (which Jackson references in his short film), produced and screened in one of the most racially volatile moments in American history.[16] An insightful overview of how Jackson's view toward black people and Africans was exhibited and how it was interpreted largely by the mainstream media in 1992 is given in Grant's *Visual Documentary*, for example:

> The trip was a "public relations disaster for Michael." Truth: It was a triumph in which he drew more spectators in Gabon than Nelson Mandela and more in the Ivory Coast than the Pope . . .
>
> He refused to shake hands with Africans. Truth: He shook the hands of hundreds of people, hugged and kissed children in hospitals and institutions for the mentally retarded (sic).[17]

The cultural concerns regarding Jackson's personal appearance and music were intrinsically connected to endemic and prevalent cultural issues at the heart of Americana—issues discussed in great detail in Margo Jefferson's *On Michael Jackson*.[18] Jackson was born into the discourse of slavery and prejudice that lies under the surface of his representation. It is evident that Jackson did not attempt, at any point, to erase his ethnicity. He suffered from a hereditary skin condition called vitiligo, and his autopsy report confirmed this.[19] In the book *Turning White: A Memoir of Change*, the African American journalist

Lee Thomas outlines in great detail the personal effects of the depigmentation process of vitiligo.[20] The process was featured several years earlier in an
Ebony article, "The Man Who Turned White"; interestingly enough, this article
was rarely mentioned in conjunction with Jackson.[21]

By 1991, Jackson's vitiligo had rendered his body a patchwork of pigmented
and depigmented skin, an emotionally troubling process, which Thomas both
describes and photographs, illustrating the ways it transformed his skin and
how clearly it reduced his ethnicity, on which so much significance has been
placed by history and culture. "It's more than turning white," he writes, "it's
becoming void of color."[22] This disease gave Lee "moments of despair and
lifted [him] into amazingly euphoric epiphanies . . . kept him locked behind
closed doors and sent [him] out to shout into the biggest microphone [he]
could find."[23] Furthermore, Lee asserts that "bleaching is one of the recom-
mended treatments if you have the disease over eighty percent of your body."[24]
For Jackson himself, inside the viewing glass of his role as the most observed
person on the planet, vitiligo may well have been as devastating as it was
for Lee:

> It began with tiny seeds of whiteness, mysteriously sprinkled onto my brown
> skin, that suddenly sprouted into small circles. With ravenous, ruthless hunger,
> these discs of discoloration devoured every drop of pigment along their smooth
> and scalloped edges. The whiteness blossomed across my torso . . . my nose . . .
> my lips. It twined around my hands and feet, weaving pale gloves and boots in
> its wake.[25]

Although Jackson spoke sparingly about his skin condition, he did speak
about it. The earliest occasion was 1993: "I have a skin disorder which destroys
the pigmentation of the skin, it's something that I cannot help;" but what is
more telling is how Jackson highlights the hypocrisy of America: "what about
all the millions of people who sit in the sun, to become darker, to become
other than what they are, no one says nothing about that."[26] In 1996 Jackson also briefly referred to the disorder, saying, "my skin condition has gotten worse, I hate to say it. I have vitiligo, and I'm totally completely allergic
to the sun . . . Even if I'm in the shade the sun rays can destroy my skin."[27]
Therefore, we can ascertain that Jackson did suffer from a skin-altering disease and that this disease restricted his life, as well as his ability to move freely
and express himself. The way in which Jackson managed his visual representation with makeup, to ensure his splotches and uneven skin remained hidden from the public, served to alienate audiences from believing he actually
suffered from the disorder. This became ammunition for those who were primarily horrified at the ways in which Jackson seemed to be controverting

dominant constructions of race. Jackson's transformation seemed to be producing a perplexing reversal and upturning of negative stereotypes, by showing that a black person could become white, thus threatening the construction of white identity. Kim F. Hall discusses literary whiteness in particular, and she argues that the refusal to even discuss whiteness as an ethnicity asserts that ethnic variation applies solely to non-whites.[28] This double standard pervades all of Jackson's representations and fuels his vilification when based on ethnicity.

Jackson's vitiligo aside, however, one may still ask how Afrocentric Jackson actually was, and how, if in any way, he asserted and affirmed his Afrocentricity in his music and short films. To further contextualize Jackson's ethnicity, his music became not "whiter," but "blacker," as his career progressed. He would continue to use elements of funk, soul, and gospel as intrinsic components of his compositions. He would also continue to emulate James Brown, Chuck Berry, Jackie Wilson, and even Mavis Staples for the entire breadth of his career. Jackson remained exceedingly black in all the ways that it mattered, and to illustrate this, we will consider two key texts—the short films *Remember the Time*, directed by John Singleton in 1991, and *They Don't Care About Us*, directed by Spike Lee in 1995.[29] These two texts have been chosen because, more than any others, they exemplify Jackson's blackness, in terms of musicality, physical expression, dance, and filmmaking. What is incredible, upon research of these key themes and ideas, however, is the fact that Jackson manages, through his art, to repeatedly inhabit Afrocentric ideological spaces, and every time he does so, he presents images of blackness that are of high status, ranging from his costumes in regal wear with kingly insignia, to his presentation of a black cast as part of the ruling class of ancient Egypt in his short film *Remember the Time*.[30]

REMEMBER THE TIME AND *THEY DON'T CARE ABOUT US*

Shot in Los Angeles in 1991 and directed by black director John Singleton, *Remember the Time* boasts an entirely African American cast that includes the black model Iman as the beautiful Egyptian queen, with the successful black comedian Eddie Murphy as her king.[31] In the short film, Jackson plays a maverick magician who appears in the balmy restful peace of the Egyptian palace, which is inhabited by a queen so bored that she kills subjects who fail to entertain her. The short film references the fact that ancient Egyptians were Africans and—far from depictions of Elizabeth Taylor in *Cleopatra*, with lily-white skin—were far more likely to be dark-skinned.[32] This brings to mind the Ife sculptures found in Benin in West Africa, which date back to the 14th century and feature heads with negroid features.[33] Black people do have a rich history of African autonomy and self-rule, which had long been denied by the American establishment, preferring a narrative of white supremacy and domination, supported by the flourishing of the slave trade, but this is only a small portion of Africa and the African story. Africa was, in fact, made up of black kingdoms for millennia, which traded throughout the entire world.[34] Jackson, whose personal library had extensive books on the subject, used *Remember the Time* to showcase blackness in not only a positive light, but in terms of a ruling class. He showed that there were black kings and princes, not just black servants, mammies, harlots, Mandingos, and brutes, as often seen in Hollywood cinema.[35] Jackson's depiction of Magic Johnson in a role of authority is also striking, as is the dance sequence in which all of the actors and dancers are black. Jackson showcases a cinematic world where all people are black Africans, and the cinematography is sumptuous, golden, and rich, thus arguing, similarly, that not only are black people in the ruling class of the diegesis of *Remember the Time*, they permeate all classes. Jackson's run from the black guards who work for the Pharaoh, the supreme ruler of ancient Egypt, lead him to the marketplace, where alluring women dance around him, protecting him and shielding him, and he shares a passionate embrace and kiss with the queen herself. Jackson highlights not just blackness in *Remember the Time*, but far more important, black affirmation. Through his depiction of an entire cast of black actors, as in the films *The Wiz*, *Stormy Weather*, and *Porgy and Bess*, he demonstrates that a black-only production can be performed and enacted. This is not simply because blacks and whites are societally segregated, but because blacks had a unique story to tell, a story that was entirely their own, about their time as the supreme civilization of the world, and on that they can base their own culture and sense of pride.[36]

To similar effect, Jackson displays Afrocentricity in the short films for *They Don't Care About Us*. The first was shot in Rio de Janeiro (Dona Marta in the quarter Botafogo) and Salvador de Bahia, Brazil, in February 1996 and was directed by Spike Lee.[37] The short film, set in favelas of Brazil, showcases people of African descent in diaspora, as Jackson follows the trajectory of the Africans sold in the transatlantic slave trade and transported to be chattel across the world. Slaves were taken not only to the West Indies but also to America and the sugar plantations of Brazil, where they would live, separated, cut off from their homeland, having to re-create their black culture and their black pride, though underprivileged and members of the underclass. It's a picture painted again throughout the world, from South Africa to the United States. In the short film, Jackson aligns himself with the diasporic population of the black community in Brazil and highlights the poverty in the slums and favelas of the entire world by aligning himself with his black brothers and sisters, dancing with the people in the streets and—most important—taking part in beating several dozen rhythmic drums.

These drums are significantly African in origin, and they beat out the syncopated rhythms at the heart of black and predominantly African culture. These drums form the heart of Jackson's chant, his battle cry against the injustice that he sees inflicted upon blacks (injustice that is both without any real logical basis and endemic in the systems of the world), no matter where he goes. In his dance with the black children of the favelas (and once again, filling every shot with black people), Jackson highlights the "us" as the black communities of the world, and the "they" as those who persecute black people and subjugate them for political and societal gain. It is poignant that Jackson was regarded by predominantly white journalists as a racist for his use of racial slurs in this song. Armond White rightly declares this as ignorance and dismissal thinly veiled, with Jackson's message clouded unnecessarily in a smokescreen of fake indignation.[38]

These are just two brief opportunities to discuss Jackson's evident Afrocentricity in terms of black culture, dance, song, power, and aesthetics, and they have been considered in relation to just two of his works. The theme of Afrocentricity extends to many key areas of Jackson's career, for example, giving interviews to black publications, *Ebony* and *Jet*; working closely with black artists and musicians like Quincy Jones, Greg Phillinganes, and Rodney Jerkins III; and Jackson's insistence on predominantly black sounds in his music and ethnic diversity in his short films, from Ola Ray in *Thriller* in 1983, all the way to Chris Tucker in *You Rock My World* in 2001. His Afrocentricity is evident in the track "Liberian Girl," discussed in great detail in Chapter 4—"Narrative in the Songs of Michael Jackson's *Bad*," as well as with his moonwalk, which Jackson learned from black children, because, in his words, "black children in the ghettos . . . have the most phenomenal rhythm of anybody on the Earth . . . it definitely started within the black culture. No doubt. And that's where it comes from."[39] In addition, the short film for the track "Bad," directed in 1987 by Martin Scorsese, is a testament to Jackson's dedication to Afrocentrism and shows repeated affirmations of blackness, especially the poverty often associated with being black in America and the drive to aspire to new heights.[40] Scorsese said of the short film, "we came up with this idea based on a real incident in Harlem" and "put Michael in with black actors in Harlem and we shot the dramatic sequences in black and white."[41]

The unjustified ideas that Michael Jackson did not like being black, did not affirm his blackness, or did not feel pride in being a black man were unequivocally rebuffed throughout his life. He disproved those ideas not only in his short films and in his music, but also in his interviews (which were often given intentionally to black interviewers like Jesse Jackson and Oprah Winfrey), showing how much Jackson felt comfortable among people of his own ethnicity, who he clearly felt would be more sympathetic to him. The claim that Jackson purposely changed his skin was a complete fabrication that served to justify a racist assertion that any black man would desire to become white in the first place. This racist assertion is as old as Ben Jonson's 1608 *Masque of Blackness*, which enacts the proverb of "turning the Ethiop white," making a black person apparently white (see Appendix A1—"From Object to Subject: A Critical Survey on the Representation of Blackness in the Early Modern Period" and Appendix A2—"'With All His Beauteous Race': High-Status Blacks in *The Masque of Blackness* and *The Merchant of Venice*").[42]

The claim that Jackson's music style shifted from being inherently "black" to being more "mainstream" was also a fabrication. Jackson offered a less mainstream and more rhythmic sound in his later career. In addition, Jackson's so called racial confusion was a third and final fallacy. What Jackson's work did, which was perhaps most controversial in America, was to show black people as a whole, and himself in particular, in positions of high status, which jarred greatly with the American culture of blacks as subjugated and segregated second-class citizens. However, what was spectacular about Jackson's Afrocentrism was how well articulated and consistent it was, and how little it rose up against the claims of his critics. He chose instead to remain synonymous with a message of peace and harmony. Jackson never showed a hierarchy of racial representation, and he opted instead for a message of egalitarianism for all ethnicities.

In closing, it is also important to remember that, for all the heights Jackson reached in his phenomenal career, he remained a black man from a poor neighborhood in Gary, Indiana, the eighth of 10 children. In his autobiography, Jackson writes about wanting to visit the South to get close to his roots as an American: "we had never been to the South then and wanted to visit . . . to have a sense of our roots and those of other black people."[43] Jackson remained implicitly black and explicitly homogeneous, in order to remain relatable to his wide audience. Jackson remained a proud possessor of his heritage, and he both affirmed and supported it in all the ways that were available to him, and in ways his audiences could never have expected.

CHAPTER 11

HIStory and Michael Jackson's Autobiographical Potency

As allegations of misconduct in 1993 ushered Jackson's representation into its most dangerous form, the monster persona, his reclusiveness served to further alienate him from his once-adoring public. To combat this, in 1995 Jackson followed his 1988 autobiography, *Moonwalk*, with another, in the form of his fifth adult solo studio album. This chapter begins by discussing the physical artefact of Jackson's *HIStory: Past, Present and Future, Book 1*, and considers both its artistic and cultural potency. It then considers the short films for the tracks "Scream," "They Don't Care About Us," and "Stranger in Moscow" as evidence that *HIStory* is not simply a personal disclosure of 1989–1994 and that Jackson uses his own negative experiences as conduits to explore more resonant narratives, such as isolation, depression, and mass incarceration. The chapter closes by highlighting several avenues for further academic research with regard to the *HIStory* album.

> "It was a casual accusation—as casually cruel as throwing a hangman's rope over a tree limb."
>
> —Armond White[1]

> "It encompassed all the turbulent emotions and struggles of the previous few years: it was his journal, his canvas, his rebuttal."
>
> —Joseph Vogel[2]

Michael Jackson's personal account of the years 1989–1994 was presented in the 1995 double compact disc release, *HIStory: Past, Present and Future, Book 1*. Unlike the usual silver discs, *HIStory*'s discs are gold. The significance of the golden disc is synonymous with hits, commercial success, and the connotations of a precious metal that cannot easily be altered or contaminated. Open the lush double album and you will be presented with two pristine golden discs onto which have been embossed Jackson's form. However, this isn't Jackson as we have known him. This is something quite different. He is made of incorruptible stone, an effigy of a man, a statue, a symbol. This image lacks authenticity, because it is not meant to be symbolic of the real—just as statues of all great dictators and world leaders are not meant to be authentic but immensely symbolic. Jackson uses the statue to embody the very idea of a cultural figure, one that may or may not share anything with its source material. This jarring, uncanny image of Jackson as benevolent dictator is certainly designed—like so much of Jackson's art—to be provocative.[3]

Jackson had an acute awareness and knowledge of world history and its many pivotal events. In presenting himself in statue form, he presents a unique and thought-provoking concept: What if a global, dictatorial figure could use their power for good and not ill? Or rather than using the immense power at their disposal to produce genocide and hatred, the dictator produced love and unity? On another level, by presenting himself in such a position of power, Jackson is openly defying the deafening chorus of his many detractors—those who may well be simply misinformed, confused, jaded, or bigoted; those who are overtly racist and possibly homophobic and transphobic; and no doubt jealous music critics who had slammed Jackson's work systematically between 1987 up until 1995, declaring every work post-*Thriller* as inconsequential. It is clear that Jackson's release of *HIStory* is in dialogue with someone, and that they, too, are part of Jackson's story. He does, after all, devote the entire track "Tabloid Junkie" to the magazines that made significant financial income from his image.

NOTES ON CULTURAL AND ARTISTIC SIGNIFICANCE

The cultural significance of *HIStory* is encompassed in its first half. Slipping on the golden disc, the listener is immediately catapulted into the pre-*HIStory* era, starting in 1979 with the release of *Off the Wall* and ending in 1991 with the release of *Dangerous*. We race through a carefully chosen medley of hits, as Jackson reunifies his past, skipping well-known hits like "Human Nature" and "In the Closet" for lesser-known duets and ballads. This first disc is an excellent example of Jackson's editorial skills, re-presenting his art by virtue of repositioning and authorship. In doing so, he attains a delicate balance between preferring his commercially successful hits (of which there are many) and choosing to favor compositional masterpieces such as "Billie Jean," with its killer intro, and feel-good harmonies like "Rock with You" and

"The Girl Is Mine." These are interspersed with messages of hope found in "Man in the Mirror" and "Heal the World." From the first disc we are presented with an artist who seems to be fundamentally about hope. These 15 tracks represent some of the most widely sold music of the 1980s and 1990s, the most danced-to and played, the score to the latter part of the century, and combined sales of dozens of millions to date of just four albums: *Off the Wall*, *Thriller*, *Bad*, and *Dangerous*. Culturally, Jackson's influence has been so vast that it remains particularly challenging to quantify. Nevertheless, it is fair to say that both popular music and popular culture would look incredibly different if he had stopped making music after *The Wiz*.

The second disc has far more to do with Jackson's artistic significance than his cultural influence. In these 15 tracks, balanced and equal, Jackson presents the world as he sees it now. For him, this is as relevant as all that came before; hence, "past" and "present" are balanced on two of the discs. The future is perhaps implied by his statuesque representation on the cover—an image of further world domination. In the present, as explored in the tracks of the second disc, Jackson no longer focuses on hope. Hope is a faith that continually looks forward, and it is what Jackson was made from: the hopes encompassed in the American Dream and the "I Have a Dream" speech of Dr. Martin Luther King, Jr. are the pillars on which Jackson built his empire, his Neverland.

However, like every Miller-esque hero, in *HIStory*'s present Jackson has finally come to realize that his dream is fiction.[4] We the listeners arrive in a place that is dying and, in fact, is in its dying throes. Jackson's hopefulness is almost done. Somewhere between the humiliating strip search and the stint in drug rehabilitation, Jackson was "rap[ed] of his pride," but not of his truth.[5] Truth is a notion Jackson can hold on to, and hold on he does, for dear life. Truth, in terms of verifiable facts, is contradicted time and again with popular beliefs and dominant accepted narratives. Jackson reveals in his story, as he narrates, that truth is constructed by those who believe it. Therefore, what people believe becomes the truth.

The artistic significance of this arises in the way Jackson presents his version of events from behind a smokescreen, revealing key details for those who wish to hear them and smooth tunes for those who do not. Even the title, "his story," wears a loose linguistic mask and uses typography and the italicization of *his* to make its true meaning explicit. Throughout the album Jackson presents his version of truth or fact as fiction, in order to repeatedly combat fiction that has been presented, predominantly by the tabloid press, as fact. This cloak-and-dagger representation is insightfully explored in Karin Merx's article, "From Throne to Wilderness: Michael Jackson as Foucauldian Outlaw."[6] In *HIStory* Jackson presents his life as it is from within the panopticon, and refuses to lighten it, simply because "some things in life they just don't

want to see."[7] It is this dark perspective that most likely jarred with contemporary listeners, who found the intensely autobiographical, hardened perspective too far a gulf from "Don't Stop 'Til You Get Enough." In *HIStory*
Jackson showcases the hardboiled, dank underbelly of fame and success, as in
the unreleased track from the *Bad* era that displayed the heavy price of fame.[8]

"Scream"

"Scream," performed with Jackson's younger sister, Janet Jackson, is a song
in which twin voices express a shared predicament. In *Man in the Music: The
Creative Life and Work of Michael Jackson*, Vogel highlights the added resonance of this track: it was the first duet between Janet (who was at the peak
of her career) and Michael (whose career had recently suffered its biggest
blow), who described themselves as "twins" in separate interviews throughout their lives. The closeness of their personalities, experiences, and careers
provided a mirror between them as two halves of the same coin, and personally, they experienced similar personal tragedies and triumphs. The ongoing
rumor that they were, in fact, the same person, was dispelled by Jackson at
his 1993 Grammy Awards acceptance speech. Vogel also reiterates the importance of the fact that Janet sang this particular song as a tribute to her brother
at the 2009 MTV Music Video Awards, performing with him virtually, mere
months after his passing. In the track, they rage against the system. The song
expresses at its core, anger, outrage, and disenchantment—all stemming (seemingly) from the allegations of 1993, during which Janet was particularly sup-
portive of her brother.[9]

However, more profound than the autobiographical material on which the
song draws its strength, it has a deeply metaphysical interpretation. Edvard
Munch's *Der Schrei der Natur* conveys the deeply harrowing imagery of what
some have termed "depersonalization disorder" and denotes the physical,
visceral, emotional outlet of screaming.[10] The *OED* defines a "scream" as "a
shrill piercing cry, usually expressive of pain, alarm, or other sudden emotion."
Its earliest written usage is in Shakespeare's play *Macbeth*, and it is found in
Act Two, Scene 3, when Lennox recounts "th' woeful time" to Macbeth himself, who, having just killed the king, replies, "twas a rough night."[11] In psychology, a "primal scream" is employed in order to release pent-up rage and
frustration. However, the key factor of the "scream" is that it is raw emotion
without the hindrance of language, or further, that it is an animalistic, prehu-
man expression of emotion. The human scream is akin to the howl of a dying
animal or the shriek of a captive animal.

Screaming is an action of a being that has no other recourse, and it is an
involuntary expression of uncontainable emotion, whether grief, fear, or

delight. To "scream" is to simultaneously release and convey what has not been previously expressed. Babies scream to express their most basic and fundamental needs: hunger, comfort, and care. The artist and theater director Chiara Guidi describes the "O" of the human mouth as an "indecorous opening," which causes connection and repulsion to the viewer on a primal level.[12] The opening is the break in the barrier between the world within and the world without. It is a break in the surface of the enclosed space of our bodies. As such, it is fundamentally terrifying.

In the liner notes of *HIStory*, Jackson includes the image by the artist Gottfried Helnwein, *Das Lied* (*The Song*), which features a semi-naked child screaming in a corner, staring up at the ceiling.[13] The face is obscured in darkness and Jackson's lyrics are handwritten on the image with the title, "Scream." For both Jackson and Helnwein, children were a muse.[14] However, Jackson's self-identification with this image is apparent in his signing of it with his lyrics. He is the child. Jackson (undeterred by the backlash in his life's work) also included another image by Helnwein in the liner notes, for the track "Little Susie," to represent and campaign for the underprivileged and voiceless children of the world.

"They Don't Care About Us"

"They Don't Care About Us" is arguably the most politically charged track of Michael Jackson's artistic career. The song targets a "they" who "don't care about an "us." I will posit the idea that the "us" referred to here includes the disenfranchised working class of the world and, more specifically, the African American population. The "us" are the black African Americans who still bear the signs of being separate but equal. Michael Jackson's cultural mistreatment, in both life and death, is a perfect example of this. In her article "Dancing with Michael Jackson," Toni Bowers writes about Jackson and the #*BlackLivesMatter* movement.[15] They can be said to embody a black minority, an underclass of former second-class citizens and the victims of ritual lynchings and ill treatment as subjugated by the white middle class, whose political power is enforced by both the legal system and the penal system. Much of the difficulties Jackson suffered were motivated by racial tensions. In "They Don't Care About Us," Jackson presents two alternatives: prison and/or poverty. He reminds us of the demeaning and dehumanizing treatment he has suffered ("I'm tired of being the victim of hate") at the hands of the Los Angeles Police Department, who were venomous in their ill treatment of both Jackson and his home, Neverland Valley Ranch. After this ill treatment, the completely unsubstantiated allegations of child molestation made against him were settled out of court for an undisclosed sum, upon the advice of Jackson's legal team.

In his article Vogel examines the racial climate/context into which this short film was released, contextualized within the Los Angeles race riots. Auto-biographically speaking, the song pours out: "black man, blackmail, throw the brother in jail."[16] Is Jackson incorrect in arguing that America "doesn't care" about black people? Is it too much a generalization to state that much of Jackson's persecution came from his position as an internationally influential African American artist and the most commercially successful recording artist in the world? Maybe so. However, it is certainly valid to assert that Jackson's African American heritage remains a thorny subject within the wider concept of his legacy, impact, and influence. "Some things in life they just don't want to see . . . if Martin Luther were living he wouldn't let this be," Jackson repeats in the closing ad-libs to "They Don't Care About Us," lyrics that sound like "they keep me on fire" or "we're deep in the fire," harkening back to the days of lynchings, strange fruit, and the deep-seated hatred of blacks that stem back to slavery. In Chapter 10—"Recontextualizing Michael Jackson's Blackness," I discuss Jackson's increasingly "black" sound and styling through his career, which was at odds with both his skin disorder and the continued dominant presentation of the artist as racially confused and ethnically ambiguous. "They Don't Care About Us" is a wake-up call to its listener, and a reminder that the odds are stacked against the African American population. Much in the same way, these same odds were always stacked against Jackson, and no matter how many records he sold, he could never truly garner the respect afforded to the likes of John Lennon or Elvis Presley[17]—not necessarily because of his alleged crimes, but fundamentally because of the problematic nature of his ethnicity and his perceived power and influence. It is also important to note that Jackson's androgyny was no less prominent than David Bowie's and his flamboyance no more prominent than Elton John's, but where Bowie and John are regarded as artists, Jackson does not yet garner the same level of respect.

The short film for "They Don't Care About Us," in its prison version, is characterized by several shots of violence, of political power at play, with police beatings and starving children, a reworking of the shots in the same style as employed in the *Man in the Mirror* short film years before. Jackson sits in a prison cell in prison uniform. Into the walls are grafted television sets that spew out a range of harrowing, disturbing images, the type of images that we are becoming desensitized to, that Andy Warhol used in his print work in order to bring viewers ever closer to the darkness they both saw and did not see on a daily basis.[18] Perhaps this is also Jackson's sentiment.

Though the short film was shot and produced in 1995, issues surrounding African American incarceration in America remain topical 20-plus years later. It is no coincidence that Jackson, who recently had a very close brush with the law, decided to shoot a version of *They Don't Care About Us* in a mimed penitentiary system. In *The Atlantic*'s recent animated series, sociologist Bruce Western argues that America "could have chosen a whole variety of ways to respond to that problem of crime . . . we've chosen the response of the deprivation of liberty for a historically aggrieved group whose liberty in the United States was never firmly established to begin with." Western also asserts quite clearly that incarceration may well become an inherited trait, due to the detrimental effects on young children of having a parent in incarceration.[19]

Jackson mimes being shot in the head during the early segment, just before we are catapulted into the prison canteen, where Jackson aligns himself with inmates of all races. The united indignity of the inmates is juxtaposed with images of Jackson in chains, saying "I'm tired of being the victim of shame." The lyrics "beat me, bash me" and "hit me, kick me" allude to physical attack, and are then interspersed with shots of nuclear war, water cannon, and eventually, the image of Martin Luther King, Jr. embossed onto the background as Jackson repeats his refrain that "they don't care."[20]

Jackson widens his meaning to encompass every disenfranchised person on the planet. However, it's necessary to state that the majority of the men in the prison canteen are African Americans ("black man, black mail | throw the brother in jail").[21] The "everyman" is presented in Spike Lee's short film as disposable—and the victims of injustice are discarded into prison cells to waste away their lives. Even Michael Jackson. Even the most successful artist on the planet who has devoted his life and time, not only to honing his craft but to caring for impoverished and needy children everywhere. Interestingly enough, the short film culminates in a prison riot, an uprising of anger, in which Jackson is shown alone in the canteen, upturning tables. Also, we see a final shot of Jackson in the favelas of Brazil's Rio de Janeiro, where the second version of *They Don't Care About Us* is set. We can construe the joining together of these two narratives in the character that Jackson presents, a convicted felon who has escaped prison and escaped to Brazil, where he can live amongst the favelas. The autobiographical elements of *They Don't Care About Us* are found, primarily, within the portrayal of Jackson as a criminal element, which must be contained because he is deemed dangerous. He is an angry dissident, discarded by his own culture.

"Stranger in Moscow"

In a far more subdued and less volatile mode than "Scream," and a far less militant mood than "They Don't Care About Us," "Stranger in Moscow," the third track on Jackson's *HIStory*, focuses on the anecdotal "Armageddon of the brain" that Jackson experienced during a period in 1993.[22] He charts his "swift and sudden fall from grace," and relates his loneliness and the malaise that involves drug abuse and self-medication, combined with a desperation to no longer feel anything at all.[23]

The repeated refrain has moved from enraged to simply disaffected and desperate. Fundamentally, after all the initial pain that has produced the screaming and the anger that ensues, Jackson is left "living lonely" like a "stranger in Moscow."[24] The key themes are loneliness and cold. There is an extended semantic field of death and the staccato rhythm that drives the song onward in shuffles, as if dragging its feet. Jackson is bedecked by "tombs" and "shadows" and relentless rain. The song is filled with pathetic fallacy, as his world bleeds onto the track which itself is precursory to the rain. He is "alone," "abandoned" in his fame, and "stalked."

The city of Moscow within this short film is a metaphor both for alienating environments and for emotionally draining events. In linking these two to the cinematography of his film, Jackson's world is bled of all color. The monochromatic theme is unnerving because it never lets up. Jackson links the theme back to *Scream*, but whereas *Scream*'s monochromatic cinematography represents otherworldliness and distance, the use of chiaroscuro lighting in "Stranger in Moscow" deepens the blacks and greys. There was once color in this cinematic world, but now it is long gone.

Jackson walks through streets of people who cannot see or hear him; though he is singing, no one is listening. He is imprisoned, cocooned within his own mind, with no way to communicate with the likewise isolated characters showcased in the short film, like the old man who is a beggar in the street and the lady staring through the window. The rain storm that ensues connects them all, harkening back to the bible verse "he causes his sun to rise on the evil and the good, and sends rain on the righteous and the unrighteous."[25] The film relates the loneliness and alienation he is feeling toward the general 21st-century persecution and relentless hounding. Again and again the chorus asks, "How does it feel?" Eventually it adds, "when you're alone and you're cold inside."[26] The constant questioning and use of interrogatives position Jackson as the recipient of a continual barrage of questions, requiring him to assess emotional and physical damage beyond assessing.

In *Moonwalk*, Jackson wrote that his persona and reception as a celebrity were tied intrinsically to his self-esteem.[27] So when he found his reputation in shreds in 1993, the trauma led to a life-threatening addiction to painkiller medication. The emotional state that pushes a person to medicate themselves to such an extent can only be *imagined* by those who haven't personally experienced them, but "Stranger in Moscow" gives us a glimpse into this moment of Jackson's autobiographical account. It answers questions about how it feels to be discarded by a once-adoring public and labeled a criminal and a monster. The song simulates the cry of a man on the very margins of his own mind, dehumanized by constant questioning and repeated inquiry into every aspect of what academic Karin Merx calls his "excavated abnormality."[28] Jackson's time as a criminal, his "fall from grace," has left him utterly and completely alone and numb. He is a stranger in his own land and a stranger to himself.

The relationship between autobiographical accounts and art is often a complex one. For example, some critics consider William Shakespeare's First Folio to be a kind of autobiography.[29] Of course, Shakespeare's First Folio is vital, because without its publication we may well have lost several of Shakespeare's plays. Many of these plays do not survive in their quarto versions, and some were never published in quarto in the first place. The publishers of the First Folio, John Heminges and Henry Condell, spared no expense or cost in the elaborately printed collection, a work whose production was groundbreaking for its time (1623). *The Tempest*, the first play in the Folio, presents Shakespeare as a literary dramatist, and the veneration of the artist Shakespeare begins with the Folio. In much the same way, Jackson's veneration as an artist should begin with *HIStory: Past, Present and Future, Book 1*.[30] Like Jackson's song "Stranger in Moscow," the plays *Timon of Athens* and *King Lear*, were both written about a particularly dark period of output in Shakespeare's life. *King Lear* boasts the utter obliteration of the happy ending; and just as Shakespeare wrote from borrowed source material, so, too, did Jackson. In the words of Sonia Massai, "it would be foolish to assume there is no connection between biography and art."[31]

It is through this connection between biography and art that Jackson's *HIStory* enables academics in film studies, popular culture and music, and representation and cultural studies to use it as a key piece of primary source material. Jackson's double-disc album is golden, because it carries so much significance in terms of the past, the present, and how we present ourselves in the future. It maintains far more significance in its ability to take Jackson's personal fears, neuroses, and sufferings and relate them to wider societal problems and issues, like that of mass incarceration of the African American population in America and the African diaspora throughout the world, including the favelas of Brazil. Jackson's *HIStory* is a unique physical artefact of the last decade of the 21st century, which encompasses something far more resonant than simply Jackson's version of events. However, what exactly it resonates with, and why, can only come from detailed exploration and analysis of each of the tracks musically and cinematically, along with their contexts of production and reception. I would advise future researchers to assign a specific theme or idea as a lynchpin, in order to illuminate their understanding and endeavor to present any track analyzed in light of prior research and in the context of the double-disc album itself.

The *HIStory* album marks a significant turning point in popular music and culture. After this album, Jackson would never quite produce music that was more metaphorically autobiographical than literally biographical. He would continue to be edgier and darker, more bold and unflinching. His awareness of his status as an outsider, on the periphery of what was popular, gave him a new vantage point from which to present himself and his work. His playful moments would be restricted to glimpses: "I'm resilient. I have rhinoceros skin. Nothing can hurt me. Nothing."[32] After this album, Jackson truly had said it all, and how he took harrowing experiences and repurposed them was no less magic than spinning thread into gold.

CHAPTER 12

Michael Jackson and Children Revisited

As a range of critics have noted, Michael Jackson's fascination with childhood and his upbringing proffers ample room for critical discussion[1]—especially in terms of society's construction of child stars as objects of desire. However, this chapter focuses its attention not only on Jackson's problematic childhood but also on how it may have contributed to his use of the child as a primary source of inspiration. Much like the artist Gottfried Helnwein, known for his controversial images of children, Jackson's work presented "the child" as one of its single-most recurring themes.[2] This chapter seeks to continue this highly topical, critical conversation and present opportunities for further analysis. Its unique focus is in its use of Jackson's canon as primary source material.

> "I am the product of a lack of a childhood, an absence . . ."
> —Michael Jackson[3]

In "Have You Seen His Childhood? Song, Screen, and the Queer Culture of the Child in Michael Jackson's Music," critic Tavia Nyong'o seeks to reconsider Jackson and the child in a unique context: "how his music, and in particular the schematizing of boyish innocence within and through it, relates to a larger social incoherence . . . around childhood."[4] Nyong'o's essay takes the adoration of a child in Jackson's 1995 teaser for the *HIStory: Past, Present, and Future, Book 1* album and then considers, much like Margo Jefferson in *On Michael Jackson*, whether the cultural fascination for Jackson as a child contributes to his vilification as adult: "we talk about how we think, believe, suspect Michael Jackson treats children. We don't talk about how *we* treat child stars. Child stars are abused by the culture."[5] Both Jefferson and Nyong'o consider the taboo of the child as sexual object in Western culture, and then subvert this taboo with the public adoration of precocious child stars: "there is nothing natural about the making of child stars . . . little archaeological sites, carrying layers of show-business history inside them, fragments" and "Jackson was sealed into the world of showbusiness by the age of five."[6]

Jackson's fascination with the child and childhood, matched by that of J.M. Barrie, author of *Peter Pan* (see "'The Isle is Full of Noises': Revisiting the Peter Pan of Pop") existed on two separate levels.[7] The first was in terms of personal experience. In order to begin any discussion of Jackson and the theme of "the child," it is relevant to state that Jackson was one of 10 children, for whom a large family was a main source of support and enjoyment. Jackson, in particular, was drawn to looking after his siblings from a very young age. Jackson's childhood was a time fraught with domestic abuse and familial control, discussed repeatedly by Jackson himself in interviews and in his autobiography, *Moonwalk*. Jackson's childhood was a time when he would be forced, or at least coerced, into a life into which he had been fully initiated before he could give his adult consent. This powerlessness, an abuse and violation, would continue to affect Jackson for his entire life in ways that would shock the world. As Jefferson asserts, Jackson "lives in extremis what other people have gone through . . . The damage suffered by child stars rarely shows by word or deed until they crash suddenly . . . Then comes the anger, the grief, the cynicism . . . the longing for a prime you've been past for most of your life."[8]

In addition to Jackson's self-deigned mission to "heal the world" by "healing the world's children," Jackson also saw himself very much as a child.[9] He believed that his own childlike innocence, possibly a result of his harsh and sheltered upbringing, was a positive thing, the source of his inspiration, his art, and the "creative juice" that allowed him to create to the limits of his imagination.[10] In his book *Home Coming*, John Bradshaw discusses both the wonder child, or "puer aeternus," and its many pitfalls. Bradshaw argues that on some level all adults contain their child selves, and if this childhood state is not fully integrated with the adult it can become toxic and contaminate the adult's life, resulting in rage and other antisocial behaviors. Though a fountain of creativity and self-expression, a desire to remain an eternal child can only have damaging consequences, because a child is insatiable and unable to reason the validity of its desires. To remain an eternal child is to open oneself to destruction.[11]

The same freeness Jackson found in his relationships with children, he also found in his relationships with animals and in his lifelong love affair with nature. For Jackson, animals, nature, and children were connected very much to the eternal, the divine. Bradshaw calls this an "I Am-ness," a "being-ness" that holds true to one's very nature, and his sentiments were confirmed by the words of Christ in the Bible, who said, "the kingdom of heaven belongs to ones such as these."[12] Christ often lifted children to be the chief heirs of the greatest treasure mentioned in the Bible, the paradise of heaven. Jesus goes on to say that heaven—eternal life—can only be gained by those who allow themselves to be humbled like children. To be a child is to be unaware of who one is in the eyes of the world, and to be aware of the magnificence of one's being.

The overarching theme of many of the texts to which this chapter refers is innocence and the violation of that innocence. The purity and innocence of childhood fascinated Jackson. He wrote poetry about it, sought to emulate it, and was ultimately undone by it. His own innocence was "simple and trusting like a child."[13] For Jackson, the only alternative he saw was to be "locked into a pattern of thinking and responding," allowing "his creativity to get blocked."[14] This childlike innocence was also an artistic tool, a way to capture "the freshness and magic of the moment."[15] Jackson's *Dancing the Dream* offers the artist's most frank and genuine thoughts and feelings about childhood, children, and philosophy, many of which are explored in Chapter 3—"On Michael Jackson's *Dancing the Dream*."

CHILDHOOD INNOCENCE AND SUPERIORITY

On page 51 of Jackson's collection of poetry, *Dancing the Dream: Poems and Reflections*, there is a vibrant and touching illustration; it is a reprint of a painting from Jackson's private collection and was commissioned from David Nordahl.[16] This illustration, above all, shows Jackson's overarching perspective on children. Jackson is pictured as the father of 13 children, and he reads to them from a book of "Enchanted Tales," out of which shines a magical light that illuminates all their faces; the light correlates with the kingdom of magic that lies just below the copious bed of flowers and leaves, a literary visual underworld that is home to raucous magical beings. One seems to be young Jackson himself, holding aloft his cap from his early Motown career. This is the world Jackson shares with those he has called to be his children, a world that only they can share and experience. This is a world Jackson seeks to inhabit perpetually, and only children are able to join him there.

All of the children are unique in this forest scene; they are all in the midst of a safe and warm nature scene, and they are a range of ethnicities, from the wide-eyed African American girl sitting, seeing fairies, to the Caucasian boy center-right, who has left his crutches to lean into the book Jackson is holding. This child, although he may well have a disability of some kind, is equal to all the others. Some of the children are raptly attentive, others are completely asleep. In the center, Jackson clutches his son, who reaches out to touch a fairy; behind him the star shines out its light brighter than anything else on the page.

Jackson's connection to children was repeatedly echoed in his short films. In his 1998 anthology film, *Moonwalker*, Jackson's co-stars are children. However, they don't treat Jackson particularly as an adult or even as a father figure, but as a friend. They see him and treat him as an equal, a friend who is misunderstood and attacked. The antagonist, in the "Smooth Criminal" sequence of the film, Mr. Big's evil plan (the film's narrative enigma) is that he wishes to sell drugs to the children of the world, and hence, Jackson is positioned as a child, who sometimes takes on an adult's form—for instance, while dancing suggestively with seductive ladies in the Club 90s bar; but for the most part, Jackson identifies more directly with the children in these sequences. Cinematically, the children played by Brandon Adams, Kelly Parker, and Sean Lennon are his co-stars, not supporting stars. It is the other adults in this world who are secondary to the four of them. This brings us to another way children feature in Jackson's work—as superior to, or at least equal to, all adults.

The theme of child superiority can easily be seen in the *Badder* short film, when Jackson's cast from the *Bad* short film, directed by Martin Scorsese and starring Wesley Snipes, is entirely recast as young children (including producer, writer, and actress Maurissa Tancharoen in a minor role, and the actor Brandon Adams as the star. Again, in the *Black or White* short film, a pair of babies are seen on top of the world, literally holding Jackson's diegesis in their hands. In the *Heal the World* short film, Jackson's stars are predominantly the children of the world, and the short film begins with sick and institutionalized children, and it cuts between the adults in situations typified by war, famine and pain, and the children in these situations. The children are repeatedly presented as the solution to these problems and as the way the world will be made into a "better place." The short film intercuts little black children, staring through dusty windows, on which are reflected the burning crosses of the Ku Klux Klan, with skinheads, police, and a little girl in a blue dress who runs to standing soldiers and presents them with a flower. Children of all ethnicities and from all backgrounds are shown carrying flowers, playing and running toward the adults, bringing the solution in their bright dispositions, which contrast starkly with the dark faces of the adults, who are gloomy. The short film crescendos with the soldiers throwing their guns into the air and groups of children of all ethnicities, shapes, and sizes walking together. The low-angled shots of these children presents them as being of high status. In the closing shots of the short film, the world is inhabited only by children, holding candles that illuminate their hopeful faces. They stand side by side, equal in the world, holding up their candles in solidarity with one another, as if fully aware that the solution is to wait and grow, so that they can impact their world more positively than those who have gone before. Jackson's short film *Jam* also showcases young people in a similar way; they dance and move to the beat of the music that Jackson and Michael Jordan are making, and through the course of this short film they are invigorated with life, which lifts them up from their low starting place and moves them to a place of dynamism. Thus inspired by Jordan and Jackson, the kids are encouraged to "jam," because the cultural and global dilemmas their generation is faced with "ain't too much" for them, either.

CHILDHOOD SUFFERING AND DEATH

Not only was Jackson concerned for the plight and rights of young children, their health, and their voice, he was also very much concerned in his art with the depiction of their deaths and their loss. This is construed through songs such as "The Lost Children" on the *Invincible* album, which follows a lyrical Hansel and Gretel into a place where no one can find them, and cries for "the lost children | wishing them well."[17]

The track "Gone Too Soon" and its short film present Jackson alongside a teenager, Ryan White, a hemophiliac who contracted HIV and was at the forefront of the American debate on the fear of people with the disease.[18] White was a victim of prejudice, and he was ostracized in his community, but his courage and his willingness to speak out made him a poster child and a testament to what a single person can do with the hand dealt them. Jackson's short film for the song focuses primarily on footage of Ryan and images from Ryan's life. Jackson also covered the subject of White in *Dancing the Dream*.[19] However, what was clear was that Jackson saw Ryan as a compatriot of sorts, especially since both of them were deemed strange and ostracized for their uniqueness.

One way that Jackson articulates the theme of childhood suffering and death is in the song "Little Susie." The deaths of children are often highly sensationalized in the tabloid media, and the hunts for missing children have become an uncomfortably normal part of everyday life. However, in the liner notes for the *HIStory* album, Jackson includes the work of Gottfried Helnwein.[20] It seems to present a little girl lying dead, her head bandaged and her wrists overexposed to the light. It is a sobering and uncomfortable image to look at; it confronts the viewer with the reality of violence against children, and the true incapacity of children to defend themselves if they have no champion. Jackson's song outlines the life of a little girl who simply went unnoticed and unloved until her life was over. It is reminiscent of the misogynistic violence in "Smooth Criminal" ("Annie, are you okay"?). The blood in Susie's hair suggests that her death was violent, possibly even sexual. The song highlights that Susie's death was suspicious ("dress torn," "blood in her hair"), and it reminds us of publicized cases of tragedies of young children abducted and stolen.[21] However, in Susie's case, "she knew no one cared." It is neglect that is to blame for Susie's death, the fact that fundamentally no responsibility was taken for her welfare when "father left home, poor mother died."[22] It seems that Susie was most vulnerable to attack because of her isolation and her loneliness. She was defenseless, and no one came forward to protect her.

Helnwein's art forces its viewers to confront the reality of violence against children. However, it is controversial because of the fact that it does not contextualize what are often very disturbing images. Jackson's relationship with Helnwein stems from an earlier period than this particular image in 1995, which is in black and white and is horrifying, like something from a police detective photograph. According to Helnwein's web site, the relationship stems as far back as 1988, when Helnwein was photographed with Jackson in the *Bad* era, presumably during the *Bad* tour.[23] Both Helnwein and Jackson have a particular focus on children and a particular focus on aspects of children's lives that adults may not want to be confronted with, namely, abuse and ultimately death.

Jackson utilizes another depiction by the same artist on page 33 of the *HIStory* liner notes.[24] The image in question is *Scream*, and it shows a child in its underwear, stood in a corner, as a light shines from below its head remains shrouded by shadows. The child stares up with its mouth wide open mid-scream. What torment this child is experiencing is not clear, but what is clear is that the child suffers great pain. The scream is a way to communicate what cannot be expressed through words. Furthermore, a scream is useful only if it is heard, acknowledged, and then responded to. Jackson highlights the fact that, for so many children, this is not the case. Neglect, however, is not simply the fault of incompetent or damaged parents, but of a range of people who look away and overlook poor conditions over a period of time. In many ways, Jackson's work highlights how broken childhoods serve to create broken people who never quite find their way to wholeness. In one sense, then, all broken children are, in effect, dead children, because something in them has been destroyed that can never fully be regained. Hence, for Jackson, giving a voice to voiceless children was of paramount importance, not only because he felt compelled to do so, but because the children in his world were a significant reminder of the inner child within everyone.

This chapter has continued the critical discussion of childhood and "the child" within Jackson's life and work, depictions that are numerous and multilayered. Moving beyond conjecture, childhood innocence, superiority, and violence and death are crucial to understanding Jackson's relationship with the theme of "the child." Children are evident throughout every decade of Jackson's career, from the time he was a child himself until the time his own children were born. The artist was particularly enamored of fictional child characters like Peter Pan, as discussed in the article " 'The Isle Is Full of Noises': Revisiting the Peter Pan of Pop."[25] However, Jackson's work and his music show how the artist uses the depiction and portrayal of children as a symbol for newness and growth. He also uses these images to highlight and confront the negative plight of children all around the world, and he links them to his own wounded past and his own present pain. It is vital that we seek new understandings of the societal constructions of Jackson and childhood, placing them in their unique context of a former child star.

CHAPTER 13

"Faith, Hope, and Love": The Dangerous Philosophies of Michael Jackson

On March 6, 2001, Michael Jackson, aged 42, gave a speech to an audience at the Oxford Union, Oxford University.[1] Published by *The Journal of Pan-African Studies* as "Love: The Human Family's Most Precious Legacy," his speech featured the word "love" 42 times.[2] It was a monologue that described, with haunting clarity, the detrimental effect of Jackson's youth on his life, but the speech also held a surprising optimism for the fate of broken families everywhere. This chapter deconstructs Jackson's speech to highlight how three themes—faith, hope, and love—were integral components of Jackson's art and ethos. The chapter concludes by arguing that these philosophies may also contribute to how Jackson was perceived as dangerous.

> "Three things will last forever—faith, hope, and love . . . and the greatest of these is love."
>
> —1 Corinthians 13:13[3]

> "We should note that faith, hope and love are not meant to be merely attitudes . . . faith acts, love toils and hope grips."
>
> —David Pawson[4]

The University of Oxford needs no introduction. It is one of the oldest and most prestigious universities in the world, and countless academics and scholars have walked through its doors—a fact that was not lost on Jackson: "the walls of Oxford have not only housed the greatest philosophical and scientific geniuses—they have also ushered forth some of the most cherished creators of children's literature." The Oxford Union is "the world's most prestigious debating society, with an unparalleled reputation for bringing international guests and speakers to Oxford." The Union itself has a reputation for bringing controversial and thought-provoking speakers, and its long history of speakers include "Mother Theresa, Albert Einstein, Ronald Reagan, Robert Kennedy and Malcolm X."[5]

Jackson begins his speech by focusing on the Oxford intellectuals known for their contributions to children's literature, "from J.R.R. Tolkien to C.S. Lewis."[6] Jackson highlights his own lack of "academic expertise" but then proceeds to profess his "claim to having experienced more places and cultures than most people will ever see."[7] A brief look into Jackson's touring itineraries, from his early days with Motown to his solo world tours, gives a very clear overview of Jackson's immense amount of world travel, and he truly was seeing and experiencing more people, places, and admirers than most will ever hope to. Jackson's deep interest in and fascination with world cultures is shown repeatedly in his creative work. Jackson argues that "human knowledge consists not only of libraries of parchment and ink" but also of "the volumes of knowledge that are written on the human heart, chiseled on the human soul, and engraved on the human psyche."[8]

Jackson looks at inner knowledge, a deeper knowing that goes beyond intellect. This knowledge is claimed to be universal and to belong to all, no matter their gender, race, creed, or class. For Jackson, his philosophy and the deeper knowledge gained by his own experiences and insight "can bring healing to humanity and healing to our planet."[9] Jackson's initial joke about Kermit the Frog exhibits Jackson's uncanny ability to put his audience at ease.[10]

Jackson goes on to discuss his childhood in some depth, but not without merit, for childhood and the lack of love in childhood bolsters his main point. He reveals that "the cheery five-year-old who belted out 'Rockin' Robin' and 'Ben' to adoring crowds was not indicative of the boy behind the smile."[11] For Jackson, there was "no respite," and his professional working schedule gave few of the mundane experiences every child should have. Normality was simply a venture of voyeurism that Jackson attained while witnessing his family, who took him door to door, handing out *Watchtower* magazines. For Jackson, what he witnessed were in fact "wonderful, ordinary and starry scenes of everyday life."[12]

He makes it clear that his sense of difference and alienation from the world began far earlier in his youth; being a child celebrity already made his appearance something he already had to alter in order to achieve a semblance of normality, in order to "see the magic of other people's childhood."[13]

Focusing on the lack of something highlights and exacerbates the pain of its absence, and Jackson relates the emotional disconnection and pain of child stardom with the universal experience of young people in the developed world, who "are constantly encouraged to grow up faster."[14] Jackson argues that his prior experiences of having an accelerated youth is a subject on which he is "one of the world's greatest experts."[15] Jackson also underscores the "destructive effects of denying one's children the unconditional love that is so necessary."[16] However, he acquiesces that many of the parents of these children were raised in similar environments, and that these parents, therefore are not actually capable of providing the unconditional love and acceptance needed.[17]

In the rush to discard the trappings of childhood and the immaturity of juvenility, Jackson claims that "Generation X" has given way to "Generation O," a generation who have "wealth, success, fancy clothing and fancy cars, but an aching emptiness on the inside."[18] They have a "cavity in our chests . . . barrenness at our core . . . void in our center."[19] Jackson's use of the collective noun "our" puts him squarely in a group that has an abyss where love could be. However, it is easily claimed that Jackson's perspective of poverty is rose-tinted, especially for a person who has lived in the very lap of luxury for most of his life. The claim that previous generations' homes were "lit with love" does not chime with the Victorians' alarming rates of child prostitution and appalling standards of child labor. However, Jackson goes on to assert that children should have rights of their own and that these rights could be the answer to many of the world's problems and issues.

His words are profound, and they do ring true. Many personal problems in adulthood stem from low self-esteem and self-worth. This is often why people stay in abusive situations and gravitate toward them in the first place. Jackson's speech goes on to highlight children's rights "to be loved . . . be protected . . . feel valuable . . . be listened to," et cetera, and emphasizes that these rights should be entirely unconditional. Jackson states that "the foundation of all human knowledge . . . must be that each and every one of us is an object of love."[20] Scientific studies have shown that much of the development of children occurs in the first three years of life, and Jackson echoes this sentiment: "Before you know if you have red hair or brown . . . you have to know that you are loved."[21]

Jackson illustrates his point with the story of a young fan who died at the age of 10. Jackson attempted to help the child hold on to life by giving him a glove and a jacket, but the child did not survive. Tearfully, Jackson explains that "at least when he died, he knew that he was loved."[22] For Jackson, "if you enter this world knowing you are loved and you leave this world knowing the same, then everything that happens in between can be dealt with"; if not, "you are condemned to search the world for something to fill you up."[23]

He goes on to identify the solution: a re-creation of the parent–child bond that puts the emphasis on the child to forgive the parent—which is a particularly volatile idea, that a child can thus transcend a parent's wrongdoing. In

Jackson's words, his father "had great difficulty showing affection," and he breaks into tears while recounting this fact.[24] He gives personal details about his journey to understanding his own father's behavior as a model for young people and everyone who feels they are part of Generation O, those who suffer from a prodigious lack of love because of their upbringing. However, although some might agree that forgiveness is key to letting go of the past and the resentment, guilt, and anger that are often attributed to the past; and that the only love that is truly unconditional is self-love, which can be found only through therapy, mirror work, and positive affirmations. It is a love of self that soothes the inner child and bolsters self-esteem. For Jackson, it became clear that his father "seemed intent, above all else on making [him] a commercial success," but all the money in the world did not make up for the neglect Jackson experienced in his early life.

He also says that love is now central to his hopes and intentions for his own children, and for how he would like them to remember him. He hoped they would one day say, "daddy did the best he could, given the unique circumstances that he faced."[25] It is the generational connections, from grandparent to parent to child, that Jackson seems most concerned with in the latter part of his speech. He connects his father's cruelty with the fact that he was "a poor Black man in the South, robbed of dignity, bereft of hope, struggling to become a man," and states how even "his harshness was a kind of love" that pushed Jackson to be "the first black artist to be played on MTV."[26] Within this outpouring of forgiveness as the key to true love and freedom, we see time and again his almost Gatsby-like propensity for hope and faith. He hopes that he can "put to rest the ghosts" of his childhood. He has faith that he can "step into a new relationship" with his father, "unhindered by the goblins of the past." and Jackson uses this same hope to believe that "love will finally be restored to a desolate and lonely world."[27]

It's Jackson's deepest belief that, "In a world filled with hate, we must still dare to hope. In a world filled with anger, we must still dare to comfort. In a world filled with despair, we must still dare to dream. And in a world filled with distrust, we must still dare to believe."[28] This quote is part of Paul the Apostle's first letter to the Corinthians in the New Testament (given more fully in the chapter's notes). Jackson's biblical values centered on the three simple concepts Paul explains here. A synonym of the word "love" here is "charity," and it denotes an act of selfless giving. Jackson was entered into the *Guinness Book of World Records* for donating millions of dollars to charities.[29]

The dissenting, and therefore dangerous, perception of those who embody love and charity has been particularly evident in the treatment of many missionaries and martyrs who were certainly seen as destructive and rebellious. The radical and uncontrollable nature of one who cannot be easily swayed by a desire for the self is a catastrophic component in cultures that thrive on greed, hedonism, and selfishness. Jackson found his beliefs completely at odds with dominant popular ideologies, and this often led to his ridicule. This chapter has considered Jackson's 2001 speech in detail and has deconstructed its philosophies for the deeper understanding and revelation that Jackson provides, in terms of his very own philosophical outlook.

It is this resounding monologue that demonstrates so significantly Jackson's philosophies of faith, hope, and love. They have become so integral to his person and his work that he holds to them despite his overwhelming awareness of the hatred, anger, despair, and distrust that surround him. The use of the word "dare" is particularly effective, because it implies that in so doing, he is being bold, courageous, and of course, dangerous. Jackson's hope is for a world filled with "children laughing," "children playing," and "children singing." It is also a world filled with the sound of "parents listening."[30] Jackson closes the speech with the words "I love you." However, what we are left with are harrowing images of Jackson's own childhood and the severe effect that a life in the spotlight had on him. Nevertheless, we are also left with a vivid picture of his relentless optimism and fortitude.

CHAPTER 14

From Crown to Cross: The Poisoned Chalice of *Thriller*'s Success

This chapter charts the success of Michael Jackson's 1982 *Thriller* album, especially as a precursor to several issues the artist would later face with regard to public perceptions of his work. Using the metaphor of a "poisoned chalice," it presents Jackson's *Thriller*, though seemingly the pinnacle of Jackson's career, as one of the most prevalent factors in narratives of decline that were constructed afterwards. It seeks to widen the discussion of *Thriller* as not only an astronomical success, but also an integral part of the artist's journey from "crown" (idolization) to "cross" (vilification).

> "This even-handed justice | commands th' ingredience of our poisoned chalice | To our own lips." (1.8.11)
>
> —William Shakespeare[1]

This quote appears just before a Scottish nobleman commits regicide on the early modern stage. Shakespeare's 400-year-old play challenges ambition and self-seeking behavior.[2] The poisoned chalice, also featured in Matthew 20:20 and 26:39, is the cup that one must drink, a poisoned cup referred to as the "bitter cup." The *OED* defines it as a "chalice containing wine . . . laced with poison" and "an award which appears advantageous . . . proves to be detrimental." It is this second definition that this chapter is most concerned with, but the metaphoric substance of the first definition is particularly useful for the understanding of the concept, too.

The poisoned chalice is Jackson's second solo adult album, *Thriller*. Though the highest-selling record of all time, critical views of *Thriller* range from being unanimously positive to decidedly lukewarm. Rarely does the album garner a negative review, with several critics opting to easily place the album as the very epitome of Jackson's creative output. There are opinions about the album as a work of manifest genius or as one of accidental timeliness. Much like the "discovery" of gravity, it has been called a signifier of time, a reflection of globalization, and a moment of clearly accentuated collectedness of its age. It has even been compared to the election of a black president, the emancipation of African American-ness, a moment of magic, a pinnacle, a summit.[3]

However, the perspective from within this gargantuan success, under the glistening rhinestone gloves and glowing socks, beneath the leather jackets and John Landis–directed short film, and the seemingly endless capacity to fascinate and enthrall; the enigmatic smile, and all the pomp and ceremony that was Michael Jackson, lay a deeply traumatized 24-year-old man, one who was in many ways still very much a child. Jackson was a complex artist who had survived the pitfalls of childhood stardom, but he emerged obsessed with "being the best," the greatest. Jackson was also coping with a period of intense depression. Jackson himself has stated on several occasions in interviews, and in particular in his autobiography *Moonwalk*, that his depression was overwhelming. During the recording of *Off the Wall* a few years before, Jackson suffered most deeply from the adult realization that his past had marked him for life, both mentally and physically, and that he was condemned to be perceived as "other." Simultaneously, Jackson was less than, and more than, human—a spectacle, and a figure of adoration as well as sexual attraction for his consumers. But with regard to his own feelings and emotions, he'd become anything but a human being.

By age 24, Jackson had been subsumed into the consciousness of America as a child, and for many, as the little boy he would remain. Jackson was very much a "real boy," complete with the thoughts and feelings of emerging maturity. He struggled to begin a sexually fulfilling relationship with the actress Tatum O'Neal and obsessed over his lifelong crush Diana Ross. He may have begun to realize that he "was not like other boys."[4] By this point, and with the complete manifestation of his idol persona (see Chapter 9—" 'Throwing Stones to Hide Your Hands': The Mortal Persona of Michael Jackson"), for all intents and purposes Jackson had become an American "king." The commodification of Jackson's physical image was the selling of a soul that transpired first through records and short films, then compact discs and mp3s, and no doubt via future technologies. All the while it became accustomed to leaping into more tabloids than newspapers.

If Jackson was indeed a king, then his kingdom extended way beyond America, especially later in his career (and posthumously). It was a global no-man's-land that stretched throughout all the continents—wherever people had ears to hear and chose to listen to his music. The utter pervasiveness of

Figure 14.1
Michael Jackson's Star on the Hollywood Walk of Fame,
Los Angeles, California.
The Jon B. Lovelace Collection of California Photographs in Carol M. Highsmith's
America Project. (Library of Congress)

Jackson's music is still difficult to comprehend; on any one day, one can hear his music played on several radio stations completely by chance. Jackson became a king; he also became a sufferer of the concept of the "body politic," where the body of the king becomes the preserve of and representative of the healthiness of the state. In *Macbeth*, the murder of the king results in a deep and pervasive malaise in his kingdom: "good men's lives | Expire before the flowers in their caps, | Dying or ere they sicken" (4.3.173-175).[5] Similarly, as Jackson's body seemed to change, so, too, did the world around him, digitizing and modernizing itself. To the average, casual viewer, it may well have seemed that Jackson also went from child star to adult star, mortal to eternal, and physical to digital.

Jackson was synonymous with his music, meaning that he became king wherever his subjects were fascinated with him. This fascination soon dissolved into a continual inquiry into what was "wrong" with him, because it was, in fact, a symptom of what was wrong with them, his "subjects," the public. When Jackson had no heir, and the kingdom remained undefined and turbulent and without its king, the virtual kingdom fell—hence, the posthumous ascent of the "Michael Jackson" trademark, an attempt to reaffirm a dead king's place and hold together several broken and crumbling industries. Jackson started something only he could finish. The public concern over Jackson's appearance was a simultaneous concern for self, and the outpouring of grief over the king's death was a grief for the kingdom that, without an heir, could not exist without him.

Jackson's misrepresentation, his worldwide success, and deeply personal misery began with *Thriller*.

Jackson would never be a normal person, and *Thriller*'s success guaranteed that for life. The door that had already been shut behind him—between Gary, Indiana, and his appearance on the Ed Sullivan Show—was reinforced with concrete and steel with the success of *Thriller*. Jackson's dream was cinema, and his prowess in *The Wiz* is ample evidence of his ability to act. He would profess, throughout his career, his prodigious desire to act in and produce feature-length films: "these days movies are my number one dream."[6] It would be the events that spread out from the *Thriller* explosion, poisonous, that would deny him ever achieving that dream.

Thriller stemmed directly from the Grammy snub of *Off the Wall*, undoubtedly the most successful album release of 1979, which received a single Grammy in the category for "Black Music," despite its massive mainstream success. In 1980, Jackson was the biggest-selling black artist in history, but the snub at the Grammy Awards turned him all about, and made him obsessed (by many accounts) with proving that a black man, descended from slaves in a country mired in African blood, could be the most successful recording artist in the world.

It was always Jackson's wish to sell more records than anyone else who had ever recorded music, and to destroy the walls of segregated MTV and the music publishing power that kept blacks and many ethnic minorities from getting a fair start in the industry. However, he did not come to his *Thriller* success easily. He danced so hard he drove grooves into the wood of his dance floor, and fasted into what critics would call a "balletic stick," "insect-like."[7] Jackson's dramatic weight loss would be a chronic problem for him, barely acknowledged and lurking in the background. He would write in his autobiography, "I'm a vegetarian now and I'm so much thinner. I've been on a strict diet for years."[8]

Health problems Jackson had coped with were exacerbated by the "poisoned chalice" of the *Thriller* album's success. The combined successes of *Billie Jean*, the Bob Giraldi–directed short film, and projects with Paul McCartney, Quincy Jones, and Stephen Spielberg (to top it all off) radically altered Jackson's perception of the world. These successes simultaneously altered the world's perception of him as an idol—who could be immortalized. This issue is further discussed in Chapter 9—"'Throwing Stones to Hide Your Hands': The Mortal Persona of Michael Jackson."

Jackson's perception of the world was radically altered by *Thriller*'s success because he would be chased, hounded, and mercilessly hunted by his fans for the rest of his life; he would also face continual and serious death threats and would need a significant security detail to ensure his protection and safety.[9] The power Jackson gained from *Thriller*'s success meant he was soon perceived as a cultural threat. The mass exposure of his image (which had accompanied his massive sales) made him instantly recognizable everywhere. Essentially, for him, there really was no escape.

The depression-fueled nightmare of Jackson's *Off the Wall* self had become a complete reality. The emotional struggle of a maturing sense of self, within a massive, single-handed conglomerate, would soon show up in Jackson's actions. For example, maintaining a close friendship with his animals, namely, Bubbles, a chimp who would soon seem the closest thing Jackson had to a friend. It would show, even more evidently in Jackson's music, *Bad*-hosted songs like "Smooth Criminal," explicitly written about murder and attack, with voices asking, "Are you okay?" Like "Smooth Criminal," "Leave Me Alone" marks a turning point in Jackson's artistic output. He has transitioned quickly into the enemy, and he is bad for being so commercially viable a product and for marketing and delivering himself into so many customers' hands. The swift backlash against him was relentless, as fiction after fiction would be treated as fact.

Alongside Jackson's fissuring outlook on the world—a world where he would never feel safe again—there was the world's increasingly negative perception of him. His subsequent artistic contributions could not, with regard to record sales, ever meet *Thriller*'s. Imagine Jackson's sales as a symbol of reverse inflation, and we can never forget the fact that fewer records were sold in general. We can also take into context the unbelievably bad press Jackson's reputation received, combined with an expectation that he would do something never before seen. His raw talent had been exchanged for sheer spectacle. Even Jackson himself regarded his life (his show) by 1991 to be the "greatest show on Earth."[10]

Jackson, an artistic chameleon, knew only how to change. Change and transformation were part of him and became themes in several of his creations (as discussed in detail in Chapter 8—"Thoughts on Michael Jackson's Transformations"). Change was also in Michael Jackson's genetic makeup, with his disposition toward vitiligo that irreversibly altered his skin (as early as *Off the Wall*, and it progressed through *Thriller*). Artistic change and evolution would mark each of his subsequent creative offerings—so much so that *Jackson himself* remains the single unifying theme that unites all of his art. Each of his adult solo releases is so unique—and different from one another—that in order to discuss all of them, Joseph Vogel had to divide his book *Man in the Music: The Creative Life and Work of Michael Jackson* into album-chapters. All of Jackson's subsequent releases would be dwarfed by *Thriller*, by the specter, the memory, and even the idea of *Thriller*.

Jackson was also haunted by his own specter of *Thriller*. He pushed himself to achieve sales success, as he had done with that album. Impossible dreams drove him, when what he was seeking was respect, the respect *Thriller* had promised to earn—a promise it did not fulfill. Instead, Jackson earned disrespect in the form of increasingly negative press, so even Jackson's desire for respect was an unachievable dream. Jackson earned further punishment for paving the way for subsequent black artists to gain self-respect, to become moguls like Jay-Z, and for creating a model for selling music (discussed in great detail by Zack O'Malley Greenburg in *Michael Jackson Inc.*).[11]

Thriller became synonymous with America at a time in history that was typified by a young and optimistic culture, fixed and unchanging, shiny with nostalgia and hindsight. As a result, Jackson was not permitted to change, because to evolve by creating music that moved him and his art forward would threaten that crystallized memory of the time when life was "perfect" to many of his followers (though nothing, of course, is perfect, and nothing ever has been). Jackson's career had reached a pinnacle, and a pinnacle is a collective ideology constructed in the collective societal consciousness. Furthermore, the idea that Jackson was at his peak in the early 1980s actually correlates with the fact that it was the last time he was clearly seen by his audience, without the thick smoke of public and press disapproval.

Jackson's *Thriller*, though often perceived as the pinnacle of his artistic and commercial success but also the beginning of his artistic decline, can easily be viewed as the start of his vilification and misrepresentation by the tabloid and mainstream press. It was a poisoned chalice: the album's success disguised a bitter poison that made Jackson concern himself with unachievable dreams. *Thriller*'s poison was also that its success meant every subsequent offering by Jackson would be compared to it, "no matter how you look at it, people are always going to compare . . . You can always say, 'Aw, forget *Thriller*,' but no one ever will."[12] Jackson struggled against this for the rest of his life, and once he had drunk from the poisoned cup of *Thriller*'s success, like Macbeth, he could not outlive its bitter draught.

PART III

Art beyond Life

This section focuses on Jackson's life in retrospect. It seeks to open a dialogue about Jackson's posthumous representation and ideological reconstruction. Above all, it seeks to encourage new ways of discussing Jackson's art, especially as his art is linked to his posthumous resurgence.

CHAPTER 15

Horcruxes: Michael (Split Seven Ways) Jackson

Michael Jackson was inherently unique. His uniqueness often contributes to the problem of appreciating how he lived and signified as an artist. This chapter regards Jackson as subject to reduction by way of misunderstanding. It presents Jackson using seven other artists in history as a prism through which to see him, especially in terms of biography and reception. It examines these aspects alongside those of classical composers Johann Sebastian Bach and Wolfgang Amadeus Mozart, actor and director Charlie Chaplin, filmmaker Walt Disney, and musicians James Brown, David Bowie, and Stevie Wonder. Another comparative chapter follows on Jackson and Andy Warhol.

> "You split your soul . . . hide part of it in an object outside the body . . . even if one's body is attacked or destroyed, one cannot die."
> —J.K. Rowling[1]

For those unfamiliar with a "horcrux," it is a term originated in J.K. Rowling's internationally best-selling Harry Potter series.[2] The sheer scale of Jackson's influence and impact on popular culture was really given a tangible form only upon his death in 2009, when an unprecedented volume of searches on the subject nearly "broke the Internet" and caused controversial and unexpected responses around the world.[3] Jackson's exceptional character, style, and infamy was, in the history of art and music, unprecedented. Therefore, it is useful to use new words and metaphors to describe who Jackson was, how he and his art were received, and most important, what his posthumous relevance is. Two metaphors I find particularly useful are that of the "prism" and that of the "horcrux" (see Figure 15.1 and Figure 15.2). Prisms reveal white light to be a spectrum of highly varied colors, and so does the considering of Jackson through the work of other artists and musicians. Jackson was certainly a commercially successful contemporary musician, and all the artists with whom he is compared in this chapter were also commercially successful, creating contemporary works for their time. It suffices to say that the works of Bach and Mozart were the most contemporary music of their era, and so, too, were Bowie's and Brown's. Furthermore, the brief overviews that follow are not definitive accounts; rather, they are intended as jump-off points for future researchers to consider in-depth analysis.

JOHANN SEBASTIAN BACH (1685–1750)

Bach was a musical composer and organist situated in Germany. Like Jackson, he was raised in a family of musicians in a time when musical families were immensely popular. Born in Eisenach, he was the eighth of several children, from a large family as was Jackson. However, their childhoods differ in that Bach's parents died while he was still young. Bach's musical career took him through several periods of growth and contraction (especially considering his work with choirs), and in 1717, in his early thirties, he fell out of favor in the Weimar region and even found himself in jail after protesting at an unfair dismissal:

> All in all 1717 was a turbulent year in Bach's life. It saw the first printed evidence of his rise to fame and ended in official disgrace at the Weimar Court. In between, his production of cantatas seems to have come to a standstill—either from choice or, after a show of dissent travels: to Gotha to fill in for a sick colleague and compose music at Passiontide; to Cöthen to clinch his new contract; and to Dresden in October where he had been billed as the challenger in a celebrated (much hyped, but never independently documented) bout with the French keyboard virtuoso Louis Marchand. With his opponent scratching at the last moment, Bach returned to Weimar in a black mood, smarting from the non-contest, the affront to his pride and the loss of 500 thalers in prize money somehow embezzled at source.[4]

After this, Bach would prove immensely popular with the monarchy and was particularly favored by the king himself, who supported him and his work. He had several children with two wives, and 10 of them survived until adulthood, echoing the family tradition of large families. Bach was known to hide many messages in his work, as discussed in great depth by Ruth Tatlow in *Bach and the Riddle of the Number Alphabet*. These messages were often very intellectual.[5]

While Bach performed works, he *composed* mostly for the church. Jackson's work was composed *mostly* for the masses. In later life, however, both Jackson and Bach suffered from declining health and, reportedly, poor eyesight. It is interesting that Bach died supposedly from complications after a botched eye operation.[6] (However, there are several other accounts of how Bach died.) Jackson died at the hands of an inept doctor who gave him poor care.

Bach's compositions were phenomenally beautiful, creative, and full of innovation. He lived to the grand age of 65, outliving Jackson by 15 years. He composed some of the most beautiful and well-known works, prolifically, for a range of instruments, predominantly the harpsichord, and orchestral pieces. One noteworthy parallel between Jackson and Bach is the fact that their music's reception changed greatly over time. For much of the century following his death, Bach's work was not commonly played. It was appreciated by only a small niche of connoisseurs. However, by the 19th and 20th centuries his work had a massive resurgence, and his popularity as a classical composer is now undisputed.

WOLFGANG AMADEUS MOZART (1756–1791)

Mozart is possibly most likely well known to contemporary audiences through the film *Amadeus*, directed by Milos Forman and based on the stage production written by acclaimed director Peter Shaffer.[7] Mozart was born in Salzburg, Austria, and, as with Bach, was predominantly trained by his father.[8] Much like Jackson, however, Mozart was a child prodigy. Mozart composed some of his earliest musical compositions before he was even five. Jackson began dancing at the tender age of five. Mozart would quickly outgrow the limitations of his teacher. Another parallel between Mozart and Jackson is their childhood touring; from a very young age, Mozart traveled with his father and sometimes with siblings to distant places such as Italy to perform.[9] Both Mozart and Jackson had fathers who were determined that their sons' unique abilities be displayed and exhibited for a wide range of audiences for financial gain. In 1770, aged just 14, Mozart composed his first opera, and from a particularly young age he was able to recite entire musical pieces from memory. A parallel that can be drawn here is Jackson's innate ability to sing and dance like an adult from his early adolescence.[10]

In his mid-to-late teens, Mozart was employed in Salzburg, to mixed success. However, the young Mozart grew discontented with his position there.[11] This draws some parallels with Jackson's discontent with Motown Records and subsequent move, with his brothers, to Epic. This break caused a rift in the Jackson family when Jermaine Jackson stayed with Motown. It seems that both Mozart and Jackson expressed a marked desire to grow beyond the limitations laid out for them, beyond the confines in which they had been raised. They found themselves dissatisfied with their predicaments and moved forward with an increased determination to have artistic freedom as well as social recognition.

In 1781, from his great recognition and fame, aged approximately 24, Mozart was summarily dismissed from his employment because he found himself undervalued by the archbishop, a situation where Mozart's father actually agreed with his son's opposition and thereby forced him to become a freelance composer. Mozart's tumultuous relationship with his father seems to have been one of control and manipulation, and it was with great difficulty that Mozart succeeded in receiving his father's permission to marry Constanze Weber. It was in the time following Mozart's marriage that he became heavily influenced by the work of our aforementioned composer, Bach. Mozart's personal life bore repeated tragedies, while in public his compositions went from success to success.

Some of Mozart's most well-known works are his operas *The Magic Flute*, *The Marriage of Figaro*, and *Don Giovanni*. The artist fell upon hard times toward the end of the 18th century and, much like Jackson, resorted to borrowing money to make ends meet.[12] The poor financial situation was most likely as difficult and worrisome for Mozart as it was for Jackson, especially in the lead-up to Jackson's proposed 50 performances for *This Is It*—performances he most likely would never have agreed to had he been fully solvent at the time. *The Magic Flute*, a piece of music that Jackson greatly loved throughout his life, was a piece composed during some of Mozart's most financially distressing times. It was a piece that achieved great public success in the time leading up to Mozart's death, a success he reveled in.[13]

More parallels with Jackson and Mozart include the fact that both were considered eccentric and unusual, even decadent, in their time. Alongside the fact that they both worked incredibly hard, composing and creating without abandon, both also enjoyed mingling with the aristocracy, the upper echelons of society of their time. Although the notion of celebrity was not widely used in the 17th century, Mozart would certainly have been a celebrity by modern standards, and he enjoyed playing, dancing, and keeping pets. Mozart's death has garnered much mystery, and a range of tales have sprung up about it. Though it is true that he was buried in an unmarked grave, what is not true is that he was buried in a pauper's grave. Mozart was also mourned in both Prague and Vienna. He was actually beginning to gain financial stability when he took ill. However, what is certainly true is that, at the age of just 35, his death (like Jackson's) was untimely.[14]

CHARLIE CHAPLIN (1889–1977)

Charlie Chaplin, though one of the pillars of Hollywood cinema, was in equal parts adored and reviled through his long career. It is a little known fact that Jackson was enamored of Charlie Chaplin. The inclusion of the track "Smile" on Jackson's 1995 album *HIStory: Past, Present and Future, Book 1* is very much connected with this lifelong fascination of Chaplin, particularly of Chaplin's spinning of the straw of his early life into cinematic gold. Vogel asserts that Jackson's use of "Smile" "completes a turbulent, emotionally exhausting journey."[15]

British-born Chaplin was born into an impoverished background, and his early years were steeped in hardship, which translated into his films, particularly *Modern Times* and *The Kid*. Chaplin was sent to the workhouse on two separate occasions before he was nine, and of this time in the Victorian era Chaplin said, "I was hardly aware of a crisis because we lived in a continual crisis." This meant brutal conditions that would be far below human rights standards in the present day.[16] In his youth, Chaplin was institutionalized in homes for destitute children. His mother, despite numerous attempts to get better, would continue to grow ill, and both his parents were dead before he was 30. It was in his youth, however, that Chaplin began work as both an actor and comedian, continuing in the tradition of both his parents, who had been concert hall performers in London.

Chaplin's touring stage career as a comedian gave way to a film career in silent movies in Hollywood. Here he created the persona of the Tramp, for which he would become famous. But what was of supreme fascination for Jackson was how Chaplin managed to create humor, fun, and comedy from all the painful experiences of his early life. At the age of just 29, Chaplin was one of the most well-known faces in the world. He was the cofounder of the film company United Artists, which still exists today, and his films *The Kid* and *Modern Times* were key films of the silent movie period, of which Chaplin was undoubtedly king; Jackson's success at the height of the 1980s mirrored Chaplin's.[17]

Another parallel is that Chaplin became a global brand and had a great deal of merchandise created in his image, which sold widely. He also exerted both creative and financial control over many of his productions, through his work with Essanay Film Manufacturing Company. He was offered exorbitant amounts of money for his work, and with full awareness of how much he was worth, he demanded the largest sums he could think of. Chaplin's signing bonus of $150,000 in 1915 is reminiscent of Jackson's multimillion dollar deal with Sony Records in 1991.[18]

Chaplin had an acute sense of characterization through the use of clothing, as identified through his Tramp costume. He said, "I wanted everything to be a contradiction: the pants baggy, the coat tight, the hat small and the shoes large . . . I added a small moustache, which, I reasoned, would add age without hiding my expression."[19] He created an image so iconic that it is synonymous with Hollywood today. However, for Chaplin, the high times did not last, and by the 1940s and the rise of the Second World War, Chaplin found himself at the center of great controversy. First, he was involved in a series of time-consuming litigations that included a paternity suit filed by a former lover. The media smeared Chaplin's reputation; furthermore, the close details of these trials were not often laid out, so several lurid charges for which he was accused stayed in the public consciousness long after his acquittal. For Chaplin, the litigious process dampened his creative spark. His reputation in the United States never fully recovered from the negative media coverage. For years, suspicion grew of Chaplin's communist leanings, and it was not long before he was served papers to appear before the famous House Un-American Activities Committee. Chaplin left America in 1952 and wrote, "whether I re-entered that unhappy country or not was of little consequence to me. I would like to have told them that the sooner I was rid of that hate-beleaguered atmosphere the better, that I was fed up of America's insults and moral pomposity."[20] It would take 25 years before America would recant its hasty expulsion of one of its greatest film stars. In his later life, he received an Honorary Award from the Academy of Motion Arts and Sciences; however, American

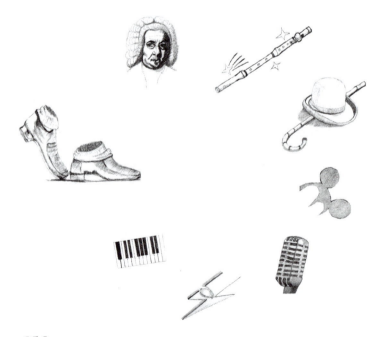

Figure 15.1
A Visual Representation of Michael Jackson as Seven Horcruxes.
(Artwork by Karin Merx)

cinema did not benefit from his work in later life, and its attempts to stamp out his liberty resulted in stamping out a light of creativity for the general public's enjoyment. Jackson's lost years parallel Chaplin's lost years, and, as in Chaplin's case, Jackson's lost years may well have been some of his most prolific. Charles Chaplin died in 1977, aged 88.

WALT DISNEY (1901–1966)

Born in 1901 in Chicago, Walt Disney was the fourth of five children, and from his early years he showed a prodigious interest in cartoon strips. An interesting comparison between Jackson and Disney in their early years is their shared love of trains. As Jackson's brother writes, "Michael had built himself the biggest electric train set you could imagine."[21] Jackson and Disney both loved trains throughout their lives; in Jackson's case, this was exhibited mostly at his home, Neverland Valley Ranch. Disney's early years were marked by a smattering of creative endeavors, attempts at art school, and lessons in drawing.[22] Unlike Jackson and Mozart, Disney was not driven as a child prodigy by an overbearing father. However, a key parallel between Jackson and Disney is their relatively humble beginnings. Disney's animating career really took off with the studio Ubbe Iwerks, and by the mid-1920s he was working in Hollywood. Disney's creative works captured the public imagination. He married in 1925 and would stay married to the same woman, Lilian Bounds, for the rest of his life.[23]

The character Mickey Mouse was born in the late 1920s and, voiced by Disney himself, would grow to become one of the world's most well-known and iconic characters. It is occasionally said that Jackson had a desire to be Mickey Mouse, to become both the iconic cartoon character and the international brand.[24] However, it is important to understand that by saying so, Jackson was also saying that he wished to become Disney, who was Mickey Mouse, since Disney was the voice of the character and breathed life into it.[25] By 1932, Disney received an Academy Award for the creation of Mickey Mouse, his first of 22 Oscars. For Disney, the late 1930s and early 1940s marked the greatest creative expansion and success. A key parallel between Disney and Jackson is their investments. Like Jackson, investing an exorbitant amount of money in the *Thriller* short film in 1983, Disney spent a massive amount of money on the feature-length film *Snow White*, enough to bankrupt his entire organization.[26] Of course, both *Snow White* and the *Thriller* short film were unequivocal successes. Disney supported the arts with his fortune, funding the education of many artists in a range of educational institutions.

Another equivalent with Jackson is that Disney grew more controversial in his later years. For example, during the House Un-American Activities

Committee in the late 1940s, he named some of his animators as communists and was also named by the FBI as a special agent.[27] In 1949 Disney moved to the Holmby Hills in California, in the area where Jackson died. He built the Carolwood Pacific Railroad and named his locomotive after his wife, the *Lily-Belle*.[28] He inaugurated Disneyland in the mid-1950s, pioneering the theme park; and, of him Jackson writes, "I have such admiration for Mr. Disney and what he accomplished . . . I am in awe."[29] Walt Disney was certainly an inspiration for Jackson, far more because of his realization that the images and animations that appeal to the child also appeal to the child within us all. Disney commodified that idea in a hitherto unseen way, and it was this monetization that Jackson learned from: "I told them that Walt Disney was a hero of mine and that I was interested in Disney's history and philosophy . . . I had read a number of books about Walt Disney and his creative empire."[30]

Accusations of racism against Disney continue, and they are as persistent as the cryogenic freezing rumors (see below). In fact, Disney did associate with those who were openly anti-Semitic, and this may be why. The racist values and archetypes showcased in some Disney films may also have far more to do with collective ideologies than with Disney's personal specific leanings. It is also important to note that not only did Disney donate money to Jewish charities, he also hired black animator Floyd Norman. He also championed the awarding of actor James Baskett, the first black actor to win an Honorary Academy Award.[31]

Disney died in 1966, aged 65. His cause of death was circulatory collapse, and he had been a smoker. Disney's death was beleaguered with rumors, the most famous of which were those of cryogenic freezing. In truth, Disney was cremated.[32] Also parallel to Jackson, Disney's legacy spread long after his death, and he created a brand from his work and exploits that continues to flourish, inspiring the pioneers of Pixar, for example, and the Disney company continues to produce blockbuster films and expand its theme parks throughout the world. One final parallel between Jackson and Disney is that both were exemplary in commercial success, they were two of the most widely awarded creative artists, garnering hundreds of awards, and they both left a profound impact on the world.

JAMES BROWN (1933–2006)

To say that James Brown was Michael Jackson's greatest hero is a wild understatement. Jackson said, "Brown is my greatest inspiration ever since I was a small child . . . when I saw him move I was mesmerized."[33] Brown, also known as the "godfather of soul," is the most sampled artist of all time. Born in 1933 in South Carolina, Brown was allegedly stillborn in abject poverty, far poorer than Jackson's humble beginnings in Indiana. Brown's early life parallels Charlie Chaplin's, pockmarked with poverty; Brown was moved into one of his aunt's brothels at a very young age, exposing him before his fifth birthday to a world of sexual exploitation and violence. He was abandoned by his mother; born into such a poor background, he had to struggle to get by and spent much of his time alone.[34]

To be successful, Brown had to both out-dance and out-sing his competition. As a teenager he boxed, and he was briefly detained for robbery. However, it was music that, much as in the case of Quincy Jones, saved him from a life of crime. Brown's first hit was the song "Please, Please" in 1956 (two years before Jackson was born).[35] Jackson's stage performances from childhood, and especially during the live performances (particularly for the *Bad* tour in 1987) recall the energy and spark of a live James Brown performance, and Jackson molded and styled himself directly after Brown: "No spotlight could keep up with him when he skidded across the stage—you had to *flood* it! I wanted to be that good."[36] However, Brown rightly wanted to cross over; he resented the lack of respect he received but also accepted where he stood culturally.

The year 1964 was of particular importance in the lives of both Jackson and Brown; it was the year of the Civil Rights Act. Jackson was only six years old at the time; the world was radically changing for black men and women, and it would never quite be the same. Jackson would go on to emulate much of Brown's stylistic nuances. For instance, his costumier, Michael Bush, would throw a cape over Jackson in performance in a state of falsified apotheosis, before Jackson rose phoenix-like from the ashes, revived by the music, introducing tension and drama into his performance.

By the time of the Civil Rights Act, James Brown was already a millionaire. He showcased his foot slide at the *T.A.M.I* show, a slide Jackson would emulate and perfect from youth. The release of "Papa's Got A Brand New Bag" in 1965 signaled the birth of funk, born out of Brown's love of live performance and albums of live recordings.[37] Jackson, conversely, would bring his songs from the studio to the stage and rework them, perfecting songs for years until he felt they were ready. Another musical parallel between Jackson and Brown is the passion they both had for syncopated rhythms and drums. Composer Rod Temperton, who wrote a series of songs for Jackson for *Off the Wall*, would later say that he knew Jackson required a staccato rhythm that would enable him to dance and inhabit the song.[38]

Along with his musical success, Brown also had his demons. He was known as a tyrant. He set the bar high for his band and his backing singers. They were never, under any circumstances, allowed to mess up; they were required to keep a strict regime of clothing; they had to be beautifully turned out every time; and he was very particular about stage decorum, pride, and black empowerment. He was to be called "Mr." at all times, in order to set an example, and, like Jackson, he saw himself as both a business and a show. Brown, watching the likes of Berry Gordy, who founded Motown Records, wanted to be like that. However, his business ventures, like many of Jackson's, had mixed success. He had a particularly successful touring career, but it was tempered by the fact that he had occasional issues with the IRS in America for failing to pay his taxes. Also parallel to Jackson, Brown began to be far more popular out of America than he was within it in the early 1970s, and this had much to do with his support of Richard Nixon in the 1972 elections.[39]

Brown's career, one could argue, had fallen into a slow decline in the years that followed. However, he did leave an undeniable mark on the music world. He continued to work and perform on stage into his later life, attending events and reveling in his status as a national icon. He made cameo appearances in a series of films, also. However, like Jackson post-1995, Brown would never again reach the lofty heights of the 1960s. The negative effects on his career of his political leanings may well be why Jackson never sided with any specific political party. In a 1983 concert at the Beverly Theater in Los Angeles with legendary blues man B.B. King, during which Brown introduced a 25-year-old Jackson, hot on the heels of his *Thriller* success, to join him onstage, Brown said, "I have a surprise for ya, a young man I watched grow and grow . . . he's very quiet and very humble and very meek and just full of talent it's running out of his ears."[40] Brown then beckoned Jackson up onto the stage for a brief and stunning performance. The delight on both Brown's and Jackson's faces is palpable as Jackson performs a slide, a spin, a moonwalk, and then embraces Brown. Twenty years later in 2003, Jackson presented Brown with a BET (Black Entertainment Television) Lifetime Achievement Award, saying, "What is a genius? A genius is one who inspires change . . . no one has influenced me more than this man right here . . . since I was a child, six years old, he was the one I looked up to more than any entertainer and I still do today."[41] Brown died in 2006 at the age of 73, and Jackson attended his funeral.

DAVID BOWIE (1948–2016)

David Bowie, born David Jones in Brixton, England, in 1948, had a reputation as a fighter from a young age. In 1962 one of his fights left him with a permanently dilated pupil. Bowie started playing in bands from an early age, forming his first at just 15.[42] However, it was following his first album release in 1968 that Bowie became immersed in drama and performance, which would lead to his forming his dramatic persona Ziggy Stardust. A key parallel with Bowie is that Jackson had a penchant for the theatrical, for heavy makeup, and an androgynous style.[43] However, a key difference between the two was that despite several claims about his homosexuality, Bowie clearly had sexual relationships with women, emphasized by his rock-star lifestyle and marriage to Angela Barnett in 1969.[44] However, Bowie continued to dress and present himself along a very fine line of gender identification.

Bowie produced albums far more prolifically than Jackson did, and the fact that he was British, and not American, may well have helped him to be understood and welcomed in critical circles. Furthermore, the fact that Bowie was not, like Jackson and Mozart, a child prodigy, gave him more freedom to change his appearance and his presentations of self to his audiences. He would wear a range of different personas during his career, from Ziggy Stardust, the Alien from Mars, to the Thin White Duke, famously dictating fashionable style and clothing in his own way.[45] By the 1980s, when Jackson was at the very height of his success, Bowie was entering the New Wave phase of his career and also branching into popular music with hits like "Let's Dance." Guitarist Nile Rodgers, who played on "Let's Dance," also performed on Jackson's *HIStory* album in 1995.[46]

Both Jackson and Bowie purported a style of smooth, frail fragility; and as Jackson's skin was whitened by vitiligo, he leaned more toward Bowie's striking but delicate makeup and cosmetic style. Bowie's rate of musical output was prolific, and he released no fewer than 25 studio albums, the last of which, *Blackstar*, was released just two days before his death.[47] Bowie also starred in a number of films, including *Basquiat*, *The Last Temptation of Christ*, and the most famous, *Labyrinth*.[48] In so doing, he made himself incredibly iconic. Bowie has been (and quite rightly so) the subject of exhibitions, such as the recent one at the Victoria and Albert Museum in London.[49] However, where he did not rival Jackson was in unanimity and in global domination, and, of course, in record sales. Nevertheless, Bowie achieved *artistic* recognition in a way that Jackson has yet to do.

STEVIE WONDER (1950–)

Stevie Wonder, born Stevland Hardaway Morris, is our final horcrux in this chapter and, of course, the only living artist in this chapter. Wonder is, in effect, a conclusion to this chapter, because he so closely parallels Jackson. Born just eight years apart, they are parallel in terms of child stardom, ethnicity, and musical achievements. Born in 1950, Wonder's premature birth resulted in his loss of eyesight, and at a young age his father left the family; thus, Wonder was brought up predominantly by his mother, with whom he had a very close relationship.[50]

Wonder was discovered as a young boy, playing his harmonica on the streets of Detroit, and he was soon signed up to Motown Records as Little Stevie

Wonder, because he had a talent that could only be described as wonderful. The tracks from *The Jazz Soul of Little Stevie*, his first album, show the unbridled talent of a young boy, who easily matches Jackson's ability to express joy through music and the sheer exuberance of his voice. Wonder released albums year after year and became one of the biggest stars in the world. A key parallel in Wonder's youth to that of Jackson is of being a working professional. However, Wonder always had his mother close for support. Jackson was chaperoned by his father. Wonder and Jackson toured and achieved hit singles in their youth and had to transition from cherubic boys, with talents that far surpassed their years, into solo adult musicians. In addition, both artists struggled with Motown boss Berry Gordy for self-control and for autonomy. While Jackson eventually chose to leave Motown altogether, Wonder took a very different route and chose to produce his work independently, for a time. The albums in question are *Music of My Mind* and *Talking Book*, which, unlike Motown's usual pop crossover sound, took listeners on journeys through auditory landscapes. Wonder's music explored mature themes, such as existentialism. Of this time, Jackson wrote, "Though Stevie [Wonder] and Marvin [Gaye] were still in the Motown camp, they had fought for—and won—the right to make their own songs."[51] Jackson was also at Motown, just 14 years old, and he was invited along to see Wonder at work in the studio. This invaluable experience profoundly affected the way that Jackson produced and recorded music, and it certainly challenged how Jackson used sound. Jackson would often go on to regard Wonder unequivocally as a "musical prophet" and "genius."

Wonder's music expanded the limits of popular music production, and he also appealed, like Jackson, across ethnicities and cultures, achieving worldwide success and an almost panoramic appeal. The artistic flourishing in the 1970s increased commercial success in the early 1980s, and Wonder also collaborated with Paul McCartney on the hit "Ebony and Ivory." Wonder, like Jackson, is also well known for his political activism; he campaigned for the offical designation of "Martin Luther King, Jr. Day" for several years, lending his name and voice to the outcry for civil rights for African Americans. Jackson and Wonder would also duet on the *Bad* album, on the track "Just Good Friends," where they play love rivals for the same girl.[52]

Wonder and Jackson remained friends for Jackson's entire life, and, at several times throughout Wonder's career, he was the single voice to stand up for him and show the respect that he felt Jackson should be accorded for his contribution to music (especially with regard to the 1993 allegations), and to speak to the unfortunate portrayal of Jackson by Eminem in the music video for "Just Lose It."[53] However, the most poignant moment in Jackson and Wonder's crossing was perhaps at Jackson's funeral in 2009, where Wonder played two songs, "They Won't Go" and "I Never Dreamed You'd Leave in

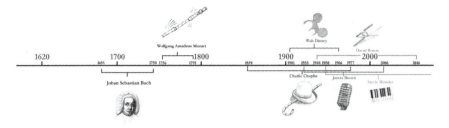

Figure 15.2
A Timeline Showing Michael Jackson's Life in Relation to Seven Artists.
(Artwork by Karin Merx)

Summer," evocative of Elton John's playing "Candle in the Wind" for Princess Diana in 1997. And also evocative of a deeply haunting refrain: that Jackson was vulnerable and innocent, that his childlike sense of wonder and imagination left him open to attack. Wonder's heartfelt renditions of these songs were a moment of true outpouring of affection for his friend.[54] Wonder continues to record music and perform, to this day, to sold-out shows. He is widely respected and known; however, what he lacks, like Jackson, is academic and authorial attention that much of his white counterparts have received. Nonetheless, Wonder lays claim to an astonishing back catalogue of unparalleled hits.

This chapter was written to model the ways in which Jackson, his reception, and his presentation are complex subjects—especially in a posthumous context. Jackson's fame was unprecedented. Whereas David Bowie could walk the average street, Jackson grew to become a prisoner of his own fame. We often underestimate the magnitude of Jackson's fame and how much this level of fame skewed the presentation of the artist. It's also true that there was very little that was normal or average about Jackson's existence, and similarly, academics may find it very useful to use new metaphors and analogies to discuss him, especially in terms of the magnitude of his personas and the depth of his brand. In terms of Jackson's philanthropy and artistry, it is a real wonder that he still managed to produce such a range of successful albums and short films. It is confusing that Jackson seems more alive now than he seemed in the last 10 years of his life, and this further reiterates the power of his legacy. Although Jackson was denied any semblance of a normal life, he still showed tremendous wisdom and a desire to learn and grow. We are now taking the time to reassess the meteor that struck our collective consciousness and to deal with the sheer size and scale of the shadow Jackson cast.[55] In this reassessment, we draw parallels between Jackson and a great number of artists through our history, which can be of great value to help us understand how Michael Jackson signifies for us now and how he will continue to signify for us.

CHAPTER 16

"Through the Looking Glass": Notes on Michael Jackson and Andy Warhol

This chapter is an extension of Chapter 15—"Horcruxes: Michael (Split Seven Ways) Jackson," in which I encourage a holistic interpretation of Jackson by using the biographies of other artists as horcruxes through which to view him. The many connections between Jackson and Andy Warhol, however, warranted a chapter of their own. There is so much to be reconstructed and reconsidered, and this can only be considered by way of elevation, rather than dismissal. This chapter seeks to further engage those who wish to embrace Jackson into the annals of music and artistic history.

> "If I'm going to sit and watch the same thing I saw the night before, I don't want it to be essentially the same—I want it to be *exactly* the same. Because the more you look at the same exact thing, the more the meaning goes away, and the better and emptier you feel."
>
> —Andy Warhol[1]

When reading *The Andy Warhol Diaries*, it does come as a surprise that two artists who so closely resemble one another had paths that would only cross superficially. Both had close relationships with their mothers, both suffered from skin disorders and depigmentation, both sought cosmetic surgery, and both were sexually ambiguous. This chapter goes beyond the superficial similarities between Jackson and Warhol, however, and seeks to consider the meta-narrative surrounding the two and their creations.

Andy Warhol, born Andy Warhola in 1928, started his early career as an illustrator. He doubtless preferred the commercial side of his industry, and this was evident in the way he became a window dresser—he predominantly preferred the democratic nature of the display, and the fact that everyone could see it, no matter who they were or whether they could afford what lay beyond the glass wall. This glass wall, also a reflective surface, mirroring society back to itself, is often known as popular culture. Warhol and Jackson were clearly enthusiasts of popular culture (often called "low culture"), and this was exhibited through their use of media that all could access.

Willa Stillwater discusses Warhol and Jackson's connection in her book *M Poetica*, highlighting primarily the ways in which Jackson is aware of the meta-narrative between the two artists.[2] What is particularly interesting here is the way that Jackson similarly uses the democratic medium of the short film, effectively turning the television into a shop window for his audience. The glass of the television screen becomes a window into another world, and in the short film for his 1995 hit single "Scream," there is a sequence in which Jackson morphs into Warhol, Jackson Pollock, and René Magritte.[3] Stillwater asserts that "the juxtaposition of Jackson and Warhol lasts only a second, yet the effect is uncanny . . . multiple reflections in that one moment: Jackson stares at Warhol, then Warhol stares back . . . we see Warhol mirrored in Jackson's expression."[4]

In addition to his democratic placement of his work on the "looking glass" of the television screen, in one form of mass entertainment, Jackson also put his music onto records, or whatever was the most widely available listening medium of his time. This grew to include compact discs and digital media. Despite believing that their work was of great artistic value, Jackson and Warhol redressed the imbalance of access to art—no longer limiting it to the special few with the educational backgrounds and other means to access their work. This democratization of culture warrants academic interest and further discussion. It is an argument about high and low culture, also posed by Pierre Bourdieu, that resurfaces time and again.[5]

The work of both Jackson and Warhol was deemed at certain times to be derivative in style, and the arguments that Warhol was "faintly perverse" in his first attempt to cross over, could also be applied to Jackson with regard to his work post-*Thriller*. Warhol and Jackson both suffered highly negative reactions to criticism of their work; for example, for Warhol, the John Butler drawings exhibition was panned. Fairfield Porter argued that Warhol was commercial and that his work should not be hung on walls and viewed as fine art.[6]

By 1960 Warhol was painting existing, printed advertisements, merging the tropes of fine art and graphic design. He would also incorporate cartoons and superheroes, of which Jackson was similarly enamored. The rumor that Michael Jackson nearly bought Marvel is well documented.[7] For Warhol, he particularly found it difficult to become as respected as the abstract expressionists, Jackson Pollock and William De Kooning, who despised popular culture and deemed it inferior. For their commerciality and eventual popularity, Warhol and Jackson were despised for embodying success and commerciality.

Furthermore, these abstract expressionists defined painting as the "tortured male psyche splattering and struggling to a higher ground." It certainly was not for the queer, not for gays, blacks, or any other ethnic minority. These macho men were often homophobic and dominant, and there was a great contempt for commerciality in general.[8] However, this attitude did not stop Warhol's Pop art from becoming an unequivocal success, in both the United States and Europe. Warhol was extremely concerned with the power of the image and what was mass-produced. In a similar way, Jackson used his music to present works that were both artistically durable and available to all. Jackson wished to further democratize the production and reception of his work, by not limiting it to a specific genre of music, instead making his work stretch to encompass as many as possible genres as possible. Hence the use of rock solos and orchestras, of a range of film and music genres in his work, and more important, a range of classical influences in his style.

Often Warhol's work was very connected to his childhood self—for example, with regard to the *Campbell's Soup Can* painting.[9] Warhol's mother often served him this soup, so the image of it in his mind was related to a mother's love and nourishment.[10] Jackson's *Thriller* also became a type of soup can, and very much so to working-class America,. It would sell as a staple of the home, like a pot or an oven, rather than in the way expected for a luxury item. It was as though every home would need to have one. What happened through this process, quite unexpectedly, was that Jackson's image, attached as packaging to his widely sold albums, triggered his ensuing immateriality. Jackson began to exist in so many ways that he barely seemed to exist at all. For him to be physically present anywhere, it was as though he had stepped off the album sleeve, out of the television, and into the world.

Jeremy Gilbert asserts, "there was an irrevocable split between Michael Jackson and 'Michael Jackson' that I was responding to . . . there is at least some limit to the number of times we can see [an] image reproduced on a daily or local basis . . . before that person actually loses the quality of being real."[11] At some point during the success of *Thriller* and subsequent releases, through the superdemocratization of his work, his short films, albums, and singles, Jackson stopped being a living, breathing artist and became a fully fledged product, a facsimile of a person, that could be reproduced at will. Is it any wonder that his literal, physical appearance garnered so much hysteria, shock, and excitement, considering how different his physical appearance was from his virtual appearance in songs and short films? Jackson effectively took Warhol's model of making the mass-produced items of everyday consumption, a Coca-Cola bottle and a soup can, into pieces of art, and turned himself into an eternally reproducible product, until "there were no longer real objects and representations of objects: there were only simulacra."[12]

Many more comparisons have been made between Jackson and Warhol, such as the fact that they became products themselves, integral to the selling of what they created. It is with this understanding that both artists reinvented themselves. They both realized that they would have to create personalities that the media would find intriguing and alluring. Jackson would soon be known for carrying around Bubbles, his pet chimp, on tours, being very softly spoken, and hiding behind large sunglasses and face mask, as much as for his music. However, unlike Jackson, Warhol, never did seem to tire of the press attention.

In the creations of their personas, Jackson and Warhol both took what could be described as their worst qualities and made out of these things an image of both interest and intrigue. Jackson even included the Peter Pan syndrome into his public persona, and he was often regarded as an eternal child, filled with boundless creativity and imagination. These things made Jackson accessible and endearing, particularly in the early part of his adult solo career. Both Warhol and Jackson were very much aware of not only *what* they wanted their audience to see in terms of artistic works, but also of *how* they desired their audience to see them.[13]

Further parallels that exist between Jackson and Warhol pertain not only to the superficial, such as their wearing of wigs, but also to the deeply philosophical, the ways that their creative works would always engender questioning and searching from the viewer. They would experiment further with their asexual personas, and Jackson's made him seem more of a child than a mature adult, while Warhol became simply an observer of sexual behavior; he would be Andy the Android or Andy the Alien. While Warhol seemed obsessed by sex without actually wanting to have sex, "Jackson seemed (up until the *Dangerous* era, at least) to be completely outside of sexuality, performing a carefully choreographed mime of sexuality in songs and short films, and then carefully counterpointing those images with scenes of games of tag and trips to Disneyland.[14]

Both Jackson and Warhol particularly enjoyed the use of religious iconography and spread it liberally throughout their art. It was the glamour aspect of celebrity combined with the devotional aspect, in a symbiosis that both Jackson and Warhol were aware of, and which was particularly American in nature. It was as if America had transferred all of its religious fixations onto its celebrities. "Heroine and heroin," referring to Marilyn Monroe, is a line in Jackson's 1995 track "Tabloid Junkie." It was the American obsession with the all-American beauty, as the all-American suicide spoke to Jackson and Warhol in deep ways. Jackson was ultra-aware that there were so many Jacksons, much in the same way that there were so many soup cans. There was only one physical Michael Jackson, and he was the only one who could be killed. In his Factory, where much of Warhol's art was produced, he would employ a production-line model, reminiscent of the studio system in classic Holly-wood cinema in its golden age.[15] In 1984 Jackson famously became a subject of Warhol's when *Time* magazine commissioned a portrait of him for its cover. This piece of art marks another look into the window for both Jackson and Warhol. Warhol's diaries chart his experience of Jackson over the years, see-ing *The Wiz* in 1979 and thinking "they made Michael Jackson ugly," and later writing, "we got there right as Michael Jackson was getting an award in the center hallway. And he talked and talked, it was a new personality," and "Michael's gotten so handsome since I saw him."[16] Through the diaries we see Jackson lurking in Warhol's periphery, and as he becomes more beautiful in Warhol's eyes, they gravitate toward one another. The famed *Time* por-trait almost never was, as Warhol writes on February 29, 1984: "they dropped the Michael cover," and then on March 1, the "cover was back on." On March 6 Warhol "worked on the Michael Jackson *Time* cover until 8:00" and by March 7 it was finished. His verdict: "I didn't like it but all the office kids did . . . the *Time* people came down to see it . . . stood around saying it should increase newsstand sales."[17]

Whereas Jackson would use the recording studio, Warhol would use his Factory. However, both would maintain the roles of overseer, closely watch-ing every single movement in their locales. Jackson even went as far as to include mechanical-sounding grooves in his later works, especially on *Dan-gerous*.[18] Jackson made imperfections an intrinsic part of this mechanized, industrial process, introducing hiccups in his recordings, staggered intakes of breath on his vocal tracks, and unpredictable whoops and cries, all of which would make his music uniquely his (see Chapter 7—" 'Instrument of Nature': The Voice of Michael Jackson"). Like Jackson, Warhol worked within mutable areas, also known as liminal spaces, between what could be defined as high art and what could be defined as low art. They each would do this in terms of form, too. For Warhol, this was predominantly between painting and pho-tography, and for Jackson this was predominantly between the production and performance of popular music and dance. However, what's true is that in regard to both artists, it is quite impossible to be truly dispassionate about them or encounter their work without thinking. In 1984 Warhol writes about a brief encounter with Jackson, "before his concert at Madison Square Gar-den," and describes him as "an apparition." By 1986, there is a change in tone in Warhol's writing: "Michael is in town again and he's wearing a brown wig and dark glasses, and a white gas mask, so if you see that coming down the street . . . ."[19]

In 1987, Warhol died quite suddenly during a routine operation, leaving a vast estate of unfinished business. Jackson, who was 30 years younger, died 22 years later, also quite suddenly. The two artists left behind a body of work that still encourages thought to this day.

In November 1986 there was an arranged meeting between Jackson and Warhol, but it was not meant to be: "by the way, Michael Jackson never did show up, he called and cancelled right before he was supposed to be there."[20] A romantic notion sees the two as mirrors of one another, on either side of a looking glass, not quite able to see each other fully, but nevertheless tied by reflections of their own making.

CHAPTER 17

Invincible: Michael Jackson's Lost Late Album

Michael Jackson's last studio album, *Invincible*, has a new resonance as Jackson's final fully realized work. It exchanges the simplicity of its creator's earlier works for a more complex and unapologetic vision. This chapter seeks to demystify the dominant reading of Jackson as a deteriorating artist, as part of a general ideology relating to lateness as a period of decline. A child star at 13, after 30 years in the industry he was seen by many to be in the later stages of his career. This chapter reconsiders *Invincible* as Jackson's lost album, with regard to the context of its initial production, and with regard to the assumed proximity to death of the work; its reception, and "Jacksonmania" as a dying religion; the album as a denouement in Jackson's career; and finally, the album as an example of general late style.

> "The attribution to late style of the status of a kind of apotheosis, an almost mythical seal attached to the life of a genius, and readings and appropriations of the late plays continue to provide instances . . . of the persistence of lateness as a controlling concept . . ."
>
> —Gordon McMullan[1]

CONTEXTS OF PRODUCTION AND PROXIMITY TO DEATH

Throughout his career, a certain level of invincibility had served Michael Jackson well, especially in his dealings with the "dishonest custodian of black wealth." Many of his artistic/financial gambles paid off: the *Thriller* short film (costing $1.2 million in 1983), his no-holds-barred Oprah Winfrey interview, and purchase of the Beatles/ATV catalogue were great achievements. Still, there were some misadventures: *Living with Michael Jackson* (dir. Martin Bashir, 2003) could have been elucidating, rather than implicating, while a revolving door of lawyers, representatives, sycophants, and shady doctors circled Jackson from 1994 to 2009.[2] Yet, the fact that *Invincible* was released just after 9/11 was inauspicious. His sold-out anniversary celebrations in Madison Square Gardens (which hosted an electric reunion of the Jacksons) were overshadowed.[3]

The title *Invincible* was not meant to be boastful; it referred primarily to the longevity of Jackson's image: "I'm resilient. I have rhinoceros skin. Nothing can hurt me. Nothing." Again, in his words, "no force of nature can shake your will to self-motivate."[4] However, it was Jackson's representation that was "invincible," not the artist himself (as discussed in Chapter 16—"'Through the Looking Glass': Notes on Michael Jackson and Andy Warhol"). Ever since the *Bad* album, Jackson had realized the need for a powerful opening statement with every new artistic effort. Hence, 1987's *Bad* was prefigured by a gritty urban short film that shouted down his detractors, 1991's *Dangerous* was heralded by an antiracism slogan, *Black or White* (dir. John Landis) contained a controversial panther dance sequence, 1995's *HIStory* was heralded by *Scream*, a futuristic vision of Jackson and his sister as celebrities-in-arms. Even 1997's *Blood on the Dance Floor* was accompanied by arguably Jackson's greatest cinematic work, *Ghosts*, a 40-minute extravaganza in which the artist exploded with brand-new dance moves that challenged all notions of what he was capable of.[5]

Invincible was designed to be the final, complete piece in Jackson's musical canon, and what it lacked in initial commercial success it made up for in sheer inventiveness. It fully embraced Jackson's unique brand of sonic sculpture, the process by which he crafted "found" sounds into musical images and narratives. The track "Unbreakable" employs the sound of smashing glass, an experimental trope that also features in "Scream," while the track "Privacy" includes the dissonant whir of a camera, the accompaniment to Jackson's public life.[6]

It is also a little-known fact that *Invincible* could have been called *Unbreakable*, and likewise, "Unbreakable," the title track, was Jackson's first choice for the first single. It would have certainly made a bigger impact. Jackson's intention for his first single in eight years, from an entirely new album, was to be a statement of his strength. Jackson planned for *Invincible* a visual feast to accompany his new sound:

> Michael wanted to release the song "Unbreakable" as the first single, and was eager to make a video for it . . . Michael even knew exactly how he wanted to open the "Unbreakable" short film. He would be on the roof of a very tall

building that was under construction, held over the edge by some thugs, and then they would let him go. He would go hurtling to the ground, seemingly dead, but slowly, his body parts would come together and he would turn into fire—dancing on fire from scaffold to scaffold as his body parts reassembled themselves. Michael envisioned creating a dance for "Unbreakable" that people would remember forever.[7]

At its core, *Invincible* represents Jackson's love for his own children ("The Lost Children," "Speechless," "You Are My Life"), antipathy for the celebrity culture that made his life unbearable ("Privacy"), his longevity ("Unbreakable" and "Threatened"), drama and musicality ("Whatever Happens," "Invincible," "Heartbreaker"), music ("2000 Watts") faith ("Cry"), and of course, love ("Break of Dawn," "Don't Walk Away," "Butterflies," "Heaven Can Wait," "You Rock My World").[8]

Perhaps one of the reasons why *Invincible*'s reception soon floundered was that the album was not simply designed to "bag it" and "sell it." *Invincible* is an album that flatly refuses to pander to critics. In Jackson's words, he simply "wrote from his heart." The track "You Are My Life" is a love letter to his children: "you brought me back to life," as is "Speechless": "I am in the light where I cannot be found."[9] The fact that these songs made it onto the finished album did not mean Jackson did not have more radio-friendly tracks up his sleeve. A "dance-hit"–worthy version of "Escape" was already mixed, while "Shout" and "Slave to the Rhythm" might also have become hits.[10] *Invincible* was poised to divide opinion. It was the crowning glory of a career cake, a career that consisted mostly of *Thriller* tiers.

Jackson's music did not sound like anyone else's because Jackson didn't make music like anyone else did: "a perfectionist has to take his time; he shapes and he molds." He could hear sounds that others couldn't and pick up on nuances that others didn't know were there. He could be infuriating in his repeat takes. He would also remember which takes were the best.[11] In the song "Crack Music," Kanye West describes creating music: "sometimes I feel the music is the only medicine . . . we cook it, cut it, measure it, bag it, sell it . . . Put the CD on your tongue." Mark Fisher, writing about "Billie Jean," puts it another way: "let it play, and you're soon bewitched by its drama, seduced into its sonic fictional space . . . Listening is like stepping onto a conveyor belt."[12] It is also addictive: "you can't escape, you're ripped by the voice's current. And it won't stop 'til you've got enough." It is likely that Jackson had synesthesia: "he told me he views music like how I view music—in shapes and colors," and kinesthesia: "it happens subliminally. When you're dancing, you know you are just interpreting the music and the sounds and the accompaniment. If there's a driving base, if there's a cello, if there's a string, you become the emotion of what that sound is . . . I'm a slave to the rhythm." He was also as much a talented singer, dancer, and composer as he was a sketch artist. Art was his intoxicant and his release.[13]

Music had changed since 1979, 1982, 1987, 1991, 1995, and finally 1997 (the dates of Jackson's key musical releases), but 1997 to 2001 was the biggest divide Jackson would ever have to cross. The rapid digitization of music heralded by Napster was transforming the industry, while the short films Jackson pioneered had already become templates for generations of artists. The popular music videos that trailed Jackson's faded into one another and lacked real innovation. Some had nostalgia value like Britney Spears' *Oops I Did It Again*, others had artistic merit like Madonna's *Vogue* and Sinead O'Connor's *Nothing Compares to You*, but rarely did a music video touch the brilliance of Michael Jackson's *Smooth Criminal, Remember the Time*, or *Black or White*.[14]

In 1982, Jackson predicted that the follow-up to his first adult solo studio album, *Off The Wall*, would be the biggest-selling record ever. Few believed him, even in light of the fact that he already had the biggest-selling album ever by a black artist. (*Thriller* is still the biggest-selling record in history.)[15] There is also great irony in the fact that America, a country with such a controversial racial heritage, embodied by its proliferation of minstrelsy, would engage in discourses that presented, as also ill-fated, Jackson's physical skin change from black to white.[16] On receiving the news of Princess Diana's death in 1997, Jackson said, "there's another one . . . I pray it's not me. Please don't let it be me."[17] According to Jackson's first wife, Lisa-Marie Presley, Jackson predicted that he would die a sudden and tragic death:

> Years ago Michael and I were having a deep conversation . . . he may have been questioning me about the circumstances of my Father's Death. At some point he paused, he stared at me very intensely and he stated with an almost calm certainty, 'I am afraid that I am going to end up like him, the way he did'.[18]

According to another account, Jackson even predicted exactly how his life would end:

> So many times Michael had told me that he would die from a shot. That was always the word he used, and whenever he said it, I inevitably thought of a gunshot, but in the end he was killed by a different kind of shot.[19]

Jackson's predictions certainly conjure the racist archetype of the "Magical Negro," which "suggests black excellence is so shocking it can only come from a source that is supernatural." However, taking into account that Jackson was "litmus paper," "always trying to learn," and "so intelligent," and that even in his last years he bought an entire bookshop worth of antique books so he could "just go in there and get lost and find interesting things to read," we see a startling connection to the concept of late works.[20] This is what McMullan terms the "proximity to death." Whether this proximity is imagined or real, it certainly influences the artist's creative works. Now, I am not claiming by any means that Jackson was psychic, but if one constantly considers the impending nature of one's death, it stands to reason that it will filter into the work produced.

Jackson was also particularly concerned with his own biography, and he read those of other celebrities prolifically: "I love experienced people. I love people who are phenomenally talented. I love people who've worked so hard and been so courageous and are the leaders in their fields. For me to meet somebody like that and learn from them and share words with them—to me that's magic."[21] Jackson's later works, *HIStory: Past, Present and Future, Book 1* and *Invincible*, hint at Jackson's conviction that his death would be untimely: "why do you go through so much . . . so you can **bury** me," "**Assassinate** and mutilate . . . the hounding media in hysteria."[22] It stands to reason, therefore, that Jackson saw most of his adult life as a necessary process of self-immortalization, "since we are given the gift of life it should be a persistent endeavor to immortalize ourselves."[23]

MICHAEL JACKSON AS DECLINING RELIGION

For many, secularism has replaced religion, and one could argue that musicians, actors, models, and rock stars are the new gods, while chart hits are the new hymns, and concerts the only places for spiritual release. In this "soulless generation," for whom the old gods were no longer relevant, Jackson was Zeus in the pantheon of mortal gods. He was the "biggest and, occasionally, the best, and always the best at being the biggest."[24] Jackson's music created devotees who dressed like and imitated their leader. They demarcated his life and death with tattoos and celebrated him in their homes with albums, posters, and ephemera. If Jackson were a religion, then, like many religions, his mass popularity waned as he was adopted globally, and his inevitable backlash produced an increasingly more devout and outspoken following. His core fan base remained healthy no matter what happened in his career, and as a result, 1995 was one of his most successful years financially.[25]

DENOUEMENT OR UNRAVELLING

The denouement is defined as an "unravelling'"(*OED*). *Invincible* is certainly underrated, and this is because it marks a denouement in Jackson's career, just as *The Tempest* can be said to mark a denouement in Shakespeare's. The denouement marks a turning point before the resolution of a narrative. Both Jackson and Shakespeare were commercially successful artists whose work was produced predominantly for a mass audience, and it is on the stage that Jackson and Shakespeare meet. The pivotal works for which both artists were most celebrated are *Off The Wall* and *Thriller*, and *Hamlet* and *Romeo & Juliet*. By the time these works were performed, the artists had already gained iconic status, and this meant that audiences knew exactly what to expect. However, *The Tempest* and *Invincible* forced audiences to reassess what they thought they knew.

Only in the context of Shakespeare's canon can *The Tempest* truly be celebrated and understood, and the same is true for *Invincible*. *The Tempest*, with its implicit criticism of colonization, continues Shakespeare's revolutionary approach (for example, where he cast Othello, a black general, as a tragic hero in 1603, at the height of the slave trade, the same year that Elizabeth I proclaimed all negroes be deported from London).[26] Shakespeare was far ahead of his time in his sensitive reading of ethnicity and gender. As an indicator of *The Tempest*'s modest success, it was never published in Shakespeare's lifetime, and only saw print in 1623 as part of the First Folio. If it were not for the Folio's publication, it may well have become one of Shakespeare's lost plays.[27]

What is an artist at the denouement, the unraveling point of their career? What will he be without the art that has so heavily defined him? As in Shakespeare's *The Tempest*, imprisonment, alienation, and entrapment are key themes. By several accounts, and indicated in his own music and words, Jackson thought he was being hounded and chased. And he was. He had been chased by crowds of adoring fans, by hysterical followers in droves, all the way up to *Invincible*'s release. *Remember the Time: Protecting Michael Jackson in His Final Days*, a biography by Jackson's bodyguards, confirmed that even in later life, Jackson's presence could still turn a leafy suburb into a mob in a few minutes. Paparazzi would stop at nothing for his picture, hiding in bushes, and also hiding cameras in toilets, to the point where Jackson's paranoia became a necessary self-defense mechanism. In the age of newly arrived smartphones and digital cameras, the value of Jackson's image had been heightened by his elusiveness. *The Tempest* also hosts characters who wander in circles, unable to escape or find one another, while the strings of their existence are being played by an unseen and malevolent force: "space enough have I in such a prison."[28]

Shakespeare's *The Tempest* is a long play. In an unabridged performance, it often drags, overstuffed with comical scenes, while its premise takes a good deal of time to find resolution. However, it remains one of Shakespeare's most iconic and quoted works, for example: "the isle is full of noises," "we are such stuff as dreams are made on," "I cried to dream again." From the drowning of magical books to a haven of heavenly music, from Caliban's unlawful entrapment to Ariel's forced servitude, *The Tempest* is a play written as much for its author as for its audience.[29]

Even after the decimation of Jackson's public image, he still sold out 50 concerts at London's O2 Arena four years later: "bury me underneath all your pain . . . steady laughin' while surfacing." It proved that his appeal had not diminished, as the mainstream press had purported. Jackson could have easily filled the arena for 100 dates had he had wanted to.[30] After Jackson's death in 2009, his record sales flourished as though his music were newly released ("I'm untouchable"). Many of the lyrics in the *Invincible* album are declarations of strength tempered with disaffection, but ultimately, Jackson's prediction was correct: False accusation, misrepresentation, not even the grave, could stop his star from shining.[31]

Invincible was *Off the Wall* without the wide-eyed optimism, *Thriller* without Quincy Jones, and Jackson's hitherto unseen libidinal dance of dramatic staccato rhythms. It was *Bad* without the record-breaking tour, *Dangerous* without the series of short films, and *HIStory* without statues floating down the Thames. In terms of academia, if *Thriller* was Michael Jackson's graduation, top of his class, then *Bad* and *Dangerous* were his Master's and *HIStory* and *Blood on the Dance Floor* his PhD. To demonstrate his genuine artistry, Jackson did not need to make *Invincible*. There was nothing left for him to prove. In the words of Berry Gordy, "he raised the bar then he broke the bar."[32]

So what were Jackson's artistic motivations for creating *Invincible*? *Invincible* was Jackson's attempt to craft his own musical world, while his multiple personas sped ahead of him: his monster persona was more hideous than ever, his idol persona more superlative, and his wacko persona even more estranged, and it was harder for his audience to relate to him than it had ever been.[33] He was well aware of this fact—that most could no longer see him behind the smoke screen of his misrepresentation. *Invincible* was Jackson's attempt to finally present the public with himself. *Invincible* was the $21 million product that had to please fans from all generations. Having spent so much on production, Sony no longer supported his ideas for short films to promote the project, and Jackson could not physically commit to a world tour. Now in his 40s, and having danced professionally for the better part of 30 years, he knew his body could no longer take the rigorous toll of all those rehearsals, flights, and performances.

Invincible may well be the least known of all Jackson's solo albums, and therein lies one of the biggest tragedies of his artistic life, that such an album, much like his book of poetry, *Dancing the Dream*, could go by relatively unnoticed for such a long time. The online campaign "MJSInvincible" was integral to making the album No. 1 for its 10th anniversary, and the events of 2009 gave it brand-new significance.[34]

It is sensitive to read *Invincible* in a context that is aware of the shadow cast by preceding works: *Thriller* was mostly instinct, made in mere months, and it took nowhere near the phenomenal effort that would go into *Bad* and the exponential growth of effort that Jackson put into subsequent works—especially in terms of expense, studio time, and perfectionism. He created *Invincible* after a lifetime in the gilded prison that his success had built for him, but the album still contains moments of pure joy ("you make me shine," "I felt the magic's all in the air"). Jackson's fame had ensured that he would never be anonymous again ("I need my privacy so paparazzi get away from me").[35] Anonymity, in many ways, is the last bastion of freedom, that unappreciated ability to move through this world without every person we meet knowing what we've accomplished, who we have loved, and what we've been accused of.

In 2011, on the 10th anniversary of *Invincible*'s release, Michael Jackson had been gone for two years. Yet, due to a successful fan campaign, his "little-known" album was No. 1 on the USA Amazon charts. It has sold an estimated 11 million copies, five million more than *Blood on the Dance Floor: HIStory in the Mix*, despite its poor promotion and lack of short films. Biographers of decline, critics, academics, musicologists, and social historians, often do not refer to *Invincible* in specific ways, and even when they do, it's often not at all within its context. *Invincible* has been largely ignored in criticism, and as a result it has become lost. Jackson's later works are often grouped into a collective degeneration. Although *Blood on the Dance Floor* is the biggest-selling remix album of all time and *HIStory* is the biggest-selling double album of all time, little attention is focused on the positive aspects of Jackson's later works. Another key issue with the narrative of decline is that the works that followed *Thriller* wildly differed from it and each other, each successor being more progressive and artistically challenging. It is largely like comparing Mozart's Symphony No. 1 to his Symphony No. 44.

Nevertheless, there was a new album in the works in 2009, another "comeback" album: *Invincible II*, one might hope, rather than *Thriller II*. It would have been a musical experience that showcased 50-year-old Jackson's accumulated learning, rather than 24-year-old Jackson's raw talent. Like Shakespeare's most dismissive critics and staunchest supporters, we will be long dead by the time *Invincible*'s fate is finally decided: "people will not understand this album right now. It's ahead of its time . . . the album will live on forever" because "music is what lives and lasts." Jackson knew that it did not matter how *Invincible*'s tale began, because "what's important is how the story ends."[36]

CHAPTER 18

Michael Jackson's Obituaries and the Shakespearean Tragic Hero

This chapter briefly considers four obituaries, published in the wake of Michael Jackson's death in 2009 and featured in *The New York Times*, *The Guardian*, and *The Daily Telegraph*.[1] It discusses the ways in which these obituaries exemplify how Jackson's biography was reconstructed and appropriated and made to signify for its audience, and it draws parallels with the narratives of Shakespearean tragedies.

> "Jackson's kind of transcendental creativity is typical of very young men; it seldom survives into manhood, when the glory fades into the light of common day."
>
> —Germaine Greer[2]

> "If ever there was an illustration of the adage that celebrity destroys what it touches, Jackson was it."
>
> —Caroline Sullivan[3]

A tragedy is "a form of drama characterized by its serious tone and unhappy ending," whose origins are found in the ancient Greek tradition and plays of Aeschylus, Euripides, and Sophocles.[4] The philosopher Aristotle gave a model for tragic action, including protagonists from high society, such as kings and nobles. In the early modern period playwrights like Shakespeare took on some of Aristotle's tragic rules and dismissed others. However, tragic theater has become part of narrative structures and the general way stories are told. The tragic narrative structure is thus: with its tragic heroes, typified by their hubris, their pride, and their fatal flaw (the one characteristic unable to escape their fate), their moment of fortune reversal, the peripeteia, which causes them to lose all they have gained, followed by their inevitable and swift downfall. The most important part of this dramatic action on the stage, however, is in the creation of catharsis for the viewer, the purging of emotion by way of learning from the hero's experience. Read any number of Jackson's obituaries, and one will find, cobbled together from incoherent fragments and fiction from a wide range of credible and incredible sources, a narrative structure that appears remarkably similar. They teem with tribulation, for example, such phrases as "his bizarre life-style and personal notoriety eclipsed his talent," and self-imposed trials, and "initially minor eccentricities escalated into grotesque changes."[5]

However, no Shakespearean tragedy is complete without an initial sense of equilibrium. According to most of Jackson's obituaries, events start out quite well: "as a solo performer, Mr. Jackson ushered in the age of pop as a global product."[6] Shakespeare's play *Othello*, begins with the eponymous character, Othello, a black general in Venice who is well loved by his wife and well respected by his peers.[7] Likewise, in *Macbeth*, the play begins with Shakespeare's Scottish lord celebrated and decorated.[8] It is this state of equilibrium that is often echoed in dominant narratives about Jackson's life.

The fiction is that somewhere during the success of *Off the Wall* and/or *Thriller*, all was well: "he began to eclipse his work with the Jacksons . . . he also found his form as a songwriter."[9] Jackson was simply living out the success that fate had brought him, and there was absolutely nothing wrong with him, the way he was perceived, or anything at all. As other chapters in this book have discussed, nothing could be further from the truth. Jackson was contending with a range of personal issues by the time of his work on *Off the Wall*, issues that were greatly exacerbated by the success of both that album and the one that followed.

Shakespeare's tragedies were derived mainly from a tragic action model, which required a unity of time, place, and action; these are lynchpins that hold the tragedy together. The primary purpose for a world in equilibrium is so that the protagonist can have their dramatic fall from grace. In the case of Jackson, obituaries mark this very spectacular fall at various moments. *The Telegraph* gives the turning point as the purchase of the Neverland Valley Ranch: "his increasingly strange transformation prompted a media frenzy . . . the more famous Jackson became, the more he retreated into his own world, and the more rumors of his increasingly odd behavior titillated the public."[10]

Brooke Barnes of *The New York Times* agrees: "soon afterward, his career started a bizarre disintegration," and Germaine Greer in *The Guardian* pits Jackson's reversal of fortune as tied intrinsically to his refusal to age: "his imagination faltered and grew dim, the fending off of maturity became desperate, demented and pointless."[11] It is intriguing the way that Greer weaves the ancient narratives of Sophocles' *Theban Plays* into Jackson's tale: "since Dionysos danced ahead of his horde of bloody-footed maenads across the rocky highlands of prehistoric Greece, dance and song have been the province of boys."[12] Nevertheless, all accounts agree that Jackson's most dramatic fall from grace was the accusation of child molestation in 1993 and 2003, "the worst crisis of his personal and professional life to that point."[13]

No Shakespearean tragedy would be complete without the fatal flaw that destroys the protagonist and the hubris that leads them to believe they can challenge the gods. The obituaries all place Jackson's fatal flaw as his desire to act like a child and live in a world of childlike fantasy with children as his close personal friends, even though he was an adult male. Barnes does state, however, that "Jackson was acquitted on all charges."[14] What is often omitted in the retelling is the fact that, despite the aggressive strategies of the prosecution, Jackson was acquitted because the case was groundless. Jackson's fatal flaw here is his naivety, or at least his refusal to fit into the requirements of an adult world that would not allow him to play by his own rules.

Shakespearean tragic action is not simply for the purposes of watching someone fail, but also to teach the audience about their own inner world, and so often we see Jackson being used as a mirror for the world in which he lived—a mirror in which we can see societal attitudes to androgyny, and constructions of race, gender, and "normal" behavior.[15] Jackson's high visibility and his widespread resonance through his music, along with the avid media coverage of him for the major part of his life, gave an unprecedented view, not of who he was, but of the societies and cultures that embraced and rejected him.

The mysterious nature of Jackson's death definitely contributed to the tragic nature of his life story, especially in its retelling by those who wrote some of his most widely read obituaries. These obituaries paint Jackson as a man who, against all odds, rises through the ranks of society to become one of its most influential people, who seemingly has everything—copious money, fame, talent, and beauty—but who squanders it all because of a simple refusal to grow up and play by the rules of an adult world. However, Jackson's story is far more complex than that. It is quite possible to be more than one thing at the same time, and Jackson, although he may have strived for perfection, was flawed, much more in the way of Arthur Miller's tragic character Willy Loman, who dreams of success despite the fact that he is simply a working-class salesman. Miller's characters were often everyday people working through mundane tragic stories.[16] Jackson's story highlights the fact that he was very human.

The dramatic nature of Jackson's death is mostly found in the fact that he died on the advent of a promised comeback, for which several million pounds of tickets had been sold. These factors indicate a resurgence that was cut short and give a sense of a lack of resolution: "annihilated on the brink of a 50-date concert tour . . . to see Michael Jackson faking it would have been heartbreaking."[17] However, Jackson as a tragic hero is also fiction, and much of this fiction is constructed in the retelling of his tale, with a view to helping it make sense to a wider audience. Much in the same way, the tragedies of Shakespeare and, subsequently of Miller, were designed to entertain and provide catharsis for the masses.

There's no telling how much the sudden and unexpected context of Jackson's death contributed to the formation of this narrative. Furthermore, the construction of a story that blurs the lines between reality and fiction is one that coincides beautifully with how Jackson lived and worked in the first place. Nevertheless, the overarching feature is that of the cathartic nature of the story of a great protagonist, a great tragic hero fallen from grace. It is supposed to purge the reader in some way, to give them a sense of cleansing, through which they can find some reason why these actions may have taken place. The attempt to draw Jackson's narrative along the lines of Shakespearean narrative structure is an attempt to neatly fold Jackson up into a simple and understandable box—to say, in effect: He was a hero, he had everything, it was his fate to fall from grace, and fall from grace he did. However, the story of Jackson's life did not simply end there. He was not so easily definable. Even as I was putting the finishing touches to this book, Jackson's Neverland Valley Ranch was still on the market, his music continues to top charts years after his death, and he remains a more lucrative brand than he was in the last 10 years of life. Hence, the story of Michael Jackson is nothing like a Shakespearean tragedy, but that doesn't mean that there isn't much we can learn from it.[18]

CHAPTER 19

Moonwalkers: Michael Jackson's Unique Fandom

As the online documentary *Michael Jackson's Moonwalkers: Then, Now, and Forever* . . . illustrates, Michael Jackson's fandom remains just as unique as he was.[1] It is due to the fact that Jackson's fans are so synonymous with him that critical attention given to them focuses on hysteria and celebrity culture.[2] This chapter seeks to open a critical conversation on Jackson's fan community as a unique subculture, complete with its own rites and sociolect. It engages with the fan community directly, featuring exclusive interviews with individual members who share their stories.

> "Michael Jackson changed the world in so many ways, with his music, with his humanitarian efforts, with his innovative dressing style . . . he had a magic that changed the world."
>
> —Tahkyia Brady, a.k.a R.E.D[3]

Michael Jackson's artistic career and global success have been measured in terms of record sales, sell-out tours, groundbreaking short films, and awards. However, one fundamentally important and relevant way to understand the phenomenon that was—and still is—is through the eyes of those who are life-long devotees to it. "Fandom" is a term commonly used to denote a group of people who are connected by their fanaticism about a particular subject. A fandom can be formed on just about anything. Among the most salient examples of fandom are the "Trekkies" devoted to *Star Trek* or the "Potter-heads" enamored of everything related to Harry Potter. With the surge of social networking and renewed connectivity, "fandoms" are now energized by the power of instant messaging and picture-sharing across continents, and by the ubiquity of related web sites and forums.

The term "moonwalker" is often used for the avid fans of Michael Jackson, This is the name of Jackson's signature dance move, as well as the name of his 1988 anthology film. The name is therefore synonymous with Jackson's creativity, and it implies that his fans are part of a collective, which *moonwalks* together:

> Indeed the more Jackson was attacked in the tabloids, the more devoted his community of fans became; loyalty to the singer in the face of adversity became its own badge of honor. Millions of listeners in dozens of countries formed an elaborate network of clubs and groups, publishing newsletters, trading memorabilia . . . What made the phenomenon of Jackson's fan base unique was not just their devotion to him, but his reciprocal embrace of them . . . he never lost his love for the people who had made him famous. The fans, Jackson believed, not the record execs and the concert promoters, were the ones responsible for his success. He felt personally indebted to each and every one. Their steadfast loyalty was something the singer had rarely experienced in his private life. And because his fans never lost faith in him, Michael Jackson never forgot about them.[4]

To begin to grasp the magnitude of Jackson's fan community, it is important to stress that casual listeners are not included within this category. The term is used for those who have a somewhat religious devotion to the artist: They observe and acknowledge the dates of his birth and death; collect and prize his releases; and include Jackson's iconography as part of their clothing, style, business names, and bodies, in the form of tattoos.[5] In so doing they make Jackson central to the fabric of their lives. Furthermore, moonwalkers embrace pilgrimages to places such as Forest Lawn Cemetery (where Michael Jackson is entombed), and Neverland Valley Ranch (where Jackson lived), leaving mementos as rites of passage (see Figure 19.1). Being a moonwalker has also become intergenerational, with fans encouraging their children to grow up as fans, too.[6]

The interview that follows is from the director of the *Moonwalkers* documentary, Tahkiya Brady.[7]

Interview 1—Tahkiya Brady, a.k.a Red, Moonwalker

Q1—*Can you tell us a little bit about yourself?*
My name is Tahkyia, but most people know me as Red. I am 36 years old and have been living in NYC until recently. I now live in Long Island, NY with my wife and my son Jackson.

Q2—*What inspired you to make your documentary,* Moonwalkers?
I usually feel the need to do something in remembrance of Michael around his anniversary and for his 5th anniversary I thought what better

Figure 19.1
Mementos Left at Michael Jackson's house, 2710 Palomino Drive,
Las Vegas, Nevada.
The Jon B. Lovelace Collection of California Photographs in Carol M. Highsmith's
America Project. (Library of Congress)

way to remember him than to do something for the fans . . . by the fans.
Any documentary I have ever seen on Michael has never been by his
true fans. . . . Moonwalkers. The term Moonwalkers was something I
came across from some of the younger fans and I adapted that as the
name for the project. I wanted to tackle topics such as the allegations
to give our answers. Our point of view. Defend our character as Michael
Jackson supporters while sharing a few facts that the media tends to
leave out.

Q3—*What do you feel is the true mark or meaning of being a moonwalker
and how is this different from what people in the general public might think
of it?*
I think for each Moonwalker that answer is different. For me, I carry
him with me every day. There isn't a person that meets me that doesn't
know what I am. . . . a huge Michael Jackson fan. Spreading his message of hope and love is something that I value and I think it is the most
important part of my duty as a Moonwalker.

Q4—*Do you think there is a place for Michael Jackson in schools and universities, and if yes, what do you think that place is?*

I do think there is a place for him. He was a complex individual with a complete method to his madness. In some ways he was childlike and innocent but in other ways he was powerful and genius. I think it was that balance that made so many people drawn to him in wonder. I would surely take Michael Jackson 101 if offered!

Q5—*If you could have studied Michael Jackson in any subject at school, what would it have been?*

I would have said English. I got straight A's in English because I loved to write. I actually wrote about him a lot and I think he would make a great essay assignment for any student.

Q6—*What are your feelings about the attempt to appropriate Jackson into academic circles now?*

I think . . . well about time. I think the world is slowly catching up to what Moonwalkers have always known. Michael IS special and he is worth being studied.

Q7—*You named your son Jackson, can you tell us a little about why you did that?*

Jackson. The love of my life. It's funny because if you watched Moonwalkers, you know that I mentioned wanting to have children one day, particularly a son so that I could name him Jackson! Just two years later I was blessed to have just that. Michael is a common name, but Jackson has that flare. And when people see me and meet my son and I say his name is Jackson, they know right away the reason. And I am the proudest mother in those moments. I will tell Jackson that he is named after a great man that helped his mom to see the world in a way that most people ignore.

Q8—*In your documentary you mention the social stigma attached to being a Michael Jackson fan. How do you think this affects people and why do you think they stay fans when it might be easier for them not to?*

That question is almost like asking why a gay person chooses to live their life openly when so many people are not accepting. Fighting who you are . . . hiding who you are is probably one of the most painful things in the world . . . and sometimes it is easier to just be open no matter who likes it or not! I am proud of being a Michael Jackson fan . . . and I am stern to any slick comments to the point where my face kind of says if you don't have anything nice to say about him. . . . we can't even have a conversation! And I am just fine with that. If you don't like Michael then you don't like me!

Q9—*Would you describe yourself as a philanthropist or a humanitarian? If yes, what influence did Michael Jackson have on you? Did he encourage you to be that?*

I do. When Michael passed in 2009 I was so devastated. People put up tributes and things but I wanted to do more. I decided to apply to volunteer at Columbia Presbyterian Hospital in the children's oncology unit. I spent one of my days of every Friday for a year doing a minimum of four hours of voluntary service in the hospital. I saw children that were so sickly . . . and I remembered Michael each time I sat by a bedside to make that child smile. . . . One little girl asked me to sew a dress for her doll. I had no idea how to do that and it came out so ugly, but she loved it. Seeing these children have so much strength under these conditions helped me to see why Michael loved them so much. If only we as adults could be so strong.

Q10—*How many books do you currently own on Michael Jackson? Are you a collector? What else do you collect?*

I own so many books I have a mini library! I would say I collect in a sense. I try to get my hands on anything Michael that I come across. I have a black fedora from the *Bad* tour . . . and a life-size *Thriller* statue.

Q11—*450 years ago, William Shakespeare was very much like Michael Jackson: successful, commercial, and contemporary. Now he is regarded as one of the most iconic artists who ever lived. What do you think will be the view on Michael Jackson in 400 years' time?*

Michael Jackson will be remembered as the greatest entertainer to ever grace the stage. Why? Because after Michael Jackson . . . every artist strives for that greatness. They may mention others along the way, but none the way they mention Michael. He is an icon and will live forever through his art, person, and lifestyle.

Q12—*Final thoughts: what does it mean to be a fan, a moonwalker, from a fan's perspective?*

A Moonwalker is someone who doesn't go one day without humming a Michael Jackson tune. . . . slipping him into daily conversations with co-workers. A Moonwalker is someone that is an independent thinker . . . who cannot be swayed to think anything of Michael Jackson other than what an amazing man he was . . . and still is to so many.

There are tons of Michael Jackson fans . . . but only a select bunch are Moonwalkers. And I am so proud to be one in that bunch.

The moonwalker community is broken up into several factions. Though this list is not meant by any means to be exhaustive, moonwalkers can be put into the following categories: academics, beLIEvers, bloggers, campaigners, collectors, emulators, followers, givers, networkers. As moonwalkers are always generally avid followers of Jackson's music and art, as well as his artistic after-life, these denominations often intersect meaning such that a fan may be part of any number of these groups at one time.

The work of academics on the subject of Michael Jackson is well documented in the Chapter 1—"A Critical Survey of Michael Jackson Studies." However, there are also many online bloggers who write and publish criticism and ideas pertaining to Jackson-related publications and ephemera. Another facet of the Michael Jackson Studies research is the practice of "Michaeling," which is to read everything and anything available about Michael Jackson. Books such as Jackson's *Dancing the Dream: Poems and Reflections*, while less well known during the artist's life, gained new traction posthumously. One of the most useful outcomes of "Michaeling" is that it culminates in a sense of rediscovery for a majority of fans, who see Jackson anew in his post-humous form. The interview that follows is from the editor of the *The Journal of Michael Jackson Academic Studies*, Karin Merx, who is also an illustrator and academic.[8]

Interview 2—Karin Merx, Academic

Q1—*Can you tell us a little bit about yourself as an artist? Your background?*
As long as I can remember, from a very young age, I knew I wanted to be an artist. I started with music, I am a classically trained flautist, but visual art and film also had my love. Later in my life I received private lessons and went to the Rietveld Academy in Amsterdam to draw and paint after life models, with Henk Huig. Currently I mainly work on specific illustrations for book covers and book illustrations, courses online, in addition to my PhD.

Q2—*What inspired you to make your portrait drawing of Jackson?*
First of all it was our talks [Author] and the enthusiasm you had for writing the book. I was floored when I read your first essay online that was the beginning of our online academic journal. You told me about the connection of Michael Jackson and Shakespeare and that to me was a very new, but also an inspiring, point of view. Michael Jackson as the Shakespeare of our time, what was kind of a challenge.

Q3—*What do you feel is the true mark or meaning of being an artist and how is this different from what people in the general public might think of it?*

First of all, artists are human beings, like anyone else. The difference is that artists have a specific skill or more than one in which they express themselves and also "entertain" other people. Artists often think outside of the box to find ways to express themselves, which can be seen as eccentric. They often walk the tightrope of what people in general believe is "normal" and "not normal." That can make it difficult for the artist because they are not always accepted as such. On the other hand, a lot of people think it is very interesting and want what you have or do, without realizing that it is hard work, or I prefer to say play, because it doesn't feel like "work" if you do what you love and love what you do.

Q4—*Do you think there is a place for Michael Jackson in schools and universities, and if yes, what do you think that place is?*

Absolutely. He deserves a place in schools and universities. An artist as versatile as he was needs to be taken seriously and can be studied on so many different subjects.

Q5—*If you could have studied Michael Jackson in any subject at school, what would it have been?*

I would have loved to study [him in] film. I absolutely love his short films.

Q6—*What are your feelings about the attempt to appropriate Jackson into academic circles now?*

That's about time. I am sure that *The Journal of Michael Jackson Academic Studies* has opened the eyes of a lot of academics as well as gave the opportunities to start studying his art. It is kind of sad that after he passed away, academic journals published special editions, but for a very small public. Still it was just a few journals, not nearly enough to cover Michael Jackson and his body of work.

Q7—*Can you tell us a bit about your process of drawing the portrait, and what you think this conveys?*

First of all you gave me a good briefing of what you wanted it to be. So I started with some sketches. Then I decided that a woodcut would take way too long and I was able to kind of replicate the Shakespeare image with pen and ink on a fine watercolor paper. After I was satisfied with the sketch I drew the outline on the paper and started carefully with the ink. It is kind of magical to see the portrait come to life, to see Michael growing out of the paper; to actually see a Jackspearean

[Jackson-Shakespearean portrait] come to life. (See Figure 19.2.) Although we all know what Michael Jackson looked like, after all he can be considered the most photographed person in the world, doesn't mean you actually know the person himself. In Shakespeare's case, we neither

Figure 19.2
The Process of Creation for the Portrait Drawing of Michael Jackson, 2014.
Ink pen on watercolor paper, Frame & Sight 44.5×34.5cm. Private Collection of Elizabeth Amisu. (Artwork by Karin Merx)

Figure 19.2 (*continued*)

know how he looked nor who he was. There is one painting in the National Gallery [in] London that has a good claim to have been painted from life, but still, no one can be sure it actually is Shakespeare. It was interesting to put Michael in this Shakespearean sphere.

Q8—*In your portrait you present Jackson as refined and regal, how do you think this challenges the way people perceive him?*

To be honest, I never thought about how this portrait could challenge the perception of other people. For me he always was a very refined

Figure 19.2 (*continued*)

artist and deserved to be treated more regally. I am sure that the people, who are shocked in whatever way, will get used to this representation of Michael Jackson, especially after reading your book. People will start to see him as I said before, as the Shakespeare of our time.

Q9—*Would you describe yourself as a philanthropist or a humanitarian? If yes, what influence did Michael Jackson have on you? Did he encourage you to be that?*
Let's say that I help people wherever I can and I have charities I support. But my biggest dream is that, at one day, I will be able to help people who really want to study with funding. I don't think Michael Jackson influenced me in that way, although I really have the utmost respect for his immense contributions.

Q10—*Tell us about your process on the illustrations that you contributed to this book. Which is the most effecting and why.*
The process doesn't differ that much from what I described before. The most effecting for me is Michael Jackson in *Ghosts*, where he pulls his jaw into this enormous mouth. I was drawing it and when I looked back it scared me. I deliberately made the mouth and the eyes darker

to emphasize them. I think everyone who knows the film recognizes him immediately. What I like about the Horcruxes illustrations is the intertextuality.

Q11—*450 years ago, William Shakespeare was very much like Michael Jackson: successful, commercial, and contemporary. Now he is regarded as one of the most iconic artists who ever lived. What do you think will be the view on Michael Jackson in 400 years' time?*

In 400 years' time, Michael Jackson will be regarded as one of the most quintessential artists from the 20th and 21st century. I know for sure that people from all over the world are studying his work and many books will be written on so many subjects. And probably archives are only accessible on request and under guidance. Michael Jackson will be taken very, very seriously, but that doesn't need 400 years I think.

Q12—*Final thoughts: what does it mean to illustrate* The Dangerous Philosophies?

First thought? It felt dangerous, but no, it means a lot to me, and I feel very honored and grateful that you chose me. I also enjoyed working with you on this very much. I absolutely loved to do it.

Shortly after Jackson's death, a new group of fans emerged who believed unequivocally that Jackson did not die but, in fact, faked his own death in order to evade the prying eyes of the world's public and the paparazzi. Commonly known as "beLIEvers," they fervently believe that Jackson is not dead and that sightings of him throughout the world confirm this: "we believe that Michael is alive and we don't hide it . . . we are open to all discussion, all exchanges of opinion."[9] In addition to YouTube videos on the subject, which definitely caters to conspiracy theorists, a popular forum also exists called *Michael Jackson Death Hoax Forum.*[10] A subculture phenomenon like the BeLIEvers may be of much interest to those interested in researching how constructions of celebrity and identity proliferate.

On a slightly less controversial note are the "campaigners." Moonwalkers in this category range from vigilantes to peace seekers. There are also campaigners who sought, while he was still alive, to spread the truth about the 1993 allegations against him, and thereby attempted to make the world aware of Jackson as a target of extortion and of his innocence of the 2003 accusations, of which he was acquitted in 2005. There are also moonwalkers who are vehemently anti-Estate (the estate of Michael Jackson, as currently managed exclusively by his lawyers and executors, John Branca and John McClain), there are those who are pro-Estate, anti-The Jackson Family, some who are pro-The Jackson Family, and some who campaign for Jackson to receive post-humous exoneration, and for truth and justice (especially with regard to the controversial nature of Jackson's death). What these various strands of the community show are how diverse and disparate its factions can be.

Another fascinating strand in Jackson fandom are the "collectors." There is an incredibly wide range of ephemera available to those who collect Jackson's music and memorabilia, as the bibliography of this book shows. Collecting is a marvelous way for fans to engage with and immerse themselves in Jackson's music; it also enables younger fans to grasp the span of Jackson's recording career. In fact, it is these younger fans who are free from the living context of Jackson's work and are able to see the artist as a whole, from his transition from child star to adult megastar, to his skin change transition through vitiligo. Alongside this, these collectors are able, through the collecting of Jackson's work holistically, to contain the flow of medium, from recording album to cassette tape and VHS, to CD and then to DVD, and lastly to the fully digital media such as mp3s. The interview that follows is from a collector of Michael Jackson memorabilia, Amber Soos.[11]

Interview 3—Amber Soos, Collector

Q1—*Can you tell us a little bit about yourself?*

As a child I was brought up in the beautiful Scottish Highlands with my three younger siblings and have been a dedicated Michael Jackson enthusiast for almost 7 years now. I discovered him amid his immensely tragic death. I began my admiration for Michael Jackson when I was ten years old in the summer of 2009. I was flicking through music channels and one particular video caught my attention, Michael's *Black or White* short film. The name sounded familiar to me although I had never seen a photo of him, or knew about his previous work. Not even *Thriller*! I was fascinated by his extraordinary style, dazzling appearance and unique voice, I had never seen anything quite like it before. I spent the remainder of the day watching more of his music videos. Ever since then I have been expanding my knowledge and devotion to Michael's work. The first addition to my collection was the "*Number Ones* CD compilation." I proceeded to collect tribute memorabilia in early 2010, as I was developing my collection I realized I wanted to collect at a more professional level. It all went on from there. When I left school at the age of 13 my parents gave me the opportunity to grow and learn in freedom. I have since taught myself Photography and Special FX Makeup. I love discovering different types of music of different genres and ethnicities.

Q2—*Do you consider yourself to be a Michael Jackson Collector?*
Yes definitely, although there is a limit to what I collect such as tabloids
and plush toys which I find unnecessary. Also, I exclude some posthumous items but Re-releases of previous albums I am ok with. I collect
what I can afford.

Q3—*What do you collect? Records, CDs or more?*
I collect three main kinds of audio formats—Cassette, Vinyl record and
Compact Disc spanning from The Jackson Five, Michael with Motown,
The Jacksons, Michael with Epic and some Michael-related releases.
Furthermore, I collect a wide variety of Michael's solo albums both
commercial and promotional from different regions of the world, various re-issues, limited edition items and box sets. I have a more altered
set of rules when it comes to collecting the Jackson Five and the Jacksons
albums. I don't collect too many of the same album as my main focus
is Michael's solo work with both Motown and Epic labels. My collection
includes only a few compilation and greatest hits albums. Commercial
and Promotional Singles are the next items that I look for. I own many
of the same singles with either alternative cover art, imports from other
countries, limited editions and collectable promo singles. I only like to
own commercial 7-inch vinyl singles with an accompanying picture
sleeve. I have yet to obtain the more rare and sought after music formats
such as the mini-disc and the controversial long box CD design which
was popular in the 80s and 90s. There are also the 3-inch CD singles from
Japan which I have yet to collect. The three video formats that I collect
are DVDs and Video cassettes, both commercial and promotional.

Moving on, I collect books that were published both before and after
Michael's death but I am very particular over what I read and purchase.
I collect both official and unofficial books like biographies, books by
Michael himself, catalogues and photo books, I am also very selective
when it comes to purchasing magazines. I primarily collect lifestyle,
music, entertainment and general interest magazines with Michael on
the front cover from a photo-shoot. Fanzines are another kind of magazine that I love. I buy very few commemorative magazines and I also like
to have interesting magazines clippings and advertisements. The many
tour items that I collect are souvenir programs, tour books, posters,
badges, tickets, backstage passes, Pepsi cups and cans and tour clothing.
The majority of paper items I collect are commercial and promotional
posters, flyers, cardboard displays and cutouts, official calendars, photos
and postcards, trading cards from 1984 and 1996, stamps and novelties

like stickers. The last few miscellaneous items I collect are accessories that are very similar to Michael's, fabric flag posters and jigsaw puzzles.

Q4—*How many individual items do you own in your collection?*
I own around 552 items in my collection, from badges to unlimited rare items.

Q5—*What inspires you to collect Michael Jackson Memorabilia?*
I am inspired to collect simply because I find Michael so interesting as both a person and a performer. His music is timeless. I love the impression of going back in time when I obtain certain memorabilia. I think of them as pieces of history, marking the years of Michael's career. When designing albums artists can express themselves through their art, which Michael has demonstrated countless times. The possibilities are limitless when you compare physical album releases to just a digital download. The quality also contributes to a good song, playing CDs or records on a large stereo system really does add to the quality of sound.

Q6—*Where do you get it from?*
First and foremost I am an eBay fanatic! I think about 90% of my collection has come from winning auctions and purchasing items from eBay. I also occasionally buy from an online marketplace called Discogs and from Amazon. Now and again I look in charity shops, attend any car boot sales and check in my local music shops.

Q7—*How do you fund your collection?*
I make money by either selling goods, saving up, self-funding, and doing odd jobs to help out.

Q8—*Do you think there is a place for Michael Jackson in schools and universities, and if yes, what do you think that place is?*
Yes, I do think there should be more talk on Michael's genius in subjects like Music and History. In universities I believe there should be a choice to learn literature through Michael's poetic work.

Q9—*Do you think collecting is a learning experience? If so, in what way?*
Yes I definitely think so. I learn about the many different kinds of musical formats and it gives me an insight into the history of how popular music was in the 70s, 80s, 90s and 20th century was distributed. I also learn about world currency through buying items internationally. I build up an archive in my head of knowing exactly where to look on labels,

determining if an item is a rare one of its kind. My computer skills have improved from constant researching. Layout design is another beneficial outcome of collecting, being creative with how to display and showcase memorabilia well.

Q10—*What are your feelings about the trend towards making Michael Jackson an academic subject?*

I think that would be great. It is agreeable to say that Michael should be taken more seriously and not be linked to the fictional character he was made out to be through media. When people want to study him academically, they can discover the many aspects in his life that are groundbreaking. People can learn so much if they look past the stereotypical image of Michael and see his true potential.

Q11—*Tell us about your top ten items in your collection. [See Figure 19.3. What are they? When do they date from? How did you get them and why are they special to you?*

My top ten items in no particular order:

- 3-LP set of *HIStory—Past Present And Future Book 1*, 1995. One of my best moments for being a collector was when I won a scarce Brazilian pressing of *HIStory* on eBay for £58. It was cheap considering how much money they go for nowadays. It will always hold a special place in my heart because it is one of my favorite albums of Michael's.
- Double-sided promotional poster for the *Invincible* album from 2001. It is 24×30 inches and is from the USA. The front of the poster is the LP cover in silver. The back has the four-colored limited edition CDs and on the bottom it reads "Michael Jackson *Invincible*. Available in Original Silver Edition and Four Collectible Limited Edition Colour Covers." I won this in an auction on eBay for a ridiculously cheap price. It is special to me because I feel like a VIP when I have things that were not originally for sale. It is very eye-catching too!
- *Dangerous Collector's Edition* "Pop Up" CD Box Set released in November 1991. A Special gold CD comes in a 10"×10" black box with the *Dangerous* eyes. It opens up into a beautiful 3-D "LP Cover" display, also with a Dangerous lyric booklet. I won it on eBay in December 2013 and it is one of my favorite pieces of memorabilia because of its creative design for the album. The *Dangerous* cover art leaves me astonished.

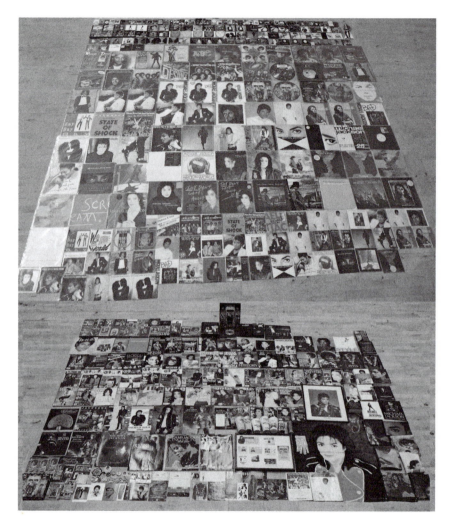

Figure 19.3
A Photograph of Michael Jackson Memorabilia Collection.
(Artwork by Amber Soos)

- The Jacksons Victory 1984 Tour Book from the USA. A fan from Canada whom I met online sent it to me while I sent something to her. It will always feel special to me because I love exchanging gifts to one another and the bond it creates.
- *The King of Style: Dressing Michael Jackson* Book. Published in 2012. When the book was available for sale, I purchased it as fast as I could

from Amazon because I had always wished for there to be a book about Michael's clothing. I was so overwhelmed when I received the book in the mail. The photographs of Michael's clothes are breathtaking. I will treasure the book for years to come.

- Another item that I bought off of eBay is *The Ghosts Deluxe Collector's Box Set* (UK) It Includes the *Ghosts* VHS tape, *Blood On The Dance Floor* CD, Limited Edition Mini-Max CD with *On the Line* and an A5 *Ghosts* program. It was one of the very first box sets I owned in my collection.
- VIBE magazine dating back to June/July 1995 with Michael, dressed in hip-hop clothing on the front cover. I won it on eBay and the reason why it's special to me is because of the magazine's rarity and I just adore the photography.
- The Jacksons *Destiny* Commercial LP Album (UK) Released in 1978. I purchased it from my local record shop and the guy gave me a discount. A very awesome thing that the LP has on the bottom left is a gold embossment reading: PROPERTY OF CBS, DEMONSTRATION ONLY, Not For Sale. It is the embossment that makes it feel more special to me.
- A 20" × 17" framed poster of Michael wearing a studded leather arm guard for a photo shoot in 1988. I saw it hanging on the wall in a charity shop and bought it for only a few pounds. There are memories attached to it. I remember carrying it around with me to other charity shops. An elderly woman noticed it and began talking about him in such a sweet manner. It made me feel happy that other people feel the same way as I do.
- *Thriller* Limited Millennium CD Edition. It was part of the Millennium Series issued by Sony in 1999. It consists of a gatefold cardboard CD case that is slightly larger than a normal plastic jewel case. It comes with a foldout lyric booklet. The front and back of the CD sleeve feature the two drawings MJ did for the original release. It comes in a clear jacket with a fold-over cardboard title insert. I really like the clean product design and that it's almost like a miniature vinyl LP.

Q12—*Can you tell us a little more about the process of collecting?*
When I want a specific item, I will look it up on eBay and then compare prices from various sources. I have my own handmade book with lists of memorabilia I want to collect. I then tick off the items I receive and whisper to myself "welcome to the family."

Q13—*Are there groups of collectors?*
Yes, I think there are. Some people only just collect his signed memorabilia, others have enough money to own personal belongings of Michael's such as his famous glove.

Q14—*How do you share your collecting with the world? Why do you do this?*
I share my collection on mostly Instagram and sometimes on Tumblr and YouTube too. I do this because I love connecting with those who share the same passion and love for Michael as I am thankful to those who boost my confidence by praising my dedication and hard work. It gives me that little lift to continue doing what I do when people praise my efforts.

Q15—*How big do you envision your collection becoming?*
I often wonder to myself just how large my collection will grow into or what lies ahead. I guess I will have to wait and see. I focus on living in the moment.

Q16—*What do you want to do with it in ten years' time?*
Ten years is long time for me to think about. I have always had aspirations to have some sort of museum or a larger space to display my collection in a more professional and pristine manner.

Q17—*Final thoughts: What do you feel is the true mark or meaning of being a Michael Jackson fan and how is this different from what people in the general public might think of it?*
I think being a Michael Jackson fan is far more than just being a fan of his music. He was such a beautiful and fragile soul. He really wanted to do more than just be a musical genius. He was all about helping, loving and caring for one another, and no matter how many times people tried to ridicule, belittle, hurt and destroy him, Michael never lost his ability to love and his deep desire to help others. It is also the connection he had and still has between his fans. Michael thought of his fans as a second family and never looked down on them as his inferiors. He sacrificed his entire life for his art and beliefs. He was outstandingly educated and so highly intelligent.

Also called impersonators, emulators of Jackson are not limited to those who dress, wear makeup, and dance in imitation of the artist. Lorena Turner wrote a fascinating and engaging book on Jackson impersonators called *The Michael Jacksons*, "both a monograph, featuring over 35 MJ represservers who live and work around the US, and an ethnography that seeks to deconstruct and understand the motivations of these fascinating people."[12] Several noteworthy musicians are widely known celebrity emulators of Jackson. There are also everyday people who use much of Jackson's style in their own lives and work. This appears not only in the form of homage, because it can be directly stolen without crediting Jackson as source. Jackson is widely emulated in popular music and culture today; furthermore, his moves and sounds are often easily recognized.

"Followers" purposely followed Jackson around the world in his adult life and sought him out wherever they could. It was reported in the biography *Remember the Time: Protecting Michael Jackson in His Final Days*, that Jackson knew some of these followers personally and that he was always kind and appreciative of them, understanding that they felt drawn to him and wanted to be near him: "the more die-hard among them followed Jackson from country to country wherever he went. And during his months-long trial in 2005, hundreds of them converged to stand vigil outside the courthouse, cheering his every coming and going and praying for his acquittal."[13]

One of the most inspired ways that moonwalkers express themselves is in their philanthropic efforts. This group has been categorized as "givers." There are several examples of this, such as the charity "Legendary Michael Jackson," but one of the most heartfelt is the "oneRoseforMJJ" campaign, which enables fans from around the world to send a rose to Jackson's grave every year on the anniversary of his death.[14] Proceeds from this venture are given to charity in Jackson's honor. The author, Zack O'Malley Greenburg, was inspired to donate a proportion of the proceeds from his book to charity, after his research into Jackson's finances revealed that he had given much of his financial revenue to charities all around the world:

> Every time someone buys a copy of this book, a person in need will receive a free meal through the United Nations' World Food Programme. Why? Michael Jackson donated tens of millions of dollars to various charities over the course of his life and left 20 percent of his financial legacy to good causes. I figured it would only be fitting to make a contribution from my author royalties.[15]

Networkers share pictures of Jackson, news about Jackson's estate and music, and little-known facts and quotations about Jackson via their social networks, such as Tumblr, Facebook, Instagram, and Twitter. These are often shared by those interested in the subject, and they are a way of keeping Jackson alive. One of the most interesting ways how this is done is by the marking of a day in Jackson's life; so, for example, *on this date in 1986, Michael Jackson arrived at such place for such reason* or *on this date Jackson was the recipient of such award.* This often has powerful reverberations along social networking lines, and for this reason Jackson's name often trends around the days of his birthday, the anniversary of his death, and the anniversaries of his solo adult album releases. This in turn helps his releases continue to chart and gain revenue for his estate.

Michael Jackson fans are not quite like any other fan group in the world. This is firstly in terms of the sheer scale of their numbers. Jackson's Facebook page currently hosts 75 million likes. His fans were noted for campaigning so well that Jackson's album *Invincible* reached the top of the charts on the anniversary of the album's release in 2011.[16] Furthermore, witness the ongoing expansion of Jackson's fan base as illustrated by the growing number of social networkers, the ongoing strength of fan clubs, and the success of books like *Man in the Music: The Creative Life and Work of Michael Jackson*; as well as the success of emergent avenues of Jackson-related research like the *Journal of Michael Jackson Academic Studies*. All show that interest in Jackson has not dwindled at all. Rather, Jackson's place in popular culture is in an exciting phase of redefinition, which poses an excellent opportunity for cultural research. How this subculture functions is a wonderful subject, in motion, because it encourages us to engage with a whole range of perspectives.

CHAPTER 20

The Power of the Editor and Michael Jackson's Posthumous Releases

T his chapter discusses four of Michael Jackson's posthumous releases in relation to their production and reception. It considers the publication choices of the coexecutors of Jackson's estate as editor-publishers, and discusses the issues of agency, attribution, authenticity, and adaptation that surface from this topic. The chapter concludes with how the reappropriation of Jackson's art places it in wider contexts and causes it to signify anew.

> It wasn't just *This Is It*, though, that rocketed Jackson to arguably his highest level of popularity in a quarter of a century. His death itself, one of the most significant news events of the social media era, served to turn the eyes of millions of people to him. And instead of seeing the scandals, the plastic surgeries, the P.T. Barnum-inspired eccentricities (real or constructed), they saw the King of Pop in his prime. He has since been crowned by a new generation of fans—the ones who, along with the loyal old guard, have sent Jackson's YouTube Vevo views past 1.3 billion since 2009 (on par with Taylor Swift and Katy Perry, and twice as many as Justin Timberlake). By the end of 2013, he boasted 65 million Facebook likes, more than Justin Bieber or Lady Gaga.[1]

2009's *THIS IS IT*

Critical discourse on *This Is It* is rich and varied, and the first posthumous release offers ample opportunity to explore posthumous constructions of persona.[2] One of the most useful discussions of *This Is It* is from a financial perspective, with regard to the fiscal solvency of Jackson at the time of his death. As Zack O'Malley Greenburg writes, "all in all, there was about $12 million more going out per year than there was coming in . . . his total debts were approaching half a billion dollars."[3] The line between creating art and staying financially solvent is not always so clear to the public who received Jackson's work. However, it does suffice to say that finances were an integral part of the creative process. Fundamentally, money is what turns art into industry:

> Shortly after Jackson passed away, Branca and McClain landed a ten-project, ten-year deal with Sony worth $250 million—the most lucrative record deal of all time—to put out unreleased material and anniversary editions of Jackson's albums. The first was a two-disc set called *This Is It*, released in conjunction with the film of the same name, it became the third-bestselling album of 2009.[4]

The first way that Jackson's work is altered in this posthumous compilation is in editing. As Margaret Kidnie states in *Where Is Hamlet? Text, Performance, and Adaptation*, editors of Shakespeare have "to be clear about what it is [they] think [they] are producing when [they] edit dramatic texts that, at least with regard to stage directions, survive only as textual fragments" and that they "might desire to reconstruct the staging" or "attempt to transcribe the non-verbal codes of a particular early modern performance into a verbal code."[5]

The compilation of the songs in a new order changes their meaning in relation to one another. It is likely that the order of the songs relate to the proposed order of the set-list of the average *This Is It* concert, as was planned at the London O2 Arena in 2009. When considering posthumous releases in any detail, it is important to pay close attention to this context. In the documentary, to which the *This Is It* album is inextricably bound, "there was something undeniably riveting and enlightening about peeking 'behind the curtain' and witnessing the artist in his element. It was tragic, of course, that his full vision was never realized. But for many viewers it humanized the singer, even as it showcased his extraordinary talent."[6]

This album has been included in this chapter primarily because it features posthumously constructed material from Jackson's personal archives.

The song "This Is It" leads the documentary soundtrack, which is presented as an homage to shows that never happened, uses "footage that was never intended to be seen," and "resulted in the best-selling documentary of all time."[7] Many of the previously released tracks on the album have been remastered, including "Jam," "They Don't Care About Us," and "The Way You Make Me Feel." The album also uses both radio edits and single versions. These attempt to construct, from Jackson's known compositions and prior releases, something that feels relatively fresh to the listener. The track "Thriller," however, has been included on the album in its original form, possibly implying that this particular song defies alteration.

It is in *This Is It* that the issue of agency first arises. The audience and the editor-publishers are equally aware that Jackson is not present to agree on the compilation of this album; and the album may well not have existed had he not died. However, it is common to have albums sold at concerts as souvenirs.

This is not the first time Jackson's work was rereleased in new and altered versions. Note the albums *Michael Jackson: The Ultimate Collection*, the special-edition versions of *Off the Wall*, *Bad*, and *Thriller* in 2001, and the album *Michael Jackson Number Ones* and the first disc of the 1995 *HIStory* album. Some of these releases even included demo versions of songs, one of the most exciting being an early recording of "Don't Stop 'Til You Get Enough" with Janet Jackson and Randy Jackson playing assorted percussion.[8]

This Is It also includes three demo recordings and the poem "Planet Earth."[9] One key area where *Michael Jackson's This Is It* differs from the usual rereleased compilations by Jackson is in the song "This Is It" itself, which was posthumously produced, including the backing vocals that were recorded by Jackson's brothers, also after their brother's death. Interestingly enough, Jackson had not recorded with his brothers in several years and had not performed with them since his Madison Square Gardens 30th Anniversary show. *Michael Jackson's This Is It* highlights the issues that surround the posthumous releasing of an artist's work. Finally, with another comparison to Shakespeare, it is important to note that the First Folio, produced in 1623 and now regarded as one of the most regarded publications in the history of English literature, was also a posthumous collection.

2010's *MICHAEL*

Released in 2010, *Michael* is definitely the most contentious collection of Jackson's posthumous releases. With 10 tracks featuring producer Akon, rapper 50 Cent, and musician Lenny Kravitz, one of the most striking things about the *Michael* album is its cover. The composite album cover image includes pictures from Jackson's career, such as his performances in *Captain EO*, *Moonwalker*, *Beat It*, and *Thriller*, and in the top left-hand space we see the moon with an MTV moon landing. Most prominent in the center of the cover is an illustration of Jackson in regal costume with ruffles around his neck, what seems to be a buttoned mantel over his armor, and a crown perched above his head, held aloft by two cherubs, one black and the other white. This version of Jackson clearly originates from his early 1980s image, especially with regard to the portrait's complexion.

The cover art for the *Michael* album is one of the most striking visual representations of Jackson's immortal persona, as discussed in Chapter 9—" 'Throwing Stones to Hide Your Hands': The Mortal Persona of Michael

Jackson." The immortal persona is typified mostly as being an amalgamated version of all the positively received depictions of Jackson that came before. This image of Jackson wears a butterfly on his left shoulder (our right). A likely metaphor here is of Jackson emerging as a butterfly from a chrysalis of death. In the center page of the album's liner notes, a full version of the image can be seen where Jackson is presented in several incongruous images, such as his appearance in *The Wiz* as the Scarecrow, along with images of the Jackson 5, his performance of "Billie Jean" at the *Motown 25*, *Ghosts*, *This Is It*, Bubbles the chimp, as well as various children in the bottom right-hand corner. Images of Jackson's leading ladies also appear, from Lisa-Marie Presley to Liza Minnelli and Naomi Campbell.[10] Careful inspections of the image show far more, and an in-depth analysis of how the image reconstructs Jackson as a compiled version of all his former representations would definitely be welcome in the field of study.

Within the album's liner notes are Jackson's handwritten notes, clearly an attempt to authenticate the album's tracks as written by the artist himself.[11] It is at the point of authenticity that the release of *Michael* became extremely controversial: "fans, family members, and even some of Jackson's former collaborators contested everything from the creative license taken to complete Jackson's unfinished work, to the tracklist, to the authenticity of certain vocals."[12] As Joseph Vogel writes, posthumous releases can be incredibly notorious, and they can "present the material basically as it was found," which effectively freezes the material in the time when it was created, or "try to complete the artist's vision based on instructions and/or intuition."[13]

The quest for authentication has been evident in Shakespeare's canon for a long time. In fact, the instability of the Shakespearean canon is one of the worst-kept secrets in academic history. It is this instability that is so evident in Jackson's posthumous releases. Expectations of fans and listeners often jarred sharply with those of the producers, who included these words on the final page of the liner notes: "album conceived and inspired by The King of Pop Michael Jackson: Management of the Estate of Michael Jackson: John Branca and John McClain." Authenticity and agency are two of the most prominent factors in considering the reception of Jackson's posthumous work, and they become increasingly important as time passes. In terms of "authenticity," we are concerned primarily with how closely the product remains "true" to the conceptions and prior work of the artists from which they originated. In terms of "agency," we must also consider attribution. Agency considers how far Jackson can be claimed to be the author of works that are polished and reconstructed—in his absence—for a wider audience, and how far these works can be said to be "his" and therefore "attributed" to him. Any doubt cast upon a posthumous release's attribution, agency, and authenticity is clearly of paramount importance to the reception of the release, and the doubt can therefore color the entire album. Although there are key songs that can easily be attributed to Jackson, such as the final track "Much Too Soon," which "showcases Jackson's ability as a singer-songwriter to magnificent effect" and may certainly be "Jackson's finest ballad . . . an exquisite expression of loss and yearning that stands shoulder-to-shoulder with some of the best folk ballads of the Carpenters and the Beatles," these key songs are often overlooked among the generally negative reception of the album itself.[14]

One of the central issues in the posthumous reception of Jackson is perception and perspective. When audiences expect to listen to a Michael Jackson release (and, of course, this is not by any means unexpected since his name is on the album art and so is his image), they may well be disappointed, not necessarily by the album's content, but by how far it falls from their expectations, their memories, and their sense of authenticity. 2012's reissue of Jackson's *Bad*, however, was a rather more successful story.

2012's *BAD 25*

Released in 2012 to commemorate the 25th anniversary of Michael Jackson's *Bad* album, *Bad 25* was more of a celebratory event than a release of newly released material. The album consisted of a black box with the graffiti'd word "Bad" sprawled in red and silver, with the number 25 directly underneath and a crown above. *Bad 25*'s lush packaging was a delight to behold, a sleek, jam-packed bundle that included four discs, the first of which included Jackson's *Bad* album remastered, and a bonus disc with unreleased tracks from the *Bad* recording sessions. The box set also includes a live recording of Jackson's performance at Wembley Stadium on July 16, 1988, along with a DVD of footage from the same performance. The live recording and live album are also given their own liner notes, which include several images of Jackson during his 1987–1988 *Bad* tour, along with the dates of where and when he played different locations around the world. This booklet includes a reproduction of the tour program, which implies that its purpose is to give young audiences a sense of what it might have been like to be there, and to refresh the memories of those who *were* there more than 25 years before, of how electric, exciting, and entrancing the performances were.[15] Also included are a poster and a sticker to further enhance the nostalgia value of the album, as well as to connect it further to the documentary of the same name released in the following year.[16]

Where 2010's *Michael*'s focus was to bring Jackson forward, from his chrysalis in the past, 2012's *BAD 25*'s aim was clearly to crystalize Jackson's performances and his music in the late 1980s in the minds of its audience, and then to present this crystalized version of Jackson at his commercial height.

> And now to celebrate *BAD*'s 25th anniversary we have gone back through Michael's archives to provide a captivating look at his artistic evolution . . . It is worth noting that, even though some of the demoed songs were subsequently worked on for possible use on other later albums, the recordings included in this package reflect the songs as they existed during *BAD*'s recording sessions . . . these recordings are being shared to offer the listener a special insight into the creative process . . . [17]

The liner notes of *BAD 25* show Jackson veiled behind black lace (anecdotally, Jackson's original preference for the album's cover)—a striking image that may well contravene dominant readings of Jackson as commercial. The liner notes include, with the credits, several contemporaneous photographs (taken during the recordings of each of the original tracks). What is particularly interesting is the choice to include images of the original media on which these songs were initially shared with the world, such as tapes and records. In doing so, McClain and Branca very much take the role of editors by representing Jackson's work posthumously in light of the successful short films, record releases, and tape releases that originally presented Jackson's work. Also included is the cover album art of the single releases on vinyl, many of which were immensely successful, suggesting that Jackson's *Bad* album, which broke records in its own right, needs reconceptualizing as its own unmitigated success, rather than simply as the follow-up album to *Thriller.* This new conceptualizing of the *Bad* album is very effective, because it intercuts images of Jackson and his collaborators in the studio with images from the short films that accompanied these releases. It is another editorial decision to showcase three separate factors—the song credits, the images from the studio (behind the scenes), and frame stills from the polished short films—together. What this does is effectively link the three individual facets of Jackson's creativity, making the reader more aware of the three factors we have previously mentioned: agency, attribution, and authenticity.

The behind-the-scenes photographs and images also provide a certain warmth and nostalgia, which link them to the audience's own experience, especially with the inclusion of nonprofessionally lit photos and Polaroids. The photos give a sense of immediacy, as though all the images were taken on an ad hoc basis, capturing the magic as it took place. Furthermore, they serve to humanize Jackson greatly, showing him simply as a musician in the studio with his collaborators making music. One such image is of "the crew with Michael's snake, muscles, visiting the studio," (the caption has been written in a font that emulates neat handwriting).[18]

There are two booklets of liner notes for the *Bad 25* special edition release. The alternate booklet, with Jackson's face on the cover (overlaid with black lace) also includes previously released 'bonus' material. The liner notes confirm that the songs "Streetwalker," "Todo Mi Amor Eres Tu" ("I Just Can't Stop Loving You" in English), and "Fly Away" were already included in a separate special edition of *Bad* in 2001. The reasons that the editors chose to include those previously released bonus tracks, in addition to six newly released bonus tracks is explained in their liner notes. However, it is the explanation itself which attempts to "sell" the bonus material to the audience.[19]

This recontextualizing and reconstructing by editor-publishers is by no means a new phenomenon. From the early modern period, editor-publishers have not only been collaborating, but also adding further information to an authors' content in order to sell their work. Two such collaborators were "two very separate and distinct publishers: Richard Bonian, from Hayes, who had been apprenticed twice in nine years and Henry Walley, a third generation London stationer, born into his trade."[20]

> Richard Bonian, baptised in Hayes, Middlesex in 1581, was the third of six children, baptised between 1575 and 1587/1588.[21] He was made apprentice to Richard Watkins in 1598 until Watkins' catastrophic demise in 1599, when the formerly successful stationer became the victim of abject 'humiliation, incarceration and destitution'. The same year Bonian became Watkins' apprentice the 'patentee of valuable almanacs', was 'reduced to poor circumstances'.[22]

> Whereas the material evidence shows Bonian to be found in three separate locations in five years, Henry Walley was the son of Robert Walley and grandson of John Walley, all stationers based in Harts Horn, Foster Lane.[23] After being freed by patrimony in 1608, Walley would publish for only two years before eventually becoming a clerk in the Stationer's Company, from 1630 to 1640, active in its dealings such as the selling of the Feathers Tavern.[24]

Bonian and Walley are interesting when one considers Michael Jackson's posthumous releases because, although they did not publish Shakespeare's work posthumously (*Troilus and Cressida* was included in the Stationer's Register in 1609), they did add to its content in order to sell it to their audience:

> Although Bonian is acknowledged by scholars like David Bevington, Zachary Lesser and R.B. McKerrow for his joint-publication of Shakespeare's *Troilus and Cressida*, he also published a series of other works ranging from music to scientific texts . . . Approximately 58% of Bonian's publishing involved a partner and 91% of the time this partner was Henry Walley. Collaboration 'in publication is as old as printing itself'. Due to the economic investment required it was

'sensible to share both the outlay and the risk'. This may have been the driving force behind Bonian and Walley's partnership.[25]

Therefore, "Lesser regards Bonian and Walley as not just publishers but, in fact, critics, able to recognise and translate the wit and irony of the works they were publishing. Bonian and Walley, if this is true, can be seen as strategic publishers. Much of the literary work they published share an 'elitist emphasis on wit and classism displayed in the preface to *Troilus*'."[26] In much the same way, Jackson's editor-publishers have strategically reframed his work in order to sell it to a wider audience, and very likely the exact audience that bought much of the work the first time. The concerns that arise from how this posthumous re-creative process makes Jackson into something new will be discussed in the final section of this chapter, following a consideration of the 2014 album release *Xscape*.

2014's *XSCAPE*

As Greenburg writes in *Michael Jackson Inc.*, Jackson's estate was seemingly resurrected by his death, which in many ways breathed new life into his brand: "the resurrected Michael Jackson Inc. wasn't constrained by the struggles that plagued its founder towards the end of his career: in the last eight years of his life, Jackson did not release a new studio album or go on tour. Within just three years of his death, he would accomplish both feats, and the financial results were staggering."[27] The sheer financial impact is evident from Greenburg's estimation of Jackson's posthumous earnings: "the moment Michael Jackson's adult solo career began in earnest in 1979 through his death in 2009 he earned a whopping $1.1 billion dollars . . . the five years since then, his estate has collected over $700 million more."[28]

One way in which the brand exhibited this new lease on life was the album *Xscape*.[29] It was released in May 2014, with a deluxe version that included both a compact disc and DVD. The compact disc hosted eight previously unreleased tracks that had been "contemporized" by a range of producers, along with original versions of each song. The DVD contained recorded interviews with various producers associated with the work. However, it is interesting to note that neither the single disc nor the vinyl versions of the albums had Jackson's original versions included.

One of the tracks of the album was a posthumous duet between Justin Timberlake and Jackson, on the track "Love Never Felt So Good." Again, issues of authenticity, agency, and attribution arise, especially due to the fact that not only has the music been contemporized, new artists have been included. A duet has been constructed where no corresponding duet existed during the artist's life. The key issue that *Xscape* introduces is that of adaptation, mainly through the use of contemporizing, to describe the appropriation of Jackson's recordings to make them appear as "new" works being presented for the first time:

> "Contemporizing" Jackson's songs, then, is a kind of parallel track in keeping Jackson's legacy thriving. It is not about replacing what Jackson left behind or even about finishing a specific blueprint; without the artist here, that is impossible. Rather it is about creatively connecting with his work, about finding new and compelling ways to capture the essence, the excitement and the magic that is Michael Jackson.[30]

Shakespearean adaptation and appropriation often bring up serious concerns about the right of editor-publishers to reconstruct Shakespeare's work, and never has this been more apparent than in Song of the Goat Theatre's *Songs of Lear*, a reworking of Shakespeare's *King Lear* using rhythm, harmonies, and song.[31]

> Professor Margaret Jane Kidnie argues that Shakespeare's "plays are mutable" with "borders that have to be patrolled" and that if these boundaries "were no longer policed, they would disappear."[32] From the opening moment of the play, Bral challenged the audience to reconsider how they engage[d] with Shakespeare's text by redefining its form.[33]

Kidnie's question, of "Where is Hamlet?" can also be asked of releases like Jackson's *Xscape*. Where is Michael Jackson in *Xscape*? We are encouraged to determine where exactly Jackson's essence can be found in a posthumous recording. Does it lie in the use of his vocals, his image emblazoned on the cover, his words quoted in the liner notes, or his lyrics? Perhaps, however, we can more easily ascertain where Jackson isn't. These posthumous recordings lack the strong sense of cohesion and innovative sound engineering found in Jackson's original canon. Jackson, it seems, may lie in his own physical touch in the final stages of production and mixing, not just in the components that make up a song or album.

The posthumous attempt to resurrect and revive Jackson underscores the impossibility of doing so, and the feeble attempt reiterates just how unique an artist he truly was.

Something quite spectacular happens when a great poet dies, as Lawrence Lipking writes in *The Life of the Poet: Beginning and Ending Poetic Careers*:

> Neglected at first, eventually competed for, like Homer, by contending cities, the poet goes to meet his shades. But not unsung. With his dying breath, frequently, an industry springs up around him—memorialists, literary undertakers,

chisellers, epitaph-makers. The custodians of his fame take charge of manuscripts and the will. He enters his tomb.[34]

Editors of Shakespeare have been battling for at least a century on how exactly to present Shakespeare's work, especially when that work exists in several (often conflicting) versions.[35] Creative adaptations of Shakespeare like *Songs of Lear* challenge the dominant ideologies that revolve around what Michael D. Bristol terms "the Shakespeare myth":

> A myth is not a description of things as they are. In fact, a myth can be used to bully people and intimidate them, to make them feel ashamed of what they feel . . . the Shakespeare myth is no exception . . . continually rewritten over time . . . a complex, ironic and potentially deceptive story.[36]

In much the same way, the many myths around Michael Jackson, which are discussed in Chapter 9—" 'Throwing Stones to Hide Your Hands': The Mortal Persona of Michael Jackson," are his idol persona, wacko persona, and subsequently, his immortal persona. They can be deeply interrogated through these posthumous releases. New "editions" of Jackson's compositions have been published, complete with the remixing, posthumous layering, rearranging, and remastering of Jackson's work. They present his personas in a new light. Furthermore, not all of the ways that Jackson has been re-presented to his audience correspond to prior notions of who he was and what he created, and this is ample ground for further research and consideration.

CHAPTER 21

Epilogue: Three *Dangerous Philosophies* Articles

The following articles were published between 2014 and 2015 on the web site *Writing Eliza* as part of a series for fans.[1] They were shared on fan sites and online communities, and they encouraged debate among Jackson fans and aficionados about his art and its afterlife. The essays were translated in German and Italian and were originally presented via *The Michael Jackson Academic Studies Journal*. They were inspired by the chapters of this book and have been presented here as useful companion texts.

21.1. "THE ISLE IS FULL OF NOISES": REVISITING THE PETER PAN OF POP

I originally wrote this article based on an idea for a chapter for *The Dangerous Philosophies* called "Michael Jackson: Peter Pan, Passion and Pathology." However, as this book began to take shape, I realized that the article had already said all that I had hoped for this chapter to say. Other ideas about childhood were discussed in detail in Chapter 12—"Michael Jackson and Children Revisited," and Chapter 13—"Faith, Hope, and Love: The Dangerous Philosophies of Michael Jackson." It would have been very interesting to include the idea of comparing Jackson to *Peter Pan* author J.M. Barrie in Chapter 15—"Horcruxes: Michael (Split Seven Ways) Jackson."

The artist Michael Jackson has often been given the epithet "Peter Pan of Pop." However, this chapter presents his association with fictional characters as far more complex. It also discusses Jackson's parallels with Shakespeare's Ariel, and with the authors F. Scott Fitzgerald and Oscar Wilde.

"Be not afeard; the isle is full of noises
Sounds, and sweet airs, that give delight and hurt not."
                              —William Shakespeare[2]

Much has been made of the fact that the artist Michael Jackson identified with the fictional character Peter Pan. To his brother Jermaine, Jackson was more like Benjamin Button, while Margo Jefferson compared him to Dorian Gray. However, his relentless pursuit of seemingly impossible dreams shares far more with Jay Gatsby, a character who "believed in the green light, the orgiastic future that year by year recedes before us."[3]

Often, commentators on Jackson's career resort to fiction to characterize him. And, through the necromancy of modern media, Jackson became as much fiction as reality. To the once-adoring masses, this constructed "painting" of who he was seemed to degenerate. How far this "disintegration" went lies in the eye of the beholder, which is a conundrum that Willa Stillwater goes some way to resolve in *M Poetica: Michael Jackson's Art of Connection and Defiance*. Jackson's life story shares much more with the misunderstood-but-successful authors J.M. Barrie, F. Scott Fitzgerald, and Oscar Wilde than their creations. Barrie emigrated from the world of adults, Fitzgerald died young, and Wilde's imprisonment would now be characterized as a violation of human rights.[4]

Michael Jackson's (like Dorian Gray's) outward appearance and personality remained youthful and beautiful. He was creative to his very last day. As for his face, it had certainly changed from *Off The Wall* and, subsequently, from that of *Thriller*. This was due in some part to age, diet, two skin-altering diseases (vitiligo and lupus), bouts of injury- and stress-induced addiction to medication, and cosmetic alterations.[5]

The factors that one should not forget, in order to attribute Jackson's penchant for physical change ("I have had my nose altered twice, and I recently had a cleft added to my chin. But that's it. Period.") were the artist's stress levels after the success of *Thriller*. Stress is the silent cause of a phenomenal range of diseases, and Jackson was no stranger to its extremes. He was an artist who bore the weight of: two false allegations and the media storms that accompanied them; a never-ending cycle of lawsuits; being a single father of three; and being a one-man conglomerate who also happened to be its most lucrative product.[6]

As for Peter Pan, Tanner Colby iterates in "The Radical Notion of Michael Jackson's Humanity" that the character is tortured by night terrors and subsequently sees death as a "great adventure." Pan exorcises his frustration and anger by ruthlessly slicing off Hook's arm, and, in true *Lord of the Flies* style, almost kills one of his own for shooting Wendy down. Furthermore, Pan's relationship with Tinker Bell is characterized by bouts of lover's jealousy.[7]

So at what point did the "boy who **wouldn't** grow up" transform into the "boy who **couldn't** grow up"? During the narrative, everyone else evolves, changes, and grows, except for Peter Pan. Jackson, in one way, suffered the same fate. His childhood face and persona became a symbol and a commodity. In his later life it would be a weapon hurled at him by his detractors: *Why don't you look this way anymore?*

Just as little Michael Jackson's expressions were "not indicative of the boy behind the smile," cherub-faced Pan can be viewed as an ancient prisoner. How long has he been in Neverland? Does he even know? Does anyone? The tale begins with the loss of his shadow, and what is a shadow but the most intrinsic part of ourselves? When Pan cannot reattach it, he falls into desperate crying. Jackson, too, used to cry with loneliness. How could he "live in himself when he [was] everywhere outside . . . the world is plastered with him, he is a thousand billboards. And the tragic truth seems ancient, that only onstage can he get back inside."[8]

We are never told what caused Pan's shadow to make its bid for escape. Could it be that life was so terrible that even his shadow wanted out? It's clearly unbearable enough for Pan to steal lost boys "who fall out of their perambulators when the nurse is looking the other way." What he seems to long for most is someone to share in his otherwise lonely existence.[9]

If writers continue to use the diminutive analogy "Peter Pan of Pop" for a consummate artist like Michael Jackson, they should use the whole story, or find other more appropriate stories. Jackson's personal Neverland became a prison only after it was ransacked twice, due to false accusations. Even then, he couldn't bear to sell it, though he could no longer live there. Before that, it had been a charitable venture, a gift for himself that he shared with children who were less fortunate. He did this for decades and hardly ever drew attention to it.[10]

I would argue that the fictional character Jackson most embodies is that of Ariel, the imprisoned spirit in Shakespeare's *The Tempest*, whose presence throughout the play is a continual cry for freedom: "Remember I have done thee worthy service, | Told thee no lies, made thee no mistakings, served without grudge or grumblings" echoes Jackson's own words: "You keep changin' the rules . . . I keep playin' the game . . . can't take it much longer . . . I might go insane." The fact that Ariel is more powerful than his captor, Prospero, does not help him; after all, it is Ariel who conjured the storm after which the play is named.[11]

Ariel remains trapped within a prison of Prospero's making. He exchanges one master for another, although he is the talent. Without him, neither of his masters would have any real power.

Parallels with Jackson abound—pick a master: family, fans, audience, managers, record label, lawyers, sycophants, or the media.

The most unnerving parallel between Jackson and Ariel is that Ariel's most entrancing ability on the stage is his song and flight. Both *The Tempest* (1611) and *Peter Pan* (1904) were plays where unfolding drama became a microcosm of events that transpired in the wider world: Barrie's regression, Shakespeare's aging, and the colonization of Africa. In 1983 Barney Hoskyns described Michael Jackson as "the boy that wants to fly; on stage he soars into the unreal." In reality, Ariel "could fly but he could not fly away," while Pan could fly away but always had to fly back. Jackson, unlike Ariel and Pan, was flesh and blood, and true flight eluded him. Instead, he joined the ranks of Barrie, Wilde, and Fitzgerald, and became, like all great fiction, a work of art.[12]

21.2. CRACK MUSIC: MICHAEL JACKSON'S *INVINCIBLE*

Inspired by Chapter 17—"*Invincible*: Michael Jackson's Lost Late Album," I originally wrote "'Crack Music': Michael Jackson's Invincible" after finding much similarity with Jackson in the way rapper Kanye West was written about in the press after he achieved mainstream success, particularly with regard to his being deemed egotistical and mentally unsound. These ideas sparked within me a probing for the common ground West and Jackson shared as *artists*, despite the hype and media circus that swarmed around them. Little academic writing has been devoted to Michael Jackson's final studio album *Invincible*. This article explores *Invincible* through Kanye West's metaphor of "crack music" from his 2005 album *Late Registration*, and places it in the context of black aspiration as a threat to dominant Western ideologies.

> "Sometimes I feel the music is the only medicine
> So we cook it, cut it, measure it, bag it, sell it."
>
> —Kanye West[13]

Listen to the track "Crack Music" from Kanye West's 2005 album *Late Registration*. The political, "Ronald Reagan cooked up an answer," is intertwined with the historical, "we've been hanging from the same tree ever since," and religious, "God, how could you let this happen?" West's gospel harmonies soar, as if reaching for impossible dreams, while his lyrics remain entrenched in the gutter. A similar bittersweetness is found in the rising choruses of "Whatever Happens" and "Heaven Can Wait" from Jackson's

Invincible. Both songs deal with existential themes, and death is at the center. There is a heavenwards reach ("tell the angels no") tempered with an earth-bound fear ("if the Lord should come for me").[14]

The curious dichotomy between what nourishes us and what kills us is the stage on which all of Jackson's songs were performed. Like Jackson did years before him ("black man, blackmail, throw the brother in jail"), West continually questions how blacks can forge identity in a predominantly white Western world: "they wanna pack us all in a box like styrofoam." While Jackson encodes his sentiments in metaphor—"I'm not a ghost from Hell, but I've got a spell on you"—West laces them with taboo lexis: "that's that crack music nigga."[15]

Some critics may disparage rap music as a binary opposite of art, and "one can readily find aesthetic reasons which seem to discredit it as a legitimate art form," but West's career was made by using the form to engage in tough racial discourse. It is unsurprising, then, that both Jackson and West were soon deemed eccentric and ridiculous: "West is an idiot, so mired in a fog of narcissism and self-delusion that he doesn't realise the full implications of what he's saying."[16]

But what exactly is "crack music," and what does it have to do with Michael Jackson's final studio album? Well, although *Invincible* is the least known of all of Michael Jackson's solo albums (much like his book of poetry, *Dancing the Dream*), it was undoubtedly "explosive," "intoxicating," and an example of a black man selling "black" music to a predominantly white (Western) world. *Invincible* was also a "crack" in Jackson's career.[17]

Invincible marked the beginning of a new phase, a change of artistic and musical direction and, unsurprisingly, it jarred with contemporary music critics: "he does need to leave Michael Jacksonland, that place where every sign points back to the spectacle of himself." This particular critic simply ignores the fact that many of us were born (musically, metaphorically, and artistically) in "Michael Jacksonland" and will continue to live there as long as his unparalleled influence pervades.[18]

Performance poet Malik Yusef, who speaks about West's "Crack Music," iterates the eponym as the way "former slaves trade hooks for Grammys." However, that exchange is mired, because respect cannot be bought. Still, the black artist has no choice but to own all of it, the otherness and the fragmentation. It is the dynamic repossessing of these difficulties that transforms poison into power: "this dark diction has become America's addiction."[19]

By 2001 and *Invincible*'s release, the world of popular music had changed radically. Jackson was no stranger to leaping across the decades, but this time things were (as in the *Thriller* short film) "different." He was simultaneously a living legend, a caricature, and a has-been. Jackson's dream of beating

Thriller's phenomenal record sales was distant. Even if he ever stood a chance of accomplishing it, he could never have done so without the fair wind of public opinion. The shadow of suspicion raised by extortion decimated his reputation and, by proxy, his sales.[20]

The poison that spiked Jackson's career was "thinly veiled racism" that effectively barred him from the artistic recognition he sought and deserved. Jackson's delinquency was the outrageous notion that he was both extraordinarily successful and black. Kanye West's "crack music" is "cooks and nannies." It changes the status quo, turns poison into power, and must be silenced at all costs.[21]

For many, the *Invincible* album was a drug that did not do what it had promised. As in J.M. Barrie's *Peter Pan*, happy thoughts alone cannot give flight. Jackson recognized Tinker Bell as the true hero of her story, and he was eventually buried with her, "slinging a stream of the dust he so loved inside the right breast of [his] jacket." It is a combination of fairy dust and "happy thoughts" that convinces the wearer that he or she can fly. Perhaps the problem with "crack music" is the audacity of the aspiration that black men like Michael Jackson and Kanye West have the gall to attempt such dizzying heights.[22]

One thing is certain, in the case of a man who can fly: "it's all done in the heavens," awe must eventually turn to resentment, no matter his color. *Invincible* was Michael Jackson's successful attempt to craft his own musical world, while his multiple personas sped ahead of him. Yet, *Invincible*, though still largely relegated as a "lesser work," far surpasses much of what was released in the same year even in the same decade.[23]

Like William Shakespeare's most dismissive critics and staunchest supporters, all will be long dead by the time *Invincible*'s fate is decided, and just like in the case of Shakespeare's *Tempest*, the latter works of a great artist can be overlooked by audiences in their contemporary time. People forget that Shakespeare's plays, now so exalted, were the common entertainment of prostitutes and peasantry in the seamier side of 17th-century London.

The playhouses were far from the air-conditioned theaters of today; they were plague-filled pits that incubated disease. As our modern actors spout 400-year-old lines in "Received Pronunciation" on brand-new stages made of imported wood, after all, "we cannot recreate the stenches, the clothes of the audience, their mind-set, and the surrounding city." William Shakespeare's Thames teemed with sewage, and his lyrical constructions have more to do with "crack music" than most would like to admit. It is easy to forget how working-class Shakespeare actually was, and it took several years for him to be regarded as a genius. Let us hope it doesn't take so long for Michael, his blackness notwithstanding: "people will not understand this album right now. It's

ahead of its time . . . the album will live on forever" because "music is what
lives and lasts."[24]

21.3. "HEARD IT ON THE GRAPEVINE": ARE WE
LOSING MICHAEL JACKSON ALL OVER AGAIN?

This article was originally published in *The Journal of Michael Jackson Academic Studies* on August 29, 2014, which would have been Michael Jackson's
56th birthday. It is with this short piece on Jackson's legacy and the future of
his representation that I end this book.

From the German fortress of Ehbreitstein to the ancient city of Trier and
beyond, there is a meandering valley called the Mosel, which hosts some of
the most beautiful vineyards in the world. Reisling grapevines are draped over
doors and along winding streets.

Brothers Grimm's fairy-tale houses are adorned with ornate calligraphy.
They remind me of Neverland Valley Ranch (see Figure 21.3.1). Why? Well,

Figure 21.3.1
**Aerial view of Neverland Ranch, once the Home of Famed Singer Michael
Jackson, in the Santa Ynez Valley of Santa Barbara County, California.**
The Jon B. Lovelace Collection of California Photographs in Carol M. Highsmith's
America Project.
(Library of Congress)

around Michael Jackson's birthday, it becomes nearly impossible to write around him. He is the fallen hero as well as the singing seraphim.

A lesson I learned from Michael Jackson: Study absolutely everyone and everything. There is no such thing as useless information. Listen and learn always. Cultivate a thirst for knowledge and it will nourish you. With this inquisitiveness I spoke to a local winemaker to learn about her unique heritage.

She taught me about the relationship between the vines and the valley, the vineyards and winemakers, about the symbiotic heritage of the place. She had the grace of a classic Hollywood starlet and a wisdom that could only come from years of experience. She told me how the hands of each element of the winemaking process are held tight in a harmonic embrace: the human taking from nature and in turn tending the woodland surrounding the valley. She explained that the tourists who came to the region were providing an income that would, in turn, help preserve the environment.

You may wonder what this has to do with the popular, mainstream music of Michael Jackson. Well, the art of Michael Jackson, like the culture of winemaking in this beautiful valley, is in serious jeopardy. New generations of winemakers are choosing to leave what is a not-so-lucrative family business with hundreds of years of history, because, often, they cannot make ends meet.

I couldn't help but feel a parallel with the words that Michael Jackson spoke, the music he made, and the short films he produced. He was indeed the author of all of his work—from his live performances (and how they were presented on camera), to his clothing, appearance, and message of love and hope. He also was the architect of his struggles, and he made them our business, the struggles of the every person, the dejected, the ostracized, and the mistreated. He didn't have to do that. But he did, and it was indeed a beautiful body of work.

From "Ben" to "Cry," Michael Jackson fashioned an intricate canon that is now in jeopardy. The short films he painstakingly fashioned are being reappropriated piecemeal, extracted from their original context before our very eyes, "his activism and outcries for the plight of the environment, of the poor and sick, and of voiceless children" are already being lost in the throng.

And it has been barely seven years since he was gone.

We, the dreamers, the thinkers, the academics, and the visionaries, to whom Michael Jackson should matter, are in danger of losing sight of exactly how he was an author, director, composer, and poet. And especially, we are losing sight of the way he channeled his personal experiences and genuine love for people into both art and charitable works, what so often now seems to be the "bonus track," when it should be the main score.

Have we already forgotten that Michael Jackson was so much more than his lucrative global brand? Have we turned an activist and humanitarian in the ilk of Mandela and Lennon into a brand like McDonalds and Starbucks? Or are we on our way to doing so, by reducing Jackson's contributions and by saturating the market with mixes and releases that carry none of the weight and meaning of Michael Jackson's own message.

Like fine wine, Jackson's work was preserved in an almost timeless form. We will never have to imagine or ask others how he spun and glided; he knowingly bottled those performances, and always with a message that we could use to be better and live better. We will never have to ask him what he thought or how he felt, because he immortalized that, too, in albums, short films, interviews, and song lyrics.

But if we do not take the time to preserve a great body of work like Michael Jackson's, it is likely that we will lose it. As the song says, "time waits for no one," and time has an uncanny way of filtering out the worst as well as the best.

Some will attempt, and some have already attempted, to rewrite history (even while Michael Jackson was making history!). They discount and devalue his contribution as one of the most incredible artists of our age. He symbolizes the best in us, while his mistreatment symbolizes the worst.

All that remains is that we who make art and write discourse must not let the real Michael Jackson be lost again. This is our responsibility. We are the real gatekeepers, and we must find our own way to preserve the truth of Jackson's art for future generations.

There are just a handful of well-researched, published books focused on the staggering body of work that Michael created in his lifetime. There were none, of note, before his death, even though *Thriller* was 25 years old in 2007.

Few of those that now exist (5) are mass-published, which means that only doggedly determined fans and academics can procure them all. On the other side of the balance lie thousands of tabloid and tabloid-inspired "infotainment" pieces and articles, in hundreds of languages, based solidly in lies.

Jackson's body of work, his "gift to us," must be treated as an artistic canon. Any academic worth their salt will tell you that the canon must be treated with esteem—untampered with and untouched. Equally, we must be careful not to elevate *Thriller* above *Invincible* or forget "Stranger in Moscow" in our praise of "Billie Jean."

If we do not find our own way to preserve and revere Jackson's great art—and the truth and sentiments behind it—it will surely die.

We could still lose the gift we were given.

From Object to Subject: A Critical Survey on the Representation of Blackness in the Early Modern Period

I n *Playing in the Dark: Whiteness and the Literary Imagination*, Toni Morrison writes, "in matters of race, silence and evasion have historically ruled literary discourse."[1] Since Morrison's publication in 1992, contemporary academics, predominantly concerned with critical significance, have sought to address these silences. After outlining its terms, this survey will examine the rapidly growing study of the representation of black people in the early modern period.

The *Oxford English Dictionary (OED) Online* defines "race" as a term beset with transposable meanings: "ethnic group of common descent"; "a distinct ethnic set"; and a "major grouping . . . defined in terms of distinct physical features." Its meaning widened and gained negative denotations consistent with the expansion of the British Empire in the 16th and 17th centuries.[2] The word is now commonly replaced by "ethnicity," from the Latin "ethnicus," meaning "heathen," a word less tainted by the negative connotations of slavery and colonization.[3] The adjective "black" and the noun "blackness" are words whose "uses with negative connotations proliferate[d] in the early modern period," and they are used in this survey to designate "a member of any dark-skinned group of peoples who are "of sub-Saharan African origin or descent."[4]

Harvey Young, in his 2013 monograph *Theatre and Race*, asserts that "race and racial thinking stem from a basic human desire for orientation" and "should not be dismissed as either a mere fiction or an anachronism." Since race "did not attain widespread use until the late nineteenth century," it is one of several factors that complicate approaches to the representation of early modern blackness.[5] Young, citing Emily Bartels' "Too Many Blackamoors:

Deportation, Discrimination, and Elizabeth I" and *Speaking of the Moor: From Alcazar to Othello*, argues that "*Othello* reveals little about racial thinking in the Elizabethan era" and "there is little evidence of an unambiguous anti-black prejudice in the Elizabethan theatre."[6] Bartels, in turn, furthers the research of academic Michael Neill, by reiterating the vague term "moor" as a liminal space between religion and ethnicity.[7] She highlights the "racist" decree of Elizabeth I as a "solution to crises resulting from Anglo-Spanish conflict," and states that that the need for such a decree implies ongoing integration of blacks in English society in the period.[8]

Critics Young-Joo Choi, Cristina Malcolmson, Michael McGiffert, William Over, and Kimberly Poitevin are acutely aware of the anachronistic nature of race.[9] In their research they all contextualize the term in order to align its use with "the need for more dynamic conceptions" and "a desire for full academic acceptance/legitimacy."[10] For Young, race's "broad acceptance, seeming materiality, and staying power is anchored in its ability to provide a narrative that unifies a collective social history."[11] So, "to conceptualize race in terms of embodiment is . . . the most useful way of attending to the various manners in which it performs."[12]

In the 1960s, the "older generation" of academics (Bernard Harris, G. K. Hunter, and Eldred D. Jones) sought to establish, through early scholarship, "black presence."[13] Jones' "The Physical Representation of African Characters on the English Stage During the 16th and 17th Centuries" and "Othello's Countrymen: The African in English Renaissance Drama," exemplified how black people were viewed in the early modern period. Critic Margo Hendricks refers to these academics as "a generation of scholars increasingly ignored or dismissed in the rush to 'racialize' Shakespeare's canon."[14]

A period of relative dormancy followed, "as Shakespeare scholars and critics embraced the tenets of New Criticism, Structuralism and Russian Formalism."[15] Nonetheless, the 1970s ushered the pioneering historical and archival research of F. O. Shyllon, Peter Mark, Edward Scobie, and James Walvin.[16] This work would be advanced by Peter Fryer, David Dabydeen, Paul Edwards, and Imtiaz Habib in the following decades, focusing on the material presence and lives of blacks in the early modern period.[17] In "'Object into Object?': Some Thoughts on the Presence of Black Women in Early Modern Culture," academic Kim F. Hall rightly contests that these scholars are "less worried about the anachronistic 'problem' of race as a category," and provide resistance by "analyzing the racism within representation."[18]

In the introduction to her 1995 monograph *Things of Darkness: Economies of Race and Gender in Early Modern England*, Hall includes a subsection, "Who Is English? The Black Presence in England." Here, she draws on the work of Peter Edwards, claiming that "modern literary criticism remystifies the appearance of blackness in literary works."[19] Edwards places "England's black presence and its 'racial' consciousness much earlier" than the early modern period, finding "evidence of blacks in the Romano-British period."[20]

The rise of New Historicism and Cultural Materialism in the late 1980s gave impetus to the study of race in Shakespeare scholarship. Criticism on the representation of early modern blackness often makes use of both New Historicist and Cultural Materialist discourse. For example, Peter Erickson, in his article "Representations of Blacks and Blackness in the Renaissance," published in 1993 in *Criticism*, cites Alan Sinfield: "the stories we need to retell are the ones that trouble us, that we find hard to resolve."[21] Likewise, in the epilogue from *Early Modern Visual Culture: Representation, Race, and Empire in Renaissance England*, Erickson cites Stephen Greenblatt on both homoeroticism and black representation. Since "any reading of a literary text is a question of negotiation . . . between text and reader within the context of history or histories that cannot be closed or finalised," the ascribing of the value of and purpose for black representation in the period is, by proxy, also a conduit for the identification of Englishness.[22]

In "Surveying 'Race' in Shakespeare," the introductory chapter of *Shakespeare and Race*, published in 2000, Hendricks terms the resurgence of interest a "revival."[23] This resurgence was galvanized by the work of academics on both sides of the Atlantic, including Anthony Barthelemy, Bernadette Andrea, Mary Floyd-Wilson, Joyce Green MacDonald, and Ania Loomba.[24] These "inheritors of an intellectual, critical and political tradition" were responsible for what Hendricks terms, the " 'next generation' engagement with race."[25]

The "next generation" owed some of its success to critics like Edward Said; for with the postcolonial criticism derived from works like Said's *Orientalism*, came a revolutionary way of looking at representation of early modern blackness.[26] Said's *Orientalism* would help ignite the postcolonial criticism in literature as it appertains to the "ambiguous status of the other (racial or otherwise) that makes it so threatening, so disturbing, so dangerous."[27] In conjunction with Said, Frantz Fanon, Gayatri Spivak, and Homi Bhabha "have argued that the Western discourse of colonialism is constituted by the other subject—by alterities of race, colour or ethnic origin."[28]

Morrison's *Playing in the Dark* was particularly "interested in what prompts and makes possible this process of entering what one is estranged from."[29] In this highly influential work, through which Morrison intended "to draw a map, so to speak, of a critical geography," she exemplified the argument that the "western notions of human identity itself . . . may be recognized as a historical construct constituted by the . . . oppression of racial others'.[30] Hall, by the same token, contends that "descriptions of dark and light . . . became in the early modern period the conduit through which the English began to formulate the notions of 'self' and 'other'." In his essay *Elizabethans and Foreigners* written 30 years before, G. K. Hunter also argued that the "explanation of the black skin of the Negro which sees it as a mark of God's disfavour . . . remains potently attractive, even in an allegedly scientific world."[31]

Loomba, citing Dympna Callaghan's *Shakespeare without Women: Representing Gender and Race on the Renaissance Stage*, points out that "the representation of an idea of the Moor . . . does not simply reflect historical reality but mediates it."[32] Meanwhile, Hall, citing Loomba, ascertains that "current work in race . . . in some ways posits 'black presence' studies as the 'other' that we must distance ourselves from."[33] The issue at hand for both Loomba and Hall is that "Africans in early modern England often exist for contemporary readers of the period in the realm of the anecdote."[34]

Morrison's *Playing in the Dark*, though centered primarily on American literature, highlights how the representation of blackness is also crucial to the representation of whiteness in the early modern period, "through significant and underscored omissions, startling contradictions, heavily nuanced conflicts . . . the way writers peopled their work with the signs and bodies of this presence—one can see that a real or fabricated Africanist presence was crucial."[35] Erickson also cites Morrison in "Representations of Blacks and Blackness": "blackness in Renaissance art, including Shakespeare's often involve . . . the symbolic process by which white artists imagine relations between whites and blacks."[36] Hall, too, refers to the fact that that she is "especially concerned with just those 'shadows' and 'lines of demarcation' that Morrison outlines, rather than with the more obvious African presences."[37]

The available criticism of early modern blackness in relation to homosexuality and queer theory is limited. Erickson highlights this but rightly acknowledges that scholars of homosexuality and race share a common ground. They seek to "call attention to visual evidence that earlier criticism has passed over in silence and thus rendered invisible."[38] The books *Queering the Renaissance*, published in 1994, and *The Renaissance of Lesbianism in Early Modern England*, published in 2002, go some way to cross this divide.[39] Another field with which the study of early modern blackness frequently intersects is feminist criticism. Erickson regards the fifth chapter of Hall's *Things of Darkness* "the single most important and concentrated discussion of the visual evidence of racial motifs."[40]

Valerie Traub's *Mapping the Global Body* presents women's bodies as vehicles for creating race and gender hierarchy. Her methodology required a survey of cartographic artefacts and the images of men and women used as symbols, representative of entire countries or geographical regions. These served to enforce a hetero-normative system on all cultures.[41] Opposite to that, Andrea Stevens' *Mastering Masques of Blackness*, published in *English*

Literary Renaissance in 2009, argues that "blackness . . . is identified as both fixed and capable of reversal" and that the "*Masque of Blackness* presents African women who 'are' black but who long for a racial transformation."[42]

The 1990s also heralded a resurgence in the use of visual, literary, and historical artefacts as metaphors for and symbols of social and political power. Erickson's "Representation of Blacks and Blackness" was key in bringing together visual rhetoric and literary criticism, continuing the visual–literary approach utilized by Bernard Harris in "A Portrait of a Moor."[43] Hendricks highlights Harris' "efforts to link the English social history behind and alongside the 1600 painting of the Ambassador from Morocco."[44] Peter Erickson and Clark Hulse's edition, *Early Modern Visual Culture*, published in 2000, presented a wide range of approaches to the representation of early modern blackness. Erickson and Hulse are two of a devoted group of critics who have steadily employed both literary and visual studies. They argue that this "cross disciplinarity arises not from a transcendence or blurring of discipline but from an embracing of . . . a happy convergence and intersection of a variety of disciplinary logics."[45] Furthermore, Erickson and Hulse believe that "a fundamental substrate of visual metaphor persists in the writings that form the basis for contemporary literary and culture theory." They also refer to Norman Bryson, Michael Ann Holly, and Keith Moxey in "bring[ing] visual studies into close contact with other disciplines, especially . . . semiotic, deconstructive, new historicist, and feminist work found in literary studies."[46]

Erickson argues that painting's "nonverbal quality makes it at once so direct and so tacit" because, "the absence of blacks in painting until after the mid-1600s does not mean that images of blacks were absent from British culture prior to that point."[47] These literary/visual methodologies continue "the long-standing alliance between the literary and the art-historical study of early modern England . . . founded on the premise that visual and literary artifacts alike must be understood in relation to their social meaning."[48] They challenge the academic "to attend in a critical way to the visual dimensions at the core of" this literary and cultural field, which is especially important when the visual is so often in "danger of a subjugation of the visual to the verbal."[49]

In *Mapping the Global Body*, Valerie Traub suggests that "even the apparently aesthetic phenomena such as tropes of light and dark figure barbarism and civility through the colours of the world's peoples."[50] Her methodology utilizes maps, through whose "'marginalia' . . . the body continues to speak to and with the geography depicted within."[51] By examining these cartographical sources, Traub delineates theological rather than physical difference: "race . . . seems not to have existed in the sixteenth century as a stable category of biological difference."[52] She refers to both Hall and Erickson, "the concept of the global body enacted a powerful universalizing logic," and goes on to examine complexion as "an external manifestation of basic humoral qualities . . . affected by climatological variations."[53]

Pascale Aebischer's "Murderous Male Moors: Gazing at Race in *Titus Andronicus* and *Othello*" was published in *Shakespeare's Violated Bodies: Stage and Screen Performance* in 2004 and focuses on the language and actions of the characters Othello and Aaron.[54] In a different way from Traub, Aebischer chooses to focus on the interplay between blackness, whiteness, and theology. Aebischer chooses to employ rehearsal notebooks in order to engage with the subtleties of identification as well as the changing aspects of negotiation.

Another particularly useful example of the range of approaches is found in criticism relating to the Drake Jewel, "made with rare materials gathered from around the globe," with the figures of a black African ruler superimposed onto a white female monarch. It was given to Elizabeth I by Sir Francis Drake, and in his article for *Uncommon Sense*, David S. Shields discusses alliances between Anglo-African forces in relation to the jewel, "Drake's alliance with the Cimmarroons, runaway African slaves."[55] Karen C. C. Dalton, on the other hand, uses the jewel as a symbol of English supremacy through the metaphor of alchemy, "the blackness of the reign of Saturn . . . envelops the gold that will result from the transmutation."[56] Erickson and Hulse regard Dalton's "juxtaposition of the Drake Jewel and the image of a black emperor . . . as indexes of Elizabethan ideology."[57] Dalton insightfully claims, however, that "an image of a black emperor does not represent a demon or a black pageboy or a slave . . . It represents an emperor whose blackness is not burdened with the medieval, Christian connotations of sin, evil and death."[58] As these few examples show, methodologies are wide-ranging. Scholars have used a wide range of material, including decrees, maps, plays, jewels, art, poems, and masques with varying degrees of engagement.

In the 1970s, Stephen Orgel, in his work on the masques of Ben Jonson, would begin to reflect on the presence of what he termed an "antithetical" blackness in the Stuart Court. Orgel categorized *The Masque of Blackness* as problematic, "a measure of the immaturity of the work . . . the poet's problem."[59] The issue of gender serves to further complicate the representation of early modern blackness, as we occasionally see the representation of black females (Anne of Denmark in *The Masque of Blackness* and Rubens' *Bacchanal and Four Continents*) placed center-stage, forcing the "socially peripheral" to become "symbolically central."[60]

The last four years have seen a deceleration in output of discourse on the representation of early modern blackness. Nevertheless, if, in reference to Michel Foucault, "power is produced and reproduced in research," then the opportunity to discuss the presence of high-status representations of blacks in the early modern period is valuable, especially since "blackness is so symbolically crucial to early modern culture."[61] After all, "to enforce its invisibility through silence is to allow the black body a shadowless participation in the dominant cultural body."[62] Toni Morrison is not entirely correct in her assertion that "images of impenetrable whiteness . . . appear almost always in conjunction with representations of black or Africanist people who are dead, impotent, or under complete control."[63] Both literary and visual artefacts, such as Jonson's *Masque of Blackness*, Shakespeare's *Othello*, and the Drake Jewel—with their inherent visual rhetoric—depict blacks in positions of high status and power. The understanding of these high-status symbols sof early modern blackness offer the opportunity "to transcend the black presence . . . and inform understandings of gender, the state and political life and private existences."[64]

"With All His Beauteous Race": High-Status Blacks in *The Masque of Blackness* and *The Merchant of Venice*

Critical discourse on the early modern representation of blackness has evolved from the necessary advocacy of black presence, to more elaborate criticism that is concerned with how blacks are portrayed in relation to class and gender. In her 1992 monograph *Playing in the Dark: Whiteness and the Literary Imagination*, Toni Morrison asserted that "images of impenetrable whiteness . . . appear almost always in conjunction with representations of black or Africanist people who are dead, impotent, or under complete control."[1] Although Morrison's work focuses primarily on contemporary literature, several early modernists, like Kim F. Hall and Peter Erickson, have cited her, in a range of works that explore how white authors represent black people.[2]

This research explores high-status representations of blacks in the early modern period, using two primary texts: Ben Jonson's 1608 quarto, *The Masque of Blackness*, and William Shakespeare's 1600 quarto, *The Merchant of Venice*. It focuses its analysis on two minor black characters, Niger and the Prince of Morocco, whose high-status representations offer the opportunity "to transcend the black presence . . . and inform understandings of gender, the state and political life."[3] It illustrates these high-status representations by considering the ways in which the characters are depicted in text and performance, and goes further to consider how these high-status black characters are represented in terms of gender.

INTRODUCTION

Fair Niger, **son** to great Oceanus,
Now honoured thus,

With **all his beauteous race**,
Who, though but black in face,
Yet they are **bright**
And full of **life** and **light**;
To prove that beauty best,
Which **not the colour**, but the feature
Assures unto the creature (64–72)

Ben Jonson's *The Masque of Blackness* (1605) is steeped in novelty. It was the earliest masque to display a white royal as a black person, for which there is "an existing text": Jonson's first court masque, as well as his first in conjunction with the designer Inigo Jones. Most importantly for this research, however, is the fact that it is "the first recorded use of blackening to actually darken the skin of the royal maskers."[4]

In its opening lines, the text, which "celebrates Britain's difference from distant, 'darker' worlds," presents the black character Niger, who is described as "fair" (64).[5] Niger is also presented as "son to great Oceanus" (64), who, in turn, is an embodiment of the world's seas. Niger's 12 princess daughters were played by the Queen of England, Anne of Denmark, and her ladies; and they were referred to as "his beauteous race" (66).[6] Their skins were painted at the behest of the Queen herself and "in eroticised cross-cultural transit," these high-status black characters . . . penetrate[d] the aptly named Whitehall," their arrival "aswarm with submarine anxieties about gender, race and culture."[7] Within the masque, Niger's character defends the beauty of his princess daughters in his "bid to do a kind and careful father's part" (95). His daughters, "in whose sparkling and refulgent eyes | The glorious sun did still delight to rise" (99–100), are deceived by "the fabulous voices of some few | Poor brain-sick men" (115–116), which results in their desire to wash away their blackness, although Niger warns them, "how near divinity they be | That stand from passion and decay so free" (113–114). This positive characterization of blackness is both complex and exciting, because in most cases of early modern performance, "the dominant group, white men, take on the characteristics of subordinate groups, namely Africans and women."[8] However, in this masque, we have white male and female maskers depicted as Africans.

Stephen Orgel argued that Niger "must be an antimasque character merely because he is not aware of the paradoxical element in his assumption that blackness is beautiful," while critics like William Over contest that "although the speech of Niger is perhaps the most direct articulation of non-European alterity on the English Renaissance stage, it has not received appropriate critical attention."[9] Early modern scholars, as products of a postcolonial heritage, may be so expectant of depictions of blacks in positions of servitude and subjugation that we are amazed at how fervently "Niger objects to the project of cultural absorption played before the English court."[10] This research is a negotiation between these two arguments, which attempts to read both race and representation as sensitively as possible. It stems from a desire to leave the perceptions of our "twentieth century ears" because "they reflect the taxonomy of colour through which we have come to rationalize our own racial fantasies."[11]

The Masque of Blackness is this research's main primary source, and a large proportion of its analysis stems from this text. Written in 1605, as a commission from Queen Anne, and first performed at the palace at Whitehall in 1605 on January 6 (also known as Twelfth Night), it was entered in the Stationer's Register in 1608 (April 21), and it first published in quarto in the same year by Thomas Thorpe, under the title The Characters of Two Royall Masques the One of Blacknesse, the Other of Beautie.[12] A "scribal copy, signed by Jonson" exists at the British Library, and "its presence among the Royal manuscripts implies that it was presented to the King or Queen."[13] The Masque of Blackness was included in two folio collections of Jonson's works in later decades, and "the 1616 Folio text was printed from the quarto," so "the quarto, therefore represents Jonson's final thoughts."[14] The published masque is aptly described by Lynn Meskill as "a tissue of references to writing paper, ink characters, Greek terminations, hieroglyphs, and visibly, a printed document that gives shape and substance to a fleeting masque performance."[15]

Less than a decade before Jonson's Niger gave his passionate defense of blackness at the royal palace, William Shakespeare's character, the Prince of Morocco, attempted unsuccessfully to woo the fair Portia in The Merchant of Venice at the public theatre. The play "was revived in 1605," the same year of The Masque of Blackness performance. It was performed "at Whitehall before James I on Sunday 10 February, and again at his request the following Shrove Tuesday, 12 February."[16] This research's second primary source is the play The Merchant of Venice, written by William Shakespeare, and first performed c. 1596 by the Lord Chamberlain's Men.[17] It was entered in the Stationer's Register in 1598 by James Roberts and published in quarto by "I.R. for Thomas Heyes" in 1600 under the title The Most Excellent Historie of the Merchant of Venice.[18] The Merchant of Venice would be featured in three quarto editions and two folio collections in the ensuing years.[19]

While plays like The Merchant of Venice "roamed the world with the freedom of thought," masques like The Masque of Blackness, "operating in a triumphal mode, explicitly—and riskfully, returned the world to England"[20] In her analysis "The Characters of Posterity in Jonson's The Masque of Blacknesse and Shakespeare's Antony and Cleopatra," Meskill centers her analysis on both a masque and play, and I will endeavor to do the same in this research.

Its locus will remain the literary and performance features of these texts, situated in their early modern context.[21] The following similarities make the play and masque excellent companions: firstly, both texts feature high-status black characters with dialogue that focuses on their physical blackness; secondly, both texts were published and performed within the same decade in the same city, and indeed, for the King, in the same year. Thirdly, though one text is a masque written primarily for a courtly audience, and the other a play written for a mass audience, both publications were sold at "Paules Church-yard."[22]

Zachary Lesser argues that both texts would have been sold to a wide audience of readers: "playbooks that did reach the bookshops continued to be an excellent investment for publishers because they were in great demand with readers."[23] Furthermore, "print publication allowed the [masque] genre to move beyond the narrow confines of culture to a larger reading public."[24] The rationale for concentrating my analysis on the minor characters, Niger and the Prince of Morocco, is that their depictions, via publication, enable us to consider closely their dialogue, which may well have been overshadowed in the spectacle of performance, "for all kinds of reasons—contingent or designed, hermeneutic or logistical—masque receivers do not always hear what masque producers project."[25] The very same can be said for theatre audiences.

In this research, I have used modern editions of works by William Shakespeare and Ben Jonson.[26] When relevant, I have employed the original spellings of key words as they are found in the quartos of both texts, as found in *Early English Books Online*.[27] When I have done so, I have used the modern letter forms and also modernized my use of italics.

The key reason for exploring race in this research is the fact that, "to pose . . . questions about the racial implications of early modern text is also to inquire into how audiences (then and now) might have construed and recognized the concept of race and its linguistic inflections."[28] As Ania Loomba suggests, the history of "race" is "both protracted and erratic," and it consists of "a range of concepts, theories and mechanisms for assigning different values to human beings [that] arise and mutate, go dormant, resurface, relocate and adapt anew."[29] The *Oxford English Dictionary (OED) Online*'s many definitions of "race" echo the word's inchoate qualities: "ethnic group of common descent," and "a major grouping."[30]

In *Shakespeare and Race*, Margo Hendricks explains how, during the early modern period, "the meaning of 'race' varied depending upon whether a writer wanted to specify difference born of a class-based concept of genealogy, a psychological (and essentialized) nature, or group typology."[31] Dennis Britton has explored the conception of racial difference, arguing that dramatists like Shakespeare and Jonson "inherited a mode in which racial, national and religious identities were conveniently flexible."[32] We can also consider "race" in terms of religious inclination. Anthony Appiah writes, "stereotypes, which *we* might naturally think of as . . . 'racialist' [are] rooted far less in notions of inherited dispositions and far more in the idea of the Moor and the Jew as infidels."[33] This research focuses on the performative markers of blackness, predominantly dark skin, and the representation of "race" in terms of stereotypes. Harvey Young's definition in *Theatre and Race* is particularly useful, because Young examines how "race" functions within society. The word "race" is employed in this research to denote a socially constructed idea that attributes social value and status to the pigmentation of skin.[34] Therefore, it will no longer be placed in quotation marks.[35]

In "Othello Was a White Man: Properties of Race on Shakespeare's Stage," Dympna Callaghan deconstructs blackness as firstly "the display of black people themselves (exhibition)" and secondly as "the simulation of negritude (mimesis)."[36] This research is concerned primarily with the latter, as "blackness is simultaneously held as a sign that confounds knowability . . . in the symbolic, visual logic of the theatre."[37] The word "ethnicity" is used to denote nationality and general region of ethnic origin.[38] The adjective "black" and the noun "blackness" also require definition, since these are two words whose negative meanings flourished in the early modern period. In this research they are used to designate "a member of any dark-skinned group of peoples" who are "of sub-Saharan African origin or descent."[39] Early modern terms interchangeable with "black" are "blackamoor," "black-moor," "moor," and "Ethiop."[40]

As I have clarified my usage of the word "black," it is equally important to clarify the word "white." In " 'These Bastard Signs of Fair': Literary Whiteness in Shakespeare's Sonnets," Kim F. Hall remarks that in the early modern period, "England was inhabited by a large population that came to be seen as 'white', and yet we have not uncovered ways of discussing this as a factor in English identity formation."[41] She also contests that "critical practice has also tended to make early modern whiteness even more impervious to critique," by way of a "general focus on Africans, Indians and other non-Europeans," which assumes "that race somehow only accrues to minoritized peoples."[42] Likewise, Ian Smith contends that contemporary "criticism's denial of color's semantic and racial significance derives an ancillary benefit: where there is no blackness, no admission of criticism's complicity with whiteness need ever be confessed."[43] The whites to which this research refers are those of predominantly English and Scottish origin, and they are considered here as a race constructed in a mode of separation from blacks. Where it is made explicit, other European nationalities may be referred to also under the same term.

The term "high status" is used with regard to social and political hierarchy. Coincidentally, the first usage offered by the *OED Online* for "high status" is racially oriented: "white servants . . . as well as almost all Negroes, are called by their first names by the high-status whites." Both high and low status are particularly useful markers of power and social authority in performance texts. A high-status individual exists only in relation to other characters. In addition, the use of the word "gender" is used to denote not only socially constructed binaries of feminine and masculine, but also the biological term "sex," which denotes male and female.

In terms of structure, this research consists of an introduction, followed by three chapters and a conclusion, in order to answer the overarching question "How are high-status blacks represented in *The Masque of Blackness* and *The Merchant of Venice*?" The first and second chapters consist of close readings of the primary texts and call upon a wide range of criticism. The first chapter focuses on the characterization of Niger in *The Masque of Blackness*, while the second focuses on Morocco in *The Merchant of Venice*. The second chapter also brings both texts together in a preliminary conclusion. The third and final chapter answers the question "How are Niger and Morocco presented in terms of gender?" This chapter also consults a range of critics, and it considers, through close reading of the source material, how these male characters are presented primarily by way of their relationships with female characters. The last chapter is followed by a conclusion that brings together all of the main research arguments. It also poses some specific opportunities for further study and analysis.

APPENDIX A.2.1:
NIGER, A HIGH-STATUS BLACK CHARACTER
IN *THE MASQUE OF BLACKNESS*

During the staged court masque, the "theatrically impressive entrance of Queen Anne and her ladies in blackface, enhanced by the first use of Italian scenic perspective on the English stage and Jones's brilliant costumes, renders Niger a voiceless supernumerary."[1] However, in print, with Jonson's assertion of control over the text, which is stripped of spectacle and theatrics, the prominence of Niger's textual presence puts forward an unchallenged "speech against assimilation," which "remains cogent and unanswered in the play."[2]

Much of the criticism relating to the character Niger focuses on his dramatic shortcomings, as opposed to his literary prominence: "Niger is made to look foolish because he does not know where he is; and that he finds his daughters' black skin beautiful."[3] Often, Niger's 69-line speech is viewed as underdeveloped, "his viewpoint is garbled and forcefully contained."[4] Niger's speech is in rhyming couplets and iambic pentameter, which affirms his royalty and high status. He "fuses body and mind, the outward and inward aspects of human identity, since for Niger, skin color, the most external part of the body, associates with the deepest traits of character, faithfulness, and constancy."[5] The *OED Online* defines "characterization" as "the quality or character imparted to something," and with this in mind, the next two chapters focus firstly on textual characterization (including stage directions) and costuming and makeup of Niger and Morocco.

Although recent scholarship has provided much debate about the agency and authorship of *The Masque of Blackness*, to the extent that Clare MacManus names both Queen Anne and Jonson as coauthors of the text, this research (because it is predominantly concerned with how blackness is represented) regards Jonson as dramatist, even though "it was Her Majesty's will to have them black-moors at first" (13–14).[6] When the 12 princess daughters of Niger are considered in this close reading, they are viewed as extensions of his high-status representation. In terms of genealogy, they legitimize his presence within the masque, and he legitimizes theirs. William Over provides a very in-depth analysis of Niger's speech in "Alterity and Assimilation in Jonson's Masques of Blackness and Beauty," which has been employed here in order to support my assertions.[7]

NOMENCLATURE, DIALOGUE, AND CHARACTERIZATION

Niger "projects a complex identity within the masque's allegorical currents."[8] Jonson presents him as the embodiment of both place and people, "a river in Ethiopia famous by the name of Niger" (10–11) and regards the "Nigritae, now Negroes," as the "blackest nation in the world" (11–12). Niger's name has several meanings, stemming firstly from the Spanish word for the color black. It occurs as the name of the principal river of West Africa in English contexts from 1600 onward, and we see the use of the word in many postderivatives, such as various types of oil and wood that are found along the river.[9]

The quotation "Fair Niger, son to great Oceanus . . . unto the creature" (64–72), referred to in the Introduction, is an extract from the first lines of the chorused song from the masque's opening ceremony, an official song, announcing Niger's arrival. The quarto text gives "fayre," which the *OED*

Online defines as "beautiful, agreeable," "of attractive appearance," especially in terms of "a person, or a person's face." In later usage the word became more closely associated with women. Niger's inherent "fairness also denotes inner qualities of character, and most significantly his faithfulness to African identity," declaring Jonson's advocacy of disposition over appearance, because "what concerns him is exoticism, not a linkage between skin tone and differential human essence."[10] This song begins the masque by also describing Niger's daughters as "his beauteous race" (66) whose beauty is not marred by their blackness, who are, while black, also "full of life and light" (69). The word "beauteous" in this context means "highly pleasing to the senses," especially in terms of being visually pleasing. It also defined as both "sensuously alluring" and "voluptuous." Jonson goes on to assert that it is "not the colour, but the feature" (71) that "assures unto the creature" (72) its beauty, thus arguing that beauty is better expressed by disposition than by outward appearances. Mary Floyd-Wilson interprets this internalized beauty as "a certain freedom in the relationship between body and soul."[11] The internal qualities of Niger and his daughters supersede their physical blackness and its negative connotations, which is not so remarkable because dark "skin, despite symbolic linkage of black with death and evil, carried few generalized negative connotations" in the previous centuries "for a medieval Europe with little contact with blacks."[12] Niger and his daughters are "beauteous" and "fair" because they are inherently, intrinsically beautiful and also, outwardly and visually beautiful. This correlates with Anu Kornohen's argument that, to whites, "black skin looked exotic and erotic, and it produced mixed pleasures of the senses."[13]

Structurally, Niger's speech is also elevated, as the rest of the masque's dialogue is, "in regular heroic couplets," except for one of Niger's replies (85–92), where he refers to "the immortal souls of creatures mortal" (86), asserting "that a single body does not form the limits of the higher power, or soul."[14] This stanza's irregularity is a precursor to Niger's main defense. In this defense, he responds to an address from his father, Oceanus, with a complex speech that begins by commending his daughters' blackness, as a result of the sun's adoration, before explaining how Western poets have marred the presentation of blackness in their eyes. Niger's "arguments for the priority of black physicality include evidence for the ever youthful appearance of the black body," and it "supports the endurance of blackness against the threat of European expansion."[15] Thus, linking the world of the masque to the world of expanding trade and colonial interests beyond. Niger's speech goes further to reveal the anguished response of his daughters, before recalling the apparition that is his reason for setting forth on the journey that has brought him to the court of Albion.

"Of these my beloved daughters, my most lovéd birth;
Who, though they were the first-formed dames of earth,
And in whose sparkling and refulgent eyes
The glorious sun did still delight to rise;
Though he (the best judge, and most formal cause
Of all dames' beauties) in their firm hues draws
Signs of his fervent'st love; and thereby shows
That in their black the perfect'st beauty grows" (97–104)

As illustrated by the above quotation, Niger's ensuing "authoritative praise of blackness raises questions . . . about the degree to which blackness expresses or belies truth about interior states."[16] The first part of Niger's argument is formed in terms of primacy: "first-formed dames" (98); the second states the fact that black skin has "firm hues" (102); the third is that black skin is a manifestation of the sun's love, "signs of his fervent'st love" (103). The very fact that dark skin is fixed means it hosts a more honest and true disposition, and in Niger's defense lies the masque's duplicity. From its first line, it identifies "blackness . . . as both fixed and capable of reversal."[17]

The words: "sparkling," "refulgent," "delight," and "glorious" (99–100) create a semantic field relating to brightness, joy, and light, which, contrary to what one might expect, is not presented in stark contrast to blackness but as synonymous with it. The princesses, according to Niger, are light and bright, not despite their blackness, but because "black skin signifies divine blessing."[18] For Niger, his daughters' blackness is a reason for them to be even more beautiful, rather than to be considered less: "in their black the perfect'st beauty grows." Niger praises his daughters' complexions and his "arguments, which masque critics ignore as merely fitting anti-masque parody of true order, posit a world of immortal forms."[19] This is, in fact, the assertions of white writers: "Poor brain-sick men, styled poets here with you, | Have with such envy of their graces sung" (116–117), which have poisoned the minds of the princesses and made them weep "such ceaseless tears" (130). Jonson goes further to argue that it is the whites that have "painted beauties" (118), whose women are only made truly beautiful through the use of cosmetics. Eventually, Jonson neutralizes much of Niger's defense with, "I with so much strength | Of argument resisted" (189–190), and a vision the princesses have that they will be transformed, "And sure they saw't for Ethiops never dream" (145).

COSTUME, MAKEUP, AND PERFORMANCE

The costuming and makeup for court masques was designed to leave a lasting impression on viewers, exploiting "the fashion for luxurious and heavily embellished clothes, together with an erotic emphasis on the body."[20] Niger first appears:

> ". . . in form and colour of an Ethiop; his hair and rare beard curled, shadowed with a blue and bright mantle, his front, neck, and wrists adorned with pearl, and crowned with an artificial wreath of cane and paper rush." (31–33)

Critics are not entirely clear about the social status of the actor who may have played Niger in performance, "in the form and colour of an Ethiop" (31), whether a professional actor or member of the nobility. It was common for professionals to be included in casts of courtly masques in the period, especially for speaking parts: "the performers . . . were usually aristocrats or high-status gentry."[21] However, what distinguishes the actor who would have played Niger is in "material methods," as the emulation of blackness was "simulate[d] with paint, rather than with masks, gloves, and leggings typically worn by performers in previous court masques."[22] This use of "blackface reduces the distance" between black and white "by showcasing the features of the face, while also requiring more labor than masks or fabric to remove."[23] The surviving portrait gives us some sense of how Niger may have been depicted, especially in terms of blackface paint.[24] The complexion depicted in the portrait is a dark brown, rather than the color black, and exemplifies the ethnicity of sub-Saharan Africans.

Although only "two of the costume designs by Inigo Jones survive," Niger's stage-directed costuming and appearance clearly mark him out as a character with both authority and royal status.[25] Niger's "front, neck and wrists" are "adorned with pearl" (31), objects of high value and the fruits of the ocean, which is in keeping with "the world of the masque, [where] priceless fabric—often actually made of gold or silver—and cheap fakery becomes ontologically equivalent and sometimes even inversely related."[26] Niger is presented wearing a "blue and bright mantle." ("mantle' being from the Latin word "mantellum" meaning "cloak" or "covering." Jonson also uses the word "mantle" in a similar context in *The Fountain of Self-Love (or Cynthia's Revels)*: "the third, in discoul ur'd | Mantle spangled all ouer."[27] Niger's costuming affirms his position of importance and high status. His authority and power are displayed through the wearing of the mantle. Its color gives Niger a further connection to his father, Oceanus, who is "presented in a human form, the colour of his flesh blue" (38). The portrait of one of the Oceaniae is one of the two remaining illustrations from *The Masque of Blackness*. From it, we can imagine what may have been the skin color of Oceanus, in performance.[28]

The fantastical element of the masque, "on sides of the shell did swim six huge sea-monsters" (40), serves to nullify Niger's legitimacy to some extent, especially as Oceanus is presented as both a deity and a work of the imagina-tion, carrying a "trident," defined as a "three-pronged fish-spear or sceptre" and "the attribute of the sea-god Poseidon or Neptune," and the trident also has later associations with Britannia (*OED Online*). Oceanus signifies the world's oceans, and thereby, he exists outside of the construction of race, with his blue skin that can also be interpreted as both preracial and panracial, because Oceanus encompasses all races. Their shared lineage also implies that Niger is the equal counterpart to Albion, as Oceanus is the father of all.

The word "artificial" is a positive term in this context, meaning the crown has been wrought with a large amount of expertise and craftsmanship. Niger's "crown of cane gives him mercantile associations, since sugar was an early trad-ing item in the West Indies."[29] The crowning of Niger further supports his case for a high-status character. In addition, his adornments have more com-plex meanings, such as the "paper rush," which we now call "papyrus," which is specific to the North African region of Egypt. Meskill argues that although the text "is ostensibly concerned with black Africans, many of the masque's descriptions of the culture and history of 'Aethiopia' and its inhabitants are actually of Egypt and Egyptian culture."[30] Floyd-Wilson also acknowledges that "though we have recognized an incipient racialism in the Ethiopians' quest . . . we have missed how the masque also equates the transmission of ancient wisdom northward—from Ethiopia to Egypt to Britannia."[31] Black-ness has, within *The Masque of Blackness*, far less relevance than social status and gender. Niger is only black, as much as Oceanus is blue, and from this perspective, Jonson's "narrative may be viewed as kind of progress of poesy from the ancient source of writing, in black Africa, to the new home of writ-ing, Britain."[32]

The princesses' vision provides a rationale for the arrival of the ensemble before the royal court: "the northward progression of Niger and his daughters maps a direct correspondence between coloration and environment."[33] It is the culmination of their journey throughout all the nations or "princedoms" (156) with "Sounds–tania" (150). The journey begins in "Black Mauritania" (158), a Moorish part of North Africa, followed by "Swarth Lusitania" (159), or Portugal, then "Rich Acquitania" (160), the south of France, before their arrival in "Britainia" (205).[34] Niger's geographical language denotes the tran-sition from the nations with the darkest inhabitants to the lightest in com-plexion. Floyd-Wilson asserts that the modifiers "black," "swarth," and "rich" are all terms that refer to pronounced, evident skin tones, exhibiting difference from whites.[35]

Martin Butler's "'The Masque of Blackness' and Stuart Court Culture" gives a comprehensive overview of the culture of masques and the Stuart court.[36] Butler highlights the fact that "masques were ideally attuned to

articulating the . . . ideology of the Jacobean state," and their "various meanings . . . cannot be understood without . . . the web of social customs, political expectations, and artistic patronage that determined masquing practice."[37]
So I will briefly outline some key contextual features surrounding the production of the text, to further illuminate the extraordinary nature of Niger's
depiction.

The masque in this period had a particularly political function, which was
inextricably linked to monarchical rule. *The Masque of Blackness* "was used to
honour the Spanish ambassador who was seated by the King and invited to
dance publicly with Queen Anne."[38] These masques were "expensive, but they
made a statement, and they did so before audiences that combined a cross-
section of England's social elites . . . with invited guests from the community
of foreign diplomats and agents residing in London."[39] They were, therefore,
"one means by which the Stuarts drew attention to themselves as monarchs
with whom to be reckoned."[40]

The Masque of Blackness's "interplay of poetics and politics both enriches
and complicates any quiet, critical closure" with regard to the masque. It "tor-
tuously celebrates the margins of power and represents the merging of distinct ethnic and gendered realms."[41] Niger's defense "censures European
literary efforts to negate African identity" and "objects to the project of cultural absorption played before the English court."[42] As Over suggests, through
the physical depiction of Niger, "Jonson constructs an intercultural discourse
wherein the African figures are fashioned as familiar."[43] Niger is a conduit
through which Jonson presents an opposing argument, retaining "a strongly
argued voice of cultural opposition—even while valorizing Queen Anne and
King James."[44]

Therefore, within the complex signification in the exhibition of a single
masque, and its ensuing publication, lie political functions: "peace with Spain
was good for trade, and it kept England out of wars she could not afford";
internal ideological functions: "James struggled with his own recalcitrant
Queen . . . he too, would have to account for the internalized outsideness that
shaped his reign"; as well as issues of belonging within a new unified England
and Scotland.[45] In addition, *The Masque of Blackness* "foregrounds the problematic status of English women's political, domestic, and textual agency" and
authority.[46]

To conclude, Niger's high status as a character in the masque is depicted
through his name, dialogue, and appearance, along with his genealogy (in
relation to Oceanus and his princess daughters). Where *The Masque of Blackness* is unique is in the fact that Niger provides an unchallenged defense of
blackness, and his speech, which "counters the transformative agenda of Albion
by prioritizing blackness" is "rhetorically brilliant." In its original performance

it was very likely to have been "theatrically weak."[47] However, what this analysis reveals is that through close reading of the text, a character situated in the narrative periphery, like Niger, helps us further define the ways in how the enactment of blackness functions. Further conclusions will be drawn on Niger's portrayal at the end of the following chapter.

APPENDIX A.2.2:
MOROCCO, A HIGH-STATUS BLACK
CHARACTER IN *THE MERCHANT OF VENICE*

In *The Merchant of Venice*, we are also presented with a high-status black character, the Prince of Morocco. He is one of Portia's three suitors, and he is rejected after failing to successfully complete the casket test set by Portia's father: "I am glad this parcel of wooers are so reasonable, for there is not one among them but I dote on his very absence" (1.2.103–104).[1] Morocco's name, character, dialogue, and costuming will be closely read in this chapter, which will also draw conclusions on both Morocco and Niger and the depiction of high-status black characters.

NOMENCLATURE, DIALOGUE,
AND CHARACTERIZATION

The name "Morocco," like "Niger," has several meanings—it denotes a region as well as a color. It is derived from a former city capital, Marrakesh, possibly of Berber origin, after the supposed dark complexion of the people of Morocco. In the quarto version of *The Merchant of Venice*, Morocco is given the name "Morochus," which has a wide range of meanings, including from the Italian for the word "Moor," as well as "Moroglie," linked to "piles or haemorrhoids," and the word "Moróglo" from John Florio's *Queen Anna's New World of Words*, meaning "tipsy, wayward, full of wine and words."[2] John Drakakis links the name Morochus to a trick-performing horse, mentioned in a 1595 pamphlet, and highlights the fact that derogatory character names "are consistent with the practice of having marginal characters condemn themselves."[3] The name Morochus, therefore, is demeaning; however, this is more performative/theatrical, rather than racial. Morocco is trivial, not entirely by way of his blackness, but by his position as a minor character, portrayed for the entertainment of a mass audience, and part of his absurdity is the fact that he "frames his own courtship as colonial enterprise and religious pilgrimage."[4]

Morocco's dialogue goes on to regard his dark skin as the "shadowed livery of the burnished sun" (2.1.2), and the use of the word "livery" is noteworthy because it denotes the costume of a servant, which enables others to recognize who their master is. The darkness of Morocco's skin is not presented as solely negative but also a result of the sun's favor, in a similar way that the darkness of Niger's daughters' skins are symbolic of the sun's "fervent'st love" (104). Furthermore, in the same way that the "brain-sick men, styled poets" (116) recount to the daughters of Niger the tale of Phaeton, "that fired the world" (121–123), Morocco also recalls "Phoebus' fire," which "scarce thaws the icicles" (2.1.5). Phoebus is the sun god, and by mentioning him, Morocco aligns the geographical region Morocco with supernatural deities, also referred to in *The Masque of Blackness*.

The tale of Phaethon and Phoebus are another point of connection between these two texts. In the tale, Phaethon asks his mother, Clymene, to avow that Phoebus is his father, and it is Phaethon's erroneous riding of his father's chariot that "discoloured the bodies of men with a murky dark bloom, and curled their hair, fusing it by unincreasable forms of fire" (15.1.24).[5] Smith asserts that in *The Masque of Blackness*, "Ovid has metamorphosed the environmental or climactic theory," which is also evident in the dialogue of Morocco in *The Merchant of Venice*. It is the error of Pheobus' son, while searching for his legitimacy, that is "introduced as a vital term in the discourse of color, expressing the flawed state of a lost original." It "theorizes a narrative of race expressed as the Ethiopians' search for the whiteness that once was theirs," which we see in the masque.[6]

The "openness of Morocco's linguistic ethnicity allows him to be identified with, though separated from, the characters around him."[7] One such character is Portia, whose responses to Morocco are also key in terms of how his character is presented. Hall contends that Portia's response is "typical of generally negative attitudes towards blacks prevalent at the time."[8] This will be discussed briefly here, and in much more detail in Chapter 3, with relation to gender. Firstly, Portia assures Morocco that she "is not solely led | By nice direction of a maiden's eyes" (2.1.12-13). The multiple meaning of "nice direction" has sexual overtones: "Portia may here be referring obliquely to the alleged sexual proclivities of the Moor, or indeed to her own capacity for sexual desire."[9] Portia goes on to remark that the Prince stands "as fair | As any comer I have looked on yet | For my affection" (20–22), which echoes the referrals to Niger as "fair" and the eyes of his daughters as "refulgent." This also reflects on Shakespeare's *Othello*, where Desdemona says, "I saw Othello's visage in his mind" (1.3.252-254), and the Duke says, "If virtue no delighted beauty lack | Your son-in-law is far more fair than black" (1.3.291-2).[10]

Morocco defends himself in Act 2, Scene 1 by swearing on his scimitar, and in performance this "large curved sword" is matched with "an extravagant gesture," to make Morocco's high-status portrayal humorous, ridiculous, and contrived, by flourishing "his sword in a comically menacing manner."[11] The scimitar is "a synedoche of his warlike character."[12] While Niger defends blackness in terms of its primacy, "according to the order of anthropological primogeniture," Morocco makes his claim with regard to his sword, which "slew the Sophy and a Persian Prince" (25–26).[13] Morocco's political and social value is self-confessed through his military exploits. He is often regarded as egocentric; however, it is important to state that the imperialistic acquisition of land by the English is not often viewed in the same way.

COSTUME, MAKEUP, AND PERFORMANCE

Although we have limited information about the portrayal of Morocco in the original performances of *The Merchant of Venice* (c. 1596–1597), Drakakis speculates that Shylock may have been played by Richard Burbage, and he later goes on to further speculate that due to a tradition of doubling, the actor who played Shylock may well have also played Morocco, arguing that "what is common to both is the possibility of a 'black face' that brings together on the stage the 'Moor' and the Jew as types of outsider."[14] Morocco is first mentioned in 1.2.103–105, and arrives on stage in Act 2, Scene 1: "Enter [the Prince of] Morocco, a tawny Moor, all in white, and three or four Followers accordingly."

His qualification as a "tawny Moor" heightens the prominence of his skin tone, and his dialogue begins with "mislike me not for my complexion" (2.1.1), in a similar way that the ceremonial song begins by affirming Niger (64–69). Morocco may well have been physically different on stage, possibly blackened with paint or by way of costuming, such as black gloves and tights, which could easily have been removed in order to swap between a black character and another. Morocco's costume, "all in white," shows how, in the early modern period, blackness became "a spectacle . . . particularly when . . . coupled with something white, be it white skin or white clothes, or something precious or beautiful, such as gold, silver or jewels."[15] Hence, Morocco is dressed in white to contrast his physical darkness, and Niger is similarly adorned with pearls. This presentation of Morocco as exotic is still employed, as "a number of modern productions still depict [him] as an extravagant, ornately dressed African."[16] However, his attendants are perhaps more notable in the championing of his high status, power, and social value. Reimaginings, as recent as Michael Radford's 2004 film, include "an admiring and encouraging African retinue."[17] Morocco's attendants affirm his high status in that, by having servants, he certainly cannot be one. They highlight the fact that there is a kingdom beyond England with black monarchs.

A range of academics, most noticeably Emily Bartels and Kim F. Hall, have cited Elizabeth I's proclamation in 1596, calling for the deportation of "the great number of Negars and Blackamoors," who had "crept into" her "realm."[18] However, both Young and Bartels offer the reason for this as the fact that "the queen likely sought to barter the Moorish population who arrived as prisoners from the second Anglo-Spanish War for English prisoners."[19] Hall's perspective on Elizabeth I's evident aversion to her black population regards it as ironic, as it arrives "despite her earlier support of English piracy in the slave trade."[20] Through her "letters dated from 1596 to 1601," the Queen "turns the presence of 'blackamoors' within her realm into an urgent national problem and promotes their deportation as a natural and possible solution."[21]

The character of Morocco is portrayed more specifically as a Moor, "even though religion is given as a compelling reason for excluding Moors, emphasizing religious difference only clouds the political reality that the Moors' visibility . . . made them a viable target for exclusion." It was "their physical difference in association with cultural difference [that] provoke[d] their exclusion—not just their religion."[22] The term "Moor" is as capricious as "race," and "as a subject, 'the Moor' does not have a single or pure culturally or racially bounded identity."[23] In *Speaking of the Moor: From Alcazar to Othello*, Bartels questions the need to enact blackness in the form of the Moor: "returning to the Moor will help us better navigate a world of proliferating differences."[24] She also asserts that in *The Merchant of Venice*, the racism shown toward the Jew is not leveled toward the black character: "a Moroccan prince can stand beside an assortment of European lords."[25] Alas, "the discourse that the theatrical figure of Morocco seeks to counter, works against, but fails to overcome, the popular prejudices that interpret his 'otherness' in terms of blackness, promiscuity and animality," and the fact that "these attributions" were "at various points in the play, attached to the Jew," suggests that racism, as we perceive it in a modern context, though prevalent with regard to Jews, was, in this period, still being constructed with regards to blacks.[26]

Plays and masques that depict blacks are by no means new in early modern performance, but "as a result of both all-male mimesis and the production of racialized others in racially-homogenous acting companies, the problem of representation . . . becomes exacerbated in historically specific relation to femininity and racial difference."[27] The "understanding of negritude as an augment to whiteness stresses blackness as representation," and this "was corroborated in the period by a climate theory of racial difference, which proposed that blackness was an extreme form of sunburn."[28] The concept of sunburn becomes important because it is an element of skin alteration that "connects white European and black African."[29] Along this line of connection, a recommendation is made that because white skins may darken, black skin should surely whiten. The "masque's representation of Aethiopian blackness demonstrates a residual adherence to . . . traditional climate theory," while "in its deliberate fashioning of whiteness as a temperature complexion, Jonson's masque also forecasts the eventual construction of racialism."[30] The key word here is "forecast." In the masque, but not in the play, physical transformation is presented as a two-way process, and the "descriptions of dark and light" become "the conduit through which the English began to formulate the notions of 'self' and 'other'."[31]

Anthony Barthelemy asserts that the moment "a black character appears on stage, a variety of responses is possible, all of which correspond to the audience's expectations of such a character."[32] This intrinsically ties public notions of race to stage representations of both blackness and gender. The most notable traits of Niger and Morocco are illustrated by monologues that reveal early modern perspectives on their depicted race, depictions that exhibit them as prominent figures with high social status and extravagant wealth. Characters like these are "allegorical agents," which "are real enough, however ideal their referents may be, however 'unlike ourselves' they may appear."[33] Both Niger and the Prince of Morocco hold positions of political power and remain autonomous in the wielding of this power as long as they stay within their own kingdoms. They are "allegorical representations" who "have power since they can display the true nature of the world" and "are instructive and reflective." Their allegorical representations "take complex ideas, and, through virtue of the chain of being, makes these ideas legible to the common man."[34] While situated in a context of emergent racial stereotypes, Niger and Morocco, the representations of high-status blacks in *The Masque of Blackness* and *The Merchant of Venice*, have a range of positive attributes connected to themes of primacy and constancy, deity and divinity, high social status and distant, though potent, political power. This upholds the argument that "blackness is often a mutable and relative quality; in early modern England, it is less a sign of complexion than one of status," and most importantly, of difference.[35]

APPENDIX A.2.3:
GENDER AND THE DEPICTIONS OF
NIGER AND MOROCCO

In terms of gender, Niger and Morocco are clearly both male characters; however, it is through their relationships to female characters that much of their high status is presented. This chapter answers the question: "How are Niger and Morocco presented in terms of gender?" It considers, firstly, the high status of Niger in relation to his 12 princess daughters and the goddess Ethiopia; and secondly, the high status of Morocco in relation to his suit with Portia. To conclude, the chapter draws similarities between the two representations.

NIGER AND GENDER

Niger's masculinity is presented in relation to his princess daughters, who are evidence of his former virility. It is interesting that Jonson did not choose to include the goddess Tethys as a mother figure for Niger, especially since together, Oceanus and Tethys are symbolic of fertility.[1] Richmond Barbour states that the fact that the princesses "move with the masculine force of Niger's current, aggravates whatever unease viewers may take from their blackness."[2] Niger's daughters are initially described as the "first-formed dames of earth" (98), echoing the widely acknowledged belief that blacks were the first inhabitants of the world, which is reinforced in Jonson's marginalia: "a conjecture of the old ethnics that they which dwell under the south were the first begotten of the earth."[3] However, bringing this distant past to the early modern present poses a serious problem, because, although "the black man is representable . . . within Europe's symbolic order of dominance and desire, the black woman destroys the system, essentially swallowing it up within the signification of her body."[4] The two concepts of "patriarchy and imperialism meet as Jonson's masque dramatizes the collision of the dark lady tradition with the actual African difference encountered in the quest for empire."[5]

The costume designs for the princesses "involve a striking amount of décolletage and often suggest that the contours of the dancer's body can be perceived through the costume's fabric," and the problematic sexuality of Niger's daughters "lingers in the lineaments of this masque's representations, destabilizing its edifice of elevated whiteness."[6] It also helps to highlight the fact that "the black female, whose signifying capacity as a mother threatens nothing less than the wholesale negation of white authority."[7] Perhaps this is the reason Niger may have daughters but not a wife or mother. The black male here does not pose so great a threat. He is a father who cannot control his own daughters, a "somewhat paternal curmudgeon" who is "domesticated by the novel use of blackface through which the identity of a well-known Whitehall court actor or courtier can be discerned."[8] Some of the sexuality of Niger's daughters, "costumed in diaphanous, free-flowing materials," is contained by the fact that "they voluntarily leave their own father and submit themselves to the authority of another, greater fount of royal knowledge and power." Thereby, Niger's "fatherly authority disappears as much as his daughters' blackness is intended to do."[9]

A range of critics have employed the surviving letters of one contemporary spectator of *The Masque of Blackness*, Dudley Carleton, quoted in part below:

Images of Sea-Horses with other terrible Fishes, which were ridden by Moors . . . Their Apparell was rich, but too light and Curtizan-like for such great ones. Instead of Vizzards, their Faces, and Arms up to the Elbows, were painted black . . . you cannot imagine a more ugly Sight, then a Troop of leancheek'd Moors . . . the Spanish Ambassador willingly accepted, and being there, seeing no Cause to the contrary . . . at this he was taken out to dance, and footed it like a lusty old Gallant with his Country Woman. He took out the Queen, and forgot not to kiss her Hand, though there was Danger it would have left a Mark upon his Lips.[10]

Often, "what strikes readers . . . is the racist edge to Carleton's mislike."[11] However, little attention has been focused on the elevated status the Queen gives Niger, by being depicted as his black daughter, and the granddaughter of the blue-skinned Oceanus. Barbour comments that, rather than being overtly racist, "Carleton is disturbed by a breach of decorum: masquers' roles should represent the dignity of the persons performing them."[12] *The Masque of Blackness* was "the first time the court had been treated . . . to a very pregnant black Queen . . . making her final public appearance before retiring to Greenwich pending delivery."[13] Another response of Carleton's often cited by critics is a letter to John Chamberlain:

The mask at night requires much labor to be well described, but there is a pamphlet in press which will save me that pains . . . The presentation of the mask at the first drawing of the traverse was very fair and their apparel rich, but too light and courtesanlike. Their black faces and hands, which were painted and bare up the elbows, was a very loathsome sight and I am sorry that strangers should see our court so strangely disguised. The Spanish and Venetian ambassadors were both there and most of the French about the town.[14]

If Carleton's particular dislike is blackface makeup and the depiction of the Queen as a black woman, then it is significant that he does not mention the performer in the role of Niger at all. Callaghan contends that Carleton's "disapproval of blackface and costume is less the product of a racist repulsion than it is part of the general censure of women's power."[15] It may well be the case that "Carleton's anxieties spring . . . from an equation of blackness with unbridled sexuality."[16] However, if this is the case, it is also very "important to recognise that continental observers were untroubled by the disguise or dress, praising the lavishness of the play."[17] Furthermore, "Carleton's decidedly anti-Union (and anti-Scottish) position would not make him a likely 'understander' of the masque's use of blackness."[18]

Carleton's is one of few surviving accounts of the masque's viewership, and it correlates with some accepted ideas about Jacobean perceptions of blacks.

However, what much critical use of it does, is take the view of one member of the audience and expand it, so that it becomes the view of the entire court, and at times, of all of England. Here we may benefit from a more sensitive consideration of both the Queen's desire to enact blackness, and Jonson's defense of it, through Niger's speech. The "pamphlet" Carleton mentions, and the 1608 publication of *The Masque of Blackness*, can be interpreted as indicators of the masque's popularity, not its failure, and this contravenes the view that "Jonson's task of praising the Queen as black was almost an insuperable one."[19] No matter the extent to which "the trope of blackness is treated as an anomaly, ultimately inconsequential outside the framework of Jonson's text," Anne's request to have herself portrayed as a blackamoor, the subsequent publication of the text, and Niger's impassioned Afrocentric defense, all combine to form a view of this moment within the early modern period that is not as racially binary as has been previously asserted.[20]

Another female character that Niger is presented in relation to is the "Great Ethiopia, goddess of our shore" (180). Over argues that Ethiopia, referred to as a "silver star" (178), is a symbol of cleansed assimilation—"name long used by Europeans as a reductive reference to Africa and Africans," while her "whiteness indicates her previous transformation and co-optation":[21]

> Britania, whose new name makes all tongues sing,
> Might be a diamond worthy to enchase it,
> Ruled by a sun that to this height doth grace it;
> Whose beams shine day and night, and are of force
> To blanch an Ethiop and revive a corse (205–209)

The quote above is an extract from Ethiopia's speech, "to blanch an Ethiop" (209), and it affirms the irreversibility of blackness and the impossibility of cleansing black skin. It stems from a proverb "used to express impossibility and bootless labour," and is thought to have "originated with Aesop, where the image of scrubbing an Ethiopian is used to demonstrate the power and permanence of nature."[22] It serves to enhance the miraculous transformation of Niger's princess daughters. The use of the concept has a long history, and Anu Kornohen claims that the proverb "was repeated so frequently . . . that it was understandable even when either half of the sentence was omitted." It was also featured in George Whitney's widely circulated book, *A Choice of Emblemes* (1586), which features an illustration of the attempt to wash an Ethiop.[23] As a result of the proverb's wide usage, "whitening black Africans became a paradigm for all that was useless, impossible and irrational."[24] Thus, this transition from black to white, "to blanch an Ethiop" (209), is as supernaturally impossible as resurrection, to "revive a corse" (209), and through it, Jonson stages "a political and ideological miracle," managing to "put into crisis customary distinctions between black and white."[25] Jonson goes further to achieve the impossible, because it is this self-same indelibility that Niger praises in his defense of blackness. Ethiopia claims the sun of Britain has refining qualities, which can "salve the rude defects of every creature" (211). These "rude defects" are assumed to be the princesses' dark skin. Toward the latter part of the masque, Niger is effectively silenced by Ethiopia: "comfort take, | Your father, only, to the lake | Shall make return" (284–286), and his impassioned defense is forgotten.

Line 209 was used in the title of Hardin Aasand's 1992 essay " 'To Blanch an Ethiop, and Revive a Corse': Queen Anne and *The Masque of Blackness*." To Aasand, the quote is symbolic of double standards and prejudice in Jacobean culture: "though Niger argues for Ethiopian propriety and familial order, he is eventually forced to accept the arguments of . . . Ethiopia, who claims to be the source of the poet's fictions of Britannia and beauty."[26] However, the quote, and Jonson's masque, can both be interpreted as presenting positive associations of blackness, especially regarding features that are unchanging and denoting inherent qualities that should, by virtue of their fixedness, be admired.

MOROCCO AND GENDER

The Masque of Blackness and *The Merchant of Venice*, are both predominantly concerned with fathers and daughters. Whereas in the former, Niger is effectively silenced by banishment, not even death can silence Portia's father. In the latter, "dead Christian fathers do not die; rather, their live on through their progeny and speak with authority from the grave" and all "who exist outside its boundaries must be either expelled or coerced."[27]

Morocco "reveals the peril of such international competition for wealth (and beauty)," and the casket test "expands the sex/gender system by opening up the romantic quest to foreign competition."[28] This is particularly evident during the casket ceremony in 2.7, where Morocco states, "A golden mind stoops not to shows of dross; | I'll then nor give nor hazard aught for lead. | What says the silver with her virgin hue?" (20–22). Morocco "forestall[s] objections to what Venetians regard as a monstrous bed to secure a union with a white wealthy woman."[29] In her monograph *Shakespeare without Women: Representing Gender and Race on the Renaissance Stage*, Callaghan chooses to "focus on absence rather than presence because racial alterity in Shakespeare's theatre has the same status as the female body, namely absent from the process of representation," and as a result we see that both the black Prince and the female Portia are subject to the same models of societal hierarchy.[30] They are both doubly invisible, represented but not permitted to be there.

Morocco clearly asserts that he is of higher status than Portia, whom he terms a "mortal breathing saint" (2.7.40). In terms of social status, he must be, in order to be presented as one of her suitors: "From the four corners of the earth . . . princes to come view fair Portia" (2.7.39-43). Morocco "ascribes the female gender to silver (*her*) that he also associates with virginity," due to its purity in color, and "reinforces his own sense of the hierarchical order of metals" and "his sense of his own superior worth."[31] In the Prince's ensuing speech we see him assert, after reading the words "Who chooseth me shall get as much as he deserves" (2.7.23), that he "deserves" Portia: "I do in birth deserve her, and in fortunes, | In graces and in qualities of breeding" (2.7.32-33).

> Never so rich a gem
> Was set in worse than gold. They have in England
> A coin that bears the figure of an angel
> Stamped in gold: but that's insculped upon.
> But here, an angel in a golden bed (54–58)

The above quotation is taken from Morocco's speech, just before he chooses the casket of gold, which is, of course, the wrong one. The word "angel" refers to a "celestial being," and Morocco "imagines Portia's picture lying inside the golden casket" which becomes for him an erotic "golden bed" (58).[32] Morocco's choice being incorrect, he finds within the casket a "carrion death," a signifier of mortality (63). He reads the "written scroll" (64), which explains that "All that glisters is not gold . . . Fare you well, your suit is cold" (65–73). Morocco is shown to be lacking in passion, and that is why he makes the wrong choice. We are presented with a dichotomy between hot weather and hot blood and cold weather, cool blood, and temperate behavior. However, there is much irony here, especially when Morocco has so fervently affirmed his closeness to "the burnished sun" (2.1.2).[33] One of the "prominent associations, frequently made in connection with black skin," is "immoderate sexuality."[34] A further debate around blackness and sexuality in the early modern period focused on the curse of Noah's son, Ham, and "no matter how emphatically the curse of Ham was denied, it was still repeated all through the seventeenth century" and so, "the associations of blackness with lechery, lust and disobedience stuck."[35] This association was also presented in Leo Africanus' *A Geographical Historie of Africa* (translated by John Pory and published in 1600) in which blacks were regarded as "more prone to sexual transgressions . . . than any other 'nation' in the world." Despite his stereotypical licentiousness, Morocco is still not passionate enough to win Portia.[36]

As he leaves to go, having lost his suit, Morocco states, "farewell, heat, and welcome frost. | Portia adieu. I have too grieved a heart | To take a tedious leave: thus losers part." (2.7.75–77). Shakespeare presents Morocco as having his intemperate fires dampened. However, he retains his status as a prince, and his authority is not lessened by losing his suit. He leaves "[with his train]," and Portia replies, "A gentle riddance. Draw the curtains, go. | Let all of his complexion choose me so" (2.7.78–79). The same way that Niger links his daughters' beauty to the "firm hues" (102) of their skin, Portia refers to the darkness of Morocco's skin, "his complexion" (2.7.79)—a clash between the emergent racial stereotype of inherent concupiscence in blacks, and the fact that Portia's "choice itself is shown to be over-detained by an active but absent metaphysical force committed to a combination of racial purity and social hierarchy."[37] The "cultural exclusiveness, to which Portia refers in her expression of relief at Morocco's failure . . . is part of the mercantilist pressure that the play exerts upon the business of national identity."[38] It also affirms the fact that "the black-male-white-female union is . . . the ultimate romantic-transgressive model of erotic love."[39]

To conclude, the question posed at the start of this chapter was: :How are Niger and Morocco presented in terms of gender?" To answer: Because "the difference in the representation of Africans and women is . . . a result of their different roles in emergent capitalism," Niger and Morocco are depicted through their relationships to key female characters, but they still continue to exhibit positive negritude and autonomy.[40] Primarily, their function is to exhibit the exotic, and to "represent the exotic and alien in terms of blackness."[41] Both masque and play "dramatize the confrontation between peoples of different races and cultures."[42] Both Niger and Morocco show us the ways that two early modern playwrights display the exotic and the unknown while the characters still contain the transgressive nature of their masculinity. What is primarily exotic is not necessarily of lesser value, it simply exhibits difference that must be contained.

Furthermore, both Niger and Morocco were performed by white men, "re-enact[ing] the exclusionary privilege on which such representations were founded."[43] These black male characters are subject to a double invisibility. They are silenced or removed from their narratives as a result of the problematic nature of their high status and gender, with its implied sexuality. This is why Niger's daughters must be cleansed and assimilated, to avert any danger of miscegenation, because it is "in the person of the black woman that the culture's pre-existing fears . . . are realized" and they are evidence of Niger's fertility.[44] In a similar way, *The Merchant of Venice* also enacts an invalidating process with regard to Morocco and maintains an invisible boundary that separates him from Portia.

APPENDIX A.2.4: CONCLUSION

This conclusion returns to both *The Masque of Blackness* and *The Merchant of Venice*, texts that mark a point in the early modern period when blacks could be presented both positively and negatively. It explores the construction of race as a process and bases its assertions on the ways that black characters like Niger and Morocco can be considered Afrocentric, even when they are positioned in high-status roles for comedic effect or as a manifestation of monarchical display. Finally, I will put forward some avenues for further research, which include the field of visual culture.

This research was carried out in a bid to demystify the appearance of high-status black characters in two literary works, and exemplify the appearance of high-status blackness in them. The analysis of the primary texts suggests that a range of positive and negative images of blackness existed in the Elizabethan and Jacobean era. In the late 15th century "a critical mass of Black Africans appear[ed] on British shores . . . some of the abducted Africans remained slaves in the British Isles, while others became court retainers, servants and dependents, rather than chattel."[1] However, "by the mid-seventeenth century, England would be competing with the Dutch for the dubious distinction of being the world's largest slave trader."[2] It is between these two contexts that *The Masque of Blackness* and *The Merchant of Venice* lie. That "modern literary criticism remystifies the appearance of blackness in literary works by insisting that references to race are rooted in European aesthetic tradition rather than in any consciousness of racial difference" may be the reason Carleton's letter has become so influential in terms of how texts like *The Masque of Blackness* are read.[3] This is part of a legacy of criticism that generally ignores the physical presence of blacks with relation to early modern playbooks, despite the fact that "inscribed fragmentarily in legal, taxation, medical and civic archives is the varied impress of black working lives."[4]

Imtiaz Habib, in his monograph *Black Lives in the English Archives, 1500–1677*, illustrates how "even with their enigmatic brevity, such references register black lives in many visible professions . . . trumpeter, diver, royal page, entertainer, laundress, servant, and maid."[5] Habib attempts, through sifting "the ponderous substance and verbiage of sixteenth- and seventeenth-century court documents," to demystify the material presence of blacks during the period—a presence that contradicts the argument that blacks solely "exist for

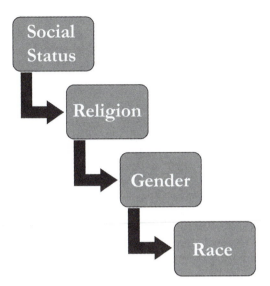

Figure A2.4.1
**Diagram Showing a Hierarchy of Character Traits in *The Masque of Blackness*
and *The Merchant of Venice*.**
(Illustration by Elizabeth Amisu and Karin Merx)

contemporary readers of the period in the realm of the anecdote."[6] It also makes the positive attributes of high-status black characters within texts like *The Merchant of Venice* and *The Masque of Blackness* far more plausible and probable.

Their "participation in the Atlantic slave trade compelled the English to deny older theories of complexion," as displayed by these texts, in "an ideological move that transformed 'blackness' into a mystery, while constructing whiteness as the temperate and unquestioned norm."[7] It is crucial to state that a majority of the slaves sold "out of and within the British Isles, even as late as the fifteenth century were Britons, mostly Celts; and when England began to compete in the trade to supply slaves to the Spanish New World colonies, the driving economic impetus behind the venture had not yet been fully vested with an ideology of racist meaning."[8] It was in fact the "erasure of Africa from the civilized world, and the reinterpretation of 'blackness' as monstrous and unnatural" that "allowed for the construction of a European race."[9] Morocco's and Niger's words challenge "current conceptions of the development of racial consciousness and awareness . . . in the late Tudor and early Stuart periods."[10] Furthermore, texts like *The Merchant of Venice* and *The Masque of Blackness* are part of a range of creative works that posit an ontology of high-status blackness that is not only positive, but affirmative: "Niger's presence in *Blackness* remains a strong anti-colonialist statement."[11]

The essay "Before Othello: Elizabethan Representations of Sub-Saharan Africans asserts that "during the second half of the sixteenth century, English representations of sub-Saharan Africans in print and performance . . . featured an unbalanced, sometimes ambiguous, but overwhelmingly derogatory picture of a segment of the world's population that the English had theretofore scarcely known at all."[12] Despite these generally negative portrayals, Alden and Virginia Vaughan concede that "by 1603–1604 . . . knowledge of Africa was far more abundant and detailed than it had been at the beginning of the Elizabethan era," so that "a black Moor could be portrayed as a hero."[13] I agree with Barbour; however, that Jonson and Shakespeare both share an "ethnocentric, even xenophobic, but not [a] racist view," because both conceive they represented blacks in their work as "a 'nation,' not a subspecies."[14] Morocco is a prince, and although he may share his name with a horse, this is as likely to be for humorous effect as it is for disparagement and mockery. The masque and play are "on the cusp—between older ethnological values and emergent racial ones."[15]

The early modern period is often considered by critics as a "pre-modern time when racial ideologies had not taken root."[16] The "critical attempts to discount the issue of racialized blackness in the interests of historical continuity or misogyny ignore the persistent presence of a discourse of blackness," especially in the court of James I.[17] The fact remains that "representations of Blacks, as well as actual Blacks, were an integral part of Scottish court entertainment" during his reign, and as such, cannot be so easily dismissed.[18] Furthermore, in the early modern period "blackness becomes the mark of bodies . . . that escape, deny or just cannot be contained by certain cultural boundaries."[19]

A more sensitive perspective can be found in viewing the early modern period as a time of formation, in which racial identities and stereotypes of blacks and whites were being configured. In light of this research, I would like to pose an academic model for early modern blackness that regards it as in flux. Like the earth spinning on its axis, from one perspective it is moving, and from another it is still. Only when there is a change in speed do we recognize that movement is occurring. Texts like *The Masque of Blackness* and *The Merchant of Venice*, and characters like Niger and Morocco, show growing perceptions of race, but do not give any ready absolutes. With regard to early modern blacks, academics should be careful not to "historicise colour consciousness, or examine a time when it had not acquired the virulent connotations of imperial times," for far more insight can be gained when we "see how such a vocabulary is transformed during this period" and how "it articulates itself through other markers of difference such as religion and gender."[20]

Jonson's citing of Leo the African, along with Pliny the Elder and Gaius Julius Solinus and the astronomer Ptolemy, "Pliny, Solinus, Ptolemy, and of late *Leo* the Africa' (10) provide "respected classical references to support many of Niger's assertions in defense of African ontology."[21] By using these sources, Jonson employs "history as a tenuous fiction," and "Pliny is indeed like a dream," in which "Jonson finds . . . a perfect vehicle for masque spectacle."[22] Smith calls race a "dream act" and argues that, in order to justify racial constructions and identities, communities must collectively imagine or "dream" that there was no time before these constructions were in play. This is "instrumental in affirming the mythic reality of a racial community that consolidates and justifies one's belonging."[23]

The depiction of "error" as "the sign under which the black Ethiopian race is born, and the accidental nature of its beginning" in both *The Masque of Blackness* and *The Merchant of Venice*, makes "blackness . . . the distortion of the original course of human nature."[24] However, "many positive European associations of blackness—including black beauty . . . must stand alongside negative conceptions," especially since "there are, indeed, no authentic 'others'—raced or gendered—of any kind, only their representations."[25] In "its denigration of outward blackness and its appropriation of internal 'blackness,' Ben Jonson's first masque captured English identity in transition."[26] Furthermore, the repeated references to African blackness we see in these texts suggest "that the sense of whiteness is being recognised by England's expanding trade and colonial ambitions."[27]

In the early modern period, knowledge was often collected and gathered, and commonplace books are evidence of this. As in a commonplace book, we see racial stereotypes constructed around blacks "formed by piling one association on top of another," the result of "an amalgam of suspicions and assumptions."[28] There was a space into which these ideas poured, a rationale for why black people were not white, and this "theoretical vacuum emphasized the mystery not only of the origins of black skin, but of black Africans in general."[29] This mystery and mythology that emerged around black skin was not only "central to the construction of black 'otherness'" but "to white identity as well."[30] How blacks were depicted, therefore, is inextricably linked to the formation of white English identity, and "we are still facing an ethnography created and appropriated by white Europeans."[31] This brings to mind Toni Morrison's question, "How does literary utterance arrange itself when it tries to imagine an Africanist other?"[32] It arranges itself through a "white gaze" that views with the acute "awareness that white skin [is] more beautiful," a gaze that is "not just dichotomizing," but "also hierarchizing."[33]

Further research of value can be found in imposing this transitionary model on a range of literary and artistic works produced in London between 1580 and 1610, which depict high-status blacks. Material artefacts such as the Drake Jewel, given to Sir Francis Drake by Queen Elizabeth I, and its "cameo with the profiles of a black emperor and a white woman," are an "excellent example of the multiple meanings an Elizabethan work can convey."[34]

The Drake Jewel also appears in "a three-quarter-length portrait slightly to the left" of Drake, who is "dressed in black, wearing leather gloves" with the jewel "hanging at waist level on a ribbon from his neck."[35] Artefacts like the jewel and the portrait can be and have been read in the literary mode by early modernists, as illustrated by Clark Hulse in "Reading Painting: Holbein, Cromwell, Wyatt," and Jonathan Gil Harris, in the monograph *Untimely Matter in the Time of Shakespeare*.[36] Much like the high-status representations Morocco and Niger, the jewel simultaneously acts as a signifier of African high status and primacy, and of English wealth and power. Finally, as Ayanna Thompson writes, I also "look forward to texts that more frankly and integrally question the relationship between the desire for historicism and the desire for social relevance," texts that situate blackness in its highly complex context, especially with regards to positive, high-status attributions, no matter how multifaceted and unfamiliar they might be.[37]

Notes

MICHAEL JACKSON: A CHRONOLOGY

1. Elizabeth Amisu, ed., *A Companion to Michael Jackson Academic Studies I* (The Journal of Michael Jackson Academic Studies [MJAS], 2015), vii–xi; Adrian Grant, *Michael Jackson: A Visual Documentary. The Official Tribute Edition* (London: Omnibus, 2009); Michael Jackson, *Moonwalk* (London: Heinemann, 2009).

CHAPTER 1. INTRODUCTION: READING, WRITING, AND REWRITING MICHAEL JACKSON

1. Ben Jonson and David Lindley, "To The Memory of My Beloved, The Author Master William Shakespeare and What He Hath Left Us," in *The Cambridge Edition of the Works of Ben Jonson, Vol. 6*, ed. David M. Bevington, Martin Butler, and Ian Donaldson (Cambridge: Cambridge University Press, 2012), 638.

2. Joseph Vogel, *Featuring Michael Jackson: Collected Writings on the King of Pop* (New York: Baldwin Books, 2012), 12.

3. Ibid., 4.

4. Ibid., 12.

5. Jonson and Lindley, "To the Memory of My Beloved, the Author Master William Shakespeare and What He Hath Left Us," 638.

6. See Appendices for the contents of this research.

7. Cultural Materialism: "a theoretical approach which states that the nature of a particular culture . . . is primarily determined by material and social conditions such as environment, technology, and economics." *OED.*

8. Charles Thomson, "Xscape: Would Michael Jackson Approve?" *Huffington Post* (2014), http://www.huffingtonpost.com/charles-thomson/xscape-would-michael -jack_b_5306640.html.

9. Michael Jackson, interview by Joy T. Bennett, December 2007.

10. Kim F. Hall, *Things of Darkness: Economies of Race and Gender in Early Modern England* (Ithaca, NY: Cornell University Press, 1995); Sonia Massai, *World-Wide Shakespeares: Local Appropriations in Film and Performance*, ed. Sonia Massai (London: Routledge, 2005).

11. Joseph Vogel, *Man in the Music: The Creative Life and Work of Michael Jackson* (New York: Sterling, 2011); Susan Fast, *Dangerous* (London: Bloomsbury, 2014).

12. Michael Jackson, *Moonwalk* (London: Heinemann, 2009); *HIStory: Past, Present and Future, Book 1* (Sony/Epic Legacy, 1995).

CHAPTER 2. A CRITICAL SURVEY OF MICHAEL JACKSON STUDIES

1. A critical survey is a useful way for academics to map an overview of the existing research (articles and books) that has been published on a specific subject, in this case, Michael Jackson. It is built around key examples and enables the reader to both use a wide range of source material to support their arguments and also identify gaps they can fill with their own research.

2. Charles Thomson, "One of the Most Shameful Episodes in Journalistic History," *Huffington Post* (2010), http://www.huffingtonpost.com/charles-thomson/one-of-the-most-shameful_b_610258.html; "Michael Jackson: It's Time for Media Outlets to Take Responsibility in Covering the Rock Star," *Huffington Post* (2010), http://www.huffingtonpost.com/charles-thomson/michael-jackson-its-time_b_482176.html.

3. Jochen Ebmeier, *Das Phänomen Michael Jackson* (Hamburg: Rasch und Rohring Verlang, 1997).

4. "Yes, I introduced the term about 3–4 years ago when I created this resource center. http://www.joevogel.net/mj-studies." Joseph Vogel, "MJ Studies," *@JoeVogel1* (2014), https://twitter.com/JoeVogel1/status/524930211323080704.

5. Mark Fisher, "'And When the Groove Is Dead and Gone': The End of Jacksonism," in *The Resistible Demise of Michael Jackson*, ed. Mark Fisher (Winchester, UK: Zero Books, 2009), 9–17.

6. "Introduction: MJ, the Symptom," in *The Resistible Demise of Michael Jackson*, ed. Mark Fisher (Winchester, UK: Zero Books, 2009), 13.

7. Susan Fast, *Dangerous* (London: Bloomsbury, 2014), 26–32.

8. Kobena Mercer, "Monster Metaphors: Notes on Michael Jackson's 'Thriller'," *Screen* 27, no. 1 (1986).

9. Dave Marsh, *Trapped: Michael Jackson and the Crossover Dream* (New York: Bantam, 1985).

10. Susan Woodward, *Otherness and Power: Michael Jackson and His Media Critics* (United States: Blackmore, 2014). *Otherness and Power* is one of the most useful available texts in terms of meta-criticism (or the analysis of the research of others) in Michael Jackson Studies, highlighting several discrepancies and false premises in a range of notable publications.

11. Ibid., 7–24.

12. Mise-en-scene: stemming from the French term meaning "scenery and properties of a stage production." *OED*. This term has been adapted in film studies to denote all that which is included visually within the cinematic frame, including the actors, lighting, cinematography, props, and costume.

13. Mercer, "Monster Metaphors: Notes on Michael Jackson's 'Thriller'," 30.

14. Michele Wallace, "Michael Jackson, Black Modernisms and the Ecstasy of Communication," *Third Text* 3, no. 7 (1989).

15. "Michael Jackson, Black Modernisms and the Ecstasy of Communication," in *Invisibility Blues* (London, New York: Verso, 2008), 77.

16. Ibid., 82.

17. Michael Eric Dyson, "Michael Jackson's Postmodern Spirituality," in *Reflecting Black: African-American Cultural Criticism* (Minneapolis: University of Minnesota Press, 1993), 35–63.

18. Wallace, "Michael Jackson, Black Modernisms and the Ecstasy of Communication," 78.

19. Dyson, "Michael Jackson's Postmodern Spirituality," 41.

20. Michael Jackson, *Moonwalk* (London: Heinemann, 2009); *Dancing the Dream: Poems & Reflections* (London: Doubleday, 1992); *HIStory: Past, Present and Future, Book 1* (Sony/Epic Legacy, 1995).

21. Joseph Vogel, "Second to None: Race, Representation and the Misunderstood Power of Michael Jackson's Music," in *Featuring Michael Jackson: Collected Writings on the King of Pop* (New York: Baldwin Books, 2012), 12–13.

22. *Man in the Music: The Creative Life and Work of Michael Jackson* (New York: Sterling, 2011), 6–8.

23. Ibid., 12.

24. Fast, *Dangerous*, 5.

25. Vogel, "Second to None: Race, Representation and the Misunderstood Power of Michael Jackson's Music," 7–14.

26. Margo Jefferson, *On Michael Jackson* (New York: Pantheon, 2006), 13.

27. Vogel, *Man in the Music: The Creative Life and Work of Michael Jackson*, 70–76. Pandora's Box: a box containing all human ills, which was opened by Pandora or, in some versions of the story, by Epimetheus. *OED*.

28. Icarus: son of Dædalus, who attempted to fly by means of artificial wings fastened with wax; Prometheus: a demigod, son of the Titan Iapetus, who is said to have made man out of clay, and to have stolen fire from Olympus and taught men how to use it, for which he was punished by Zeus by being chained to a rock in the Caucasus where an eagle fed each day upon his liver. *OED*.

29. Michael Jackson, "National Action Network Headquarters Speech" (July 9, 2002).

30. Vogel, "Second to None: Race, Representation and the Misunderstood Power of Michael Jackson's Music," 12.

31. "'Am I the Beast You Visualized?': The Cultural Abuse of Michael Jackson," 14.

32. Joseph Vogel, *Featuring Michael Jackson: Collected Writings on the King of Pop* (New York: Baldwin Books, 2012), 12; Susan Fast, interview by MJ Truth Now, October 24, 2014.

33. J. Randy Taraborrelli, *Michael Jackson: The Magic, the Madness, the Whole Story, 1958–2009* (New York: Hachette, 1991, 2003, 2009); Jackson, *Moonwalk*.

34. Francesca T. Royster, "Michael Jackson, Queer World Making, and the Trans Erotics of Voice, Gender, and Age," in *Sounding Like a No-No: Queer Sounds and Eccentric Acts in the Post-Soul Era* (Ann Arbor: University of Michigan Press, 2013); " 'Hee Hee Hee': Michael Jackson and the Transgendered Erotics of Voice," *The Journal of Michael Jackson Academic Studies* 1, no. 3 (2015).

35. Robert Burnett and Bert Deivert, "Black or White: Michael Jackson's Video as a Mirror of Popular Culture," *Popular Music and Society* 19, no. 3 (1995); Elena Oliete, "Michael Are You Ok? You've Been Hit by a Smooth Criminal: Racism, Controversy, and Parody in the Videos 'Smooth Criminal' and 'You Rock My World'," *Studies in Popular Culture* 29, no. 1 (2006); Radan Martinec, "Construction of Identity in Michael Jackson's Jam," *Social Semiotics* 10, no. 3 (2000).

36. Jefferson, *On Michael Jackson*, 13, 69.

37. "Freaks (from On Michael Jackson)," in *Michael Jackson: Grasping the Spectacle*, ed. Christopher R. Smit (Farnham, UK: Ashgate, 2012), 11–22.

38. Reid Kane, "The King of Pop's Two Bodies, or, Thriller as Allegory," in *The Resistible Demise of Michael Jackson*, ed. Mark Fisher (Winchester, UK: Zero Books, 2009), 233–42.

39. Armond White, "Screaming to Be Heard, Book I," in *Keep Moving: The Michael Jackson Chronicles* (New York: Resistance Works, 2010), 53–62.

40. Examples of essays that offer useful source material for researchers wishing to focus on negative public perceptions of Jackson: Ruchi Mital, "Tomorrow Today: Michael Jackson as Science Fiction Character, Author, and Text," in *Michael Jackson: Grasping the Spectacle*, ed. Christopher R. Smit (Farnham, UK: Ashgate, 2012), 131–44; Ian Penman, "Notes Towards a Ritual Exorcism of the Dead King," in *The Resistible Demise of Michael Jackson*, ed. Mark Fisher (Winchester, UK: Zero Books, 2009), 267–309; Chris Roberts, "True Enough: Michael in Fifty Shards," ibid.

41. Jeremy Gilbert, "The Real Abstraction of Michael Jackson," ibid.; "The Real Abstraction of Michael Jackson," in *A Companion to Michael Jackson Academic Studies I*, ed. Elizabeth Amisu (MJAS, 2015); Amy C. Billone, "Sentenced to Neverland: Michael Jackson, Peter Pan, and Queer Futurity," in *Michael Jackson: Grasping the Spectacle*, ed. Christopher R. Smit (Farnham, UK: Ashgate, 2012), 39–50.

42. Richard M. Breaux, " 'I'm a Cartoon!' The Jackson 5ive Cartoon as Comodified Civil Rights & Black Power Ideologies, 1971-1973," *The Journal of Pan African Studies* 3, no. 7 (2010); Julian Vigo, "Metaphor of Hybridity: The Body of Michael Jackson," ibid.; Matthew Delmont, "Michael Jackson & Television before Thriller," ibid.; Darryl Scriven, "Michael Jackson & the Psycho/Biology of Race," ibid.; Firpo W. Carr, "Michael Jackson Motivated," ibid.; Gershom Williams, "Michael Jackson: Color Complex and the Politics of White Supremacy," ibid.; Itibari M. Zulu, "MJ: The Man in the Mirror Analyzed," ibid.; Konrad Sidney Bayer, "The Semiosis of Soul: Michael

Jackson's Use of Popular Music Conventions," ibid., no. 7 (2010); Susan and Robert G. Weiner Hidalgo, "Wanna Be Startin' Somethin': MJ in the Scholarly Literature: A Selected Bibliographic Guide," ibid.

43. Michael Jackson, "Love: The Human Family's Most Precious Legacy," ibid., 4–13.

44. Panel, "The Cultural Phenomenon of Michael Jackson" (Society of Cinema and Media Studies, 2011); Various, "Michael Jackson: Critical Reflection on a Life & Phenomenon" (University of California, Berkeley, October 1, 2009); "Genius without Borders: A Symposium in Honor of the Genius of Michael Jackson" (Columbia College Chicago, September 24, 2010); "After the Dance: Conversations on Michael Jackson's Black America" (Schomburg Center for Research in Black Culture, June 4–5, 2010).

45. Vogel, *Featuring Michael Jackson: Collected Writings on the King of Pop*, 4.

46. *Earth Song: Inside Michael Jackson's Magnum Opus* (New York: BlakeVision Books, 2011); Vogel, *Featuring Michael Jackson: Collected Writings on the King of Pop*.

47. Susan Fast & Stan Hawkins (eds.), "Michael Jackson: Musical Subjectivities," *Popular Music & Society—Special Issue* 35, no. 2 (2012).

48. Michael Bush, *The King of Style: Dressing Michael Jackson* (San Rafael, CA: Insight Editions, 2012); Zack O'Malley Greenburg, *Michael Jackson, Inc.* (New York: Atria, 2014).

49. Fast, *Dangerous*; Karin Merx, "'Dangerous' by Dr. Susan Fast," *The Journal of Michael Jackson Academic Studies* 1, no. 1 (2014).

50. "The Journal of Michael Jackson Academic Studies," http://michaeljacksonstudies.org.

51. Fast, *Dangerous*, 16.

52. Hidalgo, "Wanna Be Startin' Somethin': MJ in the Scholarly Literature: A Selected Bibliographic Guide," 14–28.

53. Karin Merx, "From Throne to Wilderness: Michael Jackson's 'Stranger in Moscow' and the Foucauldian Outlaw," *The Journal of Michael Jackson Academic Studies* 1, no. 4 (2015).

CHAPTER 3. ON MICHAEL JACKSON'S *DANCING THE DREAM*

1. Alden T. Vaughan, Virginia Mason Vaughan, and William Shakespeare, *The Tempest* (London, UK: Arden, 2011), 276. This chapter was originally published on *Writing Eliza* in 2014, and subsequently by *The Journal of Michael Jackson Studies Online*. It has been revised slightly here. Elizabeth Amisu, "On Michael Jackson's *Dancing the Dream*," *Writing Eliza* (2014), http://elizabethamisu.com/post/910 73957802/on-michael-jacksons-dancing-the-dream-dangerous; Michael Jackson, *Dancing the Dream: Poems & Reflections* (London: Doubleday, 1992); Elizabeth Amisu, "On Michael Jackson's 'Dancing the Dream'," *The Journal of Michael Jackson Academic Studies* 1, no. 2 (2014).

2. Paul Lester, "Michael Jackson's Twenty Greatest Hits," in *The Resistible Demise of Michael Jackson*, ed. Mark Fisher (Zero Books, 2009), 36.

3. Joseph Vogel, "Second to None: Race, Representation and the Misunderstood Power of Michael Jackson's Music," in *Featuring Michael Jackson: Collected Writings on the King of Pop* (New York: Baldwin Books, 2012), 7–14.

4. A comprehensive list of books, notes, and blogs by Michael Jackson can be found in the Bibliography. *Man in the Music: The Creative Life and Work of Michael Jackson* (New York: Sterling, 2011), 141. "I wrote a book called *Dancing the Dream* . . . it came from my heart." Michael Jackson, interview by Compuserve Contributors, 1995.

5. Editors of Rolling Stone, *Michael Jackson* (Werner Media Specials, 2014), 90.

6. "I believe that all art has as its ultimate goal the union between the material and the spiritual, the human and the divine . . . I feel that this world we live in is really a big, huge, monumental symphonic orchestra." Michael Jackson, interview by Robert E. Johnson, May 1992; Jermaine Jackson, *You Are Not Alone: Michael, through a Brother's Eyes* (London: Harper Collins, 2011), 286iii.

7. Fred Schurink, "Manuscript Commonplace Books, Literature and Reading in Early Modern England," *Huntington Library Quarterly* 73, no. 3 (2010): 453–69.

8. C. H. Hereford, Percy Simpson, and Evelyn Simpson, eds. "Timber, or Discoveries." In *Ben Jonson, Vol. 8: The Poems; The Prose Works*. Oxford: Oxford University Press, 1925–52. lns. 950–55.

9. Margaret Cavendish, *The Worlds Olio Written by the Right Honorable, the Lady Margaret Newcastle* (London: EEBO Editions, 1655, 2011), 119v. "It [*Dancing the Dream*] was essays, thoughts and things that I've thought about while on tour." Jackson, "Simulchat."

10. "His [Jackson's] personal library contained more than 20,000 titles, including biographies, poetry, philosophy, psychology, and history." Vogel, *Man in the Music: The Creative Life and Work of Michael Jackson*, 6.

11. "Michael needed a book to sell primarily as a concert souvenir . . . I sat with him for hours while he dreamily wove Aesop-like tales about animals, mixed with words about music and his love of all things musical." Deepak Chopra, "A Tribute to My Friend Michael." *Huffington Post* (2009). Published electronically July 26. http://www.huffingtonpost.com/deepak-chopra/a-tribute-to-my-friend-mi_b_221268.html.

12. Various, "Dangerous: The Short Films," (MJJ Productions, 1993).

13. Jackson, *Dancing the Dream: Poems & Reflections*, 22, 39, 45, 51, 61, 66, 76, 77, 80, 81, 115.

14. Ibid., 63, 66.

15. Juliet Dusinberre and William Shakespeare, *As You Like It* (London, UK: Arden, 2006), 227; Sandra Clark, Pamela Mason, and William Shakespeare, *Macbeth* (London, UK: Arden, 2015), 161; Jackson, *Dancing the Dream: Poems & Reflections*, 1.

16. 1 Corinthians 15:52, *NIV*.

17. Jackson, *Dancing the Dream: Poems & Reflections*, 70.

18. "You will show me the path of life; In Your presence is fullness of joy; At Your right hand are pleasures forevermore." Psalm 16:11, *NKJV*. ". . . when the shock subsides and a thousand public voices recount Michael's brilliant, joyous, embattled,

enigmatic, bizarre trajectory, I hope the word 'joyous' is the one that will rise from the ashes and shine as he once did." Chopra, "A Tribute to My Friend Michael." "When I was young, my whole family attended church together in Indiana. As we grew older, this became difficult . . . I was comforted by the belief that God exists in my heart, and in music and in beauty, not only in a building. But I still miss the sense of community that I felt there." Michael Jackson, "My Childhood, My Sabbath, My Freedom," *BeliefNet.com* (2000), http://www.beliefnet.com/Faiths/2000/12/My-Childhood -My-Sabbath-My-Freedom.aspx?p=1.

19. Jackson, *Dancing the Dream: Poems & Reflections*, 75.

20. David Bevington and William Shakespeare, *Troilus and Cressida* (London, UK: Arden, 1998), 253.

21. Jackson, *Dancing the Dream: Poems & Reflections*, 91.

22. Ibid., 140.

23. Ibid., 46.

24. "Jesus' parables of the kingdom's present state explain why his kingdom comes first in a hidden way and why Israel's leaders reject him." InterVarsity Press, "Parables of the Secret Kingdom," *BibleGateway.com*, https://www.biblegateway.com/resources /commentaries/IVP-NT/Matt/Parables-Secret-Kingdom.

25. "I just believe what's in the Bible with regard to which religion is involved. I simply believe . . . I believe in it and I get down on my knees every night and thank God and ask Him to lead the way." Michael Jackson, 1976. "Each day I take time out to study the Bible, no matter where I am . . . It, somehow, makes me whole." Interview by Charles L. Sanders, September, 1979. ". . . reading the Bible, learning about God, Jesus, love. He said, 'Bring on the children,' 'Imitate the children,' 'Be like the children' and 'Take care of others'." Interview by Geraldo Rivera, 2005. "I love the Sermon on the Mount . . . the Apostles are arguing amongst themselves about who is the greatest and Jesus says, 'Unless you humble yourself . . .' I thought that was the perfect thing to say. Return to innocence." Shmuley Boteach, *The Michael Jackson Tapes: A Tragic Icon Reveals His Soul in Intimate Conversation* (New York: Vanguard Press, 2009), 112.

26. The Parable of the Bags of Gold: "14 Again, it will be like a man going on a journey, who called his servants and entrusted his wealth to them. 15 To one he gave five bags of gold, to another two bags, and to another one bag, each according to his ability. Then he went on his journey. 16 The man who had received five bags of gold went at once and put his money to work and gained five bags more. 17 So also, the one with two bags of gold gained two more. 18 But the man who had received one bag went off, dug a hole in the ground and hid his master's money . . . 29 For whoever has will be given more, and they will have an abundance. Whoever does not have, even what they have will be taken from them. 30 And throw that worthless servant outside, into the darkness, where there will be weeping and gnashing of teeth." Matthew 25:14–30, *NIV*.

27. "The same music governs the rhythm of the seasons, the pulse of our heartbeats, the migration of birds, the ebb and flow of ocean tides . . . It's music, it's rhythm . . . It's like, my purpose, it's what I'm here for." Jackson, "Michael Jackson: Crowned in Africa, Pop Music King Tells the Real Story of Controversial Trip."

28. "The Little Children and Jesus: 13 People were bringing little children to Jesus for him to place his hands on them, but the disciples rebuked them. 14 When Jesus saw this, he was indignant. He said to them, 'Let the little children come to me, and do not hinder them, for the kingdom of God belongs to such as these. 15 Truly I tell you, anyone who will not receive the kingdom of God like a little child will never enter it.'" Mark 10:13–15, *NIV*.

29. Matthew 20:16, *NIV*.

30. '"I've travelled the world over eight times. I do as many hospitals and orphanages as I do concerts. But, of course, it's not covered . . . I'm doing something that brings joy and happiness to other people." Jackson, "At Large with Geraldo Rivera"; Susan Hayward, *Cinema Studies: The Key Concepts* (New York: Routledge, 2000), 84–85.

31. Jackson, *Dancing the Dream: Poems & Reflections*, 45.

32. "The innocence of children represents to me the source of infinite creativity . . . by the time you are an adult, you're conditioned; you're so conditioned by the things about you and it goes." "Michael Jackson: Crowned in Africa, Pop Music King Tells the Real Story of Controversial Trip."

33. *Moonwalk* (London: Heinemann, 2009), 95–97, 275.

34. *Dancing the Dream: Poems & Reflections*, 99.

35. Ibid., 107, 13.

36. Ibid., 92, 20.

37. Ibid., 31.

38. Samuel Taylor and William Wordsworth Coleridge, "The Rime of the Ancyent Marinere," In *Lyrical Ballads, with a few other Poems* (London: J. & A. Arch, 1798) Reprinted in *Lyrical Ballads* (Penguin Classics, 2006), 11, 24, 25.

39. Michael Jackson, *Dangerous* (Sony/Epic Legacy, 1991), 15.

40. Willa Stillwater and Joie Collins, "Dancing with the Elephant: Conversations About Michael Jackson, His Art, and Social Change," *Dancing With the Elephant: Conversations About Michael Jackson, His Art, and Social Change* (2011–2015), http://dancingwiththeelephant.wordpress.com/.

41. Jackson, *Dancing the Dream: Poems & Reflections*, 15.

42. Ibid., 143.

43. Ibid., 143–45.

44. Jesse Schlotterbeck, "The 'Split' Biography: Man in the Mirror: The Michael Jackson Story," in *Christopher R. Smit*, ed. Michael Jackson: Grasping the Spectacle (Farnham, UK: Ashgate, 2012), 68; Jackson, *Dancing the Dream: Poems & Reflections*, 145.

45. Keir Elam and William Shakespeare, *Twelfth Night* (London, UK: Arden, 2008), 161.

46. Michael Jackson, *HIStory: Past, Present and Future, Book 1* (Sony/Epic Legacy, 1995), 11–14.

47. Vogel, *Man in the Music: The Creative Life and Work of Michael Jackson*, 107.

48. Ibid., 140–41; Chopra, "A Tribute to My Friend Michael."

49. "I always had this tug at the back of my head, the things I wanted to do, to raise children, have children." Editors of Ebony, *Ebony Special Tribute: Michael Jackson in His Own Words* (Johnson, 2009), 70.

50. Vaughan, Vaughan, and Shakespeare, *The Tempest*, 276.

51. Jackson, *Dangerous*, 1; Vogel, *Man in the Music: The Creative Life and Work of Michael Jackson*, 131.

52. Vaughan, Vaughan, and Shakespeare, *The Tempest*, 276.

53. Amy C. Billone, "Sentenced to Neverland: Michael Jackson, Peter Pan, and Queer Futurity," in *Michael Jackson: Grasping the Spectacle*, ed. Christopher R. Smit (Farnham, UK: Ashgate, 2012), 50.

54. Lester, "Michael Jackson's Twenty Greatest Hits," 34.

55. Michael Jackson, *Bad* (Epic Legacy, 1987), 6–7. Isaiah 40:3, *NIV*; John 1:23, *NIV*; Joseph Vogel, *Earth Song: Inside Michael Jackson's Magnum Opus* (New York: BlakeVision Books, 2011).

56. Jackson, *Dancing the Dream: Poems & Reflections*, 151.

CHAPTER 4. NARRATIVE IN MICHAEL JACKSON'S *BAD*

1. Michael Jackson, *Bad—Special Edition* (Sony/Epic Legacy, 2001), Voice-Over Intro Quincy Jones Interview #1.

2. For a detailed account of Jackson's touring schedule, see Adrian Grant, *Michael Jackson: A Visual Documentary. The Official Tribute Edition* (London: Omnibus, 2009).

3. Andrew Bennett and Nicholas Royle, *An Introduction to Literature, Criticism and Theory*, 4th ed. (Harlow, UK: Longman, 2009), 52–59. Bennett and Royle provide excellent and easily accessible definitions on a wide range of literary theories and concepts.

4. Plot: a basic sequence of events in any story or a storyline. It can be expressed by a series simple statements of events are occurred. *OED*.

5. Sophocles and Bernard Knox, *The Three Theban Plays: "Antigone," "Oedipus the King," "Oedipus at Colonus,"* trans. Robert Fagles (London: Penguin Classics, 1984).

6. Other key moments in plot include: conflict, resolution, climax and anti-climax. Climactic events that lead up to a peak of climactic action are often followed by a spiral into an anti-climax and/or denouement, which occurs just before the resolution of the narrative.

7. Michael Jackson, *Bad* (Epic Legacy, 1987), 10.

8. Ibid., 11.

9. Harper Lee, *To Kill a Mockingbird: 50th Anniversary Edition* (London: Arrow, 2010).

10. F. Scott Fitzgerald and Tony Tanner, *The Great Gatsby* (London: Penguin, 2000).

11. Jackson, *Bad*, 3–4.

12. These numbers are approximate and have been derived from the lyrics provided in the liner notes of *Bad*.

13. Jackson, *Bad*, 12.

14. Ibid.

15. For a more detailed look at the *Bad* short film and a focus on racial representation and Jackson's self-representation and identification with the black community, see Elizabeth Amisu, "Bad (1987)," *Writing Eliza* (2014), http://elizabethamisu.com/2014/07/20/bad-1987-genius-the-short-films-of-michael-2/; "'Bad (1987)'," *The Journal of Michael Jackson Academic Studies* 1, no. 2 (2014).

16. Jackson, *Bad*, 5.

17. Abeodu Bowen Jones, Donald Rahl Petterson, and Svend E. Holsoe, "Liberia," *Britannica.com* (2014), http://www.britannica.com/place/Liberia.

18. Kim F. Hall, "'Object into Object?': Some Thoughts on the Presence of Black Women in Early Modern Culture," in *Early Modern Visual Culture: Representation, Race, and Empire in Renaissance*, ed. Clark Hulse and Peter Erickson (Philadelphia, PA: University of Pennsylvania Press, 2000).

19. Jeremy Samuel Faust, "'When You Have to Say 'I Do' ': Orientalism in Michael Jackson's 'Liberian Girl'," *Popular Music and Society* 35, no. 2 (2012): 223.

20. The names Annie, Susie, and Debbie repeatedly feature in Jackson's songs.

21. Jackson, *Bad*, 5.

22. Ibid.

23. Ibid., 11.

24. Jamie Kinsler, "Victorian Culture and Society: Jack the Ripper as Victorian Entertainment " *The Student Historical Journal* (1999–2000).

25. Gottfried Helnwein, *Beautiful Victim I*, 1974. Watercolor on Cardboard, 53×73 cm / 20×28' in. Museum of Modern Art.

26. Colin Chilvers, Jerry Kramer, and Jim Blashfield, *Moonwalker* (MJJ Productions, 1988).

27. Jackson may also be alluding to the mirror principle. Robert Holden states that the world is a mirror of what we believe about life. This is the foundation on which practices such as "mirror-work" are based. Robert Holden, *Loveability: Knowing How to Love and Be Loved* (London: Hay House, 2013), 53–60.

28. Jackson, *Bad*, 7.

29. Ibid.

30. China Mieville, *Perdido Street Station* (London: Pan, 2011); Ursula K. Le Guin, *The Left Hand of Darkness* (London: Orbit, 2009).

31. *Speed Demon* is discussed in further detail in Chapter 7—"'Instrument of Nature': The Voice of Michael Jackson."

CHAPTER 5. IDENTITY AND IDENTIFICATION IN MICHAEL JACKSON'S *DANGEROUS*

1. Michael Jackson, *Dancing the Dream: Poems & Reflections* (London: Doubleday, 1992), 1.

2. Joseph Vogel, *Featuring Michael Jackson: Collected Writings on the King of Pop* (New York: Baldwin Books, 2012), 29; Susan Fast, *Dangerous* (London: Bloomsbury, 2014), 31.

3. Jackson's "Monster Persona" is the most vicious incarnation of Jackson's persona constructed by the tabloid coverage of child-abuse allegations levied against Jackson in the early nineties. In this persona he was often regarded as a child molester, a masterful manipulator, and a racist. See Chapter 9—" 'Throwing Stones to Hide Your Hands': The Mortal Persona of Michael Jackson."

4. Joseph Vogel, "Second to None: Race, Representation and the Misunderstood Power of Michael Jackson's Music," in *Featuring Michael Jackson: Collected Writings on the King of Pop* (New York: Baldwin Books, 2012), 12.

5. Fast, *Dangerous*, 18–19.

6. Ibid., 46.

7. Joseph Vogel, *Man in the Music: The Creative Life and Work of Michael Jackson* (New York: Sterling, 2011), 141.

8. Ibid., 143.

9. " 'I Ain't Scared of No Sheets': Re-Screening Black Masculinity in Michael Jackson's Black or White," *Journal of Popular Music Studies* 27, no. 1 (2015); " 'I Ain't Scared of No Sheets': Re-Screening Black Masculinity in Michael Jackson's Black or White," in *A Companion to Michael Jackson Academic Studies I*, ed. Elizabeth Amisu (MJAS, 2015).

10. See the Appendices: Elizabeth Amisu, "From Object to Subject: A Critical Survey on the Representation of Blackness in the Early Modern Period," Department of English (London: King's College London, 2015); " 'With All His Beauteous Race': High-Status Blacks in *The Masque of Blackness* and *The Merchant of Venice*" (Master of Arts, King's College London, 2015). For those interested in early Modern (1550–1650) constructions of blackness, see the Appendix. Also, see Hall's monograph, which provides a comprehensive and engaging source. Kim F. Hall, *Things of Darkness: Economies of Race and Gender in Early Modern England* (Ithaca, NY: Cornell University Press, 1995).

11. Michael Jackson, *Dangerous* (Sony/Epic Legacy, 1991), 6.

12. Ibid., 8.

13. Laura Mulvey, "Visual Pleasure and Narrative Cinema," in *Film Theory and Criticism: Introductory Readings*, ed. L. Braudy and M. Cohen (Oxford: Oxford University Press, 1999); Jackson, "Dangerous," 8.

14. *Dangerous*, 8.

15. Ibid., 10.

16. Ibid.

17. Ibid.

18. Ibid., 20.

19. Ibid.

20. Ibid.

21. See Chapter 4—"Narrative in Michael Jackson's '*Bad*'."

22. Jackson, *Dangerous*, 9.

23. Note Fast's examination of Jackson with regards to the Yoruba deity, Esu. Fast, *Dangerous*, 64.

24. Jackson, *Dangerous*, 3.

25. Ibid.; Fast, *Dangerous*, 35–37.

26. David Kellogg, "Jam" (1992).

27. Jackson, *Dangerous*, 17.

28. Ibid.

29. Ibid.

30. Ibid., 18.

31. Michael Eric Dyson, "Michael Jackson's Postmodern Spirituality," in *Reflecting Black: African-American Cultural Criticism* (Minneapolis: University of Minnesota Press, 1993), 36.

32. Jackson, *Dangerous*, 18.

33. Ibid., 19.

34. Ibid., 2, 11–12; *Dancing the Dream: Poems & Reflections*, 1.

35. Vogel, 'I Ain't Scared of No Sheets': Re-Screening Black Masculinity in Michael Jackson's Black or White," 93.

36. Jackson, *Dangerous*, 13.

37. Ibid., 21.

38. Ibid. A spoken recording of "Planet Earth" is included in the posthumous release: *The Ultimate Fan Extras Collection*, Deluxe ed. (iTunes: Sony Music Entertainment, 2013).

CHAPTER 6. "LIBERACE HAS GONE TO WAR": UNDRESSING MICHAEL JACKSON'S FASHION

1. Susan B. Kaiser, *Fashion and Cultural Studies* (London: Bloomsbury Academic, 2011); Ana Marta Gonzalez, ed. *Fashion and Identity: Identities through Fashion* (London: Berg, 2012); Fred Davis, *Fashion, Culture, and Identity* (Chicago: University of Chicago Press, 1994); Diana Crane, *Fashion and Its Social Agendas: Class, Gender, and Identity in Clothing* (Chicago: University of Chicago Press, 2000); Malcolm Barnard, *Fashion as Communication* (Abingdon, Oxon: Routledge, 2002).

2. Roland Barthes, *The Language of Fashion* (London: Bloomsbury Academic, 2013); *The Fashion System* (London: Random House, 2010).

3. Michael Bush, *The King of Style: Dressing Michael Jackson* (San Rafael, CA: Insight Editions, 2012), 19.

4. Malcolm Barnard, ed. *Fashion Theory: An Introduction* (Abingdon, Oxon: Routledge, 2014), 10.

5. "Balmain," *Vogue* (2008), http://www.vogue.co.uk/fashion/spring-summer -2009/ready-to-wear/balmain/full-length-photos; Julia Neel, "Michael Jackson—a Tribute," ibid. (2009), http://www.vogue.co.uk/spy/celebrity-photos/2009/06/26 /michael-jacksons-style—26062009; Boothe Moore, "Michael Jackson: King of Style," *The Los Angeles Times* (2009), http://www.latimes.com/fashion/alltherage/la-me -jackson-style26-2009jun26-story.html.

6. Michael Bush, "Dressing Michael Jackson," http://dressingmichaeljackson .com/.

7. "About the Book," (2014), http://dressingmichaeljackson.com/about-the
-book.html.

8. Barnard, *Fashion Theory: An Introduction*, 30, 36, 67.

9. Michael Jackson, *Moonwalk* (London: Heinemann, 2009), 217; Bush, *The King
of Style: Dressing Michael Jackson*, 32. Bush offers a "how-to" guide to making Jackson's
rhinestone glove and includes several images of gloves made through the years on
pages 31–39, including the one Jackson made in the 60s, as a young boy on page 34.

10. Jackson, *Moonwalk*, 217.

11. Bush, *The King of Style: Dressing Michael Jackson*, 59.

12. Ibid., 39.

13. Ibid., 3, 53–57, 62–63.

14. Ibid., 3.

15. Ibid., 63, 62.

16. Jackson, *Moonwalk*, 176.

17. *Thriller* (Epic Legacy, 1982).

18. Joseph Vogel, *Man in the Music: The Creative Life and Work of Michael Jackson*
(Sterling, 2011), 65.

19. Bush, *The King of Style: Dressing Michael Jackson*, 114.

20. See the '*Bad* (1987)' analysis online for more on the character, Daryl, who Jackson plays in the *Bad* short film and the congruity between costume, character and performance. Elizabeth Amisu, "'Bad (1987)'," *The Journal of Michael Jackson Academic
Studies* 1, no. 2 (2014); "Bad(1987)," *Writing Eliza* (2014), http://elizabethamisu
.com/2014/07/20/bad-1987-genius-the-short-films-of-michael-2/.

21. Bush, *The King of Style: Dressing Michael Jackson*, 100–01.

22. It is clear that Jackson was very aware of these symbols that typified his representation from the triptych album cover for the *Dangerous* album, discussed in-depth
in Susan Fast, *Dangerous* (London: Bloomsbury, 2014), 97–103. On this album cover
Jackson's eyes wear a masque constructed from a wide range of symbols and images.

23. Bush, *The King of Style: Dressing Michael Jackson*, 74–75. See 134 for Jackson's
sporting of the Romeo costume and 135 for images of Jackson's crown, his throne,
and royal insignia.

24. Barnard examines the multiple meaning of military/safari jackets to multiple
viewers. Barnard, *Fashion Theory: An Introduction*.

25. Bush, *The King of Style: Dressing Michael Jackson*, 133.

26. Ibid., 133–34.

27. Michael Jackson, *HIStory: Past, Present and Future, Book 1*, (Sony/Epic Legacy, 1995).

28. Vogel, *Man in the Music: The Creative Life and Work of Michael Jackson*, 182–83.

29. Bush, *The King of Style: Dressing Michael Jackson*, 195–99.

30. Ibid., 199.

31. Ibid.

32. Two examples are the Plantin-Moretus Museum in Antwerp and the Victoria
and Albert Museum in London.

33. Peter Erickson, "Representations of Blacks and Blackness in the Renaissance," *Criticism* 35, no. 4 (1993); "Invisibility Speaks: Servants and Portraits in Early Modern Visual Culture," *Journal for Early Modern Cultural Studies* 9, no. 1 (2009); David Bindman and Henry Louis Gates, *The Image of the Black in Western Art*, 5 vols. (Cambridge, Mass.: Belknap Press, 2010); Vincent Boele, Esther Schreuder, and Elmer Kolfin, *Black Is Beautiful: Rubens to Dumas* (Amsterdam: Waanders, 2008).

34. Dennis Tompkins, Karen Faye, and Michael Bush, "Michael Jackson: After Life," by Cynthia MacFadden. *20/20* (2010).

CHAPTER 7. "INSTRUMENT OF NATURE": THE VOICE OF MICHAEL JACKSON

1. In the final chapter of his biography of Michael Jackson, his brother Jermaine Jackson shares a poignant story of seeing Jackson's influence in a remote part of the world. Jermaine Jackson, *You Are Not Alone: Michael, through a Brother's Eyes* (London: Harper Collins, 2011), 444–45.

2. Susan Fast, *Dangerous* (London: Bloomsbury, 2014), 39.

3. Barney Hoskyns, "The Boy Who Would Fly: Michael Jackson (1983)," in *The Resistible Demise of Michael Jackson*, ed. Mark Fisher (Winchester, UK: Zero Books, 2009), 37–46.

4. Ibid., 39.

5. Ibid.

6. Ibid., 38.

7. Ibid., 39.

8. Sam Davies, "Glove, Socks, Zombies, Puppets: The Unheimlich Maneuvers and Undead Metonyms of Michael Jackson," ibid., 229.

9. Mel Campbell, "Saying the Unsayable: The Non-Verbal Vocalizations of Michael Jackson," *The Enthusiast* (2009); Ryan Kristobak, "Michael Jackson's Isolated Vocals for 'Man in the Mirror' Are Raw Emotion," *Huffington Post* (2013); Isabelle Stegner-Petitjean, " 'The Voice in the Mirror': Michael Jackson: From a Vocal Identity to Its Double in Sound," *Volume!* 8, no. 2 (2011); ibid.; Francesca T. Royster, " 'Hee Hee Hee': Michael Jackson and the Transgendered Erotics of Voice," *The Journal of Michael Jackson Academic Studies* 1, no. 3 (2015); Mats Johansson, "Michael Jackson and the Expressive Power of Voice-Produced Sound," *Popular Music and Society* 35, no. 2 (2012); Francesca T. Royster, "Michael Jackson, Queer World Making, and the Trans Erotics of Voice, Gender, and Age," in *Sounding Like a No-No: Queer Sounds and Eccentric Acts in the Post-Soul Era* (Ann Arbor: University of Michigan Press, 2013).

10. Joseph Vogel, *Man in the Music: The Creative Life and Work of Michael Jackson* (New York: Sterling, 2011), 11. See "Singing Beyond Language," 9–11, and "Music as Tapestry," 11–13.

11. Michele Wallace, "Michael Jackson, Black Modernisms and 'the Ecstasy of Communication'," *The Journal of Michael Jackson Academic Studies* 1, no. 4 (2015); "Michael Jackson, Black Modernisms and the Ecstasy of Communication," *Third*

Text 3, no. 7 (1989); "Michael Jackson, Black Modernisms and the Ecstasy of Communication," in *A Companion to Michael Jackson Academic Studies I*, ed. Elizabeth Amisu (MJAS, 2015); "Michael Jackson, Black Modernisms and the Ecstasy of Communication," in *Invisibility Blues* (London, New York: Verso, 2008). Royster provides an excellent overview of Michael Jackson's voice in relation to the post-soul era, gender, and racial constructions. Royster, "Michael Jackson, Queer World Making, and the Trans Erotics of Voice, Gender, and Age." Stegner-Petitjean's article also provides a clear analysis of the specific components of voice in terms of music and technical production, especially with regard to authenticity and recording choices, as well as vocal training and timbre. Stegner-Petitjean, "'The Voice in the Mirror': Michael Jackson: From a Vocal Identity to Its Double in Sound."

12. Royster, "Michael Jackson, Queer World Making, and the Trans Erotics of Voice, Gender, and Age," 117.

13. "'Hee Hee Hee': Michael Jackson and the Transgendered Erotics of Voice," 1.

14. For *Dangerous* commentary see Chapter 3—"On Michael Jackson's *Dancing the Dream*" and Chapter 5—"Identity and Identification in Michael Jackson's *Dangerous*." For *Invincible* commentary see Chapter 17—"*Invincible*: Michael Jackson's Lost Late Album."

15. Michael Jackson, *Bad* (Epic Legacy, 1987). All song quotes are taken from the track, *Speed Demon*.

16. Royster, "'Hee Hee Hee': Michael Jackson and the Transgendered Erotics of Voice," 2.

17. Jackson, *Bad*, 4–5.

18. Ibid.

19. Royster, "'Hee Hee Hee': Michael Jackson and the Transgendered Erotics of Voice," 3.

20. "Michael Jackson, Queer World Making, and the Trans Erotics of Voice, Gender, and Age," 136.

21. Jackson, *Bad*.

22. Adrian Grant, *Michael Jackson: A Visual Documentary. The Official Tribute Edition* (London: Omnibus, 2009).

23. Jerry Kramer and Will Vinton, *Speed Demon* (1988); Colin Chilvers, Jerry Kramer, and Jim Blashfield, *Moonwalker* (MJJ Productions, 1988).

CHAPTER 8. THOUGHTS ON MICHAEL JACKSON'S TRANSFORMATIONS

1. For a detailed analysis of Jackson's spending on short films see Zack O'Malley Greenburg, *Michael Jackson, Inc.* (New York: Atria, 2014).

2. Michael Jackson, *Moonwalk* (London: Heinemann, 2009), 72.

3. Mary Wollstonecraft Shelley and Maurice Hindle, *Frankenstein: Or the Modern Prometheus* (London: Penguin, 2003); Franz Kafka, Joyce Crick, and Ritchie Robertson, *The Metamorphosis and Other Stories* (Oxford: Oxford University Press, 2009).

4. Jackson, *Moonwalk*, 95.

5. Ibid., 91, 17–18.

6. Reid Kane, "The King of Pop's Two Bodies, or, Thriller as Allegory," in *The Resistible Demise of Michael Jackson*, ed. Mark Fisher (Winchester, UK: Zero Books, 2009); John Landis, *Thriller* (1983); Kobena Mercer, "Monster Metaphors: Notes on Michael Jackson's 'Thriller'," *Screen* 27, no. 1 (1986).

7. Margo Jefferson, *On Michael Jackson* (New York: Pantheon, 2006); Matthew Delmont, "Michael Jackson & Television before Thriller," *The Journal of Pan African Studies* 3, no. 7 (2010).

8. Jackson, *Moonwalk*, 96.

9. Ibid.

10. Mary A. Fischer, "Was Michael Jackson Framed?" *GQ* (Oct. 1994); *Was Michael Jackson Framed? The Untold Story That Brought Down a Superstar* (Marston, UK and New York: CreateSpace, 2012).

11. Stan Winston, "(2 Bad+Is It Scary+) Ghosts," (1997); "Michael Jackson's Ghosts," (Kingdom Entertainment, 1998).

12. See Fischer (1994) for a detailed overview of Jackson's accusations and his accusers.

13. Tim Burton, *Edward Scissorhands* (Twentieth Century Fox, 1990).

14. Various, "Michael Jackson: The Making of Ghosts," (VH1, 1997).

15. Kim F. Hall, *Things of Darkness: Economies of Race and Gender in Early Modern England* (Ithaca, NY: Cornell University Press, 1995), 4–5.

16. William Shakespeare and E. A. J. Honigmann, *Othello* (London: Arden Shakespeare), 121–22.

17. Hall, *Things of Darkness: Economies of Race and Gender in Early Modern England*, 4–5.

18. Hall, *Things of Darkness: Economies of Race and Gender in Early Modern England*, 17–22.

19. Joseph Vogel, "Am I the Beast You Visualized? The Cultural Abuse of Michael Jackson," *Huffington Post* (2011), http://www.huffingtonpost.com/joe-vogel/michael-jackson-trial-_b_1068750.html; "'Am I the Beast You Visualized?': The Cultural Abuse of Michael Jackson," in *Featuring Michael Jackson: Collected Writings on the King of Pop* (New York: Baldwin Books, 2012).

CHAPTER 9. "THROWING STONES TO HIDE YOUR HANDS": THE MORTAL PERSONA OF MICHAEL JACKSON

1. This article was original published via *Writing Eliza* and the *Journal of Michael Jackson Academic Studies*. I am very much indebted to the fans and fellow academics who read and shared it via social media. Due to their support it became the cornerstone of this book. Elizabeth Amisu, "'Throwing Stones to Hide Your Hands': Mortal Persona of Michael Jackson," *Writing Eliza* (2014), http://elizabethamisu.com/post/88515649217/throwing-stones-to-hide-your-hands-the-mortal-persona.

2. Naboth's Vineyard: Sometime later there was an incident involving a vineyard belonging to Naboth the Jezreelite. The vineyard was in Jezreel, close to the palace of Ahab, king of Samaria. 2 Ahab said to Naboth, "Let me have your vineyard to use for a vegetable garden, since it is close to my palace. In exchange I will give you a better vineyard or, if you prefer, I will pay you whatever it is worth." 3 But Naboth replied, "The Lord forbid that I should give you the inheritance of my ancestors." 4 So Ahab went home, sullen and angry because Naboth the Jezreelite had said, "I will not give you the inheritance of my ancestors." He lay on his bed sulking and refused to eat. 5 His wife Jezebel came in and asked him, "Why are you so sullen? Why won't you eat?" 6 He answered her, "Because I said to Naboth the Jezreelite, 'Sell me your vineyard; or if you prefer, I will give you another vineyard in its place.' But he said, 'I will not give you my vineyard.'" 7 Jezebel his wife said, "Is this how you act as king over Israel? Get up and eat! Cheer up. I'll get you the vineyard of Naboth the Jezreelite." 8 So she wrote letters in Ahab's name, placed his seal on them, and sent them to the elders and nobles who lived in Naboth's city with him. 9 In those letters she wrote: "Proclaim a day of fasting and seat Naboth in a prominent place among the people. 10 But seat two scoundrels opposite him and have them bring charges that he has cursed both God and the king. Then take him out and stone him to death." 11 So the elders and nobles who lived in Naboth's city did as Jezebel directed in the letters she had written to them. 12 They proclaimed a fast and seated Naboth in a prominent place among the people. 13 Then two scoundrels came and sat opposite him and brought charges against Naboth before the people, saying, "Naboth has cursed both God and the king." So they took him outside the city and stoned him to death. 14 Then they sent word to Jezebel: "Naboth has been stoned to death." 15 As soon as Jezebel heard that Naboth had been stoned to death, she said to Ahab, "Get up and take possession of the vineyard of Naboth the Jezreelite that he refused to sell you. He is no longer alive, but dead." 16 When Ahab heard that Naboth was dead, he got up and went down to take possession of Naboth's vineyard. 1 Kings 21:13, *NIV*.

3. "It's not just about thoughts and words. It's an emotion that drives through your blood. You have to feel and live it every day until you believe it." Frank Cascio, *My Friend Michael: An Ordinary Friendship with an Extraordinary Man* (London and New York: William Morrow, 2011), 96.

4. Joseph Vogel, *Man in the Music: The Creative Life and Work of Michael Jackson* (New York: Sterling, 2011), 31, 7; Michael Jackson, *Moonwalk* (London: Heinemann, 2009), 210–13.

5. Chris Roberts, "True Enough: Michael in Fifty Shards," in *The Resistible Demise of Michael Jackson*, ed. Mark Fisher (Winchester, UK: Zero Books, 2009), 107.

6. Vogel, *Man in the Music: The Creative Life and Work of Michael Jackson*, 55.

7. Jackson, *Moonwalk*, 91.

8. Jeremy Gilbert, "The Real Abstraction of Michael Jackson," in *The Resistible Demise of Michael Jackson*, ed. Mark Fisher (Winchester, UK: Zero Books, 2009), 137–49.

9. Michael Jackson, "Love: The Human Family's Most Precious Legacy," *The Journal of Pan African Studies* 3, no. 7 (2010).

10. Cascio, *My Friend Michael: An Ordinary Friendship with an Extraordinary Man*, 206.

11. Vogel, *Man in the Music: The Creative Life and Work of Michael Jackson*, 200–01; Michael Jackson, *HIStory: Past, Present and Future, Book 1* (Sony/Epic Legacy, 1995), 38–39.

12. Gilbert, "The Real Abstraction of Michael Jackson," 138.

13. Jackson, *Moonwalk*, 227.

14. Joseph Vogel, "Abortion, Fame, and 'Bad': Listening to Michael Jackson's Unreleased Demos," *The Atlantic* (2012), http://www.theatlantic.com/entertainment /archive/2012/09/abortion-fame-and-bad-listening-to-michael-jacksons -unreleased-demos/262242/.

15. "How Michael Jackson Made 'Bad'," *The Atlantic* (2012), http://www .theatlantic.com/entertainment/archive/2012/09/how-michael-jackson-made-bad /262162/2/.

16. *Man in the Music: The Creative Life and Work of Michael Jackson*, 224.

17. Adrian Grant, *Michael Jackson: A Visual Documentary. The Official Tribute Edition* (London: Omnibus, 2009), 158–59.

18. Michael Jackson, interview by Oprah Winfrey, 1993.

19. Ibid.

20. Ibid.

21. Grant, *Michael Jackson: A Visual Documentary. The Official Tribute Edition*, 111.

22. Vogel, *Man in the Music: The Creative Life and Work of Michael Jackson*, 155; John Singleton, "Remember the Time," (1992).

23. Elena Oliete, "Michael Are You Ok? You've Been Hit by a Smooth Criminal: Racism, Controversy, and Parody in the Videos "Smooth Criminal" and "You Rock My World," *Studies in Popular Culture* 29, no. 1 (2006): 57–76.

24. 1 Kings 21:13, *NIV*.

25. Jim Blashfield, "Leave Me Alone," (1989).

26. Grant, *Michael Jackson: A Visual Documentary. The Official Tribute Edition*, 159.

27. Jackson, "Michael Jackson Talks To . . . Oprah Live."

28. Randall Sullivan, *Untouchable: The Strange Life and Tragic Death of Michael Jackson* (London and New York: Grove Press, 2012), 167.

29. Cascio, *My Friend Michael: An Ordinary Friendship with an Extraordinary Man*, 73.

30. Grant, *Michael Jackson: A Visual Documentary. The Official Tribute Edition*, 55.

31. Ibid., 172.

32. Jackson, *Moonwalk*, p. 9.

33. "I've travelled the world over eight times. I do as many hospitals and orphanages as I do concerts. But, of course, it's not covered . . . I'm doing something that brings joy and happiness to other people." Michael Jackson, interview by Geraldo Rivera, 2005.

34. "Often in the past performers have been tragic figures. A lot of the truly great people have suffered or died because of pressure and drugs . . . You feel cheated as a fan . . ." *Moonwalk*, 282.

35. Grant, *Michael Jackson: A Visual Documentary. The Official Tribute Edition*, 173.

36. Mary A. Fischer, *Was Michael Jackson Framed? The Untold Story That Brought Down a Superstar* (Marston, UK and New York: CreateSpace, 2012).

37. Grant, *Michael Jackson: A Visual Documentary. The Official Tribute Edition*, 232. "I dressed Michael Jackson every day of his fourteen-week trial . . . Michael became withdrawn, cynical and tired over these years." Michael Bush, *The King of Style: Dressing Michael Jackson* (San Rafael, CA: Insight Editions, 2012), 177.

38. Oliete, 71.

39. Grant, *Michael Jackson: A Visual Documentary. The Official Tribute Edition*, 106.

40. Jackson, *Moonwalk*, 95. Sari Shepphird, "Michael Jackson & BDD: Body Dysmorphic Disorder," *Britannica.com* (2009), http://www.britannica.com/blogs/2009/07/michael-jackson-bdd-body-dysmorphic-disorder/. Jackson, *Moonwalk*, 96–97.

41. Jackson, *At Large with Geraldo Rivera*.

42. Jackson, "Love: The Human Family's Most Precious Legacy."

43. Grant, *Michael Jackson: A Visual Documentary. The Official Tribute Edition*, 275.

44. Michael Jackson, *Bad 25*, (Sony, 2012).

45. "Thriller," (Epic Legacy, 1982).

46. Grant, *Michael Jackson: A Visual Documentary. The Official Tribute Edition*, 271.

47. Ibid.

48. Various, "Michael Jackson: The Making of Ghosts," (VH1, 1997).

49. Vogel, *Man in the Music: The Creative Life and Work of Michael Jackson*, 258–59.

50. Sullivan, *Untouchable: The Strange Life and Tragic Death of Michael Jackson*, 400-04.

51. Jackson, *At Large with Geraldo Rivera*.

52. Richard Littlejohn, "Mob Grief Proves Britain Is More Wacko Than Jacko," *Daily Mail*, July 7, 2009 (http://www.dailymail.co.uk/debate/article-1196373/LITTLEJOHN-Mob-grief-proves-Britain-wacko-Jacko.html).

53. Kenny Ortega, *Michael Jackson's This Is It* (Sony, 2009).

54. Katrina K Wheeler, "Distressed Fans Commit Suicide over Michael Jackson's Death," *Examiner* (2009), http://www.examiner.com/article/distressed-fans-commit-suicide-over-michael-jackson-s-death.

55. ". . . creating an illusion that his physical presence took up more space than it really did." Bush, *The King of Style: Dressing Michael Jackson*, 61.

56. "The benchmarks went on and on." Vogel, *Man in the Music: The Creative Life and Work of Michael Jackson*, 22.

57. "I said, I'm just going to do a great album, because I love, em, the album Tchaikovsky did, *The Nutcracker Suite*, it's an album where every song is like a great song. I said I wanted to do an album where every song is like a hit record. . . ." Michael Jackson, interview by Jesse Jackson, March 27, 2005.

58. Various, "Dangerous: The Short Films," (MJJ Productions, 1993).

CHAPTER 10. RE-CONTEXTUALIZING MICHAEL JACKSON'S BLACKNESS

1. Michael Jackson, *Moonwalk* (London: Heinemann, 2009), 108.

2. Elizabeth Amisu, "From Object to Subject: A Critical Survey on the Representation of Blackness in the Early Modern Period," Department of English (London: King's College London, 2015).

3. Ania Loomba and Jonathan Burton, eds., *Race in Early Modern England: A Documentary Companion* (Basingstoke: Palgrave Macmillan, 2007), 1.

4. Mary Floyd-Wilson, *English Ethnicity and Race in Early Modern Drama* (Cambridge, England: Cambridge University Press, 2003), 19; Elizabeth Amisu, "'With All His Beauteous Race': High-Status Blacks in *The Masque of Blackness* and *The Merchant of Venice*" (Master of Arts, King's College London, 2015), 5.

5. Harvey Young, *Theatre and Race* (Basingstoke, UK: Palgrave Macmillan, 2013), 5, 6.

6. Blackface: "make-up worn by a white actor playing a black person . . . in exaggerated style." *OED*.

7. Vitiligo: "a skin disease characterized by the presence of smooth white shining tubercles on the face, neck, and other parts of the body . . . the post-natal development of sharply defined white patches that tend to grow in size." *OED*.

8. Leeds Barroll, "Theatre as Text: The Case of Queen Anna and the Jacobean Court Masque," in *The Elizabethan Theatre, XIV*, ed. A. L. Magnusson and C. E. McGee (Toronto: Meany, 1996); Ben Jonson and David Lindley, "The Masque of Blackness," in *The Cambridge Edition of the Works of Ben Jonson*, ed. David M. Bevington, Martin Butler, and Ian Donaldson (Cambridge: Cambridge University Press, 2012); Joyce Green MacDonald, "'The Force of Imagination': The Subject of Blackness in Shakespeare, Jonson, and Ravenscroft," *Renaissance Papers* (1991).

9. Harriet J. Manning, *Michael Jackson and the Blackface Mask* (Farnham, UK: Ashgate, 2013); Constance Pierce, "Book Review: H. J. Manning, 'Michael Jackson and the Blackface Mask'," (2014).

10. Young, *Theatre and Race*, 40.

11. Ibid., 42.

12. Michael Jackson, *Blood on the Dance Floor: HIStory in the Mix* (Sony/Epic Legacy, 1995), Morphine.

13. Young, *Theatre and Race*, 38; Ian Smith, "White Skin, Black Masks: Racial Cross-Dressing on the Early Modern Stage," *Renaissance Drama* 32 (2003).

14. Peter Erickson, "Representations of Blacks and Blackness in the Renaissance," *Criticism* 35, no. 4 (1993); Amisu, "'With All His Beauteous Race': High-Status Blacks in *The Masque of Blackness* and *The Merchant of Venice*."

15. Michael Jackson, interview by Oprah Winfrey, 1993.

16. Andreana Clay, "Working Day and Night: Black Masculinity and the King of Pop," *Journal of Popular Music Studies* 23, no. 1 (2011); Joseph Vogel, "'I Ain't Scared of No Sheets': Re-Screening Black Masculinity in Michael Jackson's Black or White," ibid., 27 (2015).

17. Adrian Grant, *Michael Jackson: A Visual Documentary. The Official Tribute Edition* (London: Omnibus, 2009).

18. Margo Jefferson, *On Michael Jackson* (New York: Pantheon, 2006).

19. Elissa Fleak, "Autopsy Report for Michael Jackson," (County of Los Angeles: Department of Health Services, 2009).

20. Lee Thomas, *Turning White: A Memoir of Change* (Troy, MI: Momentum Books, 2012).

21. Ron Harris, "The Man Who Turned White," Ebony 34, no. 1 (November, 1978): 165–70.

22. Thomas, *Turning White: A Memoir of Change*, 4.

23. Ibid., 5.

24. Ibid.

25. Ibid., 2.

26. Jackson, "Michael Jackson Talks To . . . Oprah Live."

27. Michael Jackson, interview by Various, November 10, 1996.

28. Kim F. Hall, " 'These Bastard Signs of Fair': Literary Whiteness in Shakespeare's Sonnets," in *Post-Colonial Shakespeares*, ed. Ania Loomba and Martin Orkin (London, England: Routledge, 1998).

29. John Singleton, *Remember the Time* (1992); Spike Lee, *They Don't Care About Us (Prison Version)* (1996); *They Don't Care About Us (Brazil Version)* (1996).

30. For an overview of Jackson's use of costume in order to present high status, see Chapter 6—" 'Liberace Has Gone to War': Undressing Michael Jackson's Fashion."

31. Singleton, *Remember the Time*.

32. Joseph L. Mankiewicz, *Cleopatra* (20th Century Fox, 1963); Francesca T. Royster, *Becoming Cleopatra: The Shifting Image of an Icon* (New York: Palgrave Macmillan, 2003).

33. "The Kingdom of Ife (pronounced ee-feh) was a powerful, cosmopolitan and wealthy city-state in West Africa (in what is now modern southwest Nigeria)." The British Museum, "Kingdom of Ife: Sculptures from West Africa," (2010), http://www.britishmuseum.org/about_us/news_and_press/press_releases/2010/kingdom_of_ife.aspx; *Head of a Negro, Probably Representing a Ruler (Oni), from Ife, Nigeria*, 12th-14th ce. Museum of Mankind.

34. For an in-depth exploration of African art, see Frank Willet, *African Art* (London: Thames and Hudson, 1995).

35. Donald Bogle, *Toms, Coons, Mulattoes, Mammies and Bucks: An Interpretive History of Blacks in American Films* (London and New York: Continuum Publishing Group, 2001).

36. Sidney Lumet, *The Wiz* (Motown Productions, 1978); Andrew L. Stone, *Stormy Weather* (20th Century Fox, 1943); George Gershwin, *Porgy and Bess* (Decca, 1993).

37. All filming locations and dates taken from: Michael Jackson, *Michael Jackson's Vision* (Epic, Legacy Recordings, MJJ Productions, 2010); Grant, *Michael Jackson: A Visual Documentary. The Official Tribute Edition*.

38. White discusses Jackson's Afrocentricity in alarming contexts throughout his collection: Armond White, "In MJ's Shadow," in *Keep Moving: The Michael Jackson*

Chronicles (New York: Resistance Works, 2010); "'How Deep Is Your Afrocentricity?' Ask Michael & Iman," in *Keep Moving: The Michael Jackson Chronicles* (New York: Resistance Works, 2010); "The Gloved One Is Not a Chump"; "Understanding Michael Jackson."

39. Michael Jackson, interview by Jesse Jackson, March 27, 2005.

40. This article discusses the themes of race and ethnicity in Jackson's *Bad* in further detail. Elizabeth Amisu, "'Bad (1987)'," *The Journal of Michael Jackson Academic Studies* 1, no. 2 (2014).

41. Martin Scorsese, David Thompson, and Ian Christie, eds., *Scorsese on Scorsese* (London: Faber, 1990), 113.

42. Anu Kornohen, "Washing the Ethiopian White: Conceptualising Black Skin in Renaissance England," in *Black Africans in Renaissance Europe*, ed. T. F. Earle and K. J. P. Lowe (Cambridge: Cambridge University Press, 2005).

43. Jackson, *Moonwalk*, 62.

CHAPTER 11. *HISTORY* AND MICHAEL JACKSON'S AUTOBIOGRAPHICAL POTENCY

1. Armond White, "Screaming to Be Heard, Book I," in *Keep Moving: The Michael Jackson Chronicles* (New York: Resistance Works, 2010), 53.

2. Joseph Vogel, *Man in the Music: The Creative Life and Work of Michael Jackson* (New York: Sterling, 2011), 171.

3. Paul Lester, "Michael Jackson's Twenty Greatest Hits," in *The Resistible Demise of Michael Jackson*, ed. Mark Fisher (Winchester, UK: Zero Books, 2009).

4. Arthur Miller (1915–2005), was an American playwright, who wrote several plays featuring every day tragic heroes, such as *The Death of a Salesman* and *A View from the Bridge*. For a detailed overview of Miller's works, see C. W. E. Bigsby, *The Cambridge Companion to Arthur Miller*, 2nd ed. (Cambridge: Cambridge University Press, 2010).

5. Michael Jackson, *HIStory: Past, Present and Future, Book 1* (Sony/Epic Legacy, 1995), "They Don't Care About Us."

6. Karin Merx, "From Throne to Wilderness: Michael Jackson's 'Stranger in Moscow' and the Foucauldian Outlaw," *The Journal of Michael Jackson Academic Studies* 1, no. 4 (2015).

7. Panopticon: "a circular prison with cells arranged around a central well, from which inmates can be observed at all times . . . the design was first proposed by Jeremy Bentham (1748–1832) in 1787." *OED*.

8. Michael Jackson, *Bad 25* (Sony, 2012), "Price of Fame."

9. "MTV Video Music Awards | 2009," http://www.mtv.com/ontv/vma/2009/.

10. Daphne Simeon and Jeffrey Abugel, *Feeling Unreal: Depersonalization Disorder and the Loss of the Self* (Oxford: Oxford University Press, 2006).

11. Sandra Clark, Pamela Mason, and William Shakespeare, *Macbeth* (London, UK: Arden, 2015); Edvard Munch, "The Scream (1895)," in *The Story of Art*, ed. E. H. Gombrich (Phaidon, 1995).

12. Chiara Guidi, " 'The Purpose of Playing': Shakespeare and/in Experimental Theatre. A Master Class with Chiara Guidi." Interview by Sonia Massai, February 10, 2015, 2015, Notes, King's College London.

13. Jackson, *HIStory: Past, Present and Future, Book 1*, 33.

14. See Chapter 12—"Michael Jackson and Children Revisited" for an analysis of Jackson's use of childhood as a longstanding theme in his artistry.

15. Toni Bowers, "Dancing with Michael Jackson," *The Los Angeles Review of Books* (2015), https://lareviewofbooks.org/essay/dancing-with-michael-jackson.

16. Jackson, *HIStory: Past, Present and Future, Book 1*, "They Don't Care About Us."

17. Joseph Vogel, "Second to None: Race, Representation and the Misunderstood Power of Michael Jackson's Music," in *Featuring Michael Jackson: Collected Writings on the King of Pop* (New York: Baldwin Books, 2012).

18. Gottfried Helnwein, *Beautiful Victim I*, 1974. Watercolor on Cardboard, 53×73 cm / 20 x 28 in. Museum of Modern Art.

19. Jackie Lay et al., "Mass Incarceration, Visualized," (*The Atlantic*, 2015).

20. Jackson, *HIStory: Past, Present and Future, Book 1*, "They Don't Care About Us."

21. Ibid.

22. Ibid., "Stranger in Moscow."

23. Ibid.

24. Ibid.

25. Matthew 5:45, *NIV*.

26. Jackson, *HIStory: Past, Present and Future, Book 1*, "Stranger in Moscow."

27. *Moonwalk* (London: Heinemann, 2009), 95.

28. Merx, "From Throne to Wilderness: Michael Jackson's 'Stranger in Moscow' and the Foucauldian Outlaw."

29. Michael D. Bristol, "Shakespeare: The Myth," in *A Companion to Shakespeare*, ed. David Scott Kastan (Oxford: Blackwell Publishers, 1999).

30. Tim Niel, "Shakespeare's First Folio," in *The Secret Life of Books*, ed. Alan Campbell (BBC Four, 2014).

31. Ibid.

32. Pharrell Williams: Music's Hottest Hitmaker Talks To The Thriller (2003).

CHAPTER 12. MICHAEL JACKSON AND CHILDREN REVISITED

1. Veronica Bassil, *That Wonder in My Youth: Michael Jackson and Childhood* (Kindle, 2013); Shmuley Boteach, *Honoring the Child Spirit* (New York: Vanguard Press, 2011); Tavia Nyong'o, "Have You Seen His Childhood? Song, Screen, and the Queer Culture of the Child in Michael Jackson's Music," *Journal of Popular Music Studies* 23, no. 1 (2011); Joseph Vogel, "Have You Seen His Childhood?" in *Featuring Michael Jackson: Collected Writings on the King of Pop* (New York: Baldwin Books, 2012).

2. Gottfried Helnwein, "Artist Helnwein," http://www.helnwein.com/.

3. Michael Jackson, "Love: The Human Family's Most Precious Legacy," *The Journal of Pan African Studies* 3, no. 7 (2010): 6.

4. Tavia Nyong'o, "Have You Seen His Childhood? Song, Screen, and the Queer Culture of the Child in Michael Jackson's Music," *Journal of Popular Music Studies* 23, no. 1, 44.

5. Margo Jefferson, *On Michael Jackson* (New York: Pantheon, 2006), 78.

6. Ibid., 53, 56.

7. Elizabeth Amisu, " 'The Isle Is Full of Noises': Revisiting the Peter Pan of Pop," *Writing Eliza* (2014), http://elizabethamisu.com/2014/08/21/the-isle-is-full-of-noises-revisiting-the/; " 'The Isle Is Full of Noises': Revisiting the Peter Pan of Pop," *The Journal of Michael Jackson Academic Studies* 1, no. 1 (2014); " ,Die Insel Ist Voller Geräusche': Erneuter Besuch Beim „Peter Pan Des Pop"," [" 'The Isle is Full of Noises': Revisiting the Peter Pan of Pop"], *The Journal of Michael Jackson Academic Studies* 1, no. 3 (2015).

8. Jefferson, *On Michael Jackson*, 74.

9. Michael Jackson, interview by Oprah Winfrey, 1993.

10. Michael Jackson, interview by Robert E. Johnson, May 1992.

11. John Bradshaw, *Home Coming: Reclaiming and Championing Your Inner Child* (London: Piatkus, 2013), 6–25.

12. Matthew, 19:14; ibid., 30–50.

13. Michael Jackson, *Dancing the Dream: Poems & Reflections* (London: Doubleday, 1992), 58.

14. Ibid.

15. Ibid.

16. Ibid., 51.

17. *Invincible* (MJJ Productions, Epic, 2001), "The Lost Children."

18. Bill DiCicco, "Gone Too Soon," (1993); Vogel, "Gone Too Soon: The Many Lives of Michael Jackson's Elegy."

19. Jackson, *Dancing the Dream: Poems & Reflections*, 75.

20. *HIStory: Past, Present and Future, Book 1* (Sony/Epic Legacy, 1995), 37.

21. Ibid., "Little Susie."

22. Ibid.

23. Helnwein, "Artist Helnwein."

24. Jackson, *HIStory: Past, Present and Future, Book 1*, 33

25. Amisu, " 'The Isle Is Full of Noises': Revisiting the Peter Pan of Pop"; " ,Die Insel Ist Voller Geräusche': Erneuter Besuch Beim "Peter Pan Des Pop"."

CHAPTER 13. FAITH, HOPE, AND LOVE: THE DANGEROUS PHILOSOPHIES OF MICHAEL JACKSON

1. Oxford Union, "About Us" (2016), https://www.oxford-union.org/about_us.

2. Michael Jackson, "Love: The Human Family's Most Precious Legacy," *The Journal of Pan African Studies* 3, no. 7 (2010); Michael Jackson, "Love: The Human

Family's Most Precious Legacy," in *A Companion to Michael Jackson Academic Studies I*, ed. Elizabeth Amisu (MJAS, 2015).

3. "Love Is Indispensable—1 If I speak in the tongues of men or of angels, but do not have love, I am only a resounding gong or a clanging cymbal. 2 If I have the gift of prophecy and can fathom all mysteries and all knowledge, and if I have a faith that can move mountains, but do not have love, I am nothing. 3 If I give all I possess to the poor and give over my body to hardship that I may boast, but do not have love, I gain nothing. 4 Love is patient, love is kind. It does not envy, it does not boast, it is not proud. 5 It does not dishonor others, it is not self-seeking, it is not easily angered, it keeps no record of wrongs. 6 Love does not delight in evil but rejoices with the truth. 7 It always protects, always trusts, always hopes, always perseveres. 8 Love never fails. But where there are prophecies, they will cease; where there are tongues, they will be stilled; where there is knowledge, it will pass away. 9 For we know in part and we prophesy in part, 10 but when completeness comes, what is in part disappears. 11 When I was a child, I talked like a child, I thought like a child, I reasoned like a child. When I became a man, I put the ways of childhood behind me. 12 For now we see only a reflection as in a mirror; then we shall see face to face. Now I know in part; then I shall know fully, even as I am fully known. 13 And now these three remain: faith, hope and love. But the greatest of these is love." 1 Corinthians 13:1–13, *NIV*.

4. David Pawson and Andy Peck, *Unlocking the Bible* (London: Marshall Pickering, 2001), 939.

5. Jackson, "Love: The Human Family's Most Precious Legacy," 4.

6. Ibid.

7. Ibid., 4–5.

8. Ibid., 5.

9. Ibid.

10. Ibid., 4.

11. Ibid., 5.

12. Ibid.

13. Ibid.

14. Ibid., 6.

15. Ibid.

16. Ibid.

17. Ibid.

18. Ibid.

19. Ibid.

20. Ibid., 7.

21. Ibid.

22. Ibid.

23. Ibid., 8.

24. Ibid., 9.

25. Ibid., 10.

26. Ibid., 11.

27. Ibid., 12.

28. Ibid.

29. *Guinness World Records* (Guinness World Records, 2000).

30. Jackson, "Love: The Human Family's Most Precious Legacy."

CHAPTER 14. FROM CROWN TO CROSS: THE POISONED CHALICE OF *THRILLER*'S SUCCESS

1. Sandra Clark, Pamela Mason, and William Shakespeare, *Macbeth* (London, UK: Arden, 2015).

2. Ibid.

3. For a range of critical views on *Thriller*, see Joseph Vogel, *Man in the Music: The Creative Life and Work of Michael Jackson* (New York: Sterling, 2011), 55–91.

4. Michael Jackson, *Moonwalk* (London: Heinemann, 2009), 165–66.

5. Clark, Mason, and Shakespeare, *Macbeth*.

6. Jackson, *Moonwalk*, 260.

7. Barney Hoskyns, "The Boy Who Would Fly: Michael Jackson (1983)," in *The Resistible Demise of Michael Jackson*, ed. Mark Fisher (Winchester, UK: Zero Books, 2009), 40.

8. Jackson, *Moonwalk*.

9. Bill Whitfield, Javon Beard and Tanner Colby, *Remember the Time: Protecting Michael Jackson in His Final Days* (Weinstein, 2014), 38–39.

10. Vogel, *Man in the Music: The Creative Life and Work of Michael Jackson*, 148.

11. Zack O'Malley Greenburg, *Michael Jackson, Inc.* (New York: Atria, 2014).

12. Jackson, *Moonwalk*, 265.

CHAPTER 15. HORCRUXES: MICHAEL (SPLIT SEVEN WAYS) JACKSON

1. J. K. Rowling, *Harry Potter and the Half-Blood Prince* (London: Blooms-bury, 2005), 464–65.

2. "Objects of great importance to Voldemort, used to conceal parts of his soul . . . Once created, the Horcruxes make the wizard immortal as long as they remain intact . . ." "Horcruxes" (2016), https://www.pottermore.com/explore-the-story/the-horcruxes.

3. Harriet J. Manning, *Michael Jackson and the Blackface Mask* (Farnham, UK: Ashgate, 2013), 168–71.

4. John Eliot Gardiner's *Music in the Castle of Heaven* is an authoritative resource on Bach's life and work and a fantastic point of reference. John Eliot Gardiner, *Music in the Castle of Heaven: A Portrait of Johann Sebastian Bach* (London: Allen Lane, 2013), 45, 187.

5. Ruth Tatlow, *Bach and the Riddle of the Number Alphabet* (Cambridge: Cambridge University Press, 1991).

6. For an account of Bach's later life and death see Gardiner, *Music in the Castle of Heaven: A Portrait of Johann Sebastian Bach*, 525–58.

7. Milos Forman, *Amadeus* (Warner Home Video, 1984).

8. Spaethling's *Mozart's Letter, Mozart's Life* considers the artist's life and career in great detail. Robert Spaethling, *Mozart's Letters, Mozart's Life* (London: Faber & Faber, 2004), 447.

9. Ibid., 447–48.

10. Mozart's early years are charted through his letters and editorial commentary in ibid., 3–52.

11. Ibid.

12. Zack O'Malley Greenburg, *Michael Jackson, Inc.* (New York: Atria, 2014), 225–28.

13. Spaethling, *Mozart's Letters, Mozart's Life*, 452; Joseph Vogel, *Man in the Music: The Creative Life and Work of Michael Jackson* (New York: Sterling, 2011), 258.

14. Spaethling, *Mozart's Letters, Mozart's Life*, 447, 381–444.

15. Vogel, *Man in the Music: The Creative Life and Work of Michael Jackson*, 205.

16. Charles Chaplin and David Robinson, *Charles Chaplin: My Autobiography* (London: Penguin Modern Classics, 2003), 10.

17. Ibid., 221.

18. Ibid., 177; Greenburg, *Michael Jackson, Inc.*, 156.

19. Chaplin and Robinson, *Charles Chaplin: My Autobiography*, 145.

20. Ibid., 455.

21. Jermaine Jackson, *You Are Not Alone: Michael, through a Brother's Eyes* (London: Harper Collins, 2011), 9.

22. Michael Barrier, *The Animated Man: A Life of Walt Disney* (Los Angeles: University of California Press, 2007), 21.

23. Ibid., 24, 43.

24. Ibid., 56–57.

25. Ibid., 62.

26. Ibid., 100–133.

27. Ibid., 200.

28. Ibid., 210.

29. Michael Jackson, *Moonwalk* (London: Heinemann, 2009), 99.

30. Ibid., 258.

31. Karl F. Cohen, *Forbidden Animation: Censored Cartoons and Blacklisted Animators in America* (Jefferson, NC, London: McFarland & Company, 1997), 61.

32. Barrier, *The Animated Man: A Life of Walt Disney*, 317.

33. "Michael Jackson at James Brown's Funeral," (YouTube: CNN, 2006).

34. "James Brown: Mr Dynamite," (BBC2, 2015).

35. Ibid.

36. Jackson, *Moonwalk*, 50.

37. "James Brown: Mr Dynamite."

38. *Off the Wall—Special Edition* (Sony/Epic Legacy, 2001), interview with Rod Temperton.

39. "James Brown: Mr Dynamite."

40. "Michael Jackson—Live at the Beverly Theater 1983" (YouTube 2015).

41. "Michael Jackson and James Brown" (YouTube: BET Awards 2003, 2014).

42. Danny Lewis, *David Bowie Style* (London: Bloomsbury, 2012), 6.

43. Both Harriet Manning and Marjorie Garber consider Jackson's androgynous style in detail. See Marjorie Garber, "Androgyny and Its Discontents," in *Bisexuality and the Eroticism of Everyday Life* (2000); Harriet J. Manning, "The Burden of Ambiguity," in *Michael Jackson and the Blackface Mask* (Farnham, UK: Ashgate, 2013).

44. Lewis, *David Bowie Style*, 8–9.

45. Philip Auslander, *Performing Glam Rock: Gender and Theatricality in Popular Music* (Ann Arbor: The University of Michigan Press, 2006); Victoria Broackes and Geoff Marsh, *David Bowie Is the Subject* (London: V&A Publishing, 2013); Lewis, *David Bowie Style*.

46. Michael Jackson, *HIStory: Past, Present and Future, Book 1* (Sony/Epic Legacy, 1995).

47. David Bowie, *Blackstar* (Columbia, 2016).

48. Julian Schnable, *Basquiat* (Twentieth Century Fox, 1996); Jim Henson, *Labyrinth* (Sony Pictures Home Entertainment, 1986); Martin Scorsese, *The Last Temptation of Christ* (Universal Pictures, 1988).

49. Broackes and Marsh, *David Bowie Is the Subject*.

50. James E. Perone, *The Sound of Stevie Wonder: His Words and Music* (Santa Barbara, CA and Westport, CT: Praeger, 2006), xiv.

51. Jackson, *Moonwalk*, 114.

52. Ibid., 268.

53. Manning, "Just Using It: Eminem, the Mask and a Fight for Authenticity."

54. Vogel, *Man in the Music: The Creative Life and Work of Michael Jackson*, 26–28.

55. Ben Okri, "A Meteor Streaks Our Collective Consciousness," *The Times*, June 27, 2009; Armond White, "In MJ's Shadow," *New York Press* (2009), http://nypress.com/in-mjrsquos-shadow/.

CHAPTER 16. "THROUGH THE LOOKING GLASS": NOTES ON MICHAEL JACKSON AND ANDY WARHOL

1. Andy Warhol and Pat Hackett, *Popism: The Warhol '60s* (London: Penguin Modern Classics, 2007), 64.

2. Willa Stillwater, *M Poetica: Michael Jackson's Art of Connection and Defiance* (Kindle, 2011, 2013), 52.

3. Mark Romanek, *Scream* (1995).

4. Stillwater, *M Poetica: Michael Jackson's Art of Connection and Defiance*, 52.

5. Pierre Bourdieu, "The Field of Cultural Production," in *Essays on Art and Literature*, ed. Randal Johnson (Cambridge: Polity, 1993), 29–58.

6. Chris Rodley, *Andy Warhol: The Complete Picture* (BFS Entertainment, 2003).

7. Zack O'Malley Greenburg, *Michael Jackson, Inc.* (New York: Atria, 2014), 172–73.

8. Rodley, *Andy Warhol: The Complete Picture*.

9. Andy Warhol, *Campbell's Soup Cans,* 1962. Synthetic polymer paint on thirty-two canvases, 50.8×40.6 cm. Museum of Modern Art.

10. Rodley, *Andy Warhol: The Complete Picture.*

11. Jeremy Gilbert, "The Real Abstraction of Michael Jackson," in *The Resistible Demise of Michael Jackson,* ed. Mark Fisher (Winchester, UK: Zero Books, 2009), 137-38; "The Real Abstraction of Michael Jackson," in *A Companion to Michael Jackson Academic Studies I,* ed. Elizabeth Amisu (MJAS, 2015).

12. "The Real Abstraction of Michael Jackson," 138. Simulacra: "something having merely the form or appearance of a certain thing, without possessing its substance or proper qualities." *OED.*

13. Rodley, *Andy Warhol: The Complete Picture*; Willa Stillwater, Joie Collins, and Lisha McDuff, "Warhol," *Dancing With the Elephant,* http://dancingwiththeelephant .wordpress.com/?s=warhol.

14. Rodley, *Andy Warhol: The Complete Picture.*

15. H. Benshoff and S. Griffin, *America on Film: Representing Race, Class, Gender, and Sexuality at the Movies* (United Kingdom: Blackwell, 2004), 33–39.

16. Andy Warhol, *The Andy Warhol Diaries* (London: Penguin Modern Classics, 2009), 275, 561.

17. Ibid., 771–73.

18. Susan Fast, *Dangerous* (London: Bloomsbury, 2014), 17–41.

19. Warhol, *The Andy Warhol Diaries,* 822, 1077.

20. Ibid., 1078.

CHAPTER 17. *INVINCIBLE*: MICHAEL JACKSON'S LOST LATE ALBUM

1. Gordon McMullan, *Shakespeare and the Idea of Late Writing Authorship in the Proximity of Death* (Cambridge: Cambridge University Press, 2007), 5.

2. Michael Jackson, *Moonwalk* (London: Heinemann, 2009), 277; Zack O'Malley Greenburg, *Michael Jackson, Inc.* (New York: Atria, 2014), 74–75, 158, 96–09, 92–93, 210–22; Mary A. Fischer, *Was Michael Jackson Framed? The Untold Story That Brought Down a Superstar* (Marston, UK and New York: CreateSpace, 2012), 28–30; James Baldwin, *The Price of the Ticket* (New York: Macmillan, 1985), 689.

3. Joseph Vogel, *Man in the Music: The Creative Life and Work of Michael Jackson* (New York: Sterling, 2011), 229–30.

4. Michael Jackson, *HIStory: Past, Present and Future, Book 1* (Sony/Epic Legacy, 1995), 'HIStory."

5. Elizabeth Amisu, "Bad(1987)," *Writing Eliza* (2014), http://elizabethamisu .com/2014/07/20/bad-1987-genius-the-short-films-of-michael-2/; "'Bad (1987)'," *The Journal of Michael Jackson Academic Studies* 1, no. 2 (2014).

6. Willa Stillwater, Joie Collins, et al., "Summer Rewind 2014: Trust in Me," *Dancing With the Elephant* (2014), http://dancingwiththeelephant.wordpress.com /2014/08/21/summer-rewind-2014-trust-in-me-2/.

7. Frank Cascio, *My Friend Michael: An Ordinary Friendship with an Extraordinary Man* (London and New York: William Morrow, 2011), 201–02.

8. Michael Jackson, *Invincible* (MJJ Productions, Epic, 2001).

9. Barney Hoskyns, "The Boy Who Would Fly: Michael Jackson (1983)," in *The Resistible Demise of Michael Jackson*, ed. Mark Fisher (Winchester, UK: Zero Books, 2009), 38; Jackson, "Invincible," 'You Are My Life'.

10. Vogel, *Man in the Music: The Creative Life and Work of Michael Jackson*, 247–48.

11. Jackson, *Moonwalk*, 262; Various, "Post Here If You Worked on Michael Jackson's Dangerous," *GearSlutz.com* (2009), http://www.gearslutz.com/board/so-much-gear-so-little-time/403276-post-here-if-you-worked-michael-jacksons-dangerous-album.html.

12. Kanye West, *Late Registration* (Roc-a-Fella/Def-Jam, 2005); Mark Fisher, 'And When the Groove Is Dead and Gone': The End of Jacksonism," in *The Resistible Demise of Michael Jackson*, ed. Mark Fisher (Winchester, UK: Zero Books, 2009), 15.

13. Jackson, *Invincible*; Ne-Yo, "Out of Harm's Way," *Ebony Special Tribute: Michael Jackson In His Own Words* (2009); Neil McCormick, "Michael Jackson Remembered by His Band: 'The Most Alive Person You Could Ever Meet'," *The Telegraph* (2011), http://blogs.telegraph.co.uk/culture/neilmccormick/100056639/michael-jackson-remembered-by-his-band-the-most-alive-person-you-could-ever-meet/; Mike Senior, "Bruce Swedien: Recording Michael Jackson," *Sound on Sound* (2009), http://www.soundonsound.com/sos/nov09/articles/swedien.html.

14. Vogel, *Man in the Music: The Creative Life and Work of Michael Jackson*, 219–35.

15. Ibid., 59–60.

16. Harriet J. Manning, " 'Black or White': From Jim Crow to Michael Jackson," in *Michael Jackson and the Blackface Mask* (Farnham, UK: Ashgate, 2013).

17. Michael Jackson, interview by Barbara Walters, September, 1997; Vogel, *Man in the Music: The Creative Life and Work of Michael Jackson*, 224.

18. *Man in the Music: The Creative Life and Work of Michael Jackson*, 28; Lisa Marie Presley, "He Knew," *MySpace.com*, no. 27 June 2009 (2009), http://www.myspace.com/lisamariepresley/blog/497035326. http://www.elvis.com.au/presley/printer/lisa_marie_presley_michael_jackson.shtml.

19. Cascio, *My Friend Michael: An Ordinary Friendship with an Extraordinary Man*, 312–13.

20. Touré, "The Magical Negro Falls to Earth," *TIME* (2012), http://ideas.time.com/2012/09/26/the-magical-negro-falls-to-earth/; Michael Jackson, *Dancing the Dream: Poems & Reflections* (London: Doubleday, 1992), viii; Bill Whitfield, Javon Beard and Tanner Colby, *Remember the Time: Protecting Michael Jackson in His Final Days* (Weinstein, 2014), 120–21.

21. Vogel, *Man in the Music: The Creative Life and Work of Michael Jackson*, 106–07; Michael Jackson, interview by Pharrell Williams, Andy Warhol, and Bob Colacello, 1982, 2003.

22. *Invincible*, "Privacy"; HIStory: *Past, Present and Future, Book 1*, "Tabloid Junkie."

23. Editors of Ebony, *Ebony Special Tribute: Michael Jackson in His Own Words* (Johnson, 2009); Michael Jackson, *Handwritten Letter Regarding Moonwalker,* 1988. Three-page handwritten letter from Michael Jackson to William Pecchi Jr., written on Capitol Tokyu Hotel stationery, 10×7 in. Julien's Auctions.

24. Paul Lester, "Michael Jackson's Twenty Greatest Hits," in *The Resistible Demise of Michael Jackson,* ed. Mark Fisher (Winchester, UK: Zero Books, 2009), 22.

25. Greenburg, *Michael Jackson, Inc.*

26. Emily C. Bartels, "Too Many Blackamoors: Deportation, Discrimination, and Elizabeth I," *SEL: Studies in English Literature, 1500-1900* 46, no. 2 (2006); Queen Elizabeth I of England, "An Open Warrant to the Lord Maiour of London (1596)," in *Race in Early Modern England: A Documentary Companion,* ed. Ania Loomba and Ben Burton (Basingstoke: Palgrave Macmillan, 2007); "Licensing Caspar Van Senden to Deport Negroes (1601)," in *Race in Early Modern England: A Documentary Companion,* ed. Ania Loomba and Ben Burton (Basingstoke: Palgrave Macmillan, 2007).

27. Tim Niel, "Shakespeare's First Folio," in *The Secret Life of Books,* ed. Alan Campbell (BBC Four, 2014).

28. Alden T. Vaughan, Virginia Mason Vaughan, and William Shakespeare, *The Tempest* (London, UK: Arden, 2011), 206.

29. Ibid.

30. Jackson, *Invincible,* 3.

31. Vogel, *Man in the Music: The Creative Life and Work of Michael Jackson,* 260.

32. Jackson, *Moonwalk.*

33. Elizabeth Amisu, " 'Throwing Stones to Hide Your Hands': Mortal Persona of Michael Jackson," *Writing Eliza* (2014), http://elizabethamisu.com/post/88515 649217/throwing-stones-to-hide-your-hands-the-mortal-persona.

34. "On Michael Jackson's Dancing the Dream," *Writing Eliza* (2014), http://elizabethamisu.com/post/91073957802/on-michael-jacksons-dancing-the-dream-dangerous.

35. Jackson, *Invincible.*

36. Michael Jackson, *USA Today,* 2001. Vogel, *Man in the Music: The Creative Life and Work of Michael Jackson,* 256–59, 19; Various, *"Mjsinvincible,"* (2011), http://mjsinvincible.wordpress.com.

CHAPTER 18. MICHAEL JACKSON'S OBITUARIES AND THE SHAKESPEAREAN TRAGIC HERO

1. Caroline Sullivan, "Michael Jackson," *The Guardian* (2009); "The Legend of Wacko Jacko from Baby Dangling to Crotch Grabbing," *The Telegraph* (2009), http://www.telegraph.co.uk/news/obituaries/celebrity-obituaries/5643156/Michael-Jackson.html; Germaine Greer, "Like Orpheus, Michael Jackson Was Destroyed by His Fans," *The Guardian* (2009), http://www.theguardian.com/music/2009/jun/26/michael-jackson-death-in-la; Brooks Barnes, "A Star Haunted and Idolized, Michael Jackson Dies at 50," *The New York Times* (2009).

2. Greer, "Like Orpheus, Michael Jackson Was Destroyed by His Fans."

3. Caroline Sullivan, "Michael Jackson," ibid.

4. Jonathan Law, David Pickering, and Richard Helfer, *The New Penguin Dictionary of the Theatre*, Rev. and enlarged ed. ed. (London: Penguin, 2001), 610.

5. Sullivan, "Michael Jackson."

6. Barnes, "A Star Haunted and Idolized, Michael Jackson Dies at 50."

7. William Shakespeare and E. A. J. Honigmann, *Othello* (London: Arden Shakespeare, 2001).

8. Sandra Clark, Pamela Mason, and William Shakespeare, *Macbeth* (London, UK: Arden, 2015).

9. "The Legend of Wacko Jacko from Baby Dangling to Crotch Grabbing."

10. Ibid.

11. Greer, "Like Orpheus, Michael Jackson Was Destroyed by His Fans."

12. Ibid.

13. Caroline Sullivan, "Michael Jackson," ibid.

14. Barnes, "A Star Haunted and Idolized, Michael Jackson Dies at 50."

15. Karin Merx, "From Throne to Wilderness: Michael Jackson's 'Stranger in Moscow' and the Foucauldian Outlaw," *The Journal of Michael Jackson Academic Studies* 1, no. 4 (2015).

16. Arthur Miller, *Death of a Salesman: Certain Private Conversations in Two Acts and a Requiem*, Penguin Modern Classics (Harmondsworth, UK: Penguin, 1985).

17. Greer, "Like Orpheus, Michael Jackson Was Destroyed by His Fans."

18. Mark Pomeroy, "Sycamore Valley Ranch: The Splendor of the Santa Ynez Valley," (Sotheby's International Realty, 2014).

CHAPTER 19. MOONWALKERS: MICHAEL JACKSON'S UNIQUE FANDOM

1. Tahkiya Brady a.k.a Red, "Moonwalkers: Then, Now, and Forever . . ." (YouTube, 2014).

2. M. Hills, "Michael Jackson Fans on Trial? Documenting Emotivism and Fandom in Wacko About Jacko," *Social Semiotics* (2007).

3. Brady a.k.a Red, "Moonwalkers: Then, Now, and Forever . . .".

4. Bill Whitfield, Javon Beard and Tanner Colby, *Remember the Time: Protecting Michael Jackson in His Final Days* (Weinstein, 2014), 46.

5. Brady a.k.a Red, "Moonwalkers: Then, Now, and Forever . . .".

6. Ibid.

7. Tahkiya Brady a.k.a Red, interview by Elizabeth Amisu, 2016.

8. Karin Merx, interview by Elizabeth Amisu, 2016.

9. "MJ Believers Official," Facebook, https://www.facebook.com/MJBelievers .Official/info/?tab=page_info.

10. "Michael Jackson Death Hoax Forum," http://www.michaeljacksonhoaxforum .com/forums/.

11. Amber Soos, interview by Elizabeth Amisu, 2016.

12. Lorena Turner, *The Michael Jacksons* (Little Moth Press, 2015); "About the Project," *The Michael Jacksons* (2016), http://www.themichaeljacksons.com/about.php.

13. Whitfield, *Remember the Time: Protecting Michael Jackson in His Final Days*, 46.

14. "MJL is a charitable organisation dedicated to continuing Michael Jackson's humanitarian legacy and thereby making the world a better place. Michael Jackson inspired love, hope and compassion worldwide through his music and through his tireless humanitarian work on behalf of the suffering and underprivileged. Join us on this adventure and together we can create a better world." Various, "Michael Jackson's Legacy," (2015), http://www.michaeljacksonslegacy.org/; "One Rose for MJJ," (2014), http://onerose4mjj.blogspot.co.uk/.

15. Zack O'Malley Greenburg, *Michael Jackson, Inc.* (New York: Atria, 2014), 249.

16. Various, "*Mjsinvincible*," (2011), http://mjsinvincible.wordpress.com.

CHAPTER 20. THE POWER OF THE EDITOR AND MICHAEL JACKSON'S POSTHUMOUS RELEASES

1. Zack O'Malley Greenburg, *Michael Jackson, Inc.* (New York: Atria, 2014), 232–33.

2. Elizabeth Amisu, "Earth Song: Inside Michael Jackson's Magnum Opus by Joseph Vogel (Blake Vision, 2011)," *The Journal of Michael Jackson Academic Studies* 1, no. 1 (2014); Jason King, "Don't Stop 'Til You Get Enough: Presence, Spectacle, and Good Feeling in Michael Jackson's *This Is It*," in *Black Performance Theory*, ed. Thomas F. DeFrantz and Anita Gonzalez (Durham, London: Duke University Press, 2014); Harriet J. Manning, "This Is It," in *Michael Jackson and the Blackface Mask* (Farnham, UK: Ashgate, 2013); Kenny Ortega, *Michael Jackson's This Is It* (Sony, 2009).

3. Greenburg, *Michael Jackson, Inc.*, 212.

4. Ibid., 227–28.

5. Margaret Jane Kidnie, "Where Is Hamlet? Text, Performance, and Adaptation," in *A Companion to Shakespeare and Performance*, ed. Barbara Hodgdon and William B. Worthen (Oxford: Blackwell, 2005), 462.

6. Joseph Vogel, *Man in the Music: The Creative Life and Work of Michael Jackson* (New York: Sterling, 2011), 264.

7. Ibid.

8. Michael Jackson, *Off the Wall—Special Edition* (Sony/Epic Legacy, 2001); *Thriller—Special Edition* (Sony/Epic Legacy, 2001); *Bad—Special Edition* (Sony/Epic Legacy, 2001); *Dangerous—Special Edition* (Sony/Epic Legacy, 2001).

9. Included in the liner notes for the *Dangerous* album and the poetry collection, *Dancing the Dream. Dangerous*, (Sony/Epic Legacy, 1991), 21; *Dancing the Dream: Poems & Reflections* (London: Doubleday, 1992), 5.

10. *Michael*, (Sony, 2010), 6–7.

11. The album liner notes are not numbered; however, these handwritten notes can be found on the inside (verso) of the cover page and the final page. Ibid.

12. Vogel, *Man in the Music: The Creative Life and Work of Michael Jackson*, 264.

13. Ibid.

14. Ibid., 268.

15. Michael Jackson, *Bad 25* (Sony, 2012), Wembley Stadium Liner Notes, 31–32.

16. Spike Lee, *Bad 25* (Optimum Productions, 2013).

17. Note that John Branca and John McClain, co-executors of the Michael Jackson's Estate, choose in these liner notes to justify the use of "controversial topics" in Jackson's work by stating that he "saw potentially controversial topics . . . as an artistic challenge." Jackson, *Bad 25*, 1.

18. Ibid., 17.

19. Ibid., 29; *Bad—Special Edition.*

20. Elizabeth Amisu, "Choose an Early Modern Printer or Publisher and Look at the Place of Literary Publications within His Work as a Whole," Department of English (London: King's College London, 2014), 6.

21. Richard Bonian is recorded as being baptized in Hayes parish on December 24, 1581. "Middlesex & London Baptisms Index 1538–1882" (2013), http://www.origins.net/. A probable date of death, 1625 can be found in the "Index to Testamentary Records," in *British Record Society Vol. 89: Archdeaconry Court of London Probate Records Vol. I—1393-1649* (London: 1978), 60. This may correlate with the following sources in terms of an approximate age for Bonian to have begun his apprenticeship, as well as his father's name, "Richard," and his father's hometown of "Hayes, co. Middlesex." Ronald B. McKerrow, Harry G. Aldis, and Bibliographical Society, *A Dictionary of Printers and Booksellers in England, Scotland and Ireland, and of Foreign Printers of English Books 1557-1640* (London: Printed for the Bibliographical Society by Blades, East and Blades, 1968), 42. Stationers' Company (London England), Charles Robert Rivington. Edward Arber, *A Transcript of the Registers of the Company of Stationers of London: 1554-1640*, vol. 3 (London: 1875), 232, 39. The *Middlesex & London Baptisms Index 1538-1882* also gives the following as children of a Richard Bonian (snr.) in the parish of Hayes: Agnes, baptised 24 Jul 1575; John, baptised 5 Apr 1577; Richard, baptised 24 Dec 1581, William, baptised 19 Apr 1584; Thomas, baptised 28 Nov 1585; and Henry, baptised 8 Jan 1587/88. Please note that the Index does not give any further detail as to whether all these children had the same Richard Bonian (snr.) as their father, other than stating for John and Agnes, "father's name blank in original, suggested by probable siblings." The familial connection to Richard Bonian (jnr.), the stationer, is an estimation based on contiguity of location and period.

22. James Raven, *The Business of Books: Booksellers and the English Book Trade, 1450-1850* (London: Yale University Press, 2007), 296, 97; E. Gordon Duff, *A Century of the English Book Trade: Short Notices of All Printers, Stationers, Book-Binders, and Others Connected with It from the Issue of the First Dated Book in 1457 to the Incorporation of the Company of Stationers in 1557* (London: Printed for the Bibliographical society, by Blades, East & Blades, 1905), 166. *A Transcript of the Registers of the Company of Stationers of London: 1554-1640*, vol. 2 (London: 1875), 232.

23. Stationers' Company (London England), Rivington, and Arber, *A Transcript of the Registers of the Company of Stationers of London: 1554-1640*, 2, 36; ibid., 5: lxv; Henry R. Plomer, *A Dictionary of the Booksellers and Printers Who Were at Work in*

England, Scotland and Ireland from 1641 to 1667 (London: Printed for the Bibliographical Society, by Blades, East & Blades, 1907), 26.

24. Amisu, "Choose an Early Modern Printer or Publisher and Look at the Place of Literary Publications within His Work as a Whole," 4.

25. David Bevington and William Shakespeare, *Troilus and Cressida* (London, UK: Arden, 1998), 398–429; Zachary Lesser, *Renaissance Drama and the Politics of Publication: Readings in the English Book Trade* (Cambridge: Cambridge University Press, 2004), 4–8; McKerrow, Aldis, and Bibliographical Society, *A Dictionary of Printers and Booksellers in England, Scotland and Ireland, and of Foreign Printers of English Books 1557-1640*, 42; Philip Gaskell, *A New Introduction to Bibliography* (Winchester: Oak Knoll Press, 1995), 180–81; Amisu, "Choose an Early Modern Printer or Publisher and Look at the Place of Literary Publications within His Work as a Whole," 4.

26. Lesser, *Renaissance Drama and the Politics of Publication: Readings in the English Book Trade*, 1–3.

27. Greenburg, *Michael Jackson, Inc.*, 232–33.

28. Ibid., 250.

29. Michael Jackson, *Xscape* (Sony, 2014).

30. Ibid, 3.

31. Jean-Claude Acquaviva and Maciej Rychly, "Songs of Lear: Song of the Goat Theatre," (Wroclaw: Magellan Foundation, 2013); Battersea Arts Centre, "Songs of Lear at Battersea Arts Centre," (2015), https://www.bac.org.uk/content/35391/about_us/past_shows_and_events/songs_of_lear; Valenka Navea, "'Songs of Lear' at the Bac Reviewed by Valenka Navea," (2015), http://ceel.org.uk/culture/film-theatre/songs-of-lear-at-the-bac-reviewed-by-valenka-navea/; Jake Orr, "Edinburgh Fringe Review: Songs of Lear," (2012), http://www.ayoungertheatre.com/edinburgh-fringe-review-songs-of-lear-song-of-the-goat-summerhall/; Matt Trueman, "Review: Songs of Lear, Summerhall, Edinburgh Fringe," *MattTrueman.co.uk* (2012), http://matttrueman.co.uk/2012/08/review-songs-of-lear-summerhall-edinburgh-fringe.html.

32. Kidnie, "Where Is Hamlet? Text, Performance, and Adaptation," 106.

33. Elizabeth Amisu, "Song of the Goat's 'Songs of Lear'," Department of English (London: King's College London, 2015).

34. Lawrence Lipking, *The Life of the Poet: Beginning and Ending Poetic Careers* (Chicago: University of Chicago Press, 1981), 138.

35. Sonia Massai, *Shakespeare and the Rise of the Editor* (Cambridge: Cambridge University Press, 2007).

36. Michael D. Bristol, "Shakespeare: The Myth," in *A Companion to Shakespeare*, ed. David Scott Kastan (Oxford: Blackwell Publishers, 1999), 501.

CHAPTER 21. EPILOGUE: THREE *DANGEROUS PHILOSOPHIES* ARTICLES

1. Elizabeth Amisu, *Writing Eliza* http://elizabethamisu.com/.

2. Vaughan, Vaughan, and Shakespeare, *The Tempest*, 254.

3. Amy C. Billone, "Sentenced to Neverland: Michael Jackson, Peter Pan, and Queer Futurity," in *Michael Jackson: Grasping the Spectacle*, ed. Christopher R. Smit (Farnham, UK: Ashgate, 2012), 39–50; Ian Penman, "Notes Towards a Ritual Exorcism of the Dead King," in *The Resistible Demise of Michael Jackson*, ed. Mark Fisher (Winchester, UK: Zero Books, 2009), 284, 301–02; J.M. Barrie, *Peter and Wendy* (Kindle, 1911, 2004); Jermaine Jackson, *You Are Not Alone: Michael, through a Brother's Eyes* (London: Harper Collins, 2011), 9; Margo Jefferson, *On Michael Jackson* (New York: Pantheon, 2006), 15; Oscar Wilde, *The Picture of Dorian Gray*, (Kindle, 1890, 2012); F. Scott Fitzgerald, *The F. Scott Fitzgerald Collection: 2 Novels and 20 Short Stories* (Waxkeep, 2013); F. Scott Fitzgerald and Tony Tanner, *The Great Gatsby* (London: Penguin, 2000); Jeffrey Meyers and F. Scott Fitzgerald, *The Great Gatsby* (Everyman, 1993), 134.

4. Willa Stillwater, *M Poetica: Michael Jackson's Art of Connection and Defiance* (Kindle, 2011, 2013); Owen Dudley Edwards, "Wilde, Oscar Fingal O'Flahertie Wills (1854–1900)," in *Oxford Dictionary of National Biography* (http://www.oxforddnb.com/view/article/29400September 2012); R.D.S. Jack, "Barrie, Sir James Matthew, Baronet (1860–1937)," ibid. (http://www.oxforddnb.com/view/article/30617May 2014).

5. Vogel, *Man in the Music: The Creative Life and Work of Michael Jackson*, 251–62; Barrie, *Peter and Wendy*, 24; Michael Jackson, *Blood on the Dance Floor: HIStory in the Mix* (Sony/Epic Legacy, 1995), "Morphine"; *Moonwalk* (London: Heinemann, 2009), 95–97, 235–38; Jackson, *You Are Not Alone: Michael, through a Brother's Eyes*, 319–20, 31, 49–50, 72–73; Michael Jackson, interview by Oprah Winfrey, 1993; Elissa Fleak, "Autopsy Report for Michael Jackson," (County of Los Angeles: Department of Health Services, 2009).

6. Jackson, *Moonwalk*, 229, 56; Martha Davis, Elizabeth Eshelman and Matthew McKay, *The Relaxation and Stress Reduction Workbook* (New Harbinger, 2008), 3–4; Tanner Colby, "The Radical Notion of Michael Jackson's Humanity," *Slate.com* (2014), http://www.slate.com/articles/arts/culturebox/2014/06/michael_jackson _death_anniversary_we_recall_thriller_and_bad_but_what_about.html.

7. Barrie, *Peter and Wendy*, 51–53, 23.

8. Jackson, *Moonwalk*, 164; "Love: The Human Family's Most Precious Legacy," *The Journal of Pan African Studies* 3, no. 7 (2010): 5; "Michael Jackson Talks To . . . Oprah Live."; Barney Hoskyns, "The Boy Who Would Fly: Michael Jackson (1983)," in *The Resistible Demise of Michael Jackson*, ed. Mark Fisher (Winchester, UK: Zero Books, 2009), 45.

9. Barrie, *Peter and Wendy*, 24.

10. Zack O'Malley Greenburg, *Michael Jackson, Inc.* (New York: Atria, 2014), 157, 85, 06.

11. Vaughan, Vaughan, and Shakespeare, *The Tempest*, 189; *Jackson, HIStory: Past, Present and Future, Book 1*, "Scream."

12. Hoskyns, "The Boy Who Would Fly: Michael Jackson (1983)," 46; Leslie and Alan Riding Dunton-Downer, *Essential Shakespeare Handbook* (London: Dorling Kindersley, 2004), 436.

13. Kanye West, *Late Registration* (Roc-a-Fella/Def-Jam, 2005), 'Crack Music'.

14. Michael Jackson, *Invincible* (MJJ Productions, Epic, 2001), "Heaven Can Wait."

15. *HIStory: Past, Present and Future, Book 1* (Sony/Epic Legacy, 1995), "They Don't Care About Us"; *Invincible*, "Threatened"; West, *Late Registration*, "Crack Music."

16. Richard Shusterman, "The Fine Art of Rap," *New Literary History* 22, no. 3 (1991); Alexis Petridis, "Kanye West: Yeezus—Review," *The Guardian* (2013).

17. Elizabeth Amisu, "On Michael Jackson's Dancing the Dream," *Writing Eliza* (2014), http://elizabethamisu.com/post/91073957802/on-michael-jacksons-dancing-the-dream-dangerous; "On Michael Jackson's 'Dancing the Dream'," *The Journal of Michael Jackson Academic Studies* 1, no. 2 (2014).

18. Conversation with Karin Merx, Academic/Musician, September 27, 2014; James Hunter, "Invincible," *Rolling Stone* (2001); Hampton Stevens, "Michael Jackson's Unparalleled Influence," *The Atlantic* (2010).

19. West, *Late Registration*, "Crack Music."

20. Joseph Vogel, *Man in the Music: The Creative Life and Work of Michael Jackson* (Sterling, 2011), 219–35; "Second to None: Race, Representation and the Misunderstood Power of Michael Jackson's Music," in *Featuring Michael Jackson: Collected Writings on the King of Pop* (New York: Baldwin Books, 2012), 7–14.

21. Armond White, *Keep Moving: The Michael Jackson Chronicles* (New York: Resistance Works, 2010), 106; West, *Late Registration*, "Crack Music."

22. Michael Bush, *The King of Style: Dressing Michael Jackson* (California: Insight Editions, 2012), 196; Elizabeth Amisu, "'The Isle Is Full of Noises': Revisiting the Peter Pan of Pop," *The Journal of Michael Jackson Academic Studies* 1, no. 1 (2014).

23. Michael Jackson, March, 2002; Elizabeth Amisu, "'Throwing Stones to Hide Your Hands': Mortal Persona of Michael Jackson," *Writing Eliza* (2014), http://elizabethamisu.com/post/88515649217/throwing-stones-to-hide-your-hands-the-mortal-persona.

24. Alden T. Vaughan, Virginia Mason Vaughan, and William Shakespeare, *The Tempest* (London, UK: Arden, 2011), 1–2, 112–26; Rowan Moore, "Sam Wanamaker Playhouse—Review," *The Guardian* (2014), http://www.theguardian.com/artanddesign/2014/jan/12/sam-wanamaker-playhouse-globe-review; Vogel, *Man in the Music: The Creative Life and Work of Michael Jackson*, 219, 56–59; Michael Jackson, interview by Edna Gunderson, November 1, 2001.

APPENDIX A.1. FROM OBJECT TO SUBJECT: A CRITICAL SURVEY ON THE REPRESENTATION OF BLACKNESS IN THE EARLY MODERN PERIOD

1. Toni Morrison, *Playing in the Dark: Whiteness and the Literary Imagination* (Cambridge, MA: Harvard University Press, 1992), 9.

2. *OED* Online (Oxford: Oxford University Press, 2014), http://www.oed.com.

3. Ibid.

4. Ibid.

5. Harvey Young, *Theatre and Race* (Basingstoke, UK: Palgrave Macmillan, 2013), 5–6.

6. Ibid., 26, 31; Emily C. Bartels, "Too Many Blackamoors: Deportation, Discrimination, and Elizabeth I," *SEL: Studies in English Literature, 1500–1900* 46, no. 2 (2006): 305–22; *Speaking of the Moor: From Alcazar to Othello* (Philadelphia, PA: University of Pennsylvania Press, 2008).

7. Michael Neill, "'Mulattos,' 'Blacks,' and 'Indian Moors': Othello and Early Modern Constructions of Human Difference," *Shakespeare Quarterly* 49, no. 4 (1998): 361–74.

8. Bartels, "Too Many Blackamoors: Deportation, Discrimination, and Elizabeth I," 319.

9. Young-Joo Choi, "Reading Shakespeare's Othello within the Discourse of Early Modern Age: Centering on the Issues, 'Class, Race and Sexuality'," *Journal of English Language and Literature* 45, no. 1 (1999): 75–96; Cristina Malcolmson, "Race and Early Modern Studies: The Power of an Illusion and Its Genesis," *CLIO: A Journal of Literature, History, and the Philosophy of History* 33, no. 4 (2004): 439–49; Michael McGiffert, "Constructing Race: Differentiating Peoples in the Early Modern World," *William and Mary Quarterly: A Magazine of Early American History and Culture* 54, no. 1 (1997); William Over, "Race, Culture, and Openness: An Early Modern Precedent," *Partial Answers: Journal of Literature and the History of Ideas* 3, no. 2 (2005): 1–22; Kimberly Poitevin, "Making up Race in Early Modern England," PhD diss., University of Illinois, Urbana, 2004.

10. Kim F. Hall, "'Object into Object?': Some Thoughts on the Presence of Black Women in Early Modern Culture," in *Early Modern Visual Culture: Representation, Race, and Empire in Renaissance*, ed. Clark Hulse and Peter Erickson (Philadelphia, PA: University of Pennsylvania Press, 2000), 349.

11. Young, *Theatre and Race*, 4–6.

12. Ibid., 9.

13. Bernard Harris, "A Portrait of a Moor," *Shakespeare Survey* 11 (1958): 89–97; G. K. Hunter, "Elizabethans and Foreigners," *Shakespeare Survey: An Annual Survey of Shakespeare Studies and Production* 17 (1964): 37–52; Eldred D. Jones, "African Figures in Elizabethan and Jacobean Drama" (PhD Thesis) (Durham University, 1962); "The Physical Representation of African Characters on the English Stage During the 16th and 17th Centuries," *Theatre Notebook* 17 (1962); *Othello's Countrymen: The African in English Renaissance Drama* (London: Oxford University Press, 1965).

14. Margo Hendricks, "Surveying 'Race' in Shakespeare," in *Shakespeare and Race*, ed. Stanley Wells and Catherine M. S. Alexander (Cambridge, UK: Cambridge University Press, 2000), 2.

15. Ibid., 11.

16. Folarin Olawale Shyllon, *Black Slaves in Britain* (London: Oxford University Press, 1974); *Black People in Britain, 1555–1833* (London: Oxford University Press for the Institute of Race Relations, 1977); Peter Mark, *Africans in European Eyes: The Portrayal of Black Africans in Fourteenth and Fifteenth Century Europe*

(Syracuse, NY: Syracuse University, 1974); Edward Scobie, *Black Britannia: A History of Blacks in Britain* (Chicago: Johnson, 1972); James Walvin, *The Black Presence: A Documentary History of the Negro in England, 1555–1860* (London: Orbach and Chambers, 1971).

17. David Dabydeen, *Hogarth's Blacks: Images of Blacks in Eighteenth Century English Art* (Kingston-upon-Thames, UK: Dangaroo, 1985); *The Black Presence in English Literature* (Manchester, UK: Manchester University Press, 1985); Paul Edwards and James Walvin, *Black Personalities in the Era of the Slave Trade* (London: Macmillan, 1983); Imtiaz H. Habib, *Black Lives in the English Archives, 1500–1677: Imprints of the Invisible* (Aldershot, UK: Ashgate, 2008).

18. Kim F. Hall, *Things of Darkness: Economies of Race and Gender in Early Modern England* (Ithaca, NY: Cornell University Press, 1995), 348.

19. Ibid., 1.

20. Ibid., 3.

21. Peter Erickson, "Representations of Blacks and Blackness in the Renaissance," *Criticism* 35, no. 4 (1993): 504; Alan Sinfield, *Literature, Politics and Culture in Postwar Britain* (Oxford: Basil Blackwell, 1989), 37.

22. Peter Erickson, "Epilogue," in *Early Modern Visual Culture: Representation, Race, and Empire in Renaissance England*, ed. Clark Hulse and Peter Erickson (Philadelphia, PA: University of Pennsylvania Press, 2000), 380,87; Stephen J. Greenblatt, "General Introductions," in *The Norton Shakespeare*, ed. Stephen J. Greenblatt, et al. (London: W.W. Norton, 1997), 22–23, 26–27.

23. Andrew Bennett and Nicholas Royle, *An Introduction to Literature, Criticism and Theory*, 4th ed. (Harlow: Longman, 2009), 116.

24. Hendricks, "Surveying 'Race' in Shakespeare," 11.

25. Anthony Gerard Barthelemy, *Black Face, Maligned Race: The Representation of Blacks in English Drama from Shakespeare to Southerne* (Baton Rouge: Louisiana State University Press, 1987); Bernadette Andrea, "The Ghost of Leo Africanus from the English to the Irish Renaissance," in *Postcolonial Moves: Medieval through Modern*, ed. Patricia Clare Ingham and Michelle R. Warren (New York, NY: Palgrave Macmillan, 2003), 195–215; Mary Floyd-Wilson, "Temperature, Temperance, and Racial Difference in Ben Jonson's *The Masque of Blackness*," *English Literary Renaissance* 28, no. 2 (1998): 183–209; Joyce Green MacDonald, " 'The Force of Imagination': The Subject of Blackness in Shakespeare, Jonson, and Ravenscroft," *Renaissance Papers* (1991): 53–74; Ania Loomba, " 'Delicious Traffick': Alterity and Exchange on Early Modern Stages," *Shakespeare Survey: An Annual Survey of Shakespeare Studies and Production* 52 (1999): 201–14.

26. Hendricks, "Surveying 'Race' in Shakespeare," 2.

27. Edward W. Said, *Orientalism* (Harmondsworth: Penguin, 1985, 1978).

28. Bennett and Royle, *An Introduction to Literature, Criticism and Theory*, 209.

29. Ibid., 210; Homi K. Bhabha, *Nation and Narration* (London: Routledge, 1990); "Of Mimicry and Man: The Ambivalence of Colonial Discourse," in *Modern Literary Theory: A Reader*, ed. Philip; Patricia Waugh Rice (London: Edward Arnold, 1996); Frantz Fanon, Constance Farrington, and Jean Paul Sartre, *The Wretched of*

the Earth, Penguin Classics (London: Penguin, 1967); Gayatri Chakravorty Spivak, *In Other Worlds: Essays in Cultural Politics* (London: Methuen, 1987).

30. Morrison, *Playing in the Dark: Whiteness and the Literary Imagination*, 3, 4.

31. Ibid.; Bennett and Royle, *An Introduction to Literature, Criticism and Theory*, 210.

32. Hall, *Things of Darkness: Economies of Race and Gender in Early Modern England*, 2; Hunter, "Elizabethans and Foreigners," 38.

33. Ania Loomba, *Shakespeare, Race, and Colonialism* (Oxford: Oxford University Press, 2002), 92–93; Dympna Callaghan, *Shakespeare without Women: Representing Gender and Race on the Renaissance Stage* (London: Routledge, 1999).

34. Hall, " 'Object into Object?': Some Thoughts on the Presence of Black Women in Early Modern Culture," 348.

35. *Things of Darkness: Economies of Race and Gender in Early Modern England*, 13.

36. Morrison, *Playing in the Dark: Whiteness and the Literary Imagination*, 6.

37. Erickson, "Representations of Blacks and Blackness in the Renaissance," 522.

38. Hall, *Things of Darkness: Economies of Race and Gender in Early Modern England*, 14.

39. Erickson, "Epilogue," 380.

40. Jonathan Goldberg, *Queering the Renaissance* (Duke University Press, 1994); Valerie Traub, *The Renaissance of Lesbianism in Early Modern England* (Cambridge: Cambridge University Press, 2002); Erickson, "Epilogue," 380–81.

41. "Epilogue," 380.

42. Valerie Traub, "Mapping the Global Body," ibid., ed. Peter Erickson and Clark Hulse (Philadelphia: University of Pennsylvania Press), 44–97.

43. Andrea Stevens, " Mastering Masques of Blackness: Jonson's *Masque of Blackness*, the Windsor Text of *The Gypsies Metamorphosed*, and Brome's *The English Moor*," *English Literary Renaissance* 39, no. 2 (2009): 408.

44. First published by Shakespeare Survey in 1958.

45. Hendricks, "Surveying 'Race' in Shakespeare," 2.

46. Clark Hulse and Peter Erickson, "Introduction," in *Early Modern Visual Culture: Representation, Race, and Empire in Renaissance England*, ed. Clark Hulse and Peter Erickson (Philadelphia, PA: University of Pennsylvania Press, 2000), 13.

47. Ibid., 1. Norman Bryson, Michael Ann Holly, and Keith P. F. Moxey, eds., *Visual Culture: Images and Interpretations* (Hanover: Wesleyan University Press, 1994), 2.

48. Peter Erickson, "Representations of Blacks and Blackness in the Renaissance," 503, 516.

49. Hulse and Erickson, "Introduction," 3.

50. Ibid., 12.

51. Valerie Traub, "Mapping the Global Body," ibid., ed. Peter Erickson and Clark Hulse (Philadelphia: University of Pennsylvania Press), 58.

52. Ibid., 77.

53. Ibid., 44, 58.

54. Pascale Aebischer, "Murderous Male Moors: Gazing at Race in Titus Andronicus and Othello," in *Shakespeare's Violated Bodies: Stage and Screen Performance* (Cambridge University Press, 2004), 102–50.

55. David S. Shields, "The Drake Jewel," *Uncommon Sense*, no. 128 (2010), http://oieahc.wm.edu/uncommon/118/drake.cfm.

56. Karen C. C. Dalton, "Art for the Sake of Dynasty: The Black Emperor in the Drake Jewel and Elizabethan Imperial Imagery," in *Early Modern Visual Culture: Representation, Race, and Empire in Renaissance England*, ed. Peter Erickson and Clark Hulse (Philadelphia, PA: University of Pennsylvania Press, 2000), 199.

57. Erickson and Hulse, p. 10.

58. Dalton, "Art for the Sake of Dynasty: The Black Emperor in the Drake Jewel and Elizabethan Imperial Imagery," 205.

59. Ben Jonson and Richard Harp, *Ben Jonson's Plays and Masques*, 2nd ed. (London: W.W. Norton, 2001), 488; Stephen Orgel, Inigo Jones, and Roy Strong, *Inigo Jones. The Theatre of the Stuart Court* (Los Angeles: University of California Press, 1973).

60. Barbara Babcock, quoted in Peter Stallybrass and Allon White, *The Politics and Poetics of Transgression* (London: Methuen, 1986), 20. Cited in Erickson, "Representations of Blacks and Blackness in the Renaissance," 506.

61. Bennett and Royle, *An Introduction to Literature, Criticism and Theory*, 117; Michel Foucault, "The Subject and Power," in *Michel Foucault: Beyond Structuralism and Hermeneutics*, ed. Hubert L. Dreyfus and Paul Rabinow (Chicago: Chicago University Press, 1982).

62. Morrison, *Playing in the Dark: Whiteness and the Literary Imagination*, 10.

63. Ibid., 33.

64. Ania Loomba, "The Color of Patriarchy," in *Women, 'Race' and Writing in the Early Modern Period*, ed. Margo Hendricks and Patricia Parker (London: Routledge, 1994), 25.

A.2. 'WITH ALL HIS BEAUTEOUS RACE': HIGH-STATUS BLACKS IN *THE MASQUE OF BLACKNESS* AND *THE MERCHANT OF VENICE*

1. Toni Morrison, *Playing in the Dark: Whiteness and the Literary Imagination* (Cambridge, MA: Harvard University Press, 1992), 33.

2. See Appendix I—"From Object to Subject: A Critical Survey on the Representation of Blackness in the Early Modern Period."

3. Ania Loomba, "The Color of Patriarchy: Critical Difference, Cultural Difference, and Renaissance Drama," in *Women, 'Race,' and Writing in the Early Modern Period*, ed. Margo Hendricks and Patricia Parker (London: Routledge, 1994), 25.

4. Anthony Gerard Barthelemy, *Black Face, Maligned Race: The Representation of Blacks in English Drama from Shakespeare to Southerne* (Baton Rouge: Louisiana State University Press, 1987), 20.

5. Richmond Barbour, "Britain and the Great Beyond: *The Masque of Blackness* at Whitehall," in *Playing the Globe: Genre and Geography in English Renaissance Drama*, ed. John Gillies and Virginia Mason Vaughan (London: Associated University Press, 1998), 130.

6. For a comprehensive list of the ladies in the masque see Ben Jonson and David Lindley, "The Masque of Blackness," in *The Cambridge Edition of the Works of Ben Jonson*, ed. David M. Bevington, Martin Butler, and Ian Donaldson (Cambridge: Cambridge University Press, 2012), 522. Anne Burley offers a fascinating analysis of these ladies and their relationships to one another in Anne Burley, "Courtly Personages: The Lady Masquers in Ben Jonson's Masque of Blackness," *Shakespeare and Renaissance Association of West Virginia—Selected Papers* 10 (1985): 49–61.

7. Barbour, "Britain and the Great Beyond: *The Masque of Blackness* at Whitehall," 141–43.

8. Dympna Callaghan, " 'Othello Was a White Man': Properties of Race on Shakespeare's Stage," in *Alternative Shakespeares, II*, ed. Terence Hawkes and John Drakakis (London, England: Routledge, 1996), 204.

9. Stephen Orgel, "The Jonsonian Masque," in *Ben Jonson's Plays and Masques*, ed. Ben Jonson and Richard Harp (London: W.W. Norton, 2001), 484; William Over, "Alterity and Assimilation in Jonson's Masques of Blackness and Beauty: 'I, with So Much Strength/of Argument Resisted'," *Culture, Language, and Representation— Cultural Studies Journal of Universität Jaume I* 1 (2004): 44. Ruth Cowhig (1985), Hardin Aasand (1992), Bernadette Andrea (1999), Joyce Green MacDonald (2002), Mary Floyd-Wilson (2003), and Ian Smith (2009) have all made similar assertions.

10. "Alterity and Assimilation in Jonson's Masques of Blackness and Beauty: 'I, with So Much Strength/of Argument Resisted'," 43.

11. Lynda E. Boose, " 'The Getting of a Lawful Race': Racial Discourse in Early Modern England and the Unrepresentable Black Woman," in *Women, 'Race,' and Writing in the Early Modern Period*, ed. Margo Hendricks and Patricia Parker (London: Routledge, 1994), 35.

12. Jonson and Lindley, "The Masque of Blackness," 503–28.

13. Ibid., 506. Royal MS 17 B XXXI. Gabriel Heaton's research explores how "Jonson's own relationship with royalty can be explored" through the manuscript. Gabriel Heaton, *Writing and Reading Royal Entertainments: From George Gascoigne to Ben Jonson* (Oxford: Oxford University Press, 2010), 12. See Heaton, 210–213 for an in-depth analysis of its provenance.

14. Kim F. Hall, *Things of Darkness: Economies of Race and Gender in Early Modern England* (Ithaca, NY: Cornell University Press, 1995), 128–49; Jonson and Lindley, "The Masque of Blackness," 506.

15. Lynn S. Meskill, "The Characters of Posterity in Jonson's *The Masque of Blacknesse* and Shakespeare's Antony and Cleopatra," *Huntington Library Quarterly: Studies in English and American History and Literature* 73, no. 1 (2010): 46.

16. William Shakespeare and John Drakakis, *The Merchant of Venice* (London: Arden Shakespeare, 2010), 112.

17. Ibid.

18. William Shakespeare, *The Most Excellent Historie of the Merchant of Venice* (London: 1600), STC22296.

19. Alan B. Farmer and Zachary Lesser, "DEEP: Database of Early English Playbooks," Philadelphia: University of Pennsylvania (2007), http://deep.sas.upenn.edu.

20. Barbour, "Britain and the Great Beyond: *The Masque of Blackness* at Whitehall," 129.

21. Lynn S. Meskill, "The Characters of Posterity in Jonson's *The Masque of Blacknesse* and Shakespeare's Antony and Cleopatra," *Huntington Library Quarterly: Studies in English and American History and Literature* 73, no. 1 (2010): 37–56.

22. See the title page of the 1600 quarto of Shakespeare, *The Most Excellent Historie of The Merchant of Venice*, 1r. See also the title page of Ben Jonson, *The Characters of Two Royall Masques the One of Blacknesse, the Other of Beautie* (London: 1608), 1r. STC14761.

23. Zachary Lesser, "Playbooks," in *Cheap Print in Britain and Ireland to 1660*, ed. Joad Raymond, The Oxford History of Popular Print Culture (New York: Oxford University Press, 2011), 526.

24. Ibid., 531.

25. Lauren Shohet, *Reading Masques: The English Masque and Public Culture in the Seventeenth Century* (Oxford: Oxford University Press, 2010), 25.

26. Jonson and Lindley, "The Masque of Blackness," 503–28; Shakespeare and Drakakis, *The Merchant of Venice*, 161–401.

27. ProQuest LLC, "Eebo: Early English Books Online," (2003), http://eebo.chadwyck.com/home.

28. Margo Hendricks, "Surveying 'Race' in Shakespeare," in *Shakespeare and Race*, ed. Stanley Wells and Catherine M. S. Alexander (Cambridge, UK: Cambridge University Press, 2000), 20.

29. Ania Loomba and Jonathan Burton, eds., *Race in Early Modern England: A Documentary Companion* (Basingstoke, UK: Palgrave Macmillan, 2007), 1.

30. *OED* Online, "'Race, N.6'," (Oxford University Press, 2014). All term dating, definitions, and etymological references (unless otherwise stated) have been taken from *OED* Online (Oxford: Oxford University Press, 2015), http://www.oed.com.

31. Hendricks, "Surveying 'Race' in Shakespeare," 20.

32. Dennis Austin Britton, *Consuming Difference: Race, Romance and Religion in Early Modern England*, vol. 68 (University of Wisconsin, Madison, 2008), 2.

33. Anthony Appiah, "Race," in *Critical Terms for Literary Study*, ed. Frank Lentricchia and Thomas McLaughlin (Chicago: University of Chicago Press, 1995), 278.

34. Harvey Young, *Theatre and Race* (Basingstoke, UK: Palgrave Macmillan, 2013), 5.

35. Footnote 1: Loomba states that though "the social effects of race are real and tangible, the term 'race' has been increasingly framed within quotation marks in order to signal that it is a socially constructed idea." Loomba and Burton, *Race in Early Modern England: A Documentary Companion*, 28.

36. Callaghan, "'Othello Was a White Man': Properties of Race on Shakespeare's Stage," 195.

37. Andrea Stevens, "Mastering Masques of Blackness: Jonson's *Masque of Blackness*, the Windsor Text of *The Gypsies Metamorphosed*, and Brome's *The English Moor*," *English Literary Renaissance* 39, no. 2 (2009): 411.

38. *OED* Online.

39. Ibid.

40. For a comprehensive list of terms used for blacks in the early modern period, see Eldred D. Jones, "Racial Terms for Africans in Elizabethan Usage," *Review of National Literatures* 3, no. 2 (1972): 54–89.

41. Kim F. Hall, "'These Bastard Signs of Fair': Literary Whiteness in Shakespeare's Sonnets," in *Post-Colonial Shakespeares*, ed. Ania Loomba and Martin Orkin (London: Routledge, 1998), 65.

42. Ibid., 66.

43. Ian Smith, *Race and Rhetoric in the Renaissance: Barbarian Errors*, 1st ed. (Basingstoke, UK: Palgrave Macmillan, 2009), 53.

A.2.1. NIGER, A HIGH-STATUS BLACK CHARACTER IN *THE MASQUE OF BLACKNESS*

1. William Over, "Alterity and Assimilation in Jonson's Masques of Blackness and Beauty: 'I, with So Much Strength/of Argument Resisted'," *Culture, Language, and Representation—Cultural Studies Journal of Universität Jaume I* 1 (2004): 52.

2. Ibid.

3. Richmond Barbour, "Britain and the Great Beyond: *The Masque of Blackness* at Whitehall," in *Playing the Globe: Genre and Geography in English Renaissance Drama*, ed. John Gillies and Virginia Mason Vaughan (London: Associated University Press, 1998), 137. David Lindley offers a comprehensive overview of criticism relating to *The Masque of Blackness* in his "Introduction." Ben Jonson and David Lindley, "The Masque of Blackness," in *The Cambridge Edition of the Works of Ben Jonson*, ed. David M. Bevington, Martin Butler, and Ian Donaldson (Cambridge: Cambridge University Press, 2012), 505–06.

4. Barbour, "Britain and the Great Beyond: *The Masque of Blackness* at Whitehall," 137.

5. Over, "Alterity and Assimilation in Jonson's Masques of Blackness and Beauty: 'I, with So Much Strength/of Argument Resisted'," 47.

6. Clare McManus, "Defacing the Carcass: Anne of Denmark and Jonson's Masque of Blackness," in *Refashioning Ben Jonson: Gender, Politics and the Jonsonian Canon*, ed. Julie Sanders, Kate Chedgzoy, and Susan Wiseman (Basingstoke, UK: Macmillan Press, 1998).

7. Over, "Alterity and Assimilation in Jonson's Masques of Blackness and Beauty: 'I, with So Much Strength/of Argument Resisted'," 43–54.

8. Ibid., 46.

9. Encyclopædia Britannica Online, "Niger River," *Encyclopædia Britannica* (2015), http://www.britannica.com/place/Niger-River.

10. Barbour, "Britain and the Great Beyond: *The Masque of Blackness* at White-hall," 145; Andrea Stevens, "Mastering Masques of Blackness: Jonson's *Masque of Blackness*, the Windsor Text of *The Gypsies Metamorphosed*, and Brome's *The English Moor*," *English Literary Renaissance* 39, no. 2 (2009): 408.

11. Mary Floyd-Wilson, "Temperature, Temperance, and Racial Difference in Ben Jonson's *The Masque of Blackness*," *English Literary Renaissance* 28 (1998): 203.

12. Edmund Valentine Campos, "West of Eden: American Gold, Spanish Greed, and the Discourses of English Imperialism," in *Rereading the Black Legend: The Discourses of Religious and Racial Difference in the Renaissance Empires*, ed. Margaret Rich Greer, Walter Mignolo, and Maureen Quilligan (Chicago: University of Chicago Press, 2007), 247–69.

13. Anu Kornohen, "Washing the Ethiopian White: Conceptualising Black Skin in Renaissance England," in *Black Africans in Renaissance Europe*, ed. T. F. Earle and K. J. P. Lowe (Cambridge: Cambridge University Press, 2005), 100.

14. Glenn A. Odom, "Jacobean Politics of Interpretation in Jonson's Masque of Blacknesse," *SEL: Studies in English Literature, 1500–1900* 51, no. 2 (2011): 371.

15. Over, "Alterity and Assimilation in Jonson's Masques of Blackness and Beauty: 'I, with So Much Strength/of Argument Resisted'," 46.

16. Stevens, "Mastering Masques of Blackness: Jonson's *Masque of Blackness*, the Windsor Text of *The Gypsies Metamorphosed*, and Brome's *The English Moor*," 410.

17. Ibid., 408.

18. Over, "Alterity and Assimilation in Jonson's Masques of Blackness and Beauty: 'I, with So Much Strength/of Argument Resisted'," 47.

19. Hardin Aasand, " 'To Blanch an Ethiop, and Revive a Corse': Queen Anne and *The Masque of Blackness*," *SEL: Studies in English Literature, 1500–1900* 32, no. 2 (1992): 275.

20. Lesley Mickel, "Glorious Spangs and Rich Embroidery: Costume in *The Masque of Blackness* and Hymenaei," *Studies in the Literary Imagination* 36, no. 2 (2003): 3.

21. Martin Butler, "*The Masque of Blackness* and Stuart Court Culture," in *Early Modern English Drama: A Critical Companion*, ed. Garrett A. Sullivan, Jr., Patrick Cheney, and Andrew Hadfield (New York, NY: Oxford University Press, 2006), 154; Leeds Barroll, "Theatre as Text: The Case of Queen Anna and the Jacobean Court Masque," in *The Elizabethan Theatre, XIV*, ed. A. L. Magnusson and C. E. McGee (Toronto: Meany, 1996), 177–79.

22. Stevens, "Mastering Masques of Blackness: Jonson's *Masque of Blackness*, the Windsor Text of *The Gypsies Metamorphosed*, and Brome's *The English Moor*," 397.

23. Ibid., 405.

24. See the portrait of one of the daughters of Niger from *The Masque of Blackness*, by Inigo Jones. From the Devonshire Collection, Chatsworth. Stephen Orgel, Inigo Jones, and Roy Strong, *Inigo Jones. The Theatre of the Stuart Court* (Los Angeles: University of California Press, 1973), 88–99.

25. Jonson and Lindley, "The Masque of Blackness," 505.

26. Mickel, "Glorious Spangs and Rich Embroidery: Costume in *The Masque of Blackness* and Hymenaei," 46.

27. Ben Jonson, *The Fountaine of Selfe-Loue. Or Cynthias Reuels*, Early English Books, 1475–1640 (London: 1601), 39v. STC14773.

28. See a portrait of one of the Oceaniae from *The Masque of Blackness*, by Inigo Jones. From the Devonshire Collection, Chatsworth. Orgel, Jones, and Strong, *Inigo Jones. The Theatre of the Stuart Court*, 88–99.

29. Over, "Alterity and Assimilation in Jonson's Masques of Blackness and Beauty: 'I, with So Much Strength/of Argument Resisted'," 46.

30. Lynn S. Meskill, "The Characters of Posterity in Jonson's *The Masque of Blacknesse* and Shakespeare's Antony and Cleopatra," *Huntington Library Quarterly: Studies in English and American History and Literature* 73, no. 1 (2010): 41.

31. Mary Floyd-Wilson, *English Ethnicity and Race in Early Modern Drama* (Cambridge, England: Cambridge University Press, 2003), 18.

32. Meskill, "The Characters of Posterity in Jonson's *The Masque of Blacknesse* and Shakespeare's Antony and Cleopatra," 42.

33. Floyd-Wilson, "Temperature, Temperance, and Racial Difference in Ben Jonson's *The Masque of Blackness*," 187.

34. Jonson and Lindley, *The Masque of Blackness*, 518–19.

35. Floyd-Wilson, "Temperature, Temperance, and Racial Difference in Ben Jonson's *The Masque of Blackness*," 187.

36. Butler, "*The Masque of Blackness* and Stuart Court Culture," 152–63.

37. Ibid., 155, 52.

38. Ibid., 153.

39. Ibid.

40. Ibid., 154.

41. Aasand, "'To Blanch an Ethiop, and Revive a Corse': Queen Anne and *The Masque of Blackness*," 283.

42. William Over, "Familiarizing the Colonized in Ben Jonson's Masques," *Partial Answers: Journal of Literature and the History of Ideas* 2, no. 2 (2004): 27.

43. Ibid.

44. "Alterity and Assimilation in Jonson's Masques of Blackness and Beauty: 'I, with So Much Strength/of Argument Resisted'," 44.

45. Butler, "*The Masque of Blackness* and Stuart Court Culture," 55; Bernadette Andrea, "'A Noble Troop of Strangers': Masques of Blackness in Shakespeare's Henry VIII," in *Shakespeare and Immigration*, ed. Ruben Espinosa and David Ruiter (Farnham, England: Ashgate, 2014), 106. Floyd-Wilson discusses the connection between unification of Scotland and England as an allegory for transformation in *The Masque of Blackness*. Floyd-Wilson, "Temperature, Temperance, and Racial Difference in Ben Jonson's *The Masque of Blackness*," 183–209.

46. Bernadette Andrea, "Black Skin, the Queen's Masques: Africanist Ambivalence and Feminine Author(Ity) in the Masques of Blackness and Beauty," *English Literary Renaissance* 29 (1999): 247.

47. Over, "Alterity and Assimilation in Jonson's Masques of Blackness and Beauty: 'I, with So Much Strength/of Argument Resisted'," 46.

A.2.2. MOROCCO, A HIGH-STATUS BLACK CHARACTER IN *THE MERCHANT OF VENICE*

1. For a detailed analysis of the gender-related issues surrounding the casket test, see Karen Newman, "Portia's Ring: Gender, Sexuality, and Theories of Exchange in *The Merchant of Venice*," in *Essaying Shakespeare* (Minneapolis: University of Minnesota Press, 2009), 59–76.

2. John Florio, *Queen Anna's New World of Words* (London: 1611), 323.

3. William Shakespeare and John Drakakis, *The Merchant of Venice* (London: Arden Shakespeare, 2010), 164.

4. Kim F. Hall, "Guess Who's Coming to Dinner? Colonization and Miscegenation in 'The Merchant of Venice'," *Renaissance Drama* 23 (1992): 97.

5. Ovid, *Metamorphoses*, trans. A. D. Melville (Oxford: Oxford University Press, 1987); Ian Smith, *Race and Rhetoric in the Renaissance: Barbarian Errors*, 1st ed. (Basingstoke, UK: Palgrave Macmillan, 2009), 53.

6. Smith, *Race and Rhetoric in the Renaissance: Barbarian Errors*, 55.

7. Shakespeare and Drakakis, *The Merchant of Venice*, 85.

8. Hall, "Guess Who's Coming to Dinner? Colonization and Miscegenation in 'The Merchant of Venice'," 98.

9. Shakespeare and Drakakis, *The Merchant of Venice*, 223.

10. William Shakespeare and E. A. J. Honigmann, *Othello* (London: Arden Shakespeare, 2001), 151, 54.

11. Shakespeare and Drakakis, *The Merchant of Venice*, 224, 85. For a comprehensive list of recent productions see ibid., 450–51.

12. Ibid., 224.

13. Smith, *Race and Rhetoric in the Renaissance: Barbarian Errors*, 56.

14. Shakespeare and Drakakis, *The Merchant of Venice*, 112–13, 404.

15. Anu Kornohen, "Washing the Ethiopian White: Conceptualising Black Skin in Renaissance England," in *Black Africans in Renaissance Europe*, ed. T. F. Earle and K. J. P. Lowe (Cambridge: Cambridge University Press, 2005), 99.

16. Shakespeare and Drakakis, *The Merchant of Venice*, 85. Footnote 1.

17. Ibid.; Michael Radford, *The Merchant of Venice* (Sony Pictures Classics, MGM, Optimum Releasing, 2004).

18. Ania Loomba and Jonathan Burton, eds., *Race in Early Modern England: A Documentary Companion* (Basingstoke, UK: Palgrave Macmillan, 2007), 135, 36, 58; Emily C. Bartels, "Too Many Blackamoors: Deportation, Discrimination, and Elizabeth I," *SEL: Studies in English Literature, 1500–1900* 46, no. 2 (2006): 305–22; Hall, "Guess Who's Coming to Dinner? Colonization and Miscegenation in 'The Merchant of Venice'," 87–111.

19. Harvey Young, *Theatre and Race* (Basingstoke, UK: Palgrave Macmillan, 2013), 31.

20. Hall, "Guess Who's Coming to Dinner? Colonization and Miscegenation in 'The Merchant of Venice'," 90.

21. Emily C. Bartels, *Speaking of the Moor: From Alcazar to Othello* (Philadelphia, PA: University of Pennsylvania Press, 2008), 6.

22. Hall, "Guess Who's Coming to Dinner? Colonization and Miscegenation in 'The Merchant of Venice'," 92.

23. Bartels, *Speaking of the Moor: From Alcazar to Othello*, 5.

24. Ibid., 16.

25. Ibid., 162.

26. Shakespeare and Drakakis, *The Merchant of Venice*, 86.

27. Dympna Callaghan, *Shakespeare without Women: Representing Gender and Race on the Renaissance Stage*, Accents on Shakespeare (London: Routledge, 1999), 7.

28. "'Othello Was a White Man': Properties of Race on Shakespeare's Stage," in *Alternative Shakespeares, II*, ed. Terence Hawkes and John Drakakis (London, England: Routledge, 1996), 197.

29. Kim F. Hall, *Things of Darkness: Economies of Race and Gender in Early Modern England* (Ithaca, NY: Cornell University Press, 1995), 94. For an insightful overview of early modern blackness and theories of climatology see Floyd-Wilson, Mary, "Temperature, Temperance, and Racial Difference in Ben Jonson's *The Masque of Blackness.*" *English Literary Renaissance* 28, no. 2 (1998): 183–209.

30. Mary Floyd-Wilson, "Temperature, Temperance, and Racial Difference in Ben Jonson's *The Masque of Blackness*," 186.

31. Hall, *Things of Darkness: Economies of Race and Gender in Early Modern England*, 2.

32. Anthony Gerard Barthelemy, *Black Face, Maligned Race: The Representation of Blacks in English Drama from Shakespeare to Southerne* (Baton Rouge: Louisiana State University Press, 1987), 18.

33. Ibid., 18–19.

34. Glenn A. Odom, "Jacobean Politics of Interpretation in Jonson's *Masque of Blacknesse*," *SEL: Studies in English Literature, 1500–1900* 51, no. 2 (2011): 368.

35. Hall, *Things of Darkness: Economies of Race and Gender in Early Modern England*, 134.

A.2.3. GENDER AND THE DEPICTIONS OF NIGER AND MOROCCO

1. Ben Jonson and David Lindley, "The Masque of Blackness," in *The Cambridge Edition of the Works of Ben Jonson*, ed. David M. Bevington, Martin Butler, and Ian Donaldson (Cambridge: Cambridge University Press, 2012), 513.

2. Richmond Barbour, "Britain and the Great Beyond: *The Masque of Blackness* at Whitehall," in *Playing the Globe: Genre and Geography in English Renaissance Drama*, ed. John Gillies and Virginia Mason Vaughan (London: Associated University Press, 1998), 143.

3. Jonson and Lindley, "The Masque of Blackness," 527.

4. Lynda E. Boose, "'The Getting of a Lawful Race': Racial Discourse in Early Modern England and the Unrepresentable Black Woman," in *Women, 'Race,' and Writing in the Early Modern Period*, ed. Margo Hendricks and Patricia Parker (London: Routledge, 1994), 47.

5. Kim F. Hall, *Things of Darkness: Economies of Race and Gender in Early Modern England* (Ithaca, NY: Cornell University Press, 1995), 129.

6. Lesley Mickel, "Glorious Spangs and Rich Embroidery: Costume in *The Masque of Blackness* and Hymenaei," *Studies in the Literary Imagination* 36, no. 2 (2003): 48; Bernadette Andrea, "Black Skin, the Queen's Masques: Africanist Ambivalence and Feminine Author(Ity) in the Masques of Blackness and Beauty," *English Literary Renaissance* 29, no. 2 (1999): 280.

7. Boose, "'The Getting of a Lawful Race': Racial Discourse in Early Modern England and the Unrepresentable Black Woman," 46.

8. William Over, "Familiarizing the Colonized in Ben Jonson's Masques," *Partial Answers: Journal of Literature and the History of Ideas* 2, no. 2 (2004): 45; Boose, "'The Getting of a Lawful Race': Racial Discourse in Early Modern England and the Unrepresentable Black Woman," 46.

9. Andrea Stevens, "Mastering Masques of Blackness: Jonson's *Masque of Blackness*, the Windsor Text of *The Gypsies Metamorphosed*, and Brome's *The English Moor*," *English Literary Renaissance* 39, no. 2 (2009): 398; Joyce Green MacDonald, *Women and Race in Early Modern Texts* (Cambridge, England: Cambridge University Press, 2002), 7.

10. Dudley Carleton, "Letter to Sir Ralph Winwood," in *Winwood Memorials, II, P. 44, in Ben Jonson*, ed. C. H. Herford, P. Simpson, and E. Simpson (Oxford: Clarendon Press, 1941), 448.

11. Barbour, "Britain and the Great Beyond: The Masque of Blackness at Whitehall," 140.

12. Ibid.

13. Boose, "'The Getting of a Lawful Race': Racial Discourse in Early Modern England and the Unrepresentable Black Woman," 50–51.

14. Dudley Carleton, "London, January 7, 1605," in *Dudley Carleton to John Chamberlain 1603–1624. Jacobean Letters*, ed. Maurice Lee (New Brunswick, NJ: Rutgers University Press, 1972), 67–68.

15. Dympna Callaghan, "'Othello Was a White Man': Properties of Race on Shakespeare's Stage," in *Alternative Shakespeares, II*, ed. Terence Hawkes and John Drakakis (London, England: Routledge, 1996), 200.

16. Barbour, "Britain and the Great Beyond: The Masque of Blackness at Whitehall," 140.

17. Jonson and Lindley, "The Masque of Blackness," 505.

18. Mary Floyd-Wilson, "Temperature, Temperance, and Racial Difference in Ben Jonson's *The Masque of Blackness*," *English Literary Renaissance* 28, no. 2 (1998): 197.

19. Ann Cline Kelly, "The Challenge of the Impossible: Ben Jonson's Masque of Blackness," *College Language Association Journal* 20 (1977): 342.

20. Floyd-Wilson, "Temperature, Temperance, and Racial Difference in Ben Jonson's *The Masque of Blackness*," 193.

21. William Over, "Alterity and Assimilation in Jonson's Masques of Blackness and Beauty: 'I, with So Much Strength/of Argument Resisted'," *Culture, Language, and Representation—Cultural Studies Journal of Universität Jaume I* 1 (2004): 49.

22. Karen Newman, "'And Wash the Ethiop White': Femininity and the Monstrous in Othello," in *Essaying Shakespeare* (Minneapolis: University of Minnesota Press, 2009), 38.

23. "Aethiopem Lavare," in Geffrey Whitney, *A Choice of Emblemes, and Other Deuises, for the Moste Parte Gathered out of Sundrie Writers, Englished and Moralized* (Leyden: 1586), 39r.

24. Anu Kornohen, "Washing the Ethiopian White: Conceptualising Black Skin in Renaissance England," in *Black Africans in Renaissance Europe*, ed. T. F. Earle and K. J. P. Lowe (Cambridge: Cambridge University Press, 2005), 94. Jeremiah 13–23: "Can the black moor change his skin? Or the leopard his spots?'" Cited in Jonson and Lindley, "The Masque of Blackness," 521.

25. Martin Butler, "The Masque of Blackness and Stuart Court Culture," in *Early Modern English Drama: A Critical Companion*, ed. Garrett A. Sullivan, Jr., Patrick Cheney, and Andrew Hadfield (New York: Oxford University Press, 2006), 161.

26. Hardin Aasand, "'To Blanch an Ethiop, and Revive a Corse': Queen Anne and *The Masque of Blackness*," *SEL: Studies in English Literature, 1500–1900* 32, no. 2 (1992): 275.

27. William Shakespeare and John Drakakis, *The Merchant of Venice* (London: Arden Shakespeare, 2010), 85–86.

28. Kim F. Hall, "Guess Who's Coming to Dinner? Colonization and Miscegenation in 'The Merchant of Venice'," *Renaissance Drama* 23 (1992): 97.

29. Callaghan, "'Othello Was a White Man': Properties of Race on Shakespeare's Stage," 197.

30. *Shakespeare without Women: Representing Gender and Race on the Renaissance Stage*, Accents on Shakespeare (London: Routledge, 1999), 8.

31. Shakespeare and Drakakis, *The Merchant of Venice*, 263.

32. Ibid., 268.

33. Ibid.

34. Kornohen, "Washing the Ethiopian White: Conceptualising Black Skin in Renaissance England," 100.

35. Ibid., 109; Benjamin Braude, "The Sons of Noah and the Construction of Ethnic and Geographical Identities in the Medieval and Early Modern Periods," *William and Mary Quarterly: A Magazine of Early American History and Culture* 54, no. 1 (1997): 103–42.

36. Kornohen, "Washing the Ethiopian White: Conceptualising Black Skin in Renaissance England," 100; Bernadette Andrea, "The Ghost of Leo Africanus from the English to the Irish Renaissance," in *Postcolonial Moves: Medieval through Modern*, ed. Patricia Clare Ingham and Michelle R. Warren (New York: Palgrave Macmillan, 2003), 195–215; Johannes Leo Africanus, "A Geographical Historie of Africa (1600),"

in *Race in Early Modern England: A Documentary Companion*, ed. Ania Loomba and Ben Burton (Basingstoke, UK: Palgrave Macmillan, 2007), 135–57.

37. Shakespeare and Drakakis, *The Merchant of Venice*, 86.

38. Ibid., 85.

39. Boose, "'The Getting of a Lawful Race': Racial Discourse in Early Modern England and the Unrepresentable Black Woman," 41.

40. Callaghan, "'Othello Was a White Man': Properties of Race on Shakespeare's Stage," 211.

41. Lynn S. Meskill, "The Characters of Posterity in Jonson's *The Masque of Blackness*e and Shakespeare's Antony and Cleopatra," *Huntington Library Quarterly: Studies in English and American History and Literature* 73, no. 1 (2010): 37.

42. Ibid.

43. Dennis Austin Britton, *Consuming Difference: Race, Romance and Religion in Early Modern England*, vol. 68 (Madison: University of Wisconsin, 2008), 215.

44. Boose, "'The Getting of a Lawful Race': Racial Discourse in Early Modern England and the Unrepresentable Black Woman," 45–46.

A.2.4. CONCLUSION

1. Bernadette Andrea, "Black Skin, the Queen's Masques: Africanist Ambivalence and Feminine Author(Ity) in the Masques of Blackness and Beauty," *English Literary Renaissance* 29, no. 2 (1999): 257.

2. Lynda E. Boose, "'The Getting of a Lawful Race': Racial Discourse in Early Modern England and the Unrepresentable Black Woman," in *Women, 'Race,' and Writing in the Early Modern Period*, ed. Margo Hendricks and Patricia Parker (London: Routledge, 1994), 40.

3. Kim F. Hall, *Things of Darkness: Economies of Race and Gender in Early Modern England* (Ithaca, NY: Cornell University Press, 1995), 1.

4. Imtiaz H. Habib, *Black Lives in the English Archives, 1500–1677: Imprints of the Invisible* (Aldershot, UK: Ashgate, 2008), 3.

5. Ibid., 4.

6. Hall, *Things of Darkness: Economies of Race and Gender in Early Modern England*, 13.

7. Mary Floyd-Wilson, "Temperature, Temperance, and Racial Difference in Ben Jonson's *The Masque of Blackness*," *English Literary Renaissance* 28, no. 2 (1998): 208–09.

8. Boose, "'The Getting of a Lawful Race': Racial Discourse in Early Modern England and the Unrepresentable Black Woman," 36.

9. Mary Floyd-Wilson, *English Ethnicity and Race in Early Modern Drama* (Cambridge, England: Cambridge University Press, 2003), 19.

10. William Over, "Alterity and Assimilation in Jonson's Masques of Blackness and Beauty: 'I, with So Much Strength/of Argument Resisted'," *Culture, Language, and Representation—Cultural Studies Journal of Universität Jaume I* 1 (2004): 43.

11. Ibid., 44.

12. Alden T. Vaughan and Vaughan Virginia Mason, "Before Othello: Elizabethan Representations of Sub-Saharan Africans," *The William and Mary Quarterly* 54, no. 1 (1997): 44.

13. Ibid.

14. Barbour, p. 145.

15. Floyd-Wilson, *English Ethnicity and Race in Early Modern Drama*, (Cambridge, England: Cambridge University Press, 2003), 18.

16. Ania Loomba and Jonathan Burton, eds., *Race in Early Modern England: A Documentary Companion* (Basingstoke, UK: Palgrave Macmillan, 2007), 2.

17. Hall, *Things of Darkness: Economies of Race and Gender in Early Modern England*, 129.

18. "Sexual Politics and Cultural Identity in *The Masque of Blackness*," in *The Performance of Power: Theatrical Discourse and Politics*, ed. Sue-Ellen Case and Janelle Reinelt, Studies in Theatre History and Culture (Iowa City: University of Iowa Press, 1991), 4.

19. "'These Bastard Signs of Fair': Literary Whiteness in Shakespeare's Sonnets," in *Post-Colonial Shakespeares*, ed. Ania Loomba and Martin Orkin (London: Routledge, 1998), 80.

20. Ania Loomba, "'Delicious Traffick': Racial and Religious Difference on Early Modern Stages," in *Shakespeare and Race*, ed. Catherine M. S. Alexander and Stanley Wells (Cambridge, England: Cambridge University Press, 2000), 204.

21. Ben Jonson and David Lindley, "The Masque of Blackness," in *The Cambridge Edition of the Works of Ben Jonson*, ed. David M. Bevington, Martin Butler, and Ian Donaldson (Cambridge: Cambridge University Press, 2012), 512; Over, "Alterity and Assimilation in Jonson's Masques of Blackness and Beauty: 'I, with So Much Strength/ of Argument Resisted'," 44, 28; Richard Hakluyt, "The Worthy and Famous Voyage of the Master Thomas Candish Made Round About the Globe of the Earth . . . (1589)," in *Race in Early Modern England: A Documentary Companion*, ed. Ania Loomba and Ben Burton (Basingstoke, UK: Palgrave Macmillan, 2007), 123.

22. Ian Smith, *Race and Rhetoric in the Renaissance: Barbarian Errors*, 1st ed. (Basingstoke, UK: Palgrave Macmillan, 2009), 67.

23. Ibid., 58.

24. Ibid., 54.

25. Dympna Callaghan, *Shakespeare without Women: Representing Gender and Race on the Renaissance Stage*, Accents on Shakespeare (London: Routledge, 1999), 194; Hall, *Things of Darkness: Economies of Race and Gender in Early Modern England*, 117–18; Over, "Alterity and Assimilation in Jonson's Masques of Blackness and Beauty: 'I, with So Much Strength/of Argument Resisted'," 45.

26. Floyd-Wilson, "Temperature, Temperance, and Racial Difference in Ben Jonson's *The Masque of Blackness*," 208–09.

27. Hall, "'These Bastard Signs of Fair': Literary Whiteness in Shakespeare's Sonnets," 66.

28. Anu Kornohen, "Washing the Ethiopian White: Conceptualising Black Skin in Renaissance England," in *Black Africans in Renaissance Europe*, ed. T. F. Earle and K. J. P. Lowe (Cambridge: Cambridge University Press, 2005), 109.

29. Ibid., 110; Hall, *Things of Darkness: Economies of Race and Gender in Early Modern England*, 42.

30. Kornohen, "Washing the Ethiopian White: Conceptualising Black Skin in Renaissance England," 95.

31. Ibid., 11.

32. Toni Morrison, *Playing in the Dark: Whiteness and the Literary Imagination* (Cambridge, MA: Harvard University Press, 1992), 16.

33. Kornohen, "Washing the Ethiopian White: Conceptualising Black Skin in Renaissance England," 107.

34. The Drake Jewel (c. 1588). Gold and enamel with sardonyx, rubies and diamonds. From the Victoria and Albert Museum. Karen C. C. Dalton, "Art for the Sake of Dynasty: The Black Emperor in the Drake Jewel and Elizabethan Imperial Imagery," in *Early Modern Visual Culture: Representation, Race, and Empire in Renaissance England*, ed. Peter Erickson and Clark Hulse (Philadelphia, PA: University of Pennsylvania Press, 2000), 180–82.

35. Royal Museums Greenwich, "Sir Francis Drake, 1540–96," http://collections.rmg.co.uk/collections/objects/14136.html.

36. Clark Hulse, "Reading Painting: Holbein, Cromwell, Wyatt," in *Early Modern Visual Culture: Representation, Race, and Empire in Renaissance England*, ed. Peter Erickson and Clark Hulse (Philadelphia: University of Pennsylvania Press, 2000), 148–77; Jonathan Gil Harris, *Untimely Matter in the Time of Shakespeare* (Philadelphia: University of Pennsylvania Press, 2011), 3.

37. Ayanna Thompson, "The Future of Early Modern Race Studies: On Three Ambitious (Enough?) Books," *The Eighteenth Century: Theory and Interpretation* 49, no. 3 (2008): 260.

Bibliography

Aasand, Hardin. "'To Blanch an Ethiop, and Revive a Corse': Queen Anne and the Masque of Blackness." *SEL: Studies in English Literature, 1500–1900* 32, no. 2 (1992): 271–85.

Acheson, Katherine O. "Visual Rhetoric and Early Modern English Literature." *Material Readings in Early Modern Culture.* Farnham, UK: Ashgate, 2013.

Acquaviva, Jean-Claude, and Maciej Rychly. "Songs of Lear: Song of the Goat Theatre." Wroclaw: Magellan Foundation, 2013.

Aebischer, P. "Murderous Male Moors: Gazing at Race in Titus Andronicus and Othello." Chap. 3 in *Shakespeare's Violated Bodies: Stage and Screen Performance*, 102–50. Cambridge, UK: Cambridge University Press, 2004.

Aesop. "Fables (6th Century Bce)." In *Race in Early Modern England: A Documentary Companion*, edited by Ania Loomba and Ben Burton, 39. Basingstoke: Palgrave Macmillan, 2007.

Alan, Parker. *Bugsy Malone.* Carlton, 1976.

Amisu, Elizabeth. "Arrojar Piedras Y Esconder Las Manos: La Personalidad Humana De Michael Jackson." [In Spanish]. *The Journal of Michael Jackson Academic Studies* 1, no. 3 (2015): 3. http://michaeljacksonstudies.org/arrojar-piedras-y-esconder-las-manos-la-personalidad-humana-de-michael-jackson/.

Amisu, Elizabeth. "'Bad (1987)'." *The Journal of Michael Jackson Academic Studies* 1, no. 2 (2014): 4. http://michaeljacksonstudies.org/bad-1987-2/

Amisu, Elizabeth. "Bad (1987)." *Writing Eliza* (2014). Published electronically 20 July 2014. http://elizabethamisu.com/2014/07/20/bad-1987-genius-the-short-films-of-michael-2/.

Amisu, Elizabeth. "Choose an Early Modern Printer or Publisher and Look at the Place of Literary Publications within His Work as a Whole." 21. London: King's College London, 2014.

Amisu, Elizabeth, ed. *A Companion to Michael Jackson Academic Studies.* MJAS, 2015.

Amisu, Elizabeth. "'Crack Music': Michael Jackson's 'Invincible'." *The Journal of Michael Jackson Academic Studies* 1, no. 2 (2015): 1. http://michaeljacksonstudies .org/elizabeth-amisu-crack-music-michael-jacksons-invincible/.

Amisu, Elizabeth. "'Crack Music': Michael Jackson's 'Invincible'—Dangerous Philosophies 4/12." [In Italian]. *The Journal of Michael Jackson Academic Studies* 1, no. 3 (2015): 4. http://michaeljacksonstudies.org/httpjournal-culturalstudies -karinmerx-comarticlecrack-music-michael-jacksons-invincible-dangerous -philosophies-412/.

Amisu, Elizabeth. "'Crack Music': Michael Jackson's Invincible." *Writing Eliza* (2014). http://elizabethamisu.com/2014/10/23/crack-music-michael-jacksons -invincible-2/.

Amisu, Elizabeth. "The Dangerous Philosophies of Michael Jackson." [In Italian]. *The Journal of Michael Jackson Academic Studies* 1, no. 3 (2015): 4. https:// grazia28.wordpress.com/2015/01/13/the-dangerous-philosophies-of-michael -jackson-by-elizabeth-amisu/.

Amisu, Elizabeth. "'Die Insel Ist Voller Geräusche': Erneuter Besuch Beim "Peter Pan Des Pop"." [In German]. *The Journal of Michael Jackson Academic Studies* 1, no. 3 (2015): 2. http://michaeljacksonstudies.org/die-insel-ist-voller-gerausche -erneuter-besuch-beim-peter-pan-des-pop/

Amisu, Elizabeth. "Earth Song: Inside Michael Jackson's Magnum Opus Book Review." *Writing Eliza* (2014). http://elizabethamisu.com/2014/10/16/earth -song-inside-michael-jacksons-magnum-opus/.

Amisu, Elizabeth. "Earth Song: Inside Michael Jackson's Magnum Opus by Joseph Vogel (Blake Vision, 2011)." *The Journal of Michael Jackson Academic Studies* 1, no. 1 (2014): 1. http://michaeljacksonstudies.org/earth-song-inside-michael -jacksons-magnum-opus-by-joseph-vogel-blake-vision-2011/.

Amisu, Elizabeth. "Editing Task." 11. London: King's College London, 2014.

Amisu, Elizabeth. "¿Estamos Perdiendo a Michael Jackson De Nuevo?" [In Spanish]. *The Journal of Michael Jackson Academic Studies* 1, no. 3 (2015): 3. http:// michaeljacksonstudies.org/estamos-perdiendo-a-michael-jackson-de-nuevo/.

Amisu, Elizabeth. "From Object to Subject: A Critical Survey on the Representation of Blackness in the Early Modern Period." 13. London: King's College London, 2015.

Amisu, Elizabeth. "Heard It on the Grapevine." *The Journal of Michael Jackson Academic Studies* 1, no. 1 (2014): 3. http://michaeljacksonstudies.org/heard-it-on -the-grapevine/.

Amisu, Elizabeth. "'The Isle Is Full of Noises': Revisiting the Peter Pan of Pop." *Writing Eliza* (2014). http://elizabethamisu.com/2014/08/21/the-isle-is-full -of-noises-revisiting-the/.

Amisu, Elizabeth. "'The Isle Is Full of Noises': Revisiting the Peter Pan of Pop." *The Journal of Michael Jackson Academic Studies* 1, no. 1 (2014): 2. http://michael jacksonstudies.org/elizabeth-amisu-the-isle-is-full-of-noises-revisiting-the-peter -pan-of-pop/.

Amisu, Elizabeth. "On Michael Jackson Book Review." *Michael Jackson Academic Journal* 1, no. 1 (2014). http:///elizabeth-amisu-on-michael-jackson-by-margo -jefferson/.

Amisu, Elizabeth. "On Michael Jackson's *Dancing the Dream.*" *The Journal of Michael Jackson Academic Studies* 1, no. 2 (2014): 3. http://michaeljacksonstudies .org/on-michael-jacksons-dancing-the-dream/.

Amisu, Elizabeth. "On Michael Jackson's *Dancing the Dream.*" *Writing Eliza* (2014). Published electronically 7 July. http://elizabethamisu.com/post/91073957802 /on-michael-jacksons-dancing-the-dream-dangerous.

Amisu, Elizabeth. "Song of the Goat's 'Songs of Lear'." 24. London: King's College London, 2015.

Amisu, Elizabeth. "'Throwing Stones to Hide Your Hands': Mortal Persona of Michael Jackson." *Writing Eliza* (2014). Published electronically June 11. http:// elizabethamisu.com/post/88515649217/throwing-stones-to-hide-your-hands -the-mortal-persona.

Amisu, Elizabeth. "'Throwing Stones to Hide Your Hands': The Mortal Persona of Michael Jackson." *The Journal of Michael Jackson Academic Studies* 1, no. 1 (2014): 5. http://michaeljacksonstudies.org/throwing-stones-to-hide-your-hands -the-mortal-persona-of-michael-jackson/.

Amisu, Elizabeth. "'Throwing Stones to Hide Your Hands': The Mortal Persona of Michael Jackson." In *A Companion to Michael Jackson Academic Studies I,* edited by Elizabeth Amisu, 11: MJAS, 2015.

Amisu, Elizabeth. "'With All His Beauteous Race': High-Status Blacks in *The Masque of Blackness* and *The Merchant of Venice.*" Master of Arts, King's College London, 2015.

Amisu, Elizabeth. "Writing Eliza." http://elizabethamisu.com/.

Amisu, Elizabeth, Willa Stillwater, Lisha McDuff, and Karin Merx. "A Look at Neo-Noir in Michael Jackson's Short Films." (2016). Published electronically January 28. https://dancingwiththeelephant.wordpress.com/2016/01/28/a -look-at-neo-noir-in-michael-jacksons-short-films/.

Anderson, Lisa M. "When Race Matters: Reading Race in Richard III and Macbeth." In *Colorblind Shakespeare: New Perspectives on Race and Performance,* edited by Ayanna Thompson, Ania Loomba and Peter Erickson, 89–102. New York, NY: Routledge, 2006.

Andrea, Bernadette. "Black Skin, the Queen's Masques: Africanist Ambivalence and Feminine Author(Ity) in the Masques of Blackness and Beauty." *English Literary Renaissance* 29, no. 2 (1999): 246–81.

Andrea, Bernadette. "The Ghost of Leo Africanus from the English to the Irish Renaissance." In *Postcolonial Moves: Medieval through Modern,* edited by Patricia Clare Ingham and Michelle R. Warren, 195–215. New York, NY: Palgrave Macmillan, 2003.

Andrea, Bernadette. "'A Noble Troop of Strangers': Masques of Blackness in Shakespeare's Henry VIII." In *Shakespeare and Immigration,* edited by Ruben Espinosa and David Ruiter, 91–111. Farnham, England: Ashgate, 2014.

Andrea, Bernadette. "Review of "Things of Darkness: Economies of Race and Gender in Early Modern England"." *Early Modern Literary Studies* 2.2, no. 9 (1996): 1–5.

Appiah, Anthony. "Race." In *Critical Terms for Literary Study*, edited by Frank Lentricchia and Thomas McLaughlin, 274–87. Chicago: University of Chicago Press, 1995.

Arnold, Regina "Profit without Honor: Michael Jackson in and out of America, 1983–2009." *Journal of Popular Music Studies* 23, no. 1 (2011): 75–83.

Arthur, Karen. *The Jacksons: An American Dream*. Motown, 1992.

Ashcroft, B., G. Griffiths, and H. Tiffin. *The Post-Colonial Studies Reader*. Abingdon, Oxford, UK: Routledge, 2006.

Aspinall, Sarah. *Modern Masters: Andy Warhol*. BBC, 2011.

Auslander, Philip. *Performing Glam Rock: Gender and Theatricality in Popular Music*. Ann Arbor: The University of Michigan Press, 2006.

Awkward, Michael. "A Slave to the Rhythm: Essential(ist) Transmutations; or, the Curious Case of Michael Jackson." In *Negotiating Difference: Race, Gender and the Politics of Positionality*, 175–92. Chicago: University of Chicago Press, 1995.

"Balmain." *Vogue* (2008). Published electronically 28 September. http://www.vogue .co.uk/fashion/spring-summer-2009/ready-to-wear/balmain/full-length-photos.

Barbour, Richmond. "Britain and the Great Beyond: The Masque of Blackness at Whitehall." In *Playing the Globe: Genre and Geography in English Renaissance Drama*, edited by John Gillies and Virginia Mason Vaughan, 129–53. London, England: Associated University Press, 1998.

Barnard, Malcolm. *Fashion as Communication*. Abingdon, Oxford: Routledge, 2002.

Barnard, Malcolm, ed. *Fashion Theory: An Introduction*. Abingdon, Oxford: Routledge, 2014.

Barnes, Brooks. "A Star Haunted and Idolized, Michael Jackson Dies at 50." *The New York Times*, June 25, 2009.

Barrie, J. M. *Peter and Wendy*. Kindle, 1911, 2004.

Barrier, Michael. *The Animated Man: A Life of Walt Disney*. Los Angeles, CA: University of California Press, 2007.

Barroll, Leeds. "Inventing the Stuart Masque." In *The Politics of the Stuart Court Masque*, edited by David Bevington, Peter Holbrook and Leah S. Marcus, 121–43. Cambridge, England: Cambridge University Press, 1998.

Barroll, Leeds. "Theatre as Text: The Case of Queen Anna and the Jacobean Court Masque." In *The Elizabethan Theatre, XIV*, edited by A. L. Magnusson and C. E. McGee, 175–93. Toronto: Meany, 1996.

Barron, Steve. *Billie Jean*. 1983.

Bartels, Emily C. "Making More of the Moor: Aaron, Othello, and Renaissance Refashionings of Race." In *Understanding Racial Issues in Shakespeare's Othello: Selected Critical Essays*, edited by Solomon Iyasere, Marla Iyasere and Gloria Dumler, 239–71. Albany, NY: Whitston, 2008.

Bartels, Emily C. "Making More of the Moor: Aaron, Othello, and Renaissance Refashionings of Race." *Shakespeare Quarterly* 41, no. 4 (1990): 433–54.

Bartels, Emily C. "Othello and the Moor." In *Early Modern English Drama: A Critical Companion*, edited by Garrett A. Sullivan, Jr., Patrick Cheney and Andrew Hadfield, 140–51. New York, NY: Oxford University Press, 2006.

Bartels, Emily C. *Speaking of the Moor: From Alcazar to Othello*. Philadelphia: University of Pennsylvania Press, 2008.

Bartels, Emily C. "Too Many Blackamoors: Deportation, Discrimination, and Elizabeth I." *SEL: Studies in English Literature, 1500–1900* 46, no. 2 (2006): 305–22.

Barthelemy, Anthony Gerard. *Black Face, Maligned Race: The Representation of Blacks in English Drama from Shakespeare to Southerne*. Baton Rouge: Louisiana State University Press, 1987.

Barthelemy, Anthony Gerard. *Critical Essays on Shakespeare's Othello*. Boston: G.K. Hall, 1994.

Barthes, Roland. *The Fashion System*. London: Random House, 2010.

Barthes, Roland. "From Work to Text." In *Image, Music, Text*, 155–64. London: Fontana Press, 1977.

Barthes, Roland. *The Language of Fashion*. London: Bloomsbury Academic, 2013.

Barthes, Roland. "The Rhetoric of the Image." In *The Visual Culture Reader*, edited by Nicholas Mirzoeff, 129–31. London: Routledge, 1998.

Barthes, Roland. "Theory of the Text." In *Untying the Text: A Post-Structuralist Reader*, edited by Robert Young. London: Routledge, 1981.

Bassil, Veronica. *Michael Jackson's Love for Planet Earth*. Kindle, 2013. https://www.amazon.com/That-Wonder-My-Youth-Childhood-ebook/dp/B00MR5EN3Q

Bassil, Veronica. *That Wonder in My Youth: Michael Jackson and Childhood*. Kindle, 2013.

Bassil, Veronica. *Thinking Twice About Billie Jean*. Kindle, 2014.

Bate, Jonathan. "Caliban and Ariel Write Back." *Shakespeare Survey: An Annual Survey of Shakespeare Studies and Production* 48 (1995): 155–62.

Battersea Arts Centre. "Songs of Lear at Battersea Arts Centre." (2015). Published electronically 20 February. https://www.bac.org.uk/content/35391/about_us/past_shows_and_events/songs_of_lear.

Baudrillard, Jean. "Simulacra and Simulations." In *The Visual Culture Reader*, edited by Nicholas Mirzoeff, 145–46. London: Routledge, 1998.

Bayer, Konrad Sidney. "The Semiosis of Soul: Michael Jackson's Use of Popular Music Conventions." *The Journal of Pan African Studies* 3, no. 7 (2010): 45–63.

BBC. "Henry VIII." *BBC History* (2014). http://www.bbc.co.uk/history/people/henry_viii.

Beard, Adrian, and Alan Kent. *AQA English Literature B AS*. 2nd ed. Cheltenham: Nelson Thornes, 2012.

Beemer, Suzy. "Masks of Blackness, Masks of Whiteness: Coloring the (Sexual) Subject in Jonson, Cary, and Fletcher." *Thamyris: Mythmaking from Past to Present* 4, no. 2 (1997): 223–47.

Bennett, Andrew, and Nicholas Royle. *An Introduction to Literature, Criticism and Theory*. 4th ed. Harlow: Longman, 2009.

Benshoff, H., and S. Griffin. *America on Film: Representing Race, Class, Gender, and Sexuality at the Movies*. United Kingdom: Blackwell, 2004.

Berger, John. *Ways of Seeing*. London, England: Penguin Books, 1972.

Berreby, David. "Jackson Wasn't Normal. So What?" *Huffington Post* (2009). Published electronically 9 August 2009. http://www.huffingtonpost.com/david-berreby/jackson-wasnt-normal-so-w_b_228400.html.

Berry, Venise T. "Crossing Over: Musical Perceptions within Black Adolescent Culture." *Journal of Popular Music Studies* 5, no. 1 (1993): 26–38.

"Best Selling Album." *Guinness World Records* (2012). Published electronically 1 January. http://www.guinnessworldrecords.com/world-records/70133-best-selling-album.

Bevington, David, and Peter Holbrook. *The Politics of the Stuart Court Masque*. Cambridge, England: Cambridge University Press, 1998.

Bevington, David, and William Shakespeare. *Troilus and Cressida*. London, UK: Arden, 1998.

Bhabha, Homi K. *Nation and Narration*. London: Routledge, 1990.

Bhabha, Homi K. "Of Mimicry and Man: The Ambivalence of Colonial Discourse." In *Modern Literary Theory: A Reader*, edited by Patricia Waugh and Philip Rice. London: Edward Arnold, 1996.

Bigsby, C. W. E. *The Cambridge Companion to Arthur Miller*. 2nd ed. Cambridge: Cambridge University Press, 2010.

Billone, Amy C. "Sentenced to Neverland: Michael Jackson, Peter Pan, and Queer Futurity." In *Michael Jackson: Grasping the Spectacle*, edited by Christopher R. Smit, 39–50. Farnham, UK: Ashgate, 2012.

Bindman, David, and Henry Louis Gates. *The Image of the Black in Western Art*. 5 vols. Cambridge, Mass.: Belknap Press, 2010.

Blaine, Diana York. "'We Are Going to See the King': Christianity and Celebrity at Michael Jackson's Memorial." In *Michael Jackson: Grasping the Spectacle*, edited by Christopher R. Smit, 191–206. Farnham, UK: Ashgate, 2012.

Blashfield, Jim. *Badder*. 1988.

Blashfield, Jim. *Leave Me Alone*. 1989.

Block, Susan. "Sex, Death and Michael Jackson." *Counterpunch* (2009). Published electronically 3 August 2009. http://www.counterpunch.org/2009/08/03/sex-death-and-michael-jackson/.

Bloemen, Brigitte. *It's All About L.O.V.E.: Michael Jackson Stories You Were Never Meant to Read*. Kindle, 2013.

Bogle, Donald. *Toms, Coons, Mulattoes, Mammies and Bucks: An Interpretive History of Blacks in American Films*. London, New York: Continuum Publishing Group, 2001.

Boose, Lynda E. "'The Getting of a Lawful Race': Racial Discourse in Early Modern England and the Unrepresentable Black Woman." In *Women, "Race," and Writing in the Early Modern Period*, edited by Margo Hendricks and Patricia Parker, 35–54. London: Routledge, 1994.

Bordwell, D., and K. Thompson. *Film Art: An Introduction*. New York: McGraw-Hill, 1997.

Boteach, Shmuley. *Honoring the Child Spirit*. New York: Vanguard Press, 2011.

Boteach, Shmuley. *The Michael Jackson Tapes: A Tragic Icon Reveals His Soul in Intimate Conversation*. New York: Vanguard Press, 2009.

Bowen Jones, Abeodu, Donald Rahl Petterson, and Svend E. Holsoe. "Liberia." *Britannica.com* (2014). http://www.britannica.com/place/Liberia.

Bowers, Toni. "Dancing with Michael Jackson." *The Los Angeles Review of Books* (2015). Published electronically May 14, 2015. https://lareviewofbooks.org /essay/dancing-with-michael-jackson.

Bowers, Toni. "Dancing with Michael Jackson." *The Journal of Michael Jackson Academic Studies* 1, no. 4 (2015): 3.

Bowers, Toni. "Dancing with Michael Jackson." In *A Companion to Michael Jackson Academic Studies I*, edited by Elizabeth Amisu, 6: MJAS, 2015.

Bowie, David. *Blackstar*. Columbia, 2016.

Brackett, David. "Black or White? Michael Jackson and the Idea of Crossover." *Popular Music and Society* 35, no. 2 (2012): 169–85.

Bradshaw, John. *Home Coming: Reclaiming and Championing Your Inner Child*. London: Piatkus, 2013.

Brady, Tahkiya. "An Interview with Tahkiya Brady, A.K.A Red." By Elizabeth Amisu (2016).

Brady, Tahkiya. "Moonwalkers: Then, Now, and Forever . . .", 1:28:19: YouTube, 2014.

Brandt, Nicholas. *Childhood*. 1995.

Brandt, Nicholas. *Cry*. 2001.

Brandt, Nicholas. *Earth Song*. 1995.

Brandt, Nicholas. *One More Chance*. 2003.

Brandt, Nicholas. *Stranger in Moscow*. 1996.

Brannigan, John. *New Historicism and Cultural Materialism*. Basingstoke: Macmillan, 1998.

Braude, Benjamin. "The Sons of Noah and the Construction of Ethnic and Geographical Identities in the Medieval and Early Modern Periods." *William and Mary Quarterly: A Magazine of Early American History and Culture* 54, no. 1 (1997): 103–42.

Braudy, L., and M. Cohen, eds. *Film Theory and Criticism, Introductory Readings*. 5th ed. Oxford: Oxford University Press, 1999.

Breaux, Richard M. "'I'm a Cartoon!' The Jackson 5ive Cartoon as Comodified Civil Rights & Black Power Ideologies, 1971–1973." *The Journal of Pan African Studies* 3, no. 7 (2010): 79–99.

Bristol, Michael D. "Shakespeare: The Myth." Chap. 29 In *A Companion to Shakespeare*, edited by David Scott Kastan, 489–502. Oxford: Blackwell Publishers, 1999.

Britton, Dennis Austin. *Consuming Difference: Race, Romance and Religion in Early Modern England*. Vol. 68. Madison: University of Wisconsin, 2008.

Broackes, Victoria, and Geoff Marsh. *David Bowie Is the Subject*. London: V&A Publishing, 2013.

Broertjes, Andrew. " 'He's Sending His People Messages out of His Pain': Michael Jackson and the Black Community." *Popular Music and Society* 36, no. 5 (2013): 677–98.

Burley, Anne. "Courtly Personages: The Lady Masquers in Ben Jonson's Masque of Blackness." *Shakespeare and Renaissance Association of West Virginia—Selected Papers* 10 (1985): 49–61.

Burley, Anne. "The Influence of Ben Jonson's First Two Masques on the Dramatic Environment of Volpone." *Shakespeare and Renaissance Association of West Virginia—Selected Papers* 9 (1984): 21–33.

Burnett, Robert and Bert Deivert. "Black or White: Michael Jackson's Video as a Mirror of Popular Culture." *Popular Music and Society* 19, no. 3 (1995).

Burton, Ben, and Elizabeth Scott-Baumann. *The Work of Form: Poetics and Materiality in Early Modern Culture*. 1st ed. Oxford: Oxford University Press, 2014.

Burton, Tim. *Edward Scissorhands*. Twentieth Century Fox, 1990.

Bush, Michael. "About the Book." (2014). http://dressingmichaeljackson.com /about-the-book.html.

Bush, Michael. "Dressing Michael Jackson." http://dressingmichaeljackson.com/.

Bush, Michael. *The King of Style: Dressing Michael Jackson*. San Rafael, CA: Insight Editions, 2012.

Butler, Martin. "The Court Masque." *The Cambridge Edition of the Works of Ben Jonson Online* (2015). http://universitypublishingonline.org/cambridge/ben jonson/k/essays/court_msq_essay/.

Butler, Martin. "*The Masque of Blackness* and Stuart Court Culture." In *Early Modern English Drama: A Critical Companion*, edited by Garrett A. Sullivan, Jr., Patrick Cheney and Andrew Hadfield, 152–63. New York, NY: Oxford University Press, 2006.

Cadman, Chris and Craig Halstead. *Michael Jackson: For the Record*. 2nd ed.: Authors Online, 2009.

Callaghan, Dympna. " 'Othello Was a White Man': Properties of Race on Shakespeare's Stage." In *Alternative Shakespeares II*, edited by Terence Hawkes and John Drakakis, 192–215. London, England: Routledge, 1996.

Callaghan, Dympna. *Shakespeare without Women: Representing Gender and Race on the Renaissance Stage*. Accents on Shakespeare. London: Routledge, 1999.

Campbell, Lisa D. *Michael Jackson: The King of Pop's Darkest Hour*. Boston: Branden, 1994.

Campbell, Mel. "Saying the Unsayable: The Non-Verbal Vocalizations of Michael Jackson." *The Enthusiast* (2009). Published electronically 2 July 2009.

Campos, Edmund Valentine. "West of Eden: American Gold, Spanish Greed, and the Discourses of English Imperialism." In *Rereading the Black Legend: The Discourses of Religious and Racial Difference in the Renaissance Empires*, edited by Margaret Rich Greer, Walter Mignolo and Maureen Quilligan, 247–69. Chicago: University of Chicago Press, 2007.

Carleton, Dudley. "Letter to Sir Ralph Winwood." In *Winwood Memorials, II, P. 44, in Ben Jonson*, edited by C. H. Herford, P. Simpson and E. Simpson, 448. Oxford: Clarendon Press, 1941.

Carleton, Dudley. "London, January 7, 1605." In *Dudley Carleton to John Chamberlain 1603–1624. Jacobean Letters*, edited by Maurice Lee, 67–68. New Brunswick, NJ: Rutgers University Press, 1972.

Carlin, Marcello. "'. . . and Though You Fight to Stay Alive, Your Body Starts to Shiver . . .'." In *The Resistible Demise of Michael Jackson*, edited by Mark Fisher, 63–68. Winchester, UK: Zero Books, 2009.

Carlson, Jan. "Case Study: The Caricature." *Words and Violence*. 3rd ed. (2013). http://voiceseducation.org/content/case-study-caricature.

Carmody, Robin. "In Place of Strife: Michael Jackson and the British Experience of Pop." In *The Resistible Demise of Michael Jackson*, edited by Mark Fisher, 156–63. Winchester, UK: Zero Books, 2009.

Carr, Firpo W. "Michael Jackson Motivated." *The Journal of Pan African Studies* 3, no. 7 (2010): 42–44.

Carroll, Lewis. *Alice's Adventures in Wonderland*. Kindle, 1865, 2002.

Caruthers, Jakeya, and Alisa Bierria. "Stay with Me: Reflections on Michael Jackson, Sound, Sex, and (Racial) Solidarity." *Journal of Popular Music Studies* 23, no. 1 (2011): 125–32.

Cascio, Frank. *My Friend Michael: An Ordinary Friendship with an Extraordinary Man*. New York: William Morrow, 2011.

Cavendish, Margaret. *The Worlds Olio Written by the Right Honorable, the Lady Margaret Newcastle*. London: EEBO Editions, 1655, 2011.

Chaplin, Charles, and David Robinson. *Charles Chaplin: My Autobiography*. London: Penguin Modern Classics, 2003.

Chilvers, Colin. *Smooth Criminal*. 1988.

Chilvers, Colin, and Jerry Kramer. *Come Together*. 1988.

Chilvers, Colin, Jerry Kramer, and Jim Blashfield. *Moonwalker*. MJJ Productions, 1988.

Chin, Elizabeth. "Michael Jackson's Panther Dance: Double Consciousness and the Uncanny Business of Performing While Black." *Journal of Popular Music Studies* 23, no. 1 (2011): 58–74.

Choi, Young-Joo. "Reading Shakespeare's Othello within the Discourse of Early Modern Age: Centering on the Issues, 'Class, Race and Sexuality'." *Journal of English Language and Literature* 45, no. 1 (1999): 75–96.

Chomsky, Noam & Edward S. Herman. *Manufacturing Consent*. New York: Pantheon Books, 1988.

Chopra, Deepak. "A Tribute to My Friend Michael." *Huffington Post* (2009). Published electronically 26 July. http://www.huffingtonpost.com/deepak-chopra/a-tribute-to-my-friend-mi_b_221268.html.

Clark, Sandra, Pamela Mason, and William Shakespeare. *Macbeth*. London, UK: Arden, 2015.

Clay, Andreana. "Working Day and Night: Black Masculinity and the King of Pop." *Journal of Popular Music Studies* 23, no. 1 (2011): 3–18.

Clover, Joshua. "Michael Jackson at the Restaurant Vingtième Siècle." In *The Resistible Demise of Michael Jackson*, edited by Mark Fisher, 81–88. Winchester, UK: Zero Books, 2009.

Coates, Ta-Nehisi. "Black Pathology and the Closing of the Progressive Mind." *The Atlantic* (2014). Published electronically March 21, 2014.

Coates, Ta-Nehisi. "Other People's Pathologies." *The Atlantic* (2014). Published electronically March 30, 2014.

Cohen, Karl F. *Forbidden Animation: Censored Cartoons and Blacklisted Animators in America.* Jefferson, NC, London: McFarland & Company, 1997.

Colby, Tanner. "The Radical Notion of Michael Jackson's Humanity." *Slate.com* (2014). Published electronically June 24. http://www.slate.com/articles/arts /culturebox/2014/06/michael_jackson_death_anniversary_we_recall_thriller _and_bad_but_what_about.html.

Coleridge, Samuel Taylor and William Wordsworth. "The Rime of the Ancyent Marinere." In *Lyrical Ballads*. London: Penguin Classics, 2006.

Columbus, Chris. *Harry Potter and the Philosopher's Stone.* Warner Bros, 2001.

Cooper, B. Lee, and William L. Schurk. "Diana Ross Presents the Jackson 5." *Popular Music and Society* 35, no. 2 (2012): 317–19.

Cooper, Barry Michael. "Michael Jackson Agonistes: Act II of an American Pop'era'." *Huffington Post* (2009). Published electronically July 8. http://www.huffington post.com/barry-michael-cooper/michael-jackson-agonistes_b_227444.html.

Cooper, Barry Michael. "Michael Jackson Agonistes: An American Pop'era in Three Acts." *Huffington Post* (2009). Published electronically July 6. http://www .huffingtonpost.com/barry-michael-cooper/michael-jackson-agonistes_b _221156.html.

Cooper, Barry Michael. "Michael Jackson Agonistes: The Final Act of an America Pop'era'." *Hookedontheamericandream.blogspot.co.uk* (2009). Published electronically September 11. http://hookedontheamericandream.blogspot.co.uk /2009/09/michael-jackson-agonistes-final-act-of.html.

Coppola, Francis Ford. *Captain EO.* Disney, 1986.

Covach, John. "Michael Jackson: Five Years Gone and It's the Music That Endures." *Huffington Post* (2014). Published electronically June 24. http://www.huff ingtonpost.com/john-covach/michael-jackson-five-year_b_5509147.html?utm _hp_ref=tw.

Covey, William. "Review." *Film Quarterly* 52, no. 3 (1999): 64.

Covey, William B. "Review." *Journal of Film and Video* 50, no. 1 (1998): 63–66.

Cowhig, Ruth. "Blacks in Renaissance Drama and the Role of Shakespeare's Othello." In *The Black Presence in English Literature*, edited by David Dabydeen, 1–25. Manchester: Manchester University Press, 1985.

Craig, W. J. *The Complete Works of William Shakespeare.* London: Henry Pordes, 1987.

Crane, Diana. *Fashion and Its Social Agendas: Class, Gender, and Identity in Clothing.* Chicago: University of Chicago Press, 2000.

Crane, R. S. "History Versus Criticism in the Study of Literature." In *The Idea of the Humanities, and Other Essays Critical and Historical*, 3–24, 1967.

Craven, Wes. *Nightmare on Elm Street.* New Line Cinema, 1984.

Cronin, Kieran. "Morality and Self-Interest." *The Furrow* 60, no. 12 (2009): 669–76.

Crunelle-Vanrigh, Anny. "'Black Vesper's Pageants': Les Masques De Cléopâtre." *Bulletin de la Société d'Etudes Anglo-Américaines des XVIIe et XVIIIe Siècles* 53 (2001): 7–21.

Culler, J. *On Deconstruction: Theory and Criticism after Structuralism.* Ithaca, NY: Cornell University Press, 2014.

Cunningham, Phillip Lamarr. "'There's Nothing Really New under the Sun': The Fallacy of the Neo-Soul Genre." *Journal of Popular Music Studies* 22, no. 3 (2010): 240–58.

Curry, Maya. "But Did We Have a Good Time? An Examination of the Media Massacre of Michael Jackson." *Exemplary Essay Awards: Outstanding Essays from the First-Year Writing Program* (2010).

Cutrofello, A. "Foucault on Tragedy." *Philosophy & Social Criticism* 31, no. 5–6 (2005): 573–84.

Dabydeen, David, ed. *The Black Presence in English Literature.* Manchester: Manchester University Press, 1985.

Dabydeen, David. "The Black Presence in English Literature: Report on Conference Held in Wolverhampton, December 1982." Paper presented at the Wolverhampton Council for Community Relations in conjunction with The Commission for Racial Equality and Wolverhampton Education Authority, Wolverhampton, 1983.

Dabydeen, David. *Hogarth's Blacks: Images of Blacks in Eighteenth Century English Art.* Kingston-upon-Thames: Dangaroo, 1985.

Daileader, Celia R. "Casting Black Actors: Beyond Othellophilia." In *Shakespeare and Race*, edited by Catherine M. S. Alexander and Stanley Wells, 177–202. Cambridge, England: Cambridge University Press, 2000.

Dalton, Karen C. C. "Art for the Sake of Dynasty: The Black Emperor in the Drake Jewel and Elizabethan Imperial Imagery." In *Early Modern Visual Culture: Representation, Race, and Empire in Renaissance England*, edited by Peter Erickson and Clark Hulse, 178–214. Philadelphia: University of Pennsylvania Press, 2000.

Dalton, Karen C. C. *Department of Afro-American Studies Harvard University: Thirtieth Anniversary Celebration.* Cambridge, Mass.: Department of Afro-American Studies, 2000.

D'Amico, Jack. *The Moor in English Renaissance Drama.* Tampa, FL: University of South Florida, 1991.

Danielsen, Anne. "The Sound of Crossover: Micro-Rhythm and Sonic Pleasure in Michael Jackson's 'Don't Stop 'Til You Get Enough'." *Popular Music and Society* 35, no. 2 (2012): 151–68.

Dark, David. "The Unbearable Lightness of Being Michael: The Religious Witness of Michael Jackson." In *Michael Jackson: Grasping the Spectacle*, edited by Christopher R. Smit, 181–90. Farnham, UK: Ashgate, 2012.

DaSilva, Janis B. *Thrilling Moments: "#1 Authorized by Michael Jackson—My Years with Michael."* Marston, UK and New York: CreateSpace, 2012.

Davies, Sam. "Glove, Socks, Zombies, Puppets: The Unheimlich Maneuvers and Undead Metonyms of Michael Jackson." In *The Resistible Demise of Michael Jackson*, edited by Mark Fisher, 226–32. Winchester, UK: Zero Books, 2009.

Davis, Fred. *Fashion, Culture, and Identity*. Chicago: University of Chicago Press, 1994.

Davis, Martha, Elizabeth Eshelman, and Matthew McKay. *The Relaxation and Stress Reduction Workbook*. Oakland, CA: New Harbinger, 2008.

Dayal, Geeta. "The Maharaja of Pop: Michael Jackson and Bollywood." In *The Resistible Demise of Michael Jackson*, edited by Mark Fisher, 150–55. Winchester, UK: Zero Books, 2009.

Delmont, Matthew. "Michael Jackson & Television before Thriller." *The Journal of Pan African Studies* 3, no. 7 (2010): 64–78.

Delmont, Matthew. "Michael Jackson & Television before Thriller." In *A Companion to Michael Jackson Academic Studies I*, edited by Elizabeth Amisu, 2: MJAS, 2015.

Delmont, Matt, and Murray Forman. "Sonic Visions: Popular Music on Television." *Journal of Popular Music Studies* 25, no. 3 (2013): 293–300.

Denmead, Louise. "The Discovery of Blackness in the Early-Modern Bed-Trick." In *The Invention of Discovery, 1500–1700*, edited by James Dougal Fleming. *Literary and Scientific Cultures of Early Modernity* (Lscem), 153–66. Surrey, England: Farnham, UK: Ashgate, 2011.

Deroux, Margaux. "The Blackness Within: Early Modern Color-Concept, Physiology and Aaron the Moor in Shakespeare's Titus Andronicus." *Mediterranean Studies* 19 (2010): 86–101.

Deutsch, James. "Review." *American Studies International* 36, no. 1 (1998): 99–100.

DiCicco, Bill. *Gone Too Soon*. 1993.

Dictionary, Oxford English. *"Plot, N."* [In English]. Oxford University Press.

Dollimore, Jonathan, and Alan Sinfield. *Political Shakespeare: New Essays in Cultural Materialism*. Manchester: Manchester University Press, 1985.

Donner, Richard. *Superman*. Dovemead/Film Export A.G./International Film Productions, 1978.

Dubois, W.E.B. "Double Consciousness." In *The Visual Culture Reader*, edited by Nicholas Mirzoeff, 124–25. London: Routledge, 1998.

Duff, E. Gordon. *A Century of the English Book Trade: Short Notices of All Printers, Stationers, Book-Binders, and Others Connected with It from the Issue of the First Dated Book in 1457 to the Incorporation of the Company of Stationers in 1557*. London: Printed for the Bibliographical society by Blades, East & Blades, 1905.

Dunton-Downer, Leslie, and Alan Riding. *Essential Shakespeare Handbook*. London: Dorling Kindersley, 2004.

Dusinberre, Juliet, and William Shakespeare. *As You Like It*. London, UK: Arden, 2006.

Dyson, Michael Eric. "Michael Jackson's Postmodern Spirituality." In *Reflecting Black: African-American Cultural Criticism*, 35–63. Minneapolis: University of Minnesota Press, 1993.

Earle, T. F., and K. J. P. Lowe. *Black Africans in Renaissance Europe*. Cambridge: Cambridge University Press, 2005.

Easthope, A., and K. McGowan, eds. *A Critical and Cultural Theory Reader*. Toronto: University of Toronto Press, 2004.

Ebmeier, Jochen. "Das Phänomen Michael Jackson." *The Journal of Michael Jackson Academic Studies* 1, no. 2 (2014): 2.

Ebmeier, Jochen. *Das Phänomen Michael Jackson*. Hamburg: Rasch und Rohring Verlag, 1997.

Editors of Ebony. *Ebony Special Tribute: Michael Jackson in His Own Words*. Chicago: Johnson, 2009.

Editors of Rolling Stone. *Michael*. New York: It Books, 2009.

Editors of Rolling Stone. *Michael Jackson*. Werner Media Specials, 2014.

Edwards, Paul, and James Walvin. *Black Personalities in the Era of the Slave Trade*. London: Macmillan, 1983.

Elam, Keir, and William Shakespeare. *Twelfth Night*. London, UK: Arden, 2008.

Emerson, Derek. "Remember: Emerson on the King of Pop." *Finditinfondren.com* (2014). Published electronically 25 June. http://www.finditinfondren.com/2014/06/25/remember-emerson-recalls-mj-connection/.

Encyclopædia Britannica Online. "Niger River." *Encyclopædia Britannica* (2015). http://www.britannica.com/place/Niger-River.

Epstein, D. "The Face of Ruin: Evidentiary Spectacle and the Trial of Michael Jackson." In *Social Semiotics*, 441–58, 2007.

Erickson, Peter. "Epilogue." In *Early Modern Visual Culture: Representation, Race, and Empire in Renaissance England*, edited by Clark Hulse and Peter Erickson, 1–14. Philadelphia: University of Pennsylvania Press, 2000.

Erickson, Peter. "Invisibility Speaks: Servants and Portraits in Early Modern Visual Culture." *Journal for Early Modern Cultural Studies* 9, no. 1 (2009): 23–61.

Erickson, Peter. "Race Words in 'Othello'." In *Shakespeare and Immigration*, edited by Ruben Espinosa and David Ruiter, 159–76. Farnham, England: Ashgate, 2014.

Erickson, Peter. "Representations of Blacks and Blackness in the Renaissance." *Criticism* 35, no. 4 (1993): 499–527.

Espinosa, Ruben, and David Ruiter. "Introduction." In *Shakespeare and Immigration*, edited by Ruben Espinosa and David Ruiter, 1–12. Farnham, England: Ashgate, 2014.

Ewing, Tom. "After Pop." In *The Resistible Demise of Michael Jackson*, edited by Mark Fisher, 219–25. Winchester, UK: Zero Books, 2009.

Fanon, Frantz. "The Fact of Blackness." In *The Visual Culture Reader*, edited by Nicholas Mirzoeff, 129–31. London: Routledge, 1998.

Fanon, Frantz, Constance Farrington, and Jean Paul Sartre. *The Wretched of the Earth* [in Translation of: Les damnés de la terre.]. London: Penguin, 1967.

Farmer, Alan B., and Zachary Lesser, eds. "DEEP: Database of Early English Playbooks." Philadelphia: University of Pennsylvania (2007). http://deep.sas.upenn.edu.

Fast, Susan. *Dangerous*. London: Bloomsbury, 2014.

Fast, Susan. "Difference That Exceeded Understanding: Remembering Michael Jackson (1958–2009)." *Popular Music and Society* 33, no. 2 (2010): 259–66.

Fast, Susan. "Dr. Susan Fast's 'Michael Jackson's Dangerous.' " By MJ Truth Now (24 October 2014).

Fast, Susan. "Michael Jackson's Queer Musical Belongings." *Popular Music & Society* 49, no. 2 (2012): 281–300.

Fast, Susan. "Michael Jackson's 'Dangerous' (33 1/3 Excerpt)." *Genius* (2014). http://genius.com/Susan-fast-michael-jacksons-dangerous-33-1-3-excerpt-annotated.

Fast, Susan. "MJ in Memoriam: Five Years." *High Frequencies* (2014). Published electronically June 25. http://susanfast.wordpress.com/2014/06/25/mj-in-memoriam-five-years/comment-page-1.

Fast, Susan. "Noise." *Lit.Genius.com* (2014). http://lit.genius.com/Susan-fast-noise-annotated.

Fast, Susan. "Susan Fast: Michael Jacksons Dangerous Album—Kapitel 'Soul'-'Seele'." [In German]. *The Journal of Michael Jackson Academic Studies* 1, no. 4 (2015): 1.

Fast, Susan. "Telling Stories About Michael Jackson." In *A Companion to Michael Jackson Academic Studies I,* edited by Elizabeth Amisu, 1: MJAS, 2014.

Fast, Susan & Stan Hawkins (eds.). "Michael Jackson: Musical Subjectivities." *Popular Music & Society—Special Issue* Vol. 35, no. 2 (2012).

Faust, Jeremy Samuel. " 'When You Have to Say 'I Do' ': Orientalism in Michael Jackson's 'Liberian Girl'." *Popular Music and Society* 35, no. 2 (2012): 223–40.

Faust, Jeremy Samuel. " 'When You Have to Say 'I Do' ': Orientalism in Michael Jackson's 'Liberian Girl'." In *A Companion to Michael Jackson Academic Studies I,* edited by Elizabeth Amisu, 4: MJAS, 2015.

Ferguson, George. *Signs & Symbols in Christian Art.* London, Oxford, New York: Oxford University Press, 1976.

Ferguson, Margaret. "Transmuting Othello: Aphra Behn's Oroonoko." In *Cross-Cultural Performances: Differences in Women's Re-Visions of Shakespeare*, edited by Marianne Novy and Peter Erickson, 15–49. Urbana: University of Illinois Press, 1993.

Fincher, David. *Who Is It.* 1993.

Fischer, Dawn-Elissa. "Wannabe Startin' Somethin': Michael Jackson's Critical Race Representation." *Journal of Popular Music Studies* 23, no. 1 (2011): 96–107.

Fischer, Mary A. "Was Michael Jackson Framed?" *GQ*, 1994.

Fischer, Mary A. *Was Michael Jackson Framed? The Untold Story That Brought Down a Superstar.* Marston, UK and New York: CreateSpace, 2012.

Fisher, Mark. " 'And When the Groove Is Dead and Gone': The End of Jacksonism." In *The Resistible Demise of Michael Jackson*, edited by Mark Fisher, 9–17. Winchester, UK: Zero Books, 2009.

Fisher, Mark. "Introduction: MJ, the Symptom." In *The Resistible Demise of Michael Jackson*, edited by Mark Fisher, 7–8. Winchester, UK: Zero Books, 2009.

Fitzgerald, F. Scott. *The F. Scott Fitzgerald Collection: 2 Novels and 20 Short Stories.* Waxkeep, 2013. https://www.amazon.co.uk/F-Scott-Fitzgerald-Collection-Stories-ebook/dp/B00EQ95JTI

Fitzgerald, F. Scott, and Tony Tanner. *The Great Gatsby*. London: Penguin, 2000.

Fleming, Victor. *The Wizard of Oz*. Metro-Goldwyn-Meyer, 1939.

Florio, John. *Queen Anna's New World of Words*. London, 1611.

Floyd-Wilson, Mary. *English Ethnicity and Race in Early Modern Drama*. Cambridge, England: Cambridge University Press, 2003.

Floyd-Wilson, Mary. "Temperature, Temperance, and Racial Difference in Ben Jonson's the Masque of Blackness." *English Literary Renaissance* 28, no. 2 (1998): 183–209.

Forman, Milos. *Amadeus*. Warner Home Video, 1984.

Foucault, Michel. *The Order of Things—an Archaeology of the Human Sciences*. 1994.

Foucault, Michel. *"Society Must Be Defended." Lectures at the Collège De France 1975–76*. Translated by David Macey. Edited by Arnold L. Davidson. New York: Picador, 2003.

Foucault, Michel. "The Subject and Power." In *Michel Foucault: Beyond Structuralism and Hermeneutics*, edited by Hubert L. Dreyfus and Paul Rabinow. Chicago: Chicago University Press, 1982.

Foucault, Michel. "What Is an Author?" Translated by Robert Hurley. In *Michel Foucault Aesthetics, Method, and Epistemology: Essential Works of Michel Foucault 1954–1984*, edited by James D. Faubion., 202–22. London: Penguin Books, 1998.

Francis, D. *Michael Jackson: Innocent—February 28, 2005: Book 1*. Kindle, 2013.

Frith, Simon, Andrew Goodwin, and Lawrence Grossberg. *Sound and Vision: The Music Video Reader*. London: Routledge, 1993. http://kcl.eblib.com/patron/FullRecord.aspx?p=254119.

Frye, Susan. "Staging Women's Relations to Textiles in Shakespeare's Othello and Cymbeline." In *Early Modern Visual Culture: Representation, Race, and Empire in Renaissance England*, edited by Peter Erickson and Clark Hulse, 215–50. Philadelphia: University of Pennsylvania Press, 2000.

Fryer, Peter. *Staying Power: The History of Black People in Britain*. London: Pluto, 1984.

Fulcher, Jane F. *The Oxford Handbook of the New Cultural History of Music*. Oxford: Oxford University Press, 2011.

Garber, Marjorie. "Androgyny and Its Discontents." In *Bisexuality and the Eroticism of Everyday Life* 207–36. New York: Routledge, 2000.

Gardiner, John Eliot. *Music in the Castle of Heaven: A Portrait of Johann Sebastian Bach*. London: Allen Lane, 2013.

Garner, Stanton. "Rosemarine: Melville's 'Pebbles' and Ben Jonson's 'Masque of Blackness'." *Melville Society Extracts* 41 (1980): 13–14.

Gaskell, Philip. *A New Introduction to Bibliography*. Winchester: Oak Knoll Press, 1995.

Gates, Henry Louis. *Black Literature and Literary Theory*. London: Methuen, 1984.

Gates, Henry Louis. *"Race," Writing, and Difference*. Chicago: University of Chicago Press, 1986.

Gates, Henry Louis. *The Signifying Monkey: A Theory of African-American Literary Criticism*. Oxford: Oxford University Press, 1988.

Gates, Henry Louis. "Writing, 'Race' and the Difference It Makes." In *Loose Canons: Notes on the Culture Wars*, 43–69. New York: Oxford University Press, 1992.

Gauntlett, David. *Media, Gender and Identity: An Introduction*. London: Routledge, 2002.

George, Nelson. *The Michael Jackson Story*. Dell, 1993.

George, Nelson. *Thriller: The Musical Life of Michael Jackson*. Da Capo Press, 2010.

Gershwin, George. *Porgy and Bess*. Decca, 1993.

Gibney, Alex. Jam*es Brown: Mr Dynamite*. BBC2, 2015.

Gidal, Peter. *Structural Film Anthology*. 1978.

Gilbert, Jeremy. *Anticapitalism and Culture: Radical Theory and Popular Politics*. Oxford: Berg, 2008.

Gilbert, Jeremy. "The Real Abstraction of Michael Jackson." In *The Resistible Demise of Michael Jackson*, edited by Mark Fisher, 137–49. Winchester, UK: Zero Books, 2009.

Gilbert, Jeremy. "The Real Abstraction of Michael Jackson." In *A Companion to Michael Jackson Academic Studies I*, edited by Elizabeth Amisu, 12: MJAS, 2015.

Gilbert, Jeremy, and Ewan Pearson. *Discographies: Dance Music, Culture, and the Politics of Sound*. London: Routledge, 1999.

Gilbert-Rolfe, Jeremy. "Blackness as a Signifier." *Critical Inquiry* 24, no. 1 (1997): 159–75.

Gilroy, Paul. "Art of Darkness: Black Art and the Problem of Belonging to England." *Third Text* 4, no. 10 (1990/03/01 1990): 45–52.

Giraldi, Bob. *Beat It*. 1983.

Giraldi, Bob. *Say Say Say*. 1983.

Godfrey, Alex. "Back Story: Moonwalker." *Empire*, no. 261 (2011): 118–24.

Goldberg, Jonathan. *Queering the Renaissance*. Durham, NC: Duke University Press, 1994.

Gomez-Barris, M., and H. Gray. "Michael Jackson, Television, and Post-Op Disasters." *Television & New Media* 7, no. 1 (2006): 40–51.

Gondwe, Gregory. "Going Beyond the Eye: The Visual and Oral Aesthetics of Michael Jackson from an African Perspective." *Visual Communication Quarterly* 20, no. 4 (2013): 239–45.

Gonzalez, Ana Marta, ed. *Fashion and Identity: Identities through Fashion*. London: Berg, 2012.

Goodman, Melinda. "Eulogy for Michael Jackson." *Bridges* 15, no. 2 (2010): 37–38.

Gordon, D. J., and Stephen Orgel. *The Renaissance Imagination*. Berkeley, CA: University of California Press, 1980.

Gowers, Bruce. *Rock with You*. 1980.

Gowers, Bruce. *She's out of My Life*. 1980.

Grant, Adrian. *Michael Jackson: A Visual Documentary. The Official Tribute Edition*. London: Omnibus, 2009.

Gray, Todd. *Michael Jackson: Before He Was King*. San Francisco: Chronicle Books, 2009.

Greenblatt, Stephen J. "General Introductions." In *The Norton Shakespeare*, edited by Stephen J. Greenblatt, Walter Cohen, Jean E. Howard, and Katharine Eisaman Maus. London: W.W. Norton, 1997.

Greenblatt, Stephen J. *Marvelous Possessions: The Wonder of the New World*. Oxford: Clarendon, 1991.

Greenblatt, Stephen J. *Shakespearean Negotiations: The Circulation of Social Energy in Renaissance England*. Oxford: Clarendon, 1988.

Greenblatt, Stephen J. "Toward a Poetics of Culture." In *Learning to Curse: Essays in Early Modern Culture*. London: Routledge, 1990.

Greenburg, Zack O'Malley. *Michael Jackson, Inc.* New York: Atria, 2014.

Greer, Germaine. "Like Orpheus, Michael Jackson Was Destroyed by His Fans." *The Guardian* (2009). http://www.theguardian.com/music/2009/jun/26/michael -jackson-death-in-la.

Greer, Margaret Rich, Walter Mignolo, and Maureen Quilligan. *Rereading the Black Legend: The Discourses of Religious and Racial Difference in the Renaissance Empires*. Chicago: University of Chicago Press, 2007.

Guinness World Records. London: Guinness World Records, 2000.

Guins, Raiford, Joanne Morra, Marquard Smith, and Omayra Cruz. "Conversations in Visual Culture." In *The Visual Culture Reader*, edited by Nicholas Mirzoeff, 102–10. London: Routledge, 1998.

Habib, Imtiaz H. *Black Lives in the English Archives, 1500–1677: Imprints of the Invisible*. Aldershot, UK: Ashgate, 2008.

Hakluyt, Richard. "The Worthy and Famous Voyage of the Master Thomas Candish Made Round About the Globe of the Earth . . . (1589)." In *Race in Early Modern England: A Documentary Companion*, edited by Ania Loomba and Ben Burton, 123. Basingstoke: Palgrave Macmillan, 2007.

Hall, Kim F. "Guess Who's Coming to Dinner? Colonization and Miscegenation in 'The Merchant of Venice'." *Renaissance Drama* 23 (1992): 87–111.

Hall, Kim F. "'I Rather Would Wish to Be a Black-Moor': Beauty, Race, and Rank in Lady Mary Wroth's Urania." In *Women, "Race," and Writing in the Early Modern Period*, edited by Margo Hendricks and Patricia Parker, 178–94. London: Routledge, 1994.

Hall, Kim F. "'Object into Object?': Some Thoughts on the Presence of Black Women in Early Modern Culture." In *Early Modern Visual Culture: Representation, Race, and Empire in Renaissance*, edited by Clark Hulse and Peter Erickson, 346–79. Philadelphia: University of Pennsylvania Press, 2000.

Hall, Kim F. "Othello and the Problem of Blackness." In *A Companion to Shakespeare's Works, Volume I: The Tragedies*, edited by Richard Dutton and Jean E. Howard. Blackwell Companions to Literature and Culture (Blackwell Companions to Literature and Culture): 17–20, 357–74. Malden, MA: Blackwell, 2006.

Hall, Kim F. *Othello: Texts and Contexts*. Bedford Shakespeare Series (Bess). Boston, MA: Bedford, 2007.

Hall, Kim F. "Sexual Politics and Cultural Identity in the Masque of Blackness." In *The Performance of Power: Theatrical Discourse and Politics*, edited by Sue-Ellen

Case and Janelle Reinelt. Studies in Theatre History and Culture, 3–18. Iowa City: University of Iowa Press, 1991.

Hall, Kim F. " 'These Bastard Signs of Fair': Literary Whiteness in Shakespeare's Sonnets." In *Post-Colonial Shakespeares*, edited by Ania Loomba and Martin Orkin, 64–83. London, England: Routledge, 1998.

Hall, Kim F. *Things of Darkness: Economies of Race and Gender in Early Modern England*. Ithaca, NY: Cornell University Press, 1995.

Hall, Kim F., and Gwynne Kennedy. "Early Modern Women Writing Race." In *Teaching Tudor and Stuart Women Writers*, edited by Susanne Woods and Margaret P. Hannay. Options for Teaching (OFT): 17, 235–39. New York, NY: Modern Language Association of America, 2000.

Hall, Stuart. "The After-Life of Frantz Fanon: Why Fanon? Why Now? Why *Black Skin, White Masks?*". In *The Fact of Blackness: Frantz Fanon and Visual Representation*, edited by Alan Read. London: Institute of Contemporary Arts, 1996.

Harris, Bernard. "A Portrait of a Moor." *Shakespeare Survey* 11 (1958): 89–97.

Harris, Bernard. "A Portrait of a Moor." In *Shakespeare and Race*, edited by Stanley Wells and Catherine M. S. Alexander, 23–36. Cambridge: Cambridge University Press, 2000.

Harris, Jonathan Gil. *Untimely Matter in the Time of Shakespeare*. Philadelphia: University of Pennsylvania Press, 2011.

Harris, Ron. "The Man Who Turned White." *Ebony*, 1978, 165–70.

Hartle, Andrew and Surbhi Malhotra. "The Safety of Propofol." *British Medical Journal* 339, no. 7727 (2009): 928–29.

Hatherley, Owen. " 'Stalin's Tomb Won't Let Me Be': Michael Jackson as Despot." In *The Resistible Demise of Michael Jackson*, edited by Mark Fisher, 194–200. Winchester, UK: Zero Books, 2009.

Hawkins, Stan. "You Rocked Our World, Michael: Your Moves, Your Look, Your Music, Everything!" *Popular Music and Society* 35, no. 2 (2012): 145–49.

Hayward, Susan. *Cinema Studies: The Key Concepts*. New York: Routledge, 2000.

"Head of a Negro, Probably Representing a Ruler (Oni), from Ife, Nigeria." London: Museum of Mankind, 12th–14th CE.

Healy, Andy. *Michael Jackson 101: The Greatest Songs*. Andy Healy, 2013. Online. http://mj101.squarespace.com/.

Healy, Andy. *Michael Jackson 101: The Remixes*. Andy Healy, 2013. Online.

Healy, Andy. *Michael Jackson 101: The Short Films*. Andy Healy, 2013. Online.

Heaton, Gabriel. *Writing and Reading Royal Entertainments: From George Gascoigne to Ben Jonson*. Oxford: Oxford University Press, 2010.

Helmers, Marguerite. "Media, Discourse, and the Public Sphere: Electronic Memorials to Diana, Princess of Wales." *College English* 63, no. 4 (2001): 437–56.

Helnwein, Gottfried. "Artist Helnwein." http://www.helnwein.com/.

Helnwein, Gottfried. "Beautiful Victim I." Watercolor on Cardboard: Museum of Modern Art, 1974.

Helnwein, Gottfried. "Beautiful Victim II." Watercolor on Cardboard, 1974.

Helnwein, Gottfried. "The Song." Watercolor on Cardboard, 1981.

Hendricks, Margo. "Surveying 'Race' in Shakespeare." In *Shakespeare and Race*, edited by Stanley Wells and Catherine M. S. Alexander, 1–22. Cambridge, UK: Cambridge University Press, 2000.

Hendricks, Margo, and Patricia Parker, eds. *Women, "Race" and Writing in the Early Modern Period*. London: Routledge, 1994.

Hendrix, John, and Charles H. Carman. *Renaissance Theories of Vision*. Visual Culture in Early Modernity. Farnham, England: Ashgate, 2010.

Henson, Jim. *Labyrinth*. Sony Pictures Home Entertainment, 1986.

Hereford, C. H., Percy Simpson, and Evelyn Simpson. "Timber, or Discoveries." In *Ben Jonson, Vol. 8: The Poems; The Prose Works*. Oxford: Oxford University Press, 1925–52.

Herman, Edward S., and Noam Chomsky. *Manufacturing Consent*. 2002.

Herodotus. "The Histories (440 Bce)." In *Race in Early Modern England: A Documentary Companion*, edited by Ania Loomba and Ben Burton, 40. Basingstoke: Palgrave Macmillan, 2007.

Hiatt, Anna. "Michael Jackson's Personal Photographer Remembers How They Met." *New Republic* (2014). Published electronically 29 June. http://www.newrepublic.com/article/118407/michael-jackson-photographer-harrison-funk-remembers.

Hibbett, Ryan. "HIStory: Past, Present and Future, Book I." *Popular Music and Society* 35, no. 2 (2012): 315–17.

Hidalgo, Susan, and Robert G. Weiner. "Wanna Be Startin' Somethin': MJ in the Scholarly Literature: A Selected Bibliographic Guide." *The Journal of Pan African Studies* 3, no. 7 (2010): 14–28.

Hilburn, Robert. "Robert Hilburn: Michael Jackson: The Wounds, the Broken Heart." *Los Angeles Times* (2009). Published electronically June 27. http://www.latimes.com/entertainment/la-me-jackson-hilburn27-2009jun27-story.html.

Hills, M. "Michael Jackson Fans on Trial? Documenting Emotivism and Fandom in Wacko About Jacko." *Social Semiotics* (2007): 459–77.

Hogan, J. Michael. *Rhetoric and Reform in the Progressive Era*. East Lansing: Michigan State University Press, 2003.

Holden, Robert. *Loveability: Knowing How to Love and Be Loved*. London: Hay House, 2013.

Holland, Charles. "A Design for Life: Making Michael Jackson." In *The Resistible Demise of Michael Jackson*, edited by Mark Fisher, 201–09. Winchester, UK: Zero Books, 2009.

Hollander, P. "Michael Jackson, the Celebrity Cult, and Popular Culture." *Society* (2009): 1–6.

Hollings, Ken. "And Tell Sad Stories of the Death of Kings: At the End Once Again with Michael Jackson and Elvis Presley." In *The Resistible Demise of Michael Jackson*, edited by Mark Fisher, 243–60. Winchester, UK: Zero Books, 2009.

Honigmann, E. A. J. *The Texts of Othello and Shakespearian Revision*. London: Routledge, 1996.

Hoskyns, Barney. "The Boy Who Would Fly: Michael Jackson (1983)." In *The Resistible Demise of Michael Jackson*, edited by Mark Fisher, 37–46. Winchester, UK: Zero Books, 2009.

Huerta, Marisa. "Re-Reading the New World Romance: British Colonization and the Construction of 'Race' in the Early Modern Period." Providence, RI: Brown University, 2005.

Hughes, G. *Redemption: The Truth Behind the Michael Jackson Child Molestation Allegations.* Radford, VA: Branch & Vine, 2004.

Hulse, Clark. "Reading Painting: Holbein, Cromwell, Wyatt." In *Early Modern Visual Culture: Representation, Race, and Empire in Renaissance England*, edited by Peter Erickson and Clark Hulse, 148–77. Philadelphia: University of Pennsylvania Press, 2000.

Hulse, Clark, and Peter Erickson. "Introduction." In *Early Modern Visual Culture: Representation, Race, and Empire in Renaissance England*, edited by Clark Hulse and Peter Erickson, 1–14. Philadelphia: University of Pennsylvania Press, 2000.

Hunter, G. K. "Elizabethans and Foreigners." *Shakespeare Survey: An Annual Survey of Shakespeare Studies and Production* 17 (1964): 37–52.

Hunter, G. K. "Elizabethans and Foreigners." In *Shakespeare and Race*, edited by Stanley Wells and Catherine M. S. Alexander, 37–63. Cambridge: Cambridge University Press, 2000.

Hunter, G. K. "Othello and Colour Prejudice." In *Dramatic Identities and Cultural Tradition: Studies in Shakespeare and His Contemporaries: Critical Essays*, 31–59. Liverpool: Liverpool University Press, 1978.

Hunter, James "Invincible." *Rolling Stone*, Dec. 6, 2001.

Hunter, Paul. *You Rock My World.* 2001.

"Index to Testamentary Records." In *British Record Society Vol. 89: Archdeaconry Court of London Probate Records Vol. I—1393–1649.* London, 1978.

Isham, Wayne. *Whatzupwitu.* 1993.

Isham, Wayne. *You Are Not Alone.* 1995.

Iyengar, Sujata. *Shades of Difference: Mythologies of Skin Color in Early Modern England.* Philadelphia: University of Pennsylvania Press, 2005.

Izod, John. "Androgyny and Stardom: Cultural Meanings of Michael Jackson." *The San Francisco Jung Institute Library Journal* 14, no. 3 (1995): 63–74.

Oxford Dictionary of National Biography. http://www.oxforddnb.com/view/article/30617, May 2014.

Jackson, Jermaine. *You Are Not Alone: Michael, through a Brother's Eyes.* New York: Touchstone, 2011.

Jackson, Katherine. *Never Can Say Goodbye.* Long Beach, CA: Vintage Pop Media, 2010.

Jackson, Michael. "20/20 Interview with Barbara Walters." By Barbara Walters (September 1997).

Jackson, Michael. "60 Minutes Interview." By Ed Bradley. *CBS* (December 28, 2003).

Jackson, Michael. "At Large with Geraldo Rivera." By Geraldo Rivera (2005).

Jackson, Michael. *Bad*. Epic Legacy, 1987.

Jackson, Michael. *Bad 25*. Sony, 2012.

Jackson, Michael. *Bad—Special Edition*. Sony/Epic Legacy, 2001.

Jackson, Michael. *Ben*. Motown, 1972.

Jackson, Michael. *Blood on the Dance Floor: HIStory in the Mix*. Sony/Epic Legacy, 1995.

Jackson, Michael. *Dancing the Dream: Poems & Reflections*. London: Doubleday, 1992.

Jackson, Michael. *Dangerous*. Sony/Epic Legacy, 1991.

Jackson, Michael. *Dangerous—Special Edition*. Sony/Epic Legacy, 2001.

Jackson, Michael. *E.T. The Extra-Terrestrial*. MCA, 1982.

Jackson, Michael. "Ebony/Jet Interview." By Darryl Dennard (November 13, 1987).

Jackson, Michael. *Farewell My Summer Love*. Motown, 1984.

Jackson, Michael. *Forever, Michael*. Motown, 1975.

Jackson, Michael. *Got To Be There*. Motown, 1972.

Jackson, Michael. Handwritten Letter Regarding Moonwalker." Three-page handwritten letter from Michael Jackson to William Pecchi Jr., written on Capitol Tokyu Hotel stationery: Julien's Auctions, 1988.

Jackson, Michael. *HIStory: Past, Present and Future, Book 1*. Sony/Epic Legacy, 1995.

Jackson, Michael. *Immortal*. Epic, MJJ Productions, 2011.

Jackson, Michael. "Interview with Ebony Magazine." By Robert E. Johnson (October 1994).

Jackson, Michael. "Interview with Fans." By Various (November 10, 1996).

Jackson, Michael. "Interview with *The Mirror*." By Piers Morgan. *The Mirror* (April 1999).

Jackson, Michael. "Interview with TV Guide Magazine." By Mary Murphy and Jennifer Graham. *TV Guide Magazine* (2001).

Jackson, Michael. *Invincible*. MJJ Productions, Epic, 2001.

Jackson, Michael. "The Jacksons: Famed Brothers Are No Longer Little Boys." By Charles L. Sanders (September 1979).

Jackson, Michael. "The King as Pop." *Life Magazine* (1997).

Jackson, Michael. "The King of Pop and His Little Prince." *OK Magazine Interview* (1997).

Jackson, Michael. *Live at the Forum*. 2010.

Jackson, Michael. "Live at Wembley July 16, 1988." Epic, Legacy, Optimum Productions, 2012.

Jackson, Michael. "Love: The Human Family's Most Precious Legacy." *The Journal of Pan African Studies* 3, no. 7 (2010): 4–13.

Jackson, Michael. *Michael*. Sony, 2010.

Jackson, Michael. "Michael in the Mirror." By Edna Gunderson. *USA Today* (1 November 2001).

Jackson, Michael. "Michael Jackson & Friends." *Wetten, Dass . . . ?* (1999).

Jackson, Michael. "Michael Jackson Appears at Oxford University." *The Journal of Blacks in Higher Education* 31 (2001): 18.

Jackson, Michael. "Michael Jackson Interview on Steve Harvey Radio Show." By Steve Harvey. *Steve Harvey Radio Show* (March 2002).

Jackson, Michael. "Michael Jackson Talks to Access Hollywood in the Studio." By Billy Bush. *Access Hollywood* (November 2006).

Jackson, Michael. "Michael Jackson Talks To . . . Oprah Live." By Oprah Winfrey (1993).

Jackson, Michael. "Michael Jackson: Crowned in Africa, Pop Music King Tells the Real Story of Controversial Trip." By Robert E. Johnson (May 1992).

Jackson, Michael. "Michael Jackson: Life in the Magical Kingdom." By Gerri Hirshey. *Rolling Stone* (February 1983).

Jackson, Michael. *Michael Jackson's Vision*. Epic, Legacy Recordings, MJJ Productions, 2010.

Jackson, Michael. "Michael: 25 Years after Thriller." By Joy T. Bennett (December 2007).

Jackson, Michael. "Molly Meldrum Interview." By Molly Meldrum (November 19, 1996).

Jackson, Michael. *Moonwalk*. London: Heinemann, 2009. 1988.

Jackson, Michael. *Moonwalker: The Storybook*. London: Heinemann, 1988.

Jackson, Michael. *Music & Me. Motown*, 1973.

Jackson, Michael. "Music: Michael Jackson." By Pharrell Williams, Andy Warhol, and Bob Colacello (1982, 2003).

Jackson, Michael. "My Childhood, My Sabbath, My Freedom." *BeliefNet.com* (2000). http://www.beliefnet.com/Faiths/2000/12/My-Childhood-My-Sabbath-My -Freedom.aspx?p=1.

Jackson, Michael. "National Action Network Headquarters Speech." July 9, 2002.

Jackson, Michael. *Off the Wall*. Epic Legacy, 1979.

Jackson, Michael. *Off the Wall—Special Edition*. Sony/Epic Legacy, 2001.

Jackson, Michael. "The Once and Future King." By Lisa Bernhard. *TV Guide* (December 1999).

Jackson, Michael. "Online Audio Chat." By Anthony DeCurtis. *Getmusic* (October 2001).

Jackson, Michael. "Prime Time Live Interview." By Diane Sawyer. *Prime Time TV* (June 1995).

Jackson, Michael. "Radio Interview." By Jesse Jackson. *Keep Hope Alive* (27 March 2005).

Jackson, Michael. "Randy J. Taraborrelli Interview." By Randy J. Taraborrelli (1978).

Jackson, Michael. *The Remix Suites*. 2009. http://www.worldcat.org/title/michael -jackson-the-remix-suites/oclc/437315279&referer=brief_results

Jackson, Michael. "Responds to Allegations of Child Molestation." 13:42. Neverland Valley Ranch: CNN, CBS, and NBC, 1993.

Jackson, Michael. "Rick Dees Interview." By Rick Dees (10 September 2003).

Jackson, Michael. "Simulchat." By Compuserve Contributors (1995).

Jackson, Michael. *The Stripped Mixes*. 2009.

Jackson, Michael. *Thriller*. Epic Legacy, 1982.

Jackson, Michael. *Thriller—25th Anniversary Edition*. Sony/Epic Legacy, 2008.

Jackson, Michael. *Thriller—Special Edition*. Sony/Epic Legacy, 2001.

Jackson, Michael. *The Ultimate Fan Extras Collection*. Deluxe ed. iTunes: Sony Music Entertainment, 2013.

Jackson, Michael. "Vibe Magazine Interview." (March 2002).

Jackson, Michael. "Why Michael Is a Living Legend." (1976).

Jackson, Michael. *Xscape*. Sony, 2014.

Jackson, Michael, and Vincent Paterson. *Blood on the Dance Floor*. 1997.

Jackson, Michael et al. *The Wiz Soundtrack*. Motown, 1978.

Janan, Micaela. "Narcissus on the Text: Psychoanalysis, Exegesis, Ethics." *Phoenix* 61, no. 3/4 (2007): 286–95.

Jefferson, Margo. "Freaks (from On Michael Jackson)." In *Michael Jackson: Grasping the Spectacle*, edited by Christopher R. Smit, 11–22. Farnham, UK: Ashgate, 2012.

Jefferson, Margo. *On Michael Jackson*. New York: Pantheon, 2006.

Jehlen, Myra. "Gender." In *Critical Terms for Literary Study*, edited by Frank Lentricchia and Thomas McLaughlin, 263–79. Chicago: University of Chicago Press, 1995.

Johannes Leo Africanus. "A Geographical Historie of Africa (1600)." In *Race in Early Modern England: A Documentary Companion*, edited by Ania Loomba and Ben Burton, 153–57. Basingstoke: Palgrave Macmillan, 2007.

Johansson, Mats. "Michael Jackson and the Expressive Power of Voice-Produced Sound." *Popular Music and Society* 35, no. 2 (2012): 261–79.

Jones, Aphrodite. *Michael Jackson Conspiracy*. iUniverse, 2007.

Jones, Eldred D. "African Figures in Elizabethan and Jacobean Drama." Thesis (PhD), Durham University, 1962.

Jones, Eldred D. *The Elizabethan Image of Africa*. Charlottesville: University Press of Virginia, 1971.

Jones, Eldred D. "Othello—An Interpretation." In *Critical Essays on Shakespeare's Othello*, edited by Anthony Gerard Barthelemy. *Critical Essays on British Literature (CEBL)*, 39–54. New York: G. K. Hall, 1994.

Jones, Eldred D. *Othello's Countrymen: The African in English Renaissance Drama*. London: Oxford University Press, 1965.

Jones, Eldred D. "The Physical Representation of African Characters on the English Stage During the 16th and 17th Centuries." *Theatre Notebook* 17 (1962): 17–21.

Jones, Eldred D. "Racial Terms for Africans in Elizabethan Usage." *Review of National Literatures* 3, no. 2 (1972): 54–89.

Jones, Lucy. "The Incredible Way Michael Jackson Wrote Music." *NME*, 2 April 2014.

Jones, Quincy. *Q: The Autobiography of Quincy Jones*. Doubleday, 2001.

Jones, Steve, and Martin Sorger. "Covering Music: A Brief History and Analysis of Album Cover Design." *Journal of Popular Music Studies* 11–12, no. 1 (1999): 68–102.

Jonson, Ben. *The Characters of Two Royall Masques, the One of Blacknesse, the Other of Beautie*. London: 1608.

Jonson, Ben. *The Fountaine of Selfe-Loue. Or Cynthias Reuels.* Early English Books, 1475–1640. London: 1601.

Jonson, Ben. *The Workes of Beniamin Ionson.* London: 1616.

Jonson, Ben, David M. Bevington, Martin Butler, and Ian Donaldson. *The Cambridge Edition of the Works of Ben Jonson.* Cambridge: Cambridge University Press, 2012.

Jonson, Ben, and Richard Harp. *Ben Jonson's Plays and Masques.* 2nd ed. London: W.W. Norton, 2001.

Jonson, Ben, and David Lindley. "The Masque of Blackness." In *The Cambridge Edition of the Works of Ben Jonson*, edited by David M. Bevington, Martin Butler and Ian Donaldson, 503–28. Cambridge: Cambridge University Press, 2012.

Jonson, Ben, and David Lindley. "To the Memory of My Beloved, The Author Master William Shakespeare and What He Hath Left Us." In *The Cambridge Edition of the Works of Ben Jonson v.6*, edited by David M. Bevington, Martin Butler and Ian Donaldson, 638–42. Cambridge: Cambridge University Press, 2012.

"The Journal of Michael Jackson Academic Studies." http://michaeljacksonstudies .org/.

Julien, Darren. *The Collection of the King of Pop Michael Jackson: Amusement, Arcade Games & Entertainment.* 2009.

Julien, Darren. *The Collection of the King of Pop Michael Jackson: Antiques, Paintings & Fine Decorative Arts.* 2009.

Julien, Darren. *The Collection of the King of Pop Michael Jackson: Furniture & Decorative Arts.* 2009.

Julien, Darren. *The Collection of the King of Pop Michael Jackson: Garden Statuary & Outdoor Furniture.* 2009.

Kafka, Franz, Joyce Crick, and Ritchie Robertson. *The Metamorphosis and Other Stories* [Translated from the German.]. Oxford: Oxford University Press, 2009.

Kaiser, Susan B. *Fashion and Cultural Studies.* London: Bloomsbury Academic, 2011.

Kane, Reid. "The King of Pop's Two Bodies, or, Thriller as Allegory." In *The Resistible Demise of Michael Jackson*, edited by Mark Fisher, 233–42. Winchester, UK: Zero Books, 2009.

Kaplan, Paul H. D. *The Rise of the Black Magus in Western Art.* Ann Arbor: UMI Research, 1985.

Kastan, David Scott, and Peter Stallybrass. *Staging the Renaissance: Reinterpretations of Elizabethan and Jacobean Drama.* London: Routledge, 1991.

Kauffman, Barbara. "Michael Jackson on Trial Again." *Huffington Post* (2011). Published electronically 17 November. http://www.huffingtonpost.com/rev-barbara -kaufmann/michael-jackson-trial-media_b_1093132.html.

Kauffman, Barbara. "No One Else on Earth Bears the Pain of a Michael Jackson Fan." *InnerMichael.com* (2014). Published electronically 29 April. http://www.inner michael.com/2014/04/no-one-else-on-earth-bears-the-pain-of-a-michael -jackson-fan/.

Kellogg, David. *Jam.* 1992.

Kelly, Ann Cline. "The Challenge of the Impossible: Ben Jonson's Masque of Blackness." *College Language Association Journal* 20 (1977): 341–55.

Kelly, Patrick. *Another Part of Me.* 1988.

Khan, Amir. "Michael Jackson's Ressentiment: 'Billie Jean' and 'Smooth Criminal' in Conversation with Fred Astaire." *Popular Music and Society* 35, no. 2 (2012): 187–201.

Kidnie, Margaret Jane. "Where Is Hamlet? Text, Performance, and Adaptation." In *A Companion to Shakespeare and Performance*, edited by Barbara Hodgdon and William B. Worthen, 101–20. Oxford: Blackwell, 2005.

King, Jason. "An Appreciation of His Talent." In *Passed the Curve: NEXT SH*T IN RHYTHM AND BLUES, SOUL, HIP-HOP AND ELECTRONIC MUSIC*, 2009.

King, Jason. "Don't Stop 'Til You Get Enough: Presence, Spectacle, and Good Feeling in Michael Jackson's *This Is It*." Chap. 12 In *Black Performance Theory*, edited by Thomas F. DeFrantz and Anita Gonzalez, 184–203. Durham, London: Duke University Press, 2014.

King, Jason. "Form and Function: Super Stardom and Aesthetics in the Music Videos of Michael and Janet Jackson." *Velvet Light Trap* 44 (1999): 80–96.

King, Jason. *Michael Jackson Treasures.* Bellevue, WA: Becker & Mayer, 2009.

Kinsler, Jamie. "Victorian Culture and Society: Jack the Ripper as Victorian Entertainment." *The Student Historical Journal* (1999–2000).

Kirkland, Douglas. *Michael Jackson: The Making of 'Thriller': 4 Days/1983.* Filipacchi, 2010.

Kness, Katherine. *Positive Voices for MJJ Presents "Endurance": A Book Written by Fans, Friends, and Supporters of Michael Joseph Jackson the Man, the King of Pop.* Bloomington, IN: AuthorHouse, 2006.

Ko, Yu Jin, and Michael W. Shurgot. *Shakespeare's Sense of Character: On the Page and from the Stage.* Farnham, Surrey, UK: Ashgate, 2012.

Kohler, Chris. "The Remix Manifesto (Part 2)." *Joseph Vogel* (2014). http://www .joevogel.net/the-remix-manifesto-part-2.

Kohler, Chris. "The Remix Manifesto: Thoughts on the Value of Remixes." *Joevogel .net* (2014).

Kohler, Chris. "Revisiting Invincible." *Joevogel.net* (2014). http://www.joevogel.net /the-remix-manifesto-thoughts-on-the-value-of-remixes.

Kooijman, Jaap. *Fabricating the Absolute Fake. America in Contemporary Pop Culture.* Amsterdam: Amsterdam University Press, 2008.

Kornohen, Anu. "Washing the Ethiopian White: Conceptualising Black Skin in Renaissance England." In *Black Africans in Renaissance Europe*, edited by T. F. Earle and K. J. P. Lowe, 94–112. Cambridge: Cambridge University Press, 2005.

Kramer, Jerry. "The Making of Michael Jackson's Thriller." Optimum Productions/ Vestron Video, 1983.

Landis, Forbes Everett. "Does the American Dream Have to Die with Michael Jackson?" *Hub Pages* (2010). http://foreverlandis.hubpages.com/hub/Does-Ameri can-Dream-Have-to-Die-With-Michael-Jackson.

Landis, John. *Black or White*. 1991.

Landis, John. *Thriller*. 1983.

Langford, Michelle. "Review." *Australasian Journal of American Studies* 25, no. 1 (2006): 92–95.

"Larry King Live." CNN, 2009.

Law, Jonathan, David Pickering, and Richard Helfer. *The New Penguin Dictionary of the Theatre*. London: Penguin, 2001.

Lay, Jackie, Bruce Western, Kasia Cieplak-Mayr von Baldegg, and Ta-Nehisi Coates. "Mass Incarceration, Visualized." *The Atlantic*, 2015.

Le Guin, Ursula K. *The Left Hand of Darkness*. London: Orbit, 2009.

Lee, Amanda. "Dealing with Vitiligo." YouTube, 2014.

Lee, Harper. *To Kill a Mockingbird: 50th Anniversary Edition*. London: Arrow, 2010.

Lee, Spike. *Bad 25*. Optimum Productions, 2013.

Lee, Spike. *They Don't Care About Us* (Brazil Version). 1996.

Lee, Spike. *They Don't Care About Us* (Prison Version). 1996.

Lee, Summer Kim. "Alive with You: Blood Orange's Sense of Distance in Resonant Love," *Journal of Popular Music Studies* 25, no. 4 (2013): 459–75.

"The Legend of Wacko Jacko from Baby Dangling to Crotch Grabbing." *The Telegraph* (2009). http://www.telegraph.co.uk/news/obituaries/celebrity-obituaries /5643156/Michael-Jackson.html.

Leslie, Mitch. "Pass It On." *Science* 295 (2002).

Lesser, Zachary. "Playbooks." Chap. 37 In *Cheap Print in Britain and Ireland to 1660*, edited by Joad Raymond. The Oxford History of Popular Print Culture, 520– 34. New York: Oxford University Press, 2011.

Lesser, Zachary. *Renaissance Drama and the Politics of Publication: Readings in the English Book Trade*. Cambridge: Cambridge University Press, 2004.

Lester, Paul. "Michael Jackson's Twenty Greatest Hits." In *The Resistible Demise of Michael Jackson*, edited by Mark Fisher, 18–36. Winchester, UK: Zero Books, 2009.

Lewis, Danny. *David Bowie Style*. London: Bloomsbury, 2012.

Lindley, David. "*The Masque of Blackness*, *The Masque of Beauty* and the Haddington Masque: Textual Essay." *The Cambridge Edition of the Works of Ben Jonson Online* (2015). http://universitypublishingonline.org/cambridge/benjonson/k/essays /Blackness_Beauty_Haddington_textual_essay/.

Lipking, Lawrence. *The Life of the Poet: Beginning and Ending Poetic Careers*. Chicago: University of Chicago Press, 1981.

Littlejohn, Richard. "Mob Grief Proves Britain Is More Wacko Than Jacko." *Daily Mail*, 7 July 2009.

Loomba, Ania. *Colonialism-Postcolonialism*. London: Routledge, 1998.

Loomba, Ania. "The Color of Patriarchy." In *Women, "Race" and Writing in the Early Modern Period*, edited by Margo Hendricks and Patricia Parker, 17–34. London: Routledge, 1994.

Loomba, Ania. "The Color of Patriarchy: Critical Difference, Cultural Difference, and Renaissance Drama." In *Women, "Race," and Writing in the Early Modern*

Period, edited by Margo Hendricks and Patricia Parker, 17–34. London: Routledge, 1994.

Loomba, Ania. "'Delicious Traffick': Alterity and Exchange on Early Modern Stages." *Shakespeare Survey: An Annual Survey of Shakespeare Studies and Production* 52 (1999): 201–14.

Loomba, Ania. "'Delicious Traffick': Racial and Religious Difference on Early Modern Stages." In *Shakespeare and Race*, edited by Catherine M. S. Alexander and Stanley Wells, 203–24. Cambridge, England: Cambridge University Press, 2000.

Loomba, Ania. "From Gender, Race, Renaissance Drama." In *William Shakespeare: The Tempest: A Case Study in Critical Controversy*, edited by Gerald Graff and James Phelan. Case Studies in Critical Controversy (CSCC), 324–36. Boston, MA: Bedford, 2000.

Loomba, Ania. *Gender, Race, Renaissance Drama*. Manchester: Manchester University Press, 1989.

Loomba, Ania. "Othello and the Racial Question." In *Shakespeare, Race, and Colonialism*, 91–111. Oxford: Oxford University Press, 2002.

Loomba, Ania. "Shakespeare and Cultural Difference." In *Alternative Shakespeares, II*, edited by Terence Hawkes and John Drakakis. New Accents, 164–91. London, England: Routledge, 1996.

Loomba, Ania. "Shakespeare and the Racial Question." In *Where Are We Now in Shakespearean Studies? III*, edited by Graham Bradshaw, John M. Mucciolo, Tom Bishop, Angus Fletcher and Frank Kermode. Shakespearean International Yearbook: 3, 34–58. Aldershot, England: Ashgate, 2003.

Loomba, Ania. *Shakespeare, Race, and Colonialism*. Oxford: Oxford University Press, 2002.

Loomba, Ania, and Jonathan Burton, eds. *Race in Early Modern England: A Documentary Companion*. Basingstoke: Palgrave Macmillan, 2007.

Loomba, Ania, Suvir Kaul, and Matti Bunzl, eds. *Postcolonial Studies and Beyond*. Durham, NC: Duke University Press, 2005.

Lublin, Robert I. *Costuming the Shakespearean Stage: Visual Codes of Representation in Early Modern Theatre and Culture*. Farnham, England: Ashgate, 2011.

Lumet, Sidney. *The Wiz*. Motown Productions, 1978.

Luzajic, Lorette C., et al. *Michael Jackson for the Soul*. Handymaiden Books, 2011. https://www.amazon.co.uk/Michael-Jackson-Soul-fanthology-inspiration/dp/1456334646

Lynch, Christopher. "Ritual Transformation through Michael Jackson's Music Video." *Journal of Communication Inquiry* 25, no. 2 (2001): 114–31.

MacDonald, Joyce Green. "'The Force of Imagination': The Subject of Blackness in Shakespeare, Jonson, and Ravenscroft." *Renaissance Papers* (1991): 53–74.

MacDonald, Joyce Green. *Women and Race in Early Modern Texts*. Cambridge, England: Cambridge University Press, 2002.

Macdonald, Patrick. "'HIStory' Lesson: Jackson's Living on Past Glories." *The Seattle Times* (1995). http://community.seattletimes.nwsource.com/archive/?date=1995 0621&slug=212746.

MacIntyre, Jean. "Queen Elizabeth's Ghost at the Court of James I: The Masque of Blackness, Lord Hay's Masque, the Haddington Masque, and Oberon." *Ben Jonson Journal: Literary Contexts in the Age of Elizabeth, James and Charles* 5 (1998): 81–100.

MacQueen, Hector L. "'My Tongue Is Mine Ain': Copyright, the Spoken Word and Privacy." *The Modern Law Review* 68, no. 3 (2005): 349–77.

Mahmoudi, Katia. "Michael Jackson's Musical Texts: A Fanonian Study of an Inferiority Complex." Tizi Ouzou, Algeria: Mouloud Mammeri University of Tizi-Ouzou, 2014.

Malcolmson, Cristina. "Race and Early Modern Studies: The Power of an Illusion and Its Genesis." *CLIO: A Journal of Literature, History, and the Philosophy of History* 33, no. 4 (2004): 439–49.

Malik, Suhail. "Don't Stop 'Til You Beat It: Michael Jackson at the Limit of Post-Race Dialectriffs." In *The Resistible Demise of Michael Jackson*, edited by Mark Fisher, 210–18. Winchester, UK: Zero Books, 2009.

Mankiewicz, Joseph L. *Cleopatra*. 20th Century Fox, 1963.

Mann, R. S. "Neuroscience. The Michael Jackson Fly." *Science* 344, no. 6179 (Apr 4 2014): 48–9.

Manning, Harriet J. "'Black or White': From Jim Crow to Michael Jackson." In *Michael Jackson and the Blackface Mask*, 19–50. Farnham, UK: Ashgate, 2013.

Manning, Harriet J. "The Burden of Ambiguity." In *Michael Jackson and the Blackface Mask*, 137–66. Farnham: Ashgate, 2013.

Manning, Harriet J. "*Ghosts:* Racial Fantasy and the Lost Black Self." In *Michael Jackson and the Blackface Mask*, 67–94. Farnham, UK: Ashgate, 2013.

Manning, Harriet J. "Just Using It: Eminem, the Mask and a Fight for Authenticity." In *Michael Jackson and the Blackface Mask*, 117–36. Farnham, UK: Ashgate, 2013.

Manning, Harriet J. *Michael Jackson and the Blackface Mask*. Farnham, UK: Ashgate, 2013.

Manning, Harriet J. "This Is It." In *Michael Jackson and the Blackface Mask*, 167–76. Farnham, UK: Ashgate, 2013.

Marcus, Leah S. "The Two Texts of Othello and Early Modern Constructions of Race." In *Textual Performances: The Modern Reproduction of Shakespeare's Drama*, edited by Lukas Erne and Margaret Jane Kidnie, 21–36. Cambridge, England: Cambridge University Press, 2004.

Mark, Peter. *Africans in European Eyes: The Portrayal of Black Africans in Fourteenth and Fifteenth Century Europe*. Syracuse University, 1974.

Markowitz, Robin. "Ain't Nobody's Business: The Public Text of Michael Jackson." New York: City University of New York, 1992.

Marotti, Arthur F. "'Love Is Not Love': Elizabethan Sonnet Sequences and the Social Order." *ELH* 49, no. 2 (1982): 396–428.

Marriott, David. *On Black Men*. Edinburgh: Edinburgh University Press, 2000.

Marsh, Dave. *Trapped: Michael Jackson and the Crossover Dream*. New York: Bantam, 1985.

Martin, Charles D. "The Racist Freak-Show Origins of 'Wacko Jacko'." YouTube, 2009.

"Martin Scorsese: Michael Jackson Remembered: The Tributes." *Rolling Stone* (2014). http://www.rollingstone.com/music/pictures/michael-jackson-remembered -the-tributes-20140625/martin-scorsese-0100948.

Martin, Sylvia J. "From Asia to Africa, the King of Pop Emerges as a Global Platform for Philanthropy and Social Change." *OpEdNews* (2013). Published electronically June 11.

Martin, Sylvia J. "Remembering Michael Jackson: Moonwalking between Contradictions." *LearCenter.org* (2010). http://blog.learcenter.org/2010/06/remem bering_michael_jackson_mo.html.

Martin, Sylvia J. "The Roots and Routes of Michael Jackson's Global Identity." *Society* 49, no. 3 (2012): 284–90.

Martin, Sylvia J. "The Roots and Routes of Michael Jackson's Global Identity." In *A Companion to Michael Jackson Academic Studies I*, edited by Elizabeth Amisu, 9: MJAS, 2015.

Martinec, Radan. "Construction of Identity in Michael Jackson's Jam." *Social Semiotics* 10, no. 3 (2000): 313–29.

Massai, Sonia. *World-Wide Shakespeares: Local Appropriations in Film and Performance.* Edited by Sonia Massai. London: Routledge, 2005.

Maus, Katharine Eisaman, and William Shakespeare. "The Merchant of Venice." In *The Norton Shakespeare*, edited by Stephen J. Greenblatt, Walter Cohen, Jean E. Howard, and Katharine Eisaman Maus. London: W.W. Norton, 1997.

McCormick, Neil. "Michael Jackson Remembered by His Band: 'The Most Alive Person You Could Ever Meet'." *The Telegraph* (2011). Published electronically 6 October. http://blogs.telegraph.co.uk/culture/neilmccormick/100056639 /michael-jackson-remembered-by-his-band-the-most-alive-person-you-could -ever-meet/.

McCristal, Jerome. "The Michael Jackson Pill: Equality, Race, and Culture." *Michigan Law Review* 92, no. 8 (1994): 2613–44.

McGiffert, Michael. "Constructing Race: Differentiating Peoples in the Early Modern World." *William and Mary Quarterly: A Magazine of Early American History and Culture* 54, no. 1 (1997).

McKerrow, Ronald B., Harry G. Aldis, and Bibliographical Society. *A Dictionary of Printers and Booksellers in England, Scotland and Ireland, and of Foreign Printers of English Books 1557–1640.* London: Printed for the Bibliographical Society by Blades, East and Blades, 1968.

McManus, Clare. "Defacing the Carcass: Anne of Denmark and Jonson's Masque of Blackness." In *Refashioning Ben Jonson: Gender, Politics and the Jonsonian Canon*, edited by Julie Sanders, Kate Chedgzoy and Susan Wiseman, 93–113: Macmillan Press, 1998.

McManus, Clare. *Women on the Renaissance Stage: Anna of Denmark and Female Masquing in the Stuart Court (1590–1619).* Manchester: Manchester University Press, 2002.

McMullan, Gordon. *Shakespeare and the Idea of Late Writing Authorship in the Proximity of Death.* Cambridge: Cambridge University Press, 2007.

"Meaning of "Daryl"." *Meaning-Of-Names* (2004). http://www.meaning-of-names .com/english-names/daryl.asp.

Mercer, Kobena. "Ethnicity and Internationality: New British Art and Diaspora-Based Blackness." Chap. 21 In *The Visual Culture Reader*, edited by Nicholas Mirzoeff, 190–203. London: Routledge, 1998.

Mercer, Kobena. "Monster Metaphors: Notes on Michael Jackson's 'Thriller'." *Screen* 27, no. 1 (1986): 26–43.

Mercer, Kobena. "Monster Metaphors: Notes on Michael Jackson's 'Thriller'." In *A Companion to Michael Jackson Academic Studies I*, edited by Elizabeth Amisu, 3: MJAS, 2015.

Mercer, Kobena. *Welcome to the Jungle New Positions in Black Cultural Studies.* Hoboken: Taylor and Francis, 2013. http://kcl.eblib.com/patron/FullRecord .aspx?p=1397115.

Merx, Karin. "'Dangerous' Von Dr. Susan Fast." [In German]. *The Journal of Michael Jackson Academic Studies* 1, no. 3 (2015): 2.

Merx, Karin. "'Dangerous' by Dr. Susan Fast." *The Journal of Michael Jackson Academic Studies* 1, no. 1 (2014): 4.

Merx, Karin. "From Throne to Wilderness: Michael Jackson's 'Stranger in Moscow' and the Foucauldian Outlaw." *The Journal of Michael Jackson Academic Studies* 1, no. 4 (2015): 4.

Merx, Karin. "An Interview with Karin Merx." By Elizabeth Amisu (2016).

Merx, Karin. "Portrait Drawing of Michael Jackson." Ink pen on watercolor paper: Private Collection of Elizabeth Amisu, 2014.

Meskill, Lynn S. "The Characters of Posterity in Jonson's the Masque of Blacknesse and Shakespeare's Antony and Cleopatra." *Huntington Library Quarterly: Studies in English and American History and Literature* 73, no. 1 (2010): 37–56.

Meyers, Jeffrey and F. Scott Fitzgerald. *The Great Gatsby.* Everyman, 1993.

Michael, Jackson. "Love: The Human Family's Most Precious Legacy." In *A Companion to Michael Jackson Academic Studies I,* edited by Elizabeth Amisu, 7: MJAS, 2015.

"Michael Jackson and James Brown." 3:47. YouTube: BET Awards 2003, 2014.

"Michael Jackson at James Brown's Funeral." YouTube: CNN, 2006.

"Michael Jackson Death Hoax Forum." http://www.michaeljacksonhoaxforum.com /forums/.

"Michael Jackson—Live at the Beverly Theater 1983." 2:21. YouTube, 2015.

Mickel, Lesley. "Glorious Spangs and Rich Embroidery: Costume in the Masque of Blackness and Hymenaei." *Studies in the Literary Imagination* 36, no. 2 (2003): 41–59.

"Middlesex & London Baptisms Index 1538–1882." (2013). http://www.origins .net/.

Mieville, China. *Perdido Street Station.* London: Pan, 2011.

Mignolo, Walter. "Afterword: What Does the Black Legend Have to Do with Race?" In *Rereading the Black Legend: The Discourses of Religious and Racial*

Difference in the Renaissance Empires, edited by Margaret Rich Greer, Walter Mignolo, and Maureen Quilligan, 312–24. Chicago: University of Chicago Press, 2007.

Mignolo, Walter. *The Darker Side of the Renaissance: Literacy, Territoriality, and Colonization*. Ann Arbor: University of Michigan Press, 1995.

Miller, Arthur. *Death of a Salesman: Certain Private Conversations in Two Acts and a Requiem*. Penguin Modern Classics. Harmondsworth: Penguin, 1985.

Miller, Carl. "'We Are Here to Change the World': Captain EO and the Future Utopia." In *Michael Jackson: Grasping the Spectacle*, edited by Christopher R. Smit, 117–30. Farnham, UK: Ashgate, 2012.

Milton, John. *Samson Agonistes*. New York, Madras, Toronto, Tokyo: Cambridge University Press, 1925.

Miquel-Baldellou, Marta. "A Tell-Tale Thriller: An Intertextual and Structural Insight into Poe's Pop." In *De-Centring Cultural Studies: Past, Present and Future of Popular Culture*, edited by Jose-Igor Prieto-Arranz et al., 89–117. Newcastle upon Tyne: Cambridge Scholars Publishing, 2013.

Mirzoeff, Nicholas. "Coda: Fire." In *An Introduction to Visual Culture*, 255–60. London: Routledge, 1999.

Mirzoeff, Nicholas, ed. *An Introduction to Visual Culture*. London: Routledge, 1999.

Mirzoeff, Nicholas. "Introduction: What Is Visual Culture?" In *An Introduction to Visual Culture*, 1–34. London: Routledge, 1999.

Mirzoeff, Nicholas. "The Multiple Viewpoint: Diaspora and Visual Culture." In *The Visual Culture Reader*, 204–14. London: Routledge, 1998.

Mirzoeff, Nicholas. "Picture Definition: Line, Color, Vision." In *An Introduction to Visual Culture*, 37–64. London: Routledge, 1999.

Mirzoeff, Nicholas. "The Subject of Visual Culture." In *The Visual Culture Reader*, edited by Nicholas Mirzoeff, 3–23. London: Routledge, 1998.

Mirzoeff, Nicholas. "Transculture: From Kongo to the Congo." In *An Introduction to Visual Culture*, 129–61. London: Routledge, 1999.

Mirzoeff, Nicholas, ed. *The Visual Culture Reader*. London: Routledge, 1998.

Mital, Ruchi. "Tomorrow Today: Michael Jackson as Science Fiction Character, Author, and Text." In *Michael Jackson: Grasping the Spectacle*, edited by Christopher R. Smit, 131–44: Ashgate, 2012.

Mitchell, Gregory. "'Michael, Eles Não Ligam Pra Gente!' Brazilian Rentboys, Queer Affinity, and the Michael Jackson Exception." *Journal of Popular Music Studies* 23, no. 1 (2011): 109–23.

Mitchell, W. J. T. "Representation." In *Critical Terms for Literary Study*, edited by Frank Lentricchia and Thomas McLaughlin, 11–22. Chicago: University of Chicago Press, 1995.

Mittell, Jason. "A Cultural Approach to Television Genre Theory." *Cinema Journal* 40 (2001): 3–24.

MJ Academia Project. "As Jacked as It Sounds, the Whole System Sucks (Part 1 of 2)." YouTube, 2012.

MJ Academia Project. "Some Things in Life They Just Don't Want to See." YouTube, 2011.

MJ Academia Project. "You Remind Me of a Black Panther." YouTube, 2011.

"MJ BeLIEvers Official." Facebook, https://www.facebook.com/MJBelievers.Official/info/?tab=page_info.

Moharan, Andy. *Give in to Me*. 1993.

Montpellier, Ubisoft. "Michael Jackson: The Experience." Ubisoft, Triumph International, 2010.

Moore, Boothe. "Michael Jackson: King of Style." *The Los Angeles Times* (2009). Published electronically June 26. http://www.latimes.com/fashion/alltherage/la-me-jackson-style26-2009jun26-story.html.

Moore, Rowan. "Sam Wanamaker Playhouse—Review." *The Guardian* (2014). http://www.theguardian.com/artanddesign/2014/jan/12/sam-wanamaker-playhouse-globe-review.

Moore, Rich. "Stark Raving Dad—*The Simpsons* Season 3." Twentieth Century Fox, 1992.

Moriarty, Karen. *Defending a King—His Life and Legacy*. Parker, CO: Outskirts Press, 2012.

Morrison, Toni. *Playing in the Dark: Whiteness and the Literary Imagination*. Cambridge, MA: Harvard University Press, 1992.

Mortilla, Syl. "The Enigma Mirror." *SylMortilla.com* (2014). Published electronically 4 February. http://sylmortilla.com/2014/02/04/the-enigma-mirror/.

Mortilla, Syl. "Equanimity." *SylMortilla.com* (2014). Published electronically 24 September. http://sylmortilla.com/2013/09/24/equanimity/.

Mortilla, Syl. "Michael Jackson's Face." *SylMortilla.com* (2013). Published electronically 13 June. http://sylmortilla.com/2013/06/13/michael-jacksons-face/.

Mortilla, Syl. "The Mirror in the Man: An Article on What Michael Jackson Means to You." *SylMortilla.com* (2014). Published electronically 4 June. http://sylmortilla.com/2014/06/04/the-mirror-in-the-man/.

Mortilla, Syl. "The Mission: An Article on Michael Jackson and Children." *SylMortilla.com* (2014). Published electronically 15 May. http://sylmortilla.com/2014/05/15/the-mission/.

Mortilla, Syl. "Vindication." *SylMortilla.com* (2014). Published electronically 13 June. http://sylmortilla.com/2014/06/13/vindication-day/.

"MTV Video Music Awards | 1984." http://www.mtv.com/ontv/vma/1984/.

"MTV Video Music Awards | 1988." http://www.mtv.com/ontv/vma/1988/.

"MTV Video Music Awards | 2009." http://www.mtv.com/ontv/vma/2009/.

"MTV Video Music Awards | 2014." http://www.mtv.com/ontv/vma/2014/.

"MTV Video Music Awards | 2015." http://www.mtv.com/ontv/vma/2015/.

Mullaney, Steven. "Imaginary Conquests: European Material Technologies and the Colonial Mirror Stage." In *Early Modern Visual Culture: Representation, Race, and Empire in Renaissance England*, edited by Peter Erickson and Clark Hulse, 15–43. Philadelphia: University of Pennsylvania Press, 2000.

Mulvey, Laura. "Visual Pleasure and Narrative Cinema." In *Film Theory and Criticism: Introductory Readings*, edited by L. Braudy and M. Cohen, 833–44. Oxford: Oxford University Press, 1999.

Munch, Edvard. "The Scream (1895)." In *The Story of Art*, edited by E. H. Gombrich: Phaidon, 1995.

Murray, Molly. "Performing Devotion in the Masque of Blacknesse." *SEL: Studies in English Literature, 1500–1900* 47, no. 2 (2007): 427–49.

Museum, National Maritime. "Details About National Maritime Museum: The Collections Book." Woodbridge, Suffolk: Scala Publishers Ltd, 1994.

Nash, June. "Global Integration and the Commodification of Culture." *Ethnology* 39, no. 2 (2000): 129–31.

Navea, Valenka. " 'Songs of Lear' at the BAC Reviewed by Valenka Navea." (2015). http://ceel.org.uk/culture/film-theatre/songs-of-lear-at-the-bac-reviewed-by-valenka-navea/.

Neal, Mark Anthony. "Michael Jackson and the Black Performance Tradition." Duke University, 2012.

Neel, Julia. "Michael Jackson—A Tribute." *Vogue* (2009). Published electronically 26 June. http://www.vogue.co.uk/spy/celebrity-photos/2009/06/26/michael-jacksons-style—26062009.

Neill, Michael. " 'Mulattos,' 'Blacks,' and 'Indian Moors': *Othello* and Early Modern Constructions of Human Difference." *Shakespeare Quarterly* 49, no. 4 (1998): 361–74.

Nelmes, J. *Introduction to Film Studies*. London: University of Chicago Press, 1999.

Nelson, Max. "Narcissus: Myth and Magic." *The Classical Journal* 95, no. 4 (2000): 363–89.

Nero, Brian. *Race*. Basingstoke: Palgrave Macmillan, 2003.

Newman, Karen. " 'And Wash the Ethiop White': Femininity and the Monstrous in Othello." In *Critical Essays on Shakespeare's Othello*, edited by Anthony Gerard Barthelemy. *Critical Essays on British Literature (CEBL)*, 124–43. New York: G. K. Hall, 1994.

Newman, Karen. " 'And Wash the Ethiop White': Femininity and the Monstrous in *Othello*." In *Essaying Shakespeare*, 38–58: Minneapolis: University of Minnesota Press, 2009.

Newman, Karen. "Portia's Ring: Gender, Sexuality, and Theories of Exchange in *The Merchant of Venice*." In *Essaying Shakespeare*, 59–76: University of Minnesota Press, 2009.

Newman, Karen. "Reprise: Gender, Sexuality and Theories of Exchange in 'The Merchant of Venice'." In *The Merchant of Venice: Theory in Practice*, edited by Nigel Wood. Buckingham: Open University Press, 1996.

Newstok, Scott L., and Ayanna Thompson. *Weyward Macbeth: Intersections of Race and Performance*. Basingstoke: Palgrave Macmillan, 2010.

Ne-Yo. "Out of Harm's Way." *Ebony Special Tribute: Michael Jackson In His Own Words*, 2009.

Niel, Tim. "Shakespeare's First Folio." In *The Secret Life of Books*, edited by Alan Campbell, BBC Four, 2014.

Nyong'o, Tavia. "Have You Seen His Childhood? Song, Screen, and the Queer Culture of the Child in Michael Jackson's Music." *Journal of Popular Music Studies* 23, no. 1 (2011): 40–57.

Obaid, Thoraya Ahmed. "The Moor Figure in English Renaissance Drama." 1975.

O'Brien, Sandra. "Michael Jackson Story Quilt: Michael's Message in Fabric and Felt." *LMJ Magazine* (29 July 2015).

Odom, Glenn A. "Jacobean Politics of Interpretation in Jonson's Masque of Blackness." *SEL: Studies in English Literature, 1500–1900* 51, no. 2 (2011): 367–83.

OED Online. Oxford: Oxford University Press, 2015. http://www.oed.com.

O'Keeffe, Tadhg. "Performance, Materiality, and Heritage: What Does an Archaeology of Popular Music Look Like?" *Journal of Popular Music Studies* 25, no. 1 (2013): 91–113.

Okri, Ben. "A Meteor Streaks Our Collective Consciousness." *The Times*, 27 June 2009.

Oldenburg, Scott. "The Riddle of Blackness in England's National Family Romance." *Journal for Early Modern Cultural Studies* 1, no. 1 (2001): 46–62.

Oliete, Elena. "Michael Are You Ok? You've Been Hit by a Smooth Criminal: Racism, Controversy, and Parody in the Videos 'Smooth Criminal' and 'You Rock My World'." *Studies in Popular Culture* 29, no. 1 (2006): 57–76.

Optimum Productions and Michael Jackson. "Making Michael Jackson's Thriller." United States: Optimum Productions, 1983.

Orgel, Stephen. *The Illusion of Power: Political Theater in the English Renaissance*. S.l.: University of California Press, 1974.

Orgel, Stephen. *The Jonsonian Masque*. Cambridge, Mass.: Harvard University Press, 1965.

Orgel, Stephen. "The Jonsonian Masque." In *Ben Jonson's Plays and Masques*, edited by Ben Jonson and Richard Harp, 482–88. London: W.W. Norton, 2001.

Orgel, Stephen. "Marginal Jonson." In *The Politics of the Stuart Court Masque*, edited by David Bevington, Peter Holbrook and Leah S. Marcus, 144–75. Cambridge, England: Cambridge University Press, 1998.

Orgel, Stephen, John Harris, and Roy Strong. *The King's Arcadia: Inigo Jones and the Stuart Court: A Quatercentenary Exhibition Held at the Banqueting House, Whitehall . . . 1973*. London: Arts Council of Great Britain, 1973.

Orgel, Stephen, Inigo Jones, and Roy Strong. *Inigo Jones. The Theatre of the Stuart Court*. Los Angeles: University of California Press, 1973.

Orr, Jake. "Edinburgh Fringe Review: Songs of Lear." (2012). http://www.ayounger theatre.com/edinburgh-fringe-review-songs-of-lear-song-of-the-goat-summerhall/.

Ortega, Kenny. "Michael Jackson's This Is It." Sony, 2009.

Ortelius, Abraham. "Abraham Ortelius His Epitome of the Theater of the Worlde (1603)." In *Race in Early Modern England: A Documentary Companion*, edited by Ania Loomba and Ben Burton, 159–61. Basingstoke: Palgrave Macmillan, 2007.

Ostaszewska, Aneta. "Michael Jackson Death as a Social Event." In *A Companion to Michael Jackson Academic Studies I,* edited by Elizabeth Amisu, 10: MJAS, 2015.

Ostaszewska, Aneta. *Michael Jackson Jako Bohater Mityczny. Perspektywa Antropologiczna.* Wydawnictwa Akademickie I Profesjonalne, 2009.

Ostaszewska, Aneta. "Michael Jackson's Death as a Social Event." *The Journal of Michael Jackson Academic Studies* 1, no. 3 (2015): 1.

Ostaszewska, Aneta. "Michael Jackson's Death as a Social Event." In *Post Script. After Michael Jackson's Death.* Warsaw, Poland: Tauro, 2010.

Ostaszewska, Aneta. *Post Scriptum. Po Śmierci Michaela Jacksona.* Warsaw, Poland: Tauro, 2010.

Over, William. "Alterity and Assimilation in Jonson's Masques of Blackness and Beauty: 'I, with So Much Strength/of Argument Resisted'." *Culture, Language, and Representation—Cultural Studies Journal of Universitat Jaume I* 1 (2004): 43–54.

Over, William. "Familiarizing the Colonized in Ben Jonson's Masques." *Partial Answers: Journal of Literature and the History of Ideas* 2, no. 2 (2004): 27–50.

Over, William. "Race, Culture, and Openness: An Early Modern Precedent." *Partial Answers: Journal of Literature and the History of Ideas* 3, no. 2 (2005): 1–22.

Overby, L. Marvin, Robert D. Brown, John M. Bruce, Charles E. Smith Jr., and John W. Winkle III. "Justice in Black and White: Race, Perceptions of Fairness, and Diffuse Support for the Judicial System in a Southern State." *The Justice System Journal* 25, no. 2 (2004): 159–82.

Ovid. *Metamorphoses.* Translated by A. D. Melville. Oxford: Oxford University Press, 1987.

Oxford Dictionary of National Biography. http://www.oxforddnb.com/view/article/29400, September 2012.

Oxford Union. "About Us." (2016). https://www.oxford-union.org/about_us.

Panel. "The Cultural Phenomenon of Michael Jackson," Society of Cinema and Media Studies, 2011.

Parker, Patricia. "Fantasies of 'Race' and 'Gender': Africa, Othello and Bringing to Light." In *Shakespeare's Tragedies,* edited by Susan Zimmerman. New Casebooks (Neca), 167–93. New York, NY: St. Martin's, 1998.

Paterson, Susanne F. "Review." *Albion: A Quarterly Journal Concerned with British Studies* 31, no. 4 (1999): 640–41.

Paterson, Vincent. *Will You Be There?* 1993.

Pawson, David, and Andy Peck. *Unlocking the Bible.* London: Marshall Pickering, 2001.

Penman, Ian. "Notes Towards a Ritual Exorcism of the Dead King." In *The Resistible Demise of Michael Jackson,* edited by Mark Fisher, 267–309. Winchester, UK: Zero Books, 2009.

Perone, James E. *The Sound of Stevie Wonder: His Words and Music.* Barbara, CA and Westport, CT: Praeger, 2006.

Persaud, Raj. "Suicides Rise after Diana's Death." *British Medical Journal* 321, no. 7271 (2000): 1243.

Peterson, Richard S. "Icon and Mystery in Jonson's Masque of Beautie." *John Donne Journal: Studies in the Age of Donne* 5, no. 1–2 (1986): 169–99.

Petridis, Alexis "Kanye West: Yeezus—Review." *The Guardian*, 2013.

Phelps, Angela. "Memorials without Location: Creating Heritage Places." *Area* 30, no. 2 (1998): 166–68.

Pierce, Constance. "Book Review Man in the Music." *Academia.edu* (2012).

Pierce, Constance. "Book Review: H. J. Manning, Michael Jackson and the Blackface Mask." (2014).

Pierce, Constance. "Book Review: Man in the Music." (2014).

Pierce, Constance. " ' The Dance: Epiphany and Loss Water Color Series', the Fifth Art on Paper 2011." Aichi, Japan: Museum of Art, 2011.

Pierce, Constance. "Drawing Series: Will You Be There." Original series exhibited in Art on Paper 2010, Aichi, Japan: Museum of Art, Toyota City, 2009.

Pierce, Constance. "Lacrymae Rerum: Reflections of a Visual Artist Informed and Inspired by Gestures of Transcendence in the Passionate Art of Michael Joseph Jackson, Passions of the Skies in Fine Arts Expression." Cambridge, MA: Harvard University, 2011.

Pierce, Constance. "Privacy (Michael Jackson and J.D. Salinger)."

Pierce, Constance. "Ruach Hakodesh: The Epiphanic and Cosmic Nature of Imagination in the Art of Michael Jackson." In *The Cosmos and the Creative Imagination (Analecta Husserliana)*, edited by Patricia Trutty-Coohill and Anna-Teresa Tymieniecka. New York: Springer, 2016.

Pierce, Constance. "Ruach Hakodesh: The Epiphanic and Cosmic Nature of Imagination in the Art of Michael Jackson and His Influence on My Image-Making." (2013).

Pierce, Constance. "Will You Be There (Drawing Series)." Aichi, Japan: Museum of Art, Toyota City, 2009.

Pincombe, Michael, and Cathy Shrank. *The Oxford Handbook of Tudor Literature, 1485–1603.* Oxford: Oxford University Press, 2009.

Pinder, Sherrow O. "Michael Jackson and the Quandary of Black Identity." In *Michael Jackson: Grasping the Spectacle*, edited by Christopher R. Smit, 51–63: Ashgate, 2012.

Piper, Adrian. "Passing for White, Passing for Black." In *The Visual Culture Reader*, 546–55. London: Routledge, 1998.

Plasse, Marie. "Michael Jackson: Reading the King of Pop as a Cultural Text." Paper presented at the Michael Jackson: Reading the King of Pop as a Cultural Text, Merrimack College, 2014.

Pliny the Elder. "The Historie of the World (c. 77 Ce)." In *Race in Early Modern England: A Documentary Companion*, edited by Ania Loomba and Ben Burton, 45. Basingstoke: Palgrave Macmillan, 2007.

Pliny the Elder. *The History of the World.* Translated by Philemon Holland. 1601.

Plomer, Henry R. *A Dictionary of the Booksellers and Printers Who Were at Work in England, Scotland and Ireland from 1641 to 1667.* London: Printed for the Bibliographical Society, by Blades, East & Blades, 1907.

Poitevin, Kimberly. "Inventing Whiteness: Cosmetics, Race, and Women in Early Modern England." *Journal for Early Modern Cultural Studies* 11, no. 1 (2011): 59–89.

Poitevin, Kimberly. "Making up Race in Early Modern England," PhD diss., University of Illinois, Urbana, 2004.

Pomeroy, Mark. "Sycamore Valley Ranch: The Splendor of the Santa Ynez Valley." Sotheby's International Realty, 2014.

Porter, Chloe. *Making and Unmaking in Early Modern English Drama: "Spectators, Aesthetics and Incompletion".* Manchester University Press, 2014.

Poulson-Bryant, Scott. "*Michael* by Michael Jackson." *Journal of Popular Music Studies* 23, no. 2 (2011): 249–51.

ProQuest LLC. "EEBO: Early English Books Online." (2003). http://eebo.chadwyck.com/home.

Ptolemaues, Claudius. "Tetrabiblos (2nd Century Ce)." In *Race in Early Modern England: A Documentary Companion*, edited by Ania Loomba and Ben Burton, 47. Basingstoke: Palgrave Macmillan, 2007.

Pugh, Syrithe. "'Rosamarine' in the Masque of Blackness: Jonson's Herbal Medicamina Faciei?" *Notes and Queries* 52 (250), no. 2 (2005): 221–23.

Pytka, Joe. *Dirty Diana.* 1988.

Pytka, Joe. *Heal the World.* 1992.

Pytka, Joe. *The Way You Make Me Feel.* 1987.

Queen Elizabeth I of England. "Licensing Caspar Van Senden to Deport Negroes (1601)." In *Race in Early Modern England: A Documentary Companion*, edited by Ania Loomba and Ben Burton, 158. Basingstoke: Palgrave Macmillan, 2007.

Queen Elizabeth I of England. "An Open Letter to the Lord Maiour of London and Th'aldermen His Brethren (1596)." In *Race in Early Modern England: A Documentary Companion*, edited by Ania Loomba and Ben Burton, 135. Basingstoke: Palgrave Macmillan, 2007.

Queen Elizabeth I of England. "An Open Warrant to the Lord Maiour of London (1596)." In *Race in Early Modern England: A Documentary Companion*, edited by Ania Loomba and Ben Burton, 136. Basingstoke: Palgrave Macmillan, 2007.

Radford, Michael. *The Merchant of Venice.* Sony Pictures Classics, MGM, Optimum Releasing, 2004.

Ramin, Zohreh. "Shakespeare's Richard III and Macbeth: A Foucauldian Reading." *k@ta* 15, no. 2 (2013).

Raphael, Raphael. "Dancing with the Elephant Man's Bones." In *Michael Jackson: Grasping the Spectacle*, edited by Christopher R. Smit, 147–66: Farnham, UK: Ashgate, 2012.

Raven, James. *The Business of Books: Booksellers and the English Book Trade, 1450–1850.* London: Yale University Press, 2007.

Reed, Ishmael. "The Persecution of Michael Jackson." *Counter Currents* (2009).

Reed, Pamela. "Michael Jackson and the Toxicity of American Culture." *The Grio* (2009).

Ritts, Herb. *In the Closet.* 1992.

Roberts, Chris. "True Enough: Michael in Fifty Shards." In *The Resistible Demise of Michael Jackson*, edited by Mark Fisher, 96–136: Zero Books, 2009.

Roberts, Randall. "Michael Jackson's Lawyer, Bob Sanger, Talks to West Coast Sound About the Pop Star, His Life—and His Reading Habits." *LA Weekly* (2009). Published electronically 25 June. http://www.laweekly.com/westcoastsound/2009/06/25/michael-jacksons-lawyer-bob-sanger-talks-to-west-coast-sound-about-the-pop-star-his-life-and-his-reading-habits.

Roberts, Tamara. "Michael Jackson's Kingdom: Music, Race, and the Sound of the Mainstream." *Journal of Popular Music Studies* 23, no. 1 (2011): 19–39.

Roberts, Tamara, and Brandi Wilkins Catanese. "Michael Jackson in/as U.S. Popular Culture." *Journal of Popular Music Studies* 23, no. 1 (2011): 1–2.

Rodley, Chris. *Andy Warhol: The Complete Picture*. BFS Entertainment, 2003.

Rogoff, Irit. "Studying Visual Culture." In *The Visual Culture Reader*, edited by Nicholas Mirzoeff, 24–36. London: Routledge, 1998.

Romanek, Mark. *Scream*. 1995.

Rossiter, Brian. "'They Don't Care About Us': Michael Jackson's Black Nationalism." *Popular Music and Society* 35, no. 2 (2012): 203–22.

Rowling, J. K. *Harry Potter and the Half-Blood Prince*. London: Bloomsbury, 2005.

Rowling, J. K. "Horcruxes." (2016). https://www.pottermore.com/explore-the-story/the-horcruxes.

Royal Museums Greenwich. "Sir Francis Drake, 1540–96." http://collections.rmg.co.uk/collections/objects/14136.html.

Royster, Francesca. "The 'End of Race' and the Future of Early Modern Cultural Studies." *Shakespeare Studies* 26 (1998): 59–69.

Royster, Francesca. "Shakespeare's Violated Bodies: Stage and Screen Performance. By Pascale Aebischer. Cambridge: Cambridge University Press, 2004. Reviewed in *Theatre Survey* 48, no. 01 (2007): 181–83.

Royster, Francesca. *Becoming Cleopatra: The Shifting Image of an Icon*. New York: Palgrave Macmillan, 2003.

Royster, Francesca. "Fela Kuti, Bill T. Jones, and the Marketing of Black Masculine Excess on Broadway." *Biography* 34, no. 3 (2011): 492–517.

Royster, Francesca. "'Hee Hee Hee': Michael Jackson and the Transgendered Erotics of Voice." *The Journal of Michael Jackson Academic Studies* 1, no. 3 (2015): 5.

Royster, Francesca. "Michael Jackson, Queer World Making, and the Trans Erotics of Voice, Gender, and Age." In *Sounding Like a No-No: Queer Sounds and Eccentric Acts in the Post-Soul Era*, 116–41. Ann Arbor: University of Michigan Press, 2013.

Royster, Francesca. *Sounding Like a No-No: Queer Sounds and Eccentric Acts in the Post-Soul Era*. Ann Arbor: University of Michigan Press, 2013.

Rubies, Joan-Pau. "Texts, Images, and the Perception of 'Savages' in Early Modern Europe: What We Can Learn from White and Hariot." *European Visions: American Voices* (2008).

Ryan, Kiernan. *New Historicism and Cultural Materialism: A Reader*. London: Arnold, 1996.

Said, Edward W. *Beginnings: Intention and Method*. New York: Basic Books, 1975.

Said, Edward W. *Culture and Imperialism*. London: Chatto & Windus, 1993.

Said, Edward W. *Orientalism*. Harmondsworth: Penguin, 1985, 1978.

Said, Edward W. *The World, the Text, and the Critic*. London: Vintage, 1991, 1983.

Salamone, Frank A. "Persona, Identity, and Ethnicity." *Anthropos* 77, no. 3/4 (1982): 475–90.

Sale, Carolyn. "Black Aeneas: Race, English Literary History, and the 'Barbarous' Poetics of Titus Andronicus." *Shakespeare Quarterly* 62, no. 1 (2011): 25–52.

Saxton, Nick. *Don't Stop 'Til You Get Enough*. 1979.

SBU News. "Earth Song by Constance Pierce." 2011.

Schlotterbeck, Jesse. "The 'Split' Biography: Man in the Mirror: The Michael Jackson Story." In *Christopher R. Smit*, edited by Michael Jackson: Grasping the Spectacle: Farnham, UK: Ashgate, 2012.

Schlueter, June. "Martin Droeshout Redivivus Reassessing the Folio Engraving of Shakespeare." *Shakespeare Survey* 60 (2007): 237–51.

Schnable, Julian. *Basquiat*. Twentieth Century Fox, 1996.

Schurink, Fred. "Manuscript Commonplace Books, Literature and Reading in Early Modern England." *Huntington Library Quarterly* 73, no. 3 (2010): 453–69.

Scobie, Edward. *Black Britannia: A History of Blacks in Britain*. Chicago: Johnson, 1972.

Scorsese, Martin. *Bad*. 1987.

Scorsese, Martin. *Goodfellas*. Warner Bros, 1990.

Scorsese, Martin. *The Last Temptation of Christ*. Universal Pictures, 1988.

Scorsese, Martin. *Mean Streets*. Taplin-Perry-Scorsese Productions, 1973.

Scorsese, Martin. *Taxi Driver*. Bill Phillips/Italo Judeo Productions, 1976.

Scorsese, Martin, and Peter Brunette. *Martin Scorsese: Interviews*. Conversations with Filmmakers Series. Jackson: University Press of Mississippi, 1999.

Scott, Julie-Ann. "Cultural Anxiety Surrounding a Plastic Prodigy: A Performance Analysis of Michael Jackson as an Embodiment of Post-Identity Politics." In *Michael Jackson: Grasping the Spectacle*, edited by Christopher R. Smit, 167–80. Farnham, UK: Ashgate, 2012.

Scriven, Darryl. "Michael Jackson & the Psycho/Biology of Race." *The Journal of Pan African Studies* 3, no. 7 (2010): 100–05.

Semino, Matt. "Michael Jackson, the Wounded Messenger." *The Examiner* (2010). Published electronically November 29, 2010.

Senior, Mike. "Bruce Swedien: Recording Michael Jackson." *Sound on Sound* (2009). Published electronically November 2009 http://www.soundonsound.com/sos/nov09/articles/swedien.html.

Shakespeare, William. *The Most Excellent Historie of the Merchant of Venice*. London: 1600.

Shakespeare, William, and John Drakakis. *The Merchant of Venice*. London: Arden Shakespeare, 2010.

Shakespeare, William, and Katherine Duncan-Jones. *Shakespeare's Sonnets*. Rev. ed. ed. London: Arden Shakespeare, 2010.

Shakespeare, William, and E. A. J. Honigmann. *Othello*. London: Arden Shakespeare, 2001.

Shaviro, Steven. "Pop Utopia: The Promise and Disappointment of Michael Jackson." In *The Resistible Demise of Michael Jackson*, edited by Mark Fisher, 51–62. Winchester, UK: Zero Books, 2009.

Shelley, Mary Wollstonecraft, and Maurice Hindle. *Frankenstein: Or the Modern Prometheus*. London: Penguin, 2003.

Shepphird, Sari. "Michael Jackson & BDD: Body Dysmorphic Disorder." *Britannica .com* (2009). http://www.britannica.com/blogs/2009/07/michael-jackson-bdd -body-dysmorphic-disorder/.

Shields, David S. "The Drake Jewel." *Uncommon Sense*, no. 128 (2010). http://oieahc .wm.edu/uncommon/118/drake.cfm.

Shohet, Lauren. *Reading Masques: The English Masque and Public Culture in the Seventeenth Century*. Oxford: Oxford University Press, 2010.

Shusterman, Richard. "The Fine Art of Rap." *New Literary History* 22, no. 3 (1991): 613–32.

Shyllon, Folarin Olawale. *Black People in Britain, 1555–1833*. London: Oxford University Press for the Institute of Race Relations, 1977.

Shyllon, Folarin Olawale. *Black Slaves in Britain*. London: Oxford University Press, 1974.

Siddiqi, Yumna. "Dark Incontinents: The Discourse of Race and Gender in Three Renaissance Masques." *Renaissance Drama* 23 (1992): 139–63.

Silberman, Seth Clark. "Presenting Michael Jackson™." *Social Semiotics* (2007): 417–40.

Simeon, Daphne, and Jeffrey Abugel. *Feeling Unreal: Depersonalization Disorder and the Loss of the Self*. Oxford: Oxford University Press, 2006.

Sinfield, Alan. *Faultlines: Cultural Materialism and the Politics of Dissident Reading*. Oxford: Clarendon, 1992.

Sinfield, Alan. *Literature, Politics and Culture in Postwar Britain*. Oxford: Basil Blackwell, 1989.

Singh, Jyotsna G. "Introduction: The Global Renaissance." In *A Companion to the Global Renaissance: English Literature and Culture in the Era of Expansion*, edited by Jyotsna G. Singh, 1–27. Oxford: Wiley-Blackwell, 2009.

Singleton, John. *Remember the Time*. 1992.

Sinker, Mark. "'What About Death, Again?': The Dolorous Passion of the Son of Pop." In *The Resistible Demise of Michael Jackson*, edited by Mark Fisher, 164–87. Winchester, UK: Zero Books, 2009.

Smit, Christopher R. "Chasing the Spectacle of Michael Jackson." In *Michael Jackson: Grasping the Spectacle*, 1–10: Ashgate, 2012.

Smit, Christopher R., ed. *Michael Jackson: Grasping the Spectacle*: Ashgate, 2012.

Smith, Emma. "Was Shylock Jewish?" *Shakespeare Quarterly* 64, no. 2 (2013): 188–219.

Smith, Ian. "Barbarian Errors: Performing Race in Early Modern England." *Shakespeare Quarterly* 49, no. 2 (1998): 168–86.

Smith, Ian. *Race and Rhetoric in the Renaissance: Barbarian Errors.* 1st ed. Basingstoke: Palgrave Macmillan, 2009.

Smith, Ian. "White Skin, Black Masks: Racial Cross-Dressing on the Early Modern Stage." [In English]. *Renaissance Drama* 32 (2003): 33–67.

Smith, Janice L., ed. *Michael Jackson, King of Pop: A Celebration of the Life of Michael Jackson 1958–2009*: Memorial Program, 2009.

Smith, Paul, and Carolyn Wilde. *A Companion to Art Theory.* Oxford: Blackwell, 2002. http://libproxy.kcl.ac.uk/login?url=http://www.blackwellreference .com/subscriber/uid=3/book?show=all&id=g9780631207627_9780631 207627.

Sohat, Ella, and Robert Stam. "Narrativizing Visual Culture: Towards a Polycentric Aesthetics." In *The Visual Culture Reader*, edited by Nicholas Mirzoeff, 24–36. London: Routledge, 1998.

Sokol, Daniel K. "Ethics Man: Hippocrates, Michael Jackson, and Medical Ethics." *British Medical Journal* 339, no. 7720 (2009): 541.

Sollors, Werner. "Ethnicity." In *Critical Terms for Literary Study*, edited by Frank Lentricchia and Thomas McLaughlin, 300–05. Chicago: University of Chicago Press, 1995.

Sonnenfeld, Barry. *Men in Black II.* Columbia Pictures, 2002.

Soos, Amber. "An Interview with Amber Soos." By Elizabeth Amisu (2016).

Sophocles, and Bernard Knox. *The Three Theban Plays: "Antigone," "Oedipus the King," "Oedipus at Colonus."* Translated by Robert Fagles. Penguin Classics, 1984.

Sousa, Geraldo U. de. *Shakespeare's Cross-Cultural Encounters.* Basingstoke, England; New York, NY: Macmillan; St. Martin's, 1999.

Soyini, Ayana. "How Michael Got Gangsta with Sony Music over Black Music and Racism." *Golden Eyes Online*, republished by Davey D's Hip Hop Corner (2002, 2009).

Spaethling, Robert. *Mozart's Letters, Mozart's Life.* London: Faber & Faber, 2004.

Spicer, Joaneath, ed. *Revealing the African Presence in Renaissance Europe.* Baltimore: The Walters Art Museum, 2012.

Spivak, Gayatri Chakravorty. *In Other Worlds: Essays in Cultural Politics.* London: Methuen, 1987.

Stallybrass, Peter, and Allon White. *The Politics and Poetics of Transgression.* London: Methuen, 1986.

Stationers' Company (London England), Charles Robert Rivington, and Edward Arber. *A Transcript of the Registers of the Company of Stationers of London: 1554–1640.* London: 1875.

Stationers' Company (London England), Charles Robert Rivington, and Edward Arber. *A Transcript of the Registers of the Company of Stationers of London: 1554–1640.* Vol. 3, London: 1875.

Stationers' Company (London England), Charles Robert Rivington, and Edward Arber. *A Transcript of the Registers of the Company of Stationers of London: 1554–1640.* Vol. 2, London: 1875.

Stationers' Company (London England), Charles Robert Rivington, and Edward Arber. *A Transcript of the Registers of the Company of Stationers of London: 1554–1640*. Vol. 5, London: 1875.

Stegner-Petitjean, Isabelle. "'The Voice in the Mirror': Michael Jackson: From a Vocal Identity to Its Double in Sound." *Volume!* 8, no. 2 (2011): 222–53.

Stephens, Dorothy. "Review." *African American Review* 32, no. 2 (1998): 337–40.

Stevens, Andrea. "Mastering Masques of Blackness: Jonson's Masque of Blackness, the Windsor Text of the Gypsies Metamorphosed, and Brome's the English Moor." *English Literary Renaissance* 39, no. 2 (2009): 396–426.

Stevens, Hampton. "Michael Jackson's Unparalleled Influence." *The Atlantic* (2010). Published electronically June 24, 2010.

Stiegler, Zack. "Remember to Always Think Twice: The Reconciliation of Michael Jackson." In *Michael Jackson: Grasping the Spectacle* edited by Christopher R. Smit, 207–22. Farnham, UK: Ashgate, 2012.

Stillwater, Willa. *M Poetica: Michael Jackson's Art of Connection and Defiance*. Kindle, 2011, 2013.

Stillwater, Willa, and Joie Collins. "Can a Mirror Reveal the Truth?" *Dancing With the Elephant* (2014). Published electronically April 10. http://dancingwiththeele phant.wordpress.com/2014/04/10/can-a-mirror-reveal-the-truth/.

Stillwater, Willa, and Joie Collins. "A Conversation About Queerness with Susan Fast." *Dancing With the Elephant* (2012). Published electronically November 14. https://dancingwiththeelephant.wordpress.com/2012/11/14/a-conversation -about-queerness-with-susan-fast/.

Stillwater, Willa, and Joie Collins. "MJ's Art: Taking Us Higher." *Dancing With the Elephant* (2012). Published electronically April 4. http://dancingwiththeelephant .wordpress.com/2012/04/04/mjs-art-taking-us-higher/.

Stillwater, Willa, Joie Collins, and Joseph Vogel. "A Chat with Joe Vogel About Earth Song." *Dancing with the Elephant* (2011). Published electronically 9 September. https://dancingwiththeelephant.wordpress.com/2011/09/29/a-chat-with -joe-vogel-about-earth-song/.

Stillwater, Willa, and Collins. Joie. "Summer Rewind 2014: You Make Me Feel Like . . . You Make Me Feel Like. . . ." *Dancing With The Elephant* (2014).

Stillwater, Willa, Joie Collins, et al. "Celebrating Invincible, Part 4: Threatened!!!" *Dancing With the Elephant* (2011). https://dancingwiththeelephant.wordpress .com/2011/10/.

Stillwater, Willa, Joie Collins, et al. "Michael Jackson: Subverting Blackface Stereo-types." *Dancing With the Elephant* (2014). Published electronically 2 January. http://dancingwiththeelephant.wordpress.com/2014/01/02/michael-jackson -and-the-blackface-mask/.

Stillwater, Willa, Joie Collins, et al. "Rereading Michael Jackson." *Dancing With the Elephant* (2011). https://dancingwiththeelephant.wordpress.com/rereading -michael-jackson/.

Stillwater, Willa, Joie Collins, et al. "Spotlight on You Rock My World." *Dancing With the Elephant* (2011). http://dancingwiththeelephant.wordpress.com/2011 /11/17/spotlight-on-you-rock-my-world/.

Stillwater, Willa, Joie Collins, et al. "This Passion Burns inside of Me." *Dancing With the Elephant* (2012). http://dancingwiththeelephant.wordpress.com/2012/01/11/this-passion-burns-inside-of-me/.

Stillwater, Willa, Joie Collins, et al. "Summer Rewind 2014: Trust in Me." *Dancing With the Elephant* (2014). Published electronically August 21. http://dancingwiththeelephant.wordpress.com/2014/08/21/summer-rewind-2014-trust-in-me-2/.

Stoller, Bryan Michael. *Miss Cast Away and the Island Girls.* Showcase Entertainment, 2002.

Stone, Andrew L. *Stormy Weather.* 20th Century Fox, 1943.

Stubbs, David. "The 'King' Is Dead; Long Live Everything Else." In *The Resistible Demise of Michael Jackson*, edited by Mark Fisher, 69–80. Winchester, UK: Zero Books, 2009.

Sullivan, Caroline. "Michael Jackson." *The Guardian*, 2009.

Sullivan, John Jeremiah. "Back in the Day." *GQ* (2011). Published electronically October 9. http://www.gq.com/story/john-jeremiah-sullivan-remembering-michael-jackson-history.

Sullivan, Randall. *Untouchable: The Strange Life and Tragic Death of Michael Jackson.* London: Grove Press, 2012.

Swedien, Bruce. *In the Studio with Michael Jackson.* Madison, WI: Hal Leonard, 2009.

Taibbi, Matt. "Inside the Strangest Show on Earth." In *Smells Like Dead Elephants*: London: Grove Press, 2007.

Taraborrelli, J. Randy. *Michael Jackson: The Magic, the Madness, the Whole Story, 1958–2009.* New York: Hachette, 1991, 2003, 2009.

Tate, Greg. "The Man in Our Mirror." *Village Voice* (2009). Published electronically July 1. http://www.villagevoice.com/news/michael-jackson-the-man-in-our-mirror-6394480.

Tatlow, Ruth. *Bach and the Riddle of the Number Alphabet.* Cambridge: Cambridge University Press, 1991.

Tenenbaum, Sara. "I Know I Am Someone: Michael Jackson, Thriller, and American Identity." Master of Arts, Brandeis University, 2011.

The British Museum. "Kingdom of Ife: Sculptures from West Africa." (2010). http://www.britishmuseum.org/about_us/news_and_press/press_releases/2010/kingdom_of_ife.aspx.

The Jackson 5. *ABC.* Motown, 1970.

The Jackson 5. *Boogie.* Motown, 1979.

The Jackson 5. *Dancing Machine.* Motown, 1974.

The Jackson 5. *Diana Ross Presents the Jackson 5.* Motown, 1969.

The Jackson 5. *G.I.T.: Get It Together.* Motown, 1973.

The Jackson 5. *Goin' Back to Indiana.* Motown, 1971.

The Jackson 5. *Jackson 5 Christmas Album.* Motown, 1970.

The Jackson 5. *The Jackson 5 in Japan.* 1973.

The Jackson 5. *Lookin' through the Windows.* Motown, 1972.

The Jackson 5. *Maybe Tomorrow.* Motown, 1971.

The Jackson 5. *Moving Violation.* Motown, 1975.

The Jackson 5. *Skywriter.* Motown, 1973.

The Jackson 5. *Third Album.* Motown, 1970.

The Jacksons. *Destiny.* Epic Records, 1978.

The Jacksons. *Goin Places.* Epic Records, 1977.

The Jacksons. *The Jacksons.* Epic Records, 1976.

The Jacksons. *Live!* Epic Records, 1981.

The Jacksons. *Triumph.* Epic Records, 1980.

The Jacksons. *Victory.* Epic Records, 1984.

The Michael Jackson Academia Project. "You Remind Me of a Black Panther." *MJJ-Justice Project* (2012). https://mjjjusticeproject.wordpress.com/2012/05/21/the-mjap-you-remind-me-of-a-black-panther/.

Thomas, Alana M. *Letters to Michael: A Collective Goodbye.* Marston, UK and New York: CreateSpace, 2010.

Thomas, Lee. *Turning White: A Memoir of Change.* Troy, MI: Momentum Books, 2012.

Thomas, Michael R. "A Tale of Two Michaels." *Make Up Artist Magazine* (2009). Published electronically October 20. http://makeupmag.com/news/newsID/653/.

Thompson, Ayanna. "The Future of Early Modern Race Studies: On Three Ambitious (Enough?) Books." *The Eighteenth Century: Theory and Interpretation* 49, no. 3 (2008): 251–60.

Thomson, Charles. "Conjuring a Chorus of Boos: The Truth About Michael Jackson's UK Comeback." (2013). Published electronically November 17. http://charlesthomsonjournalist.blogspot.co.uk/2013/11/the-truth-about-michael-jacksons-uk.html.

Thomson, Charles. "FBI File Reveals Attempt to Convict Jackson with Racist Law." *The Diary of a Fledgling Reporter* (2010). Published electronicallyJanuary 3. http://charlesthomsonjournalist.blogspot.co.uk/2010/01/fbi-file-reveals-attempt-to-convict.html.

Thomson, Charles. "FBI Files Support Jackson's Innocence; Media Reports Otherwise." *The Diary of a Fledgling Reporter* (2010). Published electronically January 2. http://charlesthomsonjournalist.blogspot.co.uk/2010/01/fbi-files-support-jacksons-innocence.html.

Thomson, Charles. "Michael Jackson: It's Time for Media Outlets to Take Responsibility in Covering the Rock Star." *Huffington Post* (2010). http://www.huffingtonpost.com/charles-thomson/michael-jackson-its-time_b_482176.html.

Thomson, Charles. " 'One More Chance': A Dream That Turned into a Nightmare." *Sawf News* (2010). Published electronically November. http://www.charles-thomson.net/one_more_chance.html.

Thomson, Charles. "One of the Most Shameful Episodes in Journalistic History." *Huffington Post* (2010). Published electronically 13 June. http://www.huffingtonpost.com/charles-thomson/one-of-the-most-shameful_b_610258.html.

Thomson, Charles. "Play That Funky Music, White Girl." *Sawf News* (2010). Published electronically March. http://www.charles-thomson.net/jennifer-batten-interview.html.

Thomson, Charles. "Video: Thomas Mesereau Interview." *The Diary of a Fledgling Reporter* (2011). Published electronically October 17. http://charles thomsonjournalist.blogspot.co.uk/2011/10/video-thomas-mesereau-inter view.html.

Thomson, Charles. "Xscape: Would Michael Jackson Approve?" *Huffington Post* (2014). Published electronically 12 May. http://www.huffingtonpost.com/charles -thomson/xscape-would-michael-jack_b_5306640.html.

Thrasher, Steven W. "Joseph Fiennes as Michael Jackson Shows Race Problems before Oscars Row." *The Guardian* (2016). Published electronically 28 January. http:// www.theguardian.com/world/2016/jan/28/joseph-fiennes-michael-jackson -race-problems-oscarssowhite.

Thrasher, Steven W. "Joseph Fiennes to Play Michael Jackson in 9/11 Road-Trip Comedy." *The Guardian* (2016). Published electronically 26 January. http:// www.theguardian.com/tv-and-radio/2016/jan/26/joseph-fiennes-michael -jackson-9-11-road-trip-sky-arts.

Tokson, Elliot. *The Popular Image of the Black Man in English Drama, 1550–1688.* Boston, Mass.: G.K. Hall, 1982.

Tompkins, Dennis, Karen Faye, and Michael Bush. "Michael Jackson: After Life." By Cynthia MacFadden. *20/20* (2010).

Touré. "The Magical Negro Falls to Earth." *TIME* (2012). Published electronically September 26, 2012. http://ideas.time.com/2012/09/26/the-magical-negro -falls-to-earth/.

Trainor, Lauren. "Interview with Armond White, Author of Keep Moving: The Michael Jackson Chronicles." *The Jam Cafe* (2011). Published electronically August 1, 2011. http://mjtpmagazine.presspublisher.us/issue/star-dancer/article /interview-with-armond-white-author-of-keep-moving-the-michael-jackson-chro nicle-s.

Traub, Valerie. "Mapping the Global Body." In *Early Modern Visual Culture: Representation, Race, and Empire in Renaissance England,* edited by Peter Erickson and Clark Hulse, 44–97. Philadelphia: University of Pennsylvania Press, 2000.

Trbovich, Tom. *We Are the World.* 1985.

Trbovich, Tom. *We Are the World (20th Anniversary Special).* USA for Africa, 2005.

Trueman, Matt. "Review: Songs of Lear, Summerhall, Edinburgh Fringe." *MattTrueman.co.uk* (2012). Published electronically August 17. http://matttrueman.co .uk/2012/08/review-songs-of-lear-summerhall-edinburgh-fringe.html.

Turner, Lorena. "About the Project." *The Michael Jacksons* (2016). http://www .themichaeljacksons.com/about.php.

Turner, Lorena. *The Michael Jacksons.* Little Moth Press, 2015.

Typographic Etching Company. "William Shakespeare, 1564–1616 after Engraving by Maerten Droeshout.", 1 print: photograving: Library of Congress Prints and Photographs Division Washington, D.C. 20540 USA, 1882.

Van Hoesen, Brett M. "From Pop Icon to Postmodern Kitsch: Images of Michael Jackson in Contemporary Art." In *Michael Jackson: Grasping the Spectacle,* edited by Christopher R. Smit, 81–100. Ashgate, 2012.

Van Valin II, William B. *Private Conversations in Neverland with Michael Jackson*. Marston, UK and New York: CreateSpace, 2012.

Various. "After the Dance: Conversations on Michael Jackson's Black America." Schomburg Center for Research in Black Culture, 4–5 June 2010.

Various. *Dangerous: The Short Films*. MJJ Productions, 1993.

Various. "Genius without Borders: A Symposium in Honor of the Genius of Michael Jackson." Columbia College Chicago, September 24, 2010.

Various. *Greatest Hits—HIStory*. Sony Music Video Enterprises, 1995.

Various. *HIStory on Film Volume II*. Sony Music Video Enterprises, 1997.

Various. *Live in Bucharest: The Dangerous Tour*. Epic Music Video, 2005.

Various. *Michael Jackson: Critical Reflection on a Life & Phenomenon*. University of California, Berkeley, October 1, 2009.

Various. *Michael Jackson: The Making of Ghosts*. VH1, 1997.

Various. *Michael Jackson's Legacy*. (2015). http://www.michaeljacksonslegacy.org/.

Various. *Michael Jackson's Private Home Movies*. 2003.

Various. *MJsInvincible*. (2011). http://mjsinvincible.wordpress.com.

Various. *New International Version*. Colorado Springs: Biblica, 2011.

Various. "One Rose for MJJ." (2014). http://onerose4mjj.blogspot.co.uk/.

Various. "Post Here If You Worked on Michael Jackson's Dangerous." *GearSlutz.com* (2009). http://www.gearslutz.com/board/so-much-gear-so-little-time/403276 -post-here-if-you-worked-michael-jacksons-dangerous-album.html.

Various. "Vindicating Michael: People Defend the Truth About Michael Jackson." (2014). http://vindicatemj.wordpress.com/.

Various. "What More Can I Give." 2001.

Various. "The World Remembers Michael Jackson." (2014). http://theworldremembers.wordpress.com/.

Vaughan, Alden T., Virginia Mason Vaughan, and William Shakespeare. *The Tempest*. London, UK: Arden, 2011.

Vaughan, Alden T., and Vaughan Virginia Mason. "Before Othello: Elizabethan Representations of Sub-Saharan Africans." *The William and Mary Quarterly* 54, no. 1 (1997): 19–44.

Velazco y Trianosky, Gregory. "Savages, Wild Men, Monstrous Races: The Social Construction of Race in the Early Modern Era." In *Beauty Unlimited*, edited by Peg Zeglin Brand and Carolyn Korsmeyer, 45–71. Bloomington, IN: Indiana University Press, 2013.

Vernallis, Carol. "The Functions of Lyrics in Music Video." *Journal of Popular Music Studies* 14, no. 1 (2002): 11–31.

Vernallis, Carol. "Teaching Music Video: Aesthetics, Politics and Pedagogy." *Journal of Popular Music Studies* 9–10, no. 1 (1997): 93–99.

Vigo, Julian. "Metaphor of Hybridity: The Body of Michael Jackson." *The Journal of Pan African Studies* 3, no. 7 (2010): 29–41.

Vigo, Julian. "Michael Jackson and the Myth of Race and Gender." In *Michael Jackson: Grasping the Spectacle*, edited by Christopher R. Smit, 1–10. Farnham, UK: Ashgate, 2012.

Vinton, Will, and Jerry Kramer and Will. *Speed Demon.* 1988.

Vogel, Joseph. "Abortion, Fame, and 'Bad': Listening to Michael Jackson's Unreleased Demos." *The Atlantic* (2012). Published electronically September 10, 2012. http://www.theatlantic.com/entertainment/archive/2012/09/abortion-fame -and-bad-listening-to-michael-jacksons-unreleased-demos/262242/.

Vogel, Joseph. "Am I the Beast You Visualized? The Cultural Abuse of Michael Jackson." *Huffington Post* (2011). Published electronically November 2. http://www.huffingtonpost.com/joe-vogel/michael-jackson-trial-_b_1068 750.html.

Vogel, Joseph. "'Am I the Beast You Visualized?': The Cultural Abuse of Michael Jackson." In *Featuring Michael Jackson: Collected Writings on the King of Pop,* 53–60. New York: Baldwin Books, 2012.

Vogel, Joseph. "Cirque Du Soleil's Michael Jackson Immortal Takes Audience on a Dazzling Ride." In *Featuring Michael Jackson: Collected Writings on the King of Pop,* 61–66. New York: Baldwin Books, 2012.

Vogel, Joseph. "Dangerous, Nevermind and the Reinvention of Pop." In *Featuring Michael Jackson: Collected Writings on the King of Pop,* 29–36. New York: Baldwin Books, 2012.

Vogel, Joseph. "'Don't Be Messin': The Story Behind Michael Jackson's Infectious Bad-Era Demo." In *Featuring Michael Jackson: Collected Writings on the King of Pop,* 23–28. New York: Baldwin Books, 2012.

Vogel, Joseph. *Earth Song: Inside Michael Jackson's Magnum Opus.* New York: BlakeVision Books, 2011.

Vogel, Joseph. "Exclusive: Inside Michael Jackson's 'Hollywood'." *Huffington Post* (2011). Published electronically March 14.

Vogel, Joseph. *Featuring Michael Jackson: Collected Writings on the King of Pop.* New York: Baldwin Books, 2012.

Vogel, Joseph. "Gone Too Soon: The Many Lives of Michael Jackson's Elegy." In *Featuring Michael Jackson: Collected Writings on the King of Pop,* 67–74. New York: Baldwin Books, 2012.

Vogel, Joseph. "Have You Seen His Childhood?" In *Featuring Michael Jackson: Collected Writings on the King of Pop,* 75–90: Baldwin Books, 2012.

Vogel, Joseph. "How Michael Jackson Made 'Bad'." *The Atlantic* (2012). Published electronically September 10. http://www.theatlantic.com/entertainment/archive /2012/09/how-michael-jackson-made-bad/262162/2/.

Vogel, Joseph. "'I Ain't Scared of No Sheets': Re-Screening Black Masculinity in Michael Jackson's Black or White." In *A Companion to Michael Jackson Academic Studies I,* edited by Elizabeth Amisu, 8: MJAS, 2015.

Vogel, Joseph. "'I Ain't Scared of No Sheets': Re-Screening Black Masculinity in Michael Jackson's Black or White." *Journal of Popular Music Studies* 27, no. 1 (2015): 90–123.

Vogel, Joseph. "Inside Michael Jackson's "Hollywood"." In *Featuring Michael Jackson: Collected Writings on the King of Pop,* 37–42. New York: Baldwin Books, 2012.

Vogel, Joseph. "Is Crowdfunding Changing the Game for Filmmakers? A Q&A with Spike Lee." *Huffington Post* (2013). http://www.huffingtonpost.com/joe-vogel/is-crowdfunding-changing-_b_3751494.html.

Vogel, Joseph. "Joevogel.Net." *Joe Vogel.Net* (2008–2014). http://www.joevogel.net/.

Vogel, Joseph. *Man in the Music: The Creative Life and Work of Michael Jackson*. New York: Sterling, 2011.

Vogel, Joseph. "Michael Jackson, Dangerous, and the Reinvention of Pop." *Pop Matters* (2011). Published electronically September 28. http://www.popmatters.com/feature/148850-michael-jackson-dangerous-and-the-reinvention-of-pop/.

Vogel, Joseph. "Michael Jackson: Man in the Music, Part 2 (Morphine)." *Huffington Post* (2009). Published electronically July 27. http://www.huffingtonpost.com/joe-vogel/michael-jackson-man-in-th_b_221797.html.

Vogel, Joseph. "Michael Jackson: Man in the Music, Part 4 (Tabloid Junkie)." *Huffington Post* (2009). Published electronically August 2. http://www.huffingtonpost.com/joe-vogel/michael-jackson-man-in-th_b_224603.html.

Vogel, Joseph. "Michael Jackson's 'Blood on the Dance Floor,' 15 Years Later." *The Atlantic* (2012). Published electronically March 21. http://www.theatlantic.com/entertainment/archive/2012/03/michael-jacksons-blood-on-the-dance-floor-15-years-later/254877/.

Vogel, Joseph. "The Misunderstood Power of Michael Jackson's Music." *The Atlantic* (2012). Published electronically February 8. http://www.theatlantic.com/entertainment/archive/2012/02/the-misunderstood-power-of-michael-jacksons-music/252751/.

Vogel, Joseph. "MJ Studies." *@JoeVogel1* (2014). Published electronically October 22. https://twitter.com/JoeVogel1/status/524930211323080704.

Vogel, Joseph. "On Morphine." In *Featuring Michael Jackson: Collected Writings on the King of Pop*, 43–46. New York: Baldwin Books, 2012.

Vogel, Joseph. "Remembering Michael Jackson: The Story Behind His Magnum Opus." *Huffington Post* (2011). Published electronically June 24. http://www.huffingtonpost.com/joe-vogel/michael-jackson-earth-song_b_882740.html.

Vogel, Joseph. "Second to None: Race, Representation and the Misunderstood Power of Michael Jackson's Music." In *Featuring Michael Jackson: Collected Writings on the King of Pop*, 7–14. New York: Baldwin Books, 2012.

Vogel, Joseph. "The Story Behind Michael Jackson's Infectious, Newly Released Song." *The Atlantic* (2012). Published electronically 5 June 2012.

Vogel, Joseph. "The Top Ten Michael Jackson Songs of All Time." In *Featuring Michael Jackson: Collected Writings on the King of Pop*, 15–22. New York: Baldwin Books, 2012.

Wainwright, Rupert. "HIStory Teaser." 1995.

Wallace, Michele. "Michael Jackson, Black Modernisms and 'The Ecstasy of Communication'." *The Journal of Michael Jackson Academic Studies* 1, no. 4 (2015): 2.

Wallace, Michele. "Michael Jackson, Black Modernisms and the Ecstasy of Communication." *Third Text* 3, no. 7 (1989): 11–22.

Wallace, Michele. "Michael Jackson, Black Modernisms and the Ecstasy of Communication." In *Invisibility Blues*, 77–90. London, New York: Verso, 2008.

Wallace, Michele. "Michael Jackson, Black Modernisms and the Ecstasy of Communication." In *A Companion to Michael Jackson Academic Studies I*, edited by Elizabeth Amisu, 5: MJAS, 2015.

Walvin, James. *Black and White: The Negro and English Society, 1555–1945*. London: Allen Lane, 1973.

Walvin, James. *The Black Presence: A Documentary History of the Negro in England, 1555–1860*. London: Orbach and Chambers, 1971.

Warhol, Andy. *The Andy Warhol Diaries*. London: Penguin Modern Classics, 2009.

Warhol, Andy. "Campbell's Soup Cans." Synthetic polymer paint on thirty-two canvases. New York: Museum of Modern Art, 1962.

Warhol, Andy. "Michael Jackson." Synthetic polymer and silkscreen on canvas. Washington: National Portrait Gallery, Smithsonian Institution, 1984.

Warhol, Andy. "Orange Car Crash Fourteen Times." Silkscreen ink on synthetic polymer paint on two canvases. New York: Museum of Modern Art, 1963.

Warhol, Andy. *The Philosophy of Andy Warhol: From A to B and Back Again*. London: Cassell, 1975.

Warhol, Andy, and Pat Hackett. *Popism: The Warhol '60s*. London: Penguin Modern Classics, 2007.

Warwick, Jacqueline. " 'You Can't Win, Child, but You Can't Get out of the Game': Michael Jackson's Transition from Child Star to Superstar." *Popular Music and Society* 35, no. 2 (2012): 241–59.

Watson, Paul F. "The Queen of Sheba in Christian Tradition." In *Solomon & Sheba*, edited by James B. Pritchard, 115–45: London: Phaidon, 1974.

Wells, Stanley, and Catherine M. S. Alexander. *Shakespeare and Race*. Cambridge: Cambridge University Press, 2000.

West, Cornell, and Michael Eric Dyson. "Interview." By Tavis Smiley. *The Tavis Smiley Show* (June 30, 2009).

West, Kanye. *Late Registration*. Roc-a-Fella/Def-Jam, 2005.

Wheeler, Katrina K. "Distressed Fans Commit Suicide over Michael Jackson's Death." *Examiner* (2009). Published electronically June 30. http://www.examiner.com /article/distressed-fans-commit-suicide-over-michael-jackson-s-death.

White, Armond. "Earth Song Moves Music Video Mountains." Chap. 13 in *Keep Moving: The Michael Jackson Chronicles*, 76–78. New York: Resistance Works, 2010.

White, Armond. "Father Figure." In *Keep Moving: The Michael Jackson Chronicles*, 44–45. New York: Resistance Works, 2010.

White, Armond. "The Gloved One Is Not a Chump." In *Keep Moving: The Michael Jackson Chronicles*, 19–30. New York: Resistance Works, 2010.

White, Armond. "Hear, My Dears." Chap. 16 In *Keep Moving: The Michael Jackson Chronicles*, 84–85. New York: Resistance Works, 2010.

White, Armond. " 'How Deep Is Your Afrocentricity?' Ask Michael & Iman." In *Keep Moving: The Michael Jackson Chronicles*, 33–37. New York: Resistance Works, 2010.

White, Armond. "In MJ's Shadow." *New York Press* (2009). Published electronically June 30, 2009. http://nypress.com/in-mjrsquos-shadow/.

White, Armond. "In MJ's Shadow." Chap. 20 In *Keep Moving: The Michael Jackson Chronicles*, 96–101. New York: Resistance Works, 2010.

White, Armond. "Jackson and Jam-Lewis Hope Louder in New Remix." Chap. 14 in *Keep Moving: The Michael Jackson Chronicles*, 79–82. New York: Resistance Works, 2010.

White, Armond. "Jackson Pop: Music Video Artists and Hollywood Influence." Chap. 19 in *Keep Moving: The Michael Jackson Chronicles*, 93–95. New York: Resistance Works, 2010.

White, Armond. "Jackson's TV Ad Makes Rhetorical HIStory." Chap. 9 in *Keep Moving: The Michael Jackson Chronicles*, 51–52. New York: Resistance Works, 2010.

White, Armond. "Janet, the Last Black Jackson." In *Keep Moving: The Michael Jackson Chronicles*, 7–11. New York: Resistance Works, 2010.

White, Armond. *Keep Moving: The Michael Jackson Chronicles*. Resistance Works, 2010.

White, Armond. "Lists & Prizes in the Arts for 1995." Chap. 15 in *Keep Moving: The Michael Jackson Chronicles*, 83. New York: Resistance Works, 2010.

White, Armond. "Michael Takes a Bow for 'Jam'." In *Keep Moving: The Michael Jackson Chronicles*, 38–43. New York: Resistance Works, 2010.

White, Armond. "Montell and Michael Exploit/Explore Happy-Negro Fallacy." Chap. 12 in *Keep Moving: The Michael Jackson Chronicles*, 72–75. New York: Resistance Works, 2010.

White, Armond. "Moving Forward: An Introduction." In *Keep Moving: The Michael Jackson Chronicles*, 1–5. New York: Resistance Works, 2010.

White, Armond. "Remembering "Ben"." Chap. 17 in *Keep Moving: The Michael Jackson Chronicles*, 87–91. New York: Resistance Works, 2010.

White, Armond. "Screaming to Be Heard, Book I." Chap. 10 in *Keep Moving: The Michael Jackson Chronicles*, 53–62. New York: Resistance Works, 2010.

White, Armond. "Screaming to Be Heard, Book II." Chap. 11 in *Keep Moving: The Michael Jackson Chronicles*, 63–71. New York: Resistance Works, 2010.

White, Armond. "Sibling Song." In *Keep Moving: The Michael Jackson Chronicles*, 31–32. New York: Resistance Works, 2010.

White, Armond. "Song of the Day: Man in the Mirror." Chap. 18 in *Keep Moving: The Michael Jackson Chronicles*, 92. New York: Resistance Works, 2010.

White, Armond. "Table of Contents." In *Keep Moving: The Michael Jackson Chronicles*. New York: Resistance Works, 2010.

White, Armond. "Twenty-First Century Renaissance." Chap. 21 in *Keep Moving: The Michael Jackson Chronicles*, 102–06. New York: Resistance Works, 2010.

White, Armond. "Understanding Michael Jackson." In *Keep Moving: The Michael Jackson Chronicles*, 12–18. New York: Resistance Works, 2010.

White, Armond. "Video Change the Style of "Black Film"." Chap. 8 in *Keep Moving: The Michael Jackson Chronicles*, 46–50. New York: Resistance Works, 2010.

Whitfield, Bill, Javon Beard, and Tanner Colby. *Remember the Time: Protecting Michael Jackson in His Final Days*. New York: Weinstein, 2014.

Whitney, Geffrey. *A Choice of Emblemes, and Other Deuises, for the Moste Parte Gathered out of Sundrie Writers, Englished and Moralized*. Leyden: 1586.

Wilde, Oscar. *Lord Arthur Savile's Crime and Other Stories*. Kindle, 2014.

Wilde, Oscar. *The Picture of Dorian Gray*. Kindle, 1890, 2012.

Wiley, Christopher. "Putting the Music Back into Michael Jackson Studies." In *Michael Jackson: Grasping the Spectacle*, edited by Christopher R. Smit, 101–16. Farnham, UK: Ashgate, 2012.

Willet, Frank. *African Art*. London: Thames and Hudson, 1995.

Williams, Alex. "Michael's Labyrinth: A Tabloid Sublime." In *The Resistible Demise of Michael Jackson*, edited by Mark Fisher, 261–66. Winchester, UK: Zero Books, 2009.

Williams, Craig. *Michael—The Last Photo Shoots*. Noval Williams Films.

Williams, Edwina R. L., Jean Meadows, Jose Catalàn. "Death of Diana, Princess of Wales." *British Medical Journal* 315, no. 7120 (29 November 1997): 1467–68.

Williams, Evan Calder. "'You're Just Another Part of Me': Captain EO and the Metaphysics of the NGO." In *The Resistible Demise of Michael Jackson*, edited by Mark Fisher, 188–93. Winchester, UK: Zero Books, 2009.

Williams, Gershom. "Michael Jackson: Color Complex and the Politics of White Supremacy." *The Journal of Pan African Studies* 3, no. 7 (2010): 106–12.

Williams, Raymond. *Keywords: A Vocabulary of Culture and Society*. London: Routledge, 2013.

Williams, Raymond. *The Long Revolution*. London: Chatto & Windus, 1961.

Williams, Raymond. *Modern Tragedy*. London: Chatto & Windus, 1966.

Wilson, Donald. *Man in the Mirror*. 1988.

Winston, Stan. *(2 Bad + Is It Scary+) Ghosts*. 1997.

Winston, Stan. *Michael Jackson's Ghosts*. Kingdom Entertainment, 1998.

Wise, Robert, and Jerome Robbins. *West Side Story*. Twentieth Century Fox, 1961.

Wittenberg, Mark, and Willy Gijsman. "Full Report on the Michael Jackson Trial." *MJ Times Neverland Valley News* 2 (2005).

Wittenberg, Mark, and Willy Gijsman. *The MJ Times: Neverland Valley News*. Vol. 1, Holland: The Legend Continues, 2005.

Wood, Amy Louise. "Legacies of Lynching: Racial Violence and Memory." *Film Quarterly* 60, no. 2 (2006): 81.

Wood, Marcus. *Slavery, Empathy, and Pornography*. Oxford: Oxford University Press, 2002.

Woods, Raven. "'The Negro Artist and the Racial Mountain': How Langston Hughes's Seminal 1926 Essay May Help Us Better Understand Both Michael Jackson's Art and His Struggles: Pt 1." *AllForLoveBlog* (2014). Published electronically July 5. http://www.allforloveblog.com/?p=9242.

Woods, Raven. "'Remember the Time'—Review." In *AllForLoveBlog*, 2014.

Woodward, Susan. *Otherness and Power: Michael Jackson and His Media Critics*. Dorset, UK: Blackmore, 2014.

Wright, Nancy Elizabeth. "'Author Ad Librum': The Textual Authority of Ben Jonson's Masques." *Dissertation Abstracts International* 48 (1988).

Wynne-Davies, Marion. "The Queen's Masque: Renaissance Women and the Seventeenth-Century Court Masque." In *Gloriana's Face: Women, Public and Private, in the English Renaissance*, edited by S. P. Cerasano and Marion Wynne-Davies, 79–104. Detroit, MI: Wayne State University Press, 1992.

Yankovich, Weird Al. "Eat It." YouTube, 1984.

Yankovich, Weird Al. "Fat." YouTube, 1988.

Yeoh Kah Sin, Dennis. "'Did I Scare You?': The Curious Case of Michael Jackson as Gothic Narrative." *Studies in Gothic Fiction* 1, no. 1 (2009).

Young, Harvey. *Theatre and Race*. Bastingstoke: Palgrave Macmillan, 2013.

Young, Robert. *Colonial Desire: Hybridity in Theory, Culture, and Race*. London: Routledge, 1995.

Young, Robert. *Untying the Text: A Post-Structuralist Reader*. London: Routledge & Kegan Paul, 1981.

Young, Robert. *White Mythologies: Writing History and the West*. London: Routledge, 1990.

Yuan, David. "The Celebrity Freak: Michael Jackson's 'Grotesque Glory'." In *Freakery: Cultural Spectacles of the Extraordinary Body*, edited by Rosemarie Garland Thomson, 368–84. New York: New York University Press, 1996.

Yukich, Jim. *Liberian Girl*. 1989.

Zien, Katherine, and Jason Lazarus. "Carving a Sonic Path through Stratified Spaces: The Michael Jackson Memorial Procession." *Journal of Popular Music Studies* 23, no. 1 (2011): 85–93.

Ziman, Ralph. *Why*. 1996.

Ziółkowski, Marek. "Commodification of Social Life." *Polish Sociological Review*, no. 148 (2004): 385–402.

Zohny, Josephine. "In Defense of Michael." *Pop Matters* (2005). Published electronically February 9. http://www.popmatters.com/feature/050209-michaeljackson/.

Zulu, Itibari M. "MJ: The Man in the Mirror Analyzed." *Journal of Pan African Studies* 3, no. 7 (2010): 1–3.

Index

About the Author

Elizabeth Amisu holds an MA in Early Modern English Literature from King's College London, in conjunction with the British Library. She completed her teacher training at the University College London Institute of Education and has seven years' experience teaching Creative Writing, English Literature, English Language, and Film Studies. She received a First Class BA (Drama, Film, and Creative Writing) from Bucks New University and was the recipient of the award for Highest Overall Mark in the Faculty of Creativity and Culture (2008). She is cofounder and editor of *The Journal of Michael Jackson Academic Studies* online (http://michaeljacksonstudies.org/).

More at www.elizabethamisu.com.